D1605871

# Origins of Truth

# Origins of Truth

Words that Will Awaken You
to the Truth of Your Heart

## Nadia Khalil Bradley

THREE CORNERS
P R E S S

PASADENA, CALIFORNIA

THREE CORNERS
P R E S S

Three Corners Press
3579 E. Foothill Blvd. Ste. 511
Pasadena, CA 91107

Publishers Cataloging-in-Publication

Bradley, Nadia Khalil.

    Origins of truth / Nadia Khalil Bradley. — 1st ed. — Pasadena, CA : Three Corners Press, 2007.

    p. ; cm.
    ISBN: 978-0-9755585-7-7
    Includes index.
    Summary: A young Muslim woman starts hearing Jesus talking to her. What is she to do? She goes with her heart and the floodgates of love and wisdom open. "Origins of Truth" contains three books in one volume. Purity is a journal of Nadia's undeniable awakening that will fascinate and inspire the reader to a higher awareness. Love is filled with simple, clear writings of Christ, as revealed to Nadia. Truth is a wonderful dictionary of concepts that will assist the reader in understanding and navigating the process called life.

    1. Jesus Christ. 2. Private revelations. 3. Spirit writings.
4. Prayer—Christianity. 5. Angels—Christianity. 6. Spiritual life—Christianity. I. Title. II. Purity. III. Love. IV. Truth.

BT966.3 .B73 2007         2007903975
235.3—dc22          0709

Editor                   Stirling Nix Bradley
Book Consultant         Ellen Reid
Book Cover/InteriorDesign   Dotti Albertine
Copywriting             Laren Bright
Author Photographs     Dawn Katzin/Carole Forrest

Printed in the United States of America on acid-free paper

If we really believe God is one,
then we have not one excuse to limit ourselves
in what we can do as a whole.

*Editor's Note*

The punctuation appears to not be right, but it is. Some words may seem wrongly placed or misspelled, they are not. The speech is not as we speak and sometimes the words do not appear to be in the right order, but they are. Know that you will understand what you need to understand and learn what you need to learn. My heart flies to know this book is in your hands and it is yours now.

# Contents

*Foreword*

It is funny how we write. We start with an idea, it turns into something else and then it is perfect for its moment. And then time goes by and there is this phase of remembering. The "whys" before the "what happeneds."

I am forty-five. I have five brothers and sisters. My Mom and Dad came to America in the 1950s, as a result of the 1948 turnover of their homeland, Palestine. It went from being a British colony to a country called Israel. My parents came to work and to send back money to the rest of their families. They eventually brought their families to America, to live, get educated, work and prosper. My mother and father encountered a language barrier and did not understand all the cultural differences. However, they were hard workers and found many jobs that did not require knowledge of the system.

They soon learned that they could save some money like everyone else and began to understand that entrepreneurs ran America. They became educated and purchased businesses. I grew up in a succession of my father's corner grocery stores. After the 1967 war in Palestine, my parents knew that they could not go back to their country, so they bought a home and planted roots. We moved to the suburbs of Chicago in 1968. And my parents let go of their "I am just passing through" attitude.

Although I was born Arab-American, it didn't matter so much then, simply because there weren't many Arabic people in Chicago. Americans didn't know much about us. Therefore, they were allowed to love us. Isn't that interesting? And that was all I knew at that point in my life. I was an

American with Arabic influences. It was a beautiful life. I had a very strong and loving family and I lived in the freedoms of America's opportunities—to get an education and work and build a life for myself.

My Father was well known for his Chicago businesses, and he was an avid baseball fan. He never missed a Cubs game in his life. He had two TVs in his store, one in the front and one in the back. He also never saw a live game in person. He was always working. My Mother worked as well, and after my Father bought his first business they always worked together. I was left to take care of my younger sister and brother. We were a working family and eventually everyone worked in the business.

Our extended family grew as more and more of our relatives came from other countries. I loved their visits. They brought all the other parts of the world to us. My cousins and uncles and aunts traveled and went to different schools. This made international traveling, education and working all normal things to me. It taught me that just because someone is not in front of me, it didn't mean they don't love me. They would come back after long absences, and it was as if they never left. I carry that until today. Just because someone doesn't have time to get to me or me them, when we see each other, it is always without pressures or record keeping of who did what.

My Mother and Father opened our home to everyone. They paid for family members' educations, since that was always the most important thing to all of us. My Mom would cook for everyone. I was the oldest girl, so I helped her with everything—baking, cooking, cleaning and loving. As we baked, cooked and cleaned, she would speak to me about her life, about her way of loving. Many people in life have so many complaints about what their families didn't do for them, tell them, or give them. I have to say, my Mother was the most gracious of Mothers. She gave us everything. She really loved us and she never said it. She lived it. There is a difference. She really had pure will with us. So while we would be baking—in-between her telling me to make sure the cookies we were baking were golden, or not too dark, or not too light (however, if I had to err, it should be on the lighter side of the dough)—she would talk to me about intentions. What a person's intentions are. In Arabic the word for intentions is Neeya. She would tell me, even if I didn't get to speak something or do something, that my intentions are more important. That if I truly intended to do something that it is as though I did it. She didn't know this then, nor do I think she knows it now, but she was talking about energy. That the energy of intentions carries forth.

⁂

I remember a woman's husband dying and not being able to go to her. I felt really bad that her husband had passed, and she had four young children. I remember being so quiet and thinking that I could simply think of how I wanted to be there and hug them all. And it felt so beautiful to do that from the inner parts of me, of my heart. It was as though I went to them. When I did finally see them years later, I felt clear, not like I owed anything. I felt clean about it and I got to hug her then. I remember telling her how I wanted to go but I couldn't get to her, but it didn't mean I didn't love her or send her love. It was understood simply because it was true.

My Mom and Dad really loved each other and seeing this taught me love. It was nothing they ever said. My Dad taught me honesty by hitting me for lying one time. I am not saying hitting anyone is good, but he was so upset that I had lied about something. Later, he apologized and told me it hurt him more to hurt me than it could have ever hurt me. He said he would never do it again and he never did. That made me forget the entire incident, simply because he told me the truth. He lived it.

I realize now not much was said about love or truth in my family. We just all lived it. So much is understood through energy, which comes to us before any words. Energy is the universal language, no matter what language we speak, no matter what country we are from. Our intentions tell us and others who we are—as people, as parents, as children, no matter what age one is living in. We remember what is done, not what is said. My family life as a kid was a living example of living what we as people already know. And it taught me to believe in myself, even if someone disagrees with me. It just means we disagree. I learned that the same thing doesn't work for everyone, but love works for all—that the universal language need not be spoken or debated.

This book gives many examples, avenues, bridges and paths for our souls. And in each way we learn there is one universal language we all speak, and it is Love, Truth and Purity. In the same way it lives on the pages of this book, it lives in us already. This book is a reminder of who we are before race, religion and creed. It reminds us we are people, humans on a home called Earth. It reminds us, we are an US. Enjoy the journey and find your treasures. They are waiting for you.

# What Does Origin Mean?

Origin is of great importance! Origin—of Self—of Soul. It is the mark of the birth of an individual. Experience and evolvement shape Origin, and it either keeps the soul in growth or holds it back. It means you are doing what you came to Earth to do—with truth and purity. To know this gives life the meaning it needs to continue!

Some people, probably most, are held back from Origin. Many don't know why they are here or there or anywhere. These lives are filled with complaining, whining, lack of motivation, and lack of participation. Their souls have lost the memory of Origin. The very lack of Origin in their lives proves that it exists, because they know that something fundamental is missing. However, in that very first moment of existence, each soul is of Origin. Glory be to God Almighty!

*Introduction*

## JULY 19, 2006

Here I sit on a sunny southern California day at my computer. Four hundred negative in the bank and ten dollars in my purse for gas and groceries. And I trust. I trust that I saw you, Christ. I trust what you speak to me. And I trust that I am supposed to pass this on. Read and decide.

When I first saw Christ it was just like seeing people. Only more light than people, more peaceful than people. At the time, I was divorced with two children. Everything was OK, absolute, when I saw Christ. It made life on Earth explainable and giving. It made me feel like you and like me at the same time. I wanted to tell everyone. But that posed a challenge to my life, and it didn't make my Mom too happy. We are Muslim. Christ is believed to be a prophet, not the son of God as the Christians believe. Mohammed is believed to be the most important and last Prophet. It is his teachings that are the Quran.

As I said, it didn't make my Mom too happy that I saw Christ. When I called her to tell her I had seen Christ, she thought I'd turned "Christian." She asked me, "Why did you see Christ? How did you hear him? Are you a Christian now?"

I said to her, "I see Christ like I see you. I hear Christ like I hear you."

Then Christ started to speak to my Mom while I was on the phone with her. He spoke of her life, her childhood—about forgiveness, about the thoughts she could not let go of, the thoughts that had shaped her life, stemming from past hurts and misunderstandings. She started to cry, and she believed me.

Two weeks later she called me to ask if this was still happening to me. I said, "Yes."

My Mom said to me, "I went to the Mosque to ask them about you, about what you know, and they told me, 'Yes, Angels do come and speak to a person; however, it is not really an Angel. It is the devil.'" (In our background if anyone disagrees with the Muslim beliefs, then they are outcast in some way.)

&

In 2004, I wrote my first book, *Little Wing*. It touched many people. Some didn't get it all. Some thought, "Hmmm." Others got it, and read it over and over again.

I thought, "Wow, people will read this, and they will know." I held back at first because I felt odd writing about my life, about Christ. Especially once I realized Christ is a hot commodity on Earth. I realized that some people thought of Christ as un-relatable, as a fantasy, or as a judge who would come back, and the world would end. Who was I to say that that is not how it is going to be? Who was I to say that "Christ" told me? How could I prove that? What would I say?

Something had happened to me, something that was pure feeling and beautiful. There was nothing negative spoken or done. How could so much light bring so much fear in people?

Then in another conversation my Mom said to me, "I have always known who you are, who you have been all of your life. I am just too old to adjust to the change that will occur if you start revealing yourself."

And then I immediately knew she didn't believe a devil came to me. How could that be? Christ told me that there is no Hell as we know it. Hell is the lack of Love. That is what Hell means. I see evidence of that, so I have no reason to not believe him.

&

I grew up in Chicago as part of a very small Muslim community. I should say it was an Arabic community, mostly refugees from the Palestinian-Israeli war. Most had come for financial reasons, to support their families back home. My family knew only about fifty other Muslims in the Chicago area. They were mostly from the same town, very hard working people—many working two and three jobs at the same time. They loved us kids in a way that supports my heart even now. There were no big rules yet, and although religion was a part of life, it was not talked about. There were things we never did, which I just accepted—like we didn't drink alcohol or eat pork. However, we were young kids, and we had no real religious education yet on what we were supposed to be or do, or how we were different from the Christian community.

One summer when was eight years old, I went to vacation bible school with a friend. The first day they showed us a film, and, in it a house was burning. At the end of the film there was a question on the movie screen which asked, "If you die tonight, do you know if you are going to heaven?"

After the film there was a discussion about getting saved. I had no clue what they were talking about. Before that moment, I had never thought of my house burning down or about a Heaven or a Hell. I was just a happy eight-year-old girl.

My friend was not affected by the movie at all. I guess she was already used to this kind of language. I was not. Scared by this new information, I went home and asked my mom about Heaven and Hell. My mom wondered why I was asking her all of these questions after day camp. She had not known that it was a Christian camp. I told her about the film, and that it scared me. I was afraid that something could happen to us, and we would not be prepared. My Mom told me that the people at the bible camp were not like us. We were Muslim and had different beliefs about life. She spoke to my friend's mother, and I don't remember if I went back to the camp or not.

The religious differences deepend as I grew older. As the Muslim community in Chicago expanded, a "keeping up with the Jones" mentality developed. As I became more aware of these social pressures, I learned that my actions should never shame our family.

With more Muslims in my neighborhood, I felt comforted by being with people who were the same as me. My life still felt different from most of the people I knew, because I had to live two lives to cope with being a minority Muslim person in a Christian community. I could not admit things that were coming naturally to me—like being fourteen and liking boys, or wanting to go out with friends—things that were no big deal to my neighbors, but a very big deal to my family.

We all knew my siblings and I couldn't do many of the things that were very normal for them, and that someday we would have to get married without dating or knowing at times who we were really marrying—other than the obvious criteria at that time of financial stability and coming from families with "good" reputations.

I wanted both worlds—the Western world of my friends and the Muslim world of my family. I thought, "Wow, if the two worlds could join together, it truly would be the best of both worlds." I felt if the Americans would care about their families more and have much more glue to bind them together and if I were allowed to share my whole self with my family, what a wonderful world it would be. However I could not do that.

In time, even more Muslims came to Chicago. A friend of my Mom's was asked to start a Muslim Sunday school so that we could learn about our background and religion. I was Muslim by birth; however, until about eleven-years-old, it did not affect on my life. We attended that Sunday school and we were taught the thirteen small sura's or prayers, and they were so beautiful to my heart—to simply know that those thoughts existed and there was no fear in them. I wanted to know more and more. I wanted to understand the beauty of our souls, the freedoms we are afforded.

However, as I delved into the Muslim religion further, I was seeing a difference in culture, tradition and religion from most of the world around me. So I started asking questions, like, why some things were OK that were not of our religion and other things weren't? Most religions are hard to live up to, which is why so many people have to be religious or not. Religion to me was a way of life that went against the way people actually live.

I used to wonder why we would put ourselves in situations where "good" and "beauty," which made us feel like we could do anything, was not in religion. Religion was a *have to, a must, an or else*. And the *or elses* really were the questions in my head. I wanted to know more.

Once they begin, Muslims pray five times a day, every day, for the rest of their lives. It is supposed to begin around seven-years-old. However, it is rare to find a seven-year-old who can pray five times a day. Praying five times a day in a modern country that does not stop five times a day for anything, is quite a challenge.

I started praying regularly at the age of seventeen. I was in high school and had just gotten my first job at a clothing store in the local mall. I would go to school all day and then to my job. One day after I got home from work, I realized that I had been so busy that I had missed about three prayers that day. I felt anxious knowing I had to make up the three prayers and still do my homework.

I went quickly and performed wudu, which is the ritual way to clean yourself before presenting yourself to God. I love wudu. You have to wash your hands three times, your face three times, your mouth, your ears, your feet, etc. It is very humbling to know you are preparing for anything by cleaning yourself. After completing wudu, I was walking down the hallway, hoping to God I wouldn't pass gas or anything like that before I started praying, because that would invalidate all the cleansing I had just done, and I would have to go and do it all over again! (I used to wonder why the bodily functions, which are so natural, would invalidate the prayers. However, I obediently accepted the rule.) I rushed over to my prayer rug and I started to pray. I knew I had to say lot of prayers to make up for the ones I had missed earlier in the day. I started and repeated the same prayers over and over and over. By the time I was finished I was exhausted. The realization came that I couldn't remember a thing I had just said. I had been so anxious to complete the prayers, so I could go on to my huge pile of homework.

That's when it came to me that I was living in fear that God would not accept me if I did not do these prayers—that my sense of worth came from doing things that I couldn't even remember and couldn't appreciate their value, because I was not able to comfortably work the rituals into my life. The prayers were a pressure that would have been a relief to not have to do, and I didn't want to feel that way about God.

So for the first time in my life, I remember speaking directly to God. I figured that God already knew what I was thinking, and if I believed everything I had learned, then "he always knows how I feel."

So I said to God, "I am sorry that I don't feel there is a benefit to me to pray like this. I feel farther away from you rather than closer. I felt rushed saying those prayers and I don't remember a word I just said. It made me feel good to try, but if I am trying and I feel further away and I don't remember what I said, just racing to say the words, then this can't be right for me. I used to feel closer to you and free to say, 'I love you and I am happy I am on Earth.' I used to love people without thinking about it—without thinking about what is right and wrong all the time. I used to know these things in my heart, and now I feel like I know it because I am told to know it. God, I felt better before I started to pray. I want to be free and not feel forced. Feeling forced has taken away my fun with you. I want my fun back. I want my freedom back. And I hope that I can erase feeling like I have to be anything, but the love I feel for you, for my life and for everyone in it." And that was all I could say.

As I was speaking to God, I felt my body lighten and my face got warm. If I could have seen it, I'm sure it was the way we think of a face turning red. My hands were facing upward and I felt so pure in that moment, so loved in that moment. I felt like I wasn't there, that I was somewhere special, somewhere beautiful and accepting, as though I just gave the right answer to a very hard question. I felt accepted and that I had more work to do in my life, even though I couldn't conceive what it was or could be. I felt like I wanted to hug people and tell them there is so much beauty in some solitude, and to tell them to talk to God.

I had felt more heard in that moment than any other moment of my entire life. I realized that love is grander than all things we have come to know. I learned something really big in that moment and it shaped my entire life afterward. I learned that it felt great to talk to God and no matter what happens in life on Earth, there was this love, that we call God. That moment is the story behind all the stories in the books I have written to this day. It is beauty, undisputed. It is Love without boundaries. I witness people's fears of what exists and what is not known to us yet. I understand how change disables humans—how we think we are one thing because that is what we present to the world. But we actually see our real selves in an entirely different manner.

I started noticing life differently when Christ began talking to me all the time—writing with me all the time—like I have a special, invisible friend, though he is not so invisible at times. He is visible as a light that shines around me or through me. People saw him the first time I spoke publicly at Santa Anita Church in Arcadia. They said at times they could not see me at all, only light. At my first seminar, where I spoke to a whopping audience of fifteen, some of them saw him too. Again they saw him as light. Christ told me he would come through me and that people would see him in recognizable form. However, he continued to appear as light until…

One day I was at a coffee shop with a friend whose partner was in the hospital fighting cervical cancer. She had come to me in fear and desperation. I know the power of lessons and that everything that happens is to teach us something. I was seeing her partner's Cancer as a teacher. I knew it was not time for this woman to pass on to home. However, my friend really needed to know this too. So I told her, "I'm not sure you can understand what a risk it is for me to tell you that I know for certain that your partner will be ok."

It baffles me to this day, the surety in which I simply know truth for what it is. The Angels go through me like the gentlest and most loving breezes. Yet their force and their love have the strength of unabated metal. As I was speaking to my friend, and seeing in her eyes her great need of comfort, she was looking right at me. She told me that she could see two of me. While she was saying this, I looked around the room and I could not see the forms, or bodies of the people around me. All I could see was the clothes and jewelry they were wearing. And, there was one other thing I could see. It was their souls. I saw that I knew more about those people in that moment than they would have time to discover on earth. It was weird to me to know more about them than they would ever know, and never be able to tell them what I knew, or even how I came to know this.

To get back to my friend, she was saying to me, "There are two of you." Christ had told me he would come through me in a recognizable form, so it excited me that it was truth and it was happening. I was happy that I wasn't crazy—because from time to time, I did doubt my own truth. However, that moment when Christ came through me, that is eternal. Because of that moment, that showing, my friend went back to the hospital and cared for and nursed her partner with strength, love, and an endurance of the love and understanding that had come from Christ, appearing through me to her.

Love can only propel when it is pure. Perfection is love and love is perfection.

Another time, while I was sleeping, my husband looked over and saw me sitting up and watching over him. He asked me why I was staring at him and I quickly realized that I was in fact sleeping next to him and that the petite, golden, illumination was Christ. And so I believe Christ when he tells me he is within me, experiencing life on Earth, so that WE can bring the balance of love, truth and purity to the world again. I say WE and I mean WE, all of us. We are all of God, of ourselves and of God again. And God was turned into a religion. God is not a religion.

Life is like a synchronized watch. There are no mistakes. There is no soul more important than another. Love carries us and the lack of love takes away from us. There are only lessons in life to be had and all the lessons teach and grow us. And if we fight our lessons, we will repeat them until we get it. That is how God's love is revealed to us. It is the freedom of who we are, what we do, what we are honest about within ourselves. When we touch our honesty, we touch the love of God within us. And when we can't touch our own honesty it is hard to see God as a partner. We turn God into a parent and that creates distance. Male or Female, He or She, it does not matter for God is all. God is love. And we all search for that love here on Earth.

We think love is something that we do. Yet it is truly only a feeling, a passion in our hearts that drives us—an emotion that fuels us. When it is not present we live in sadness while searching for it. As we live our lives, no matter who we are, who rules us, what country we are in, we all have families, which form our early sense of identity. It is in the family that we learn to be scared and skeptical of things that appear different from what we have learned. We shy away from even knowing other ways of being, because we want to appear "normal." Today's "normal" has left us with emptiness, loneliness, and disrespect to ourselves and a lack of understanding of others and the world around us.

We react to life with murders, wars, corrupt corporations—the ripple effects of all the self-motivation we have been taught is normal. When a soul speaks truth of any kind it is deemed unsophisticated. That soul is looked upon as a fool at times and put on the news as though the truth is not truth. The media will prepare a spun story that isn't truth and make us all want to believe it.

It is time to look at truth again, to understand the role of purity in our lives. Getting that kind of love is at the bottom, at the top, and in the middle of all things. Love, truth and purity are the foundations of everything. And when one of them is awry, so are we. No matter what happens technologically, no matter what we discover, create or do, when love, truth or purity do not exist in our lives, we cannot find a resting place, nor do we feel complete.

We try to replace love, truth and purity with many substitutes. Drugs, money, sex, clothes, cars and houses only take us so far. People of courage can take themselves past all this. These souls, who start to account for themselves in a deeper, more meaningful way, look at their own roles in their lives, and start to put perspective on who they are and why. They can look at challenges that come along as lessons—rather than assuming they are bad people, and that they are being punished.

Most of us expect so much from life and we give so sparingly back—to ourselves, our families, our friends, our co-workers and our neighbors. We don't trust anyone, and go to people for help, and we find that everyone is overwhelmed with issues of trust. The problems we have or face are all of our own making. We are a family. We all have many tensions and pressures and want to alleviate them by lashing out at others. It is time to pay attention. When we kill others, we are killing ourselves. When we lie to others, we are lying to ourselves. What happens to the "least" of us happens to us "All."

There is not one soul more important than another. You will hear this many times in my writing. Our media is dominated by fear-based thinkers and thinking, by selves unaccounted for, by intentions unknown. There is purpose in every challenge and challenge in every purpose. Let's use the knowledge we have. We already know enough to move ourselves along. We simply have to take what we know and use it. Give it life and give ourselves the feelings of being alive, of wonder, and of hope again. Let's all share and not feel resentful of doing so. Sharing is a way of life. Extend life, and invite yourself into your own life, since we cannot give what we do not have. Feel life and let life feel you. It is all about choices and free will.

❧

I wear sweats most of the time and care for my six children, a blended family with three ex-spouses between my husband and me. I love to cook.

Some of the best conversations and revelations come while I am cooking a meal or baking cookies. Like…there is no way to love, love just is! And the following equations:

**Accounting plus Intentions equals Growth.** This is an equation in my head. a+i=g. Simply knowing your role in all that you do and your intent in all that you do will always lead you to growth.

**Read and Decide.** To me this is not about whether what you are reading is true or not; but rather about deciding what you are reading means to you. Why are you reading this right now? What is in it for your soul to know, to understand, to take on compassion for?

I can only extend this book as an invitation to knowledge for all of us, in a way that can and can't be explained. It is fruitful, loving and productive for our minds and our souls. We have yet to know ourselves with all of the lights on. I am proof that Christ is not just for some people. I am proof that God is not a religion. I am proof that lives can change. I am proof that time will answer every question, if only we can trust life long enough to teach us, because on Earth, time is the best teacher. Learn and Love in truth. With all my love to everyone, this book is for us!

*Part ONE*

# THE JOURNAL

# CHAPTER 1

# PURITY

DO NOT BE EMBARRASSED of your growth or anything we say to you that is for the greater good of the day of that moment. Do not feel like you can not share that part of yourself, for loves that you feel were in far away from your body, yet very close to your heart.

You are a woman of 42, and you know peoples in the ways that you do for this very reason of innocence. You embarked on the experience in fullness or partial, in order to help others in need of love with the patience we gave to you. By giving your heart its way to learning and loving you in each walking of life you took.

There is a reason you were incubated until 35. There is a reason why you did not drink alcohol or take medications or drugs. The reasons were to force you to feel internal the truest feelings that could be felt. It was not easy for you had no cushions in life.

You used to say you felt at times like someone threw you off a high rise building with no net. Yes they did. And you survived on your inner love that not a soul can take and disturb. Take heart and take on all that comes your ways. You are loved.

*Christ*

One day, I went to drive my daughter to school and there was this white dove outside of our side door. We passed it by and it didn't really move. It was gentle and very uninterrupting. I was still in my first marriage and I was very sad. I drove my daughter, came back home and it was still there. At 3:00 pm I went to pick my daughter up from school and it was still there. The next morning…it was still there.

I told my daughter maybe we should buy it some food and she said it wasn't looking for food, it was just walking up and down our pathway. So I asked her to stand by it and I took a picture of her near it. You can see in the picture that she was hesitant to get too close to it. The following day, as I had grown to expect, it was still there. I was used to it by then and it gave me great peace. It was so white, its feet, even its beak. I just loved that this bird was present.

At that time my marriage was not working out. It was an arranged marriage. I was so depressed that I would wear the same clothes for a week or so, I would pull my hair back so you couldn't tell if it was clean or dirty. I was so skinny that I wore layers of clothing on my body to keep myself warm. The only love I could feel was the love that I had for my children. I stopped eating, I stopped talking, I stopped using my mouth to do anything. I had diarrhea for about two years by then and I was sad and very lonely inside, and that is what spurred my writings to God.

So seeing this bird—as much a surprise as it was—it gave me great peace to know that beauty was still around me. On the third day, my husband was late coming home. I had finished making dinner and I thought, "I want to go outside and sit with the bird." And I did. It didn't move. It was right next to me. Imagine. It had no fear of me or me of it. It was one of the most peaceful moments I have ever known. I felt like no matter what happened in my life, no matter what it was, I would be fine within it. I would be OK. And as soon as I came to that conclusion, the bird flew away and landed on the tip of my neighbor's garage. It was immediately met by another bird and they both flew away together.

# CHAPTER 2

# THE ANGELS

*T*he following excerpts from my journal are from January of 2002, to November of 2004. Before that I had been writing many times a day for a few years. At red lights, on the side of the road, on store receipts, notepads, any paper I could find. I knew I was not alone in this world, yet it took me quite awhile to wrap my mind around the fact that I was heard. That I could hear, see and feel Angels. I was working as a salesperson for an employment firm and raising two kids as a single mom. It was my job to find jobs for other people, so I got to go to many companies and meet a lot of people.

I always knew that my life would change in my fortieth year of life. The question was how? This is the beginning of my recognition of the fact that I could ask specific questions of the Angels and that they would respond in kind.

## JANUARY 11, 2002

Please Dearest Lord, tell me, I am here and I am listening. I am really loving you Angels, Azna and Spirit Guides. It is hard for me still to grasp the actual presence of all of you. I love that you are with me. I want to feel your presence in this moment. Please come through me. I love the feeling. I did a lot of work on this end this week. It is not really work, it is my passion without doubt. If people ask me, it is God. All of you. I am writing.

Tell me now. I will just write it. I know we never did it this way before but I never felt this way before either. I am curious. I am learning to feel love back to me. Thank you for the grace. You are giving it to me through my skin. I could feel you. Can we talk, or is this the way? I am so open to you and to this…Azna, the emotion you instill in me. I am all you.

**We are here and we will stand beside you and you will know that we will be with you and take care of you always. Don't ever worry my sweet soul for I love you and you are in my hands.**

Thank you for telling me. This is the first time I ever did this consciously or knowingly. I am in such amazement. I am in some kind of glory. That is why I am alone tonight while I could still be awake. I was elated in some ways because I knew that you were there. The bustle of everyday life was taking me away mentally for some time. I missed feeling that feeling when I ask to feel you and you come through me. I love that more than you could know. I look forward to enjoying those moments. I love you.

Nadia

## January 19, 2002

My Dearest Lord,

I do have this belief. I thank you for giving me the brains to remember it and repeat it to myself. So that I remember that I am changing a way of thinking that shouldn't be in me. I am game. It is hard however I find comfort in the change of it all. I am enjoying learning. I feel the scary spots and I remember that you are there, Azna is there. And the Angels and the spirit guides. I love you Azna, Angels. I could feel you flow through me. I love you so much Allah. I am waiting in anticipation. I love this. It is such a fun way of hearing you. I will stop now. Take it over baby!

OK, here we are, we are here with you. We love you. We know you are waiting for us. Sometimes we lead you to us in funny ways. We like watching you discover all that we give to you. That is when we sing. We would stand around you and weep when your soul was suffering. And we would rejoice and sing in happiness when you would succeed by choosing the choices of love and understand in duress.

The white bird, he was one of a pair. You saw them both and you saw them fly. Only one came to your door and the other, he stood far away in which to surround you with peace as only you could have had it. Your heart in those hours, we were weeping in your pain. You would write to God and we heard you. You were willing to settle and we weren't. Your belief in us kept you there. We couldn't let you down. We love you. We only know to love you.

We are here for you now differently. You have a job to do my sweet dear. You are dear to us. You are us. We are you. Understand how powerful that is. You are in our hearts. You are the spirit of us walking this earth. This earth is in need of you. You will touch people and they will heal. You will love them and they will heal. WE know now when you recognize us in the midst of all other things that occupy a mind. We rejoice. We love you.

I am sorry, my eyes are closing. Thank you for your love and for your existence. It made a difference to me to know that you are there as you are. Goodnight.

Nadia

JANUARY 27, 2002

My Dearest Lord,

Azna, Angels, Spirit Guides, I love all of you. Thank you for this day. It has been of peace and I am growing my way into understanding what is in my heart and in my head. I went through all the stages only to come back and say, I have been through this before and I know I will be OK. I want to grow in my heart. Keep pushing me. I also understand that you told me that I wasn't supposed to be with the people I knew just because there will be no support for all that is to come.

I thank you for the interference. I thank you for stopping it. Always know if I had to choose between my life with you and that of a boy/girl relationship, you know it is all of You. Unless that person is with me, my family, and understands my commitment with You. I am trying to ease my pains with logic but you know a girl's gotta do what a girl's gotta do!!

I am learning that I can really enjoy those that cross my path, and I can wish them well, and I can love them, and that they aren't meant for me. I am the one that gets them ready for others. I am like this underlying support in life. I enjoy that part. I love that if my life touches another's that they will have greater hope after meeting me. I feel you. You must be ready. Thank you for coming into me. I am waiting.

**You sweet soul, don't think less than is possible. Everything is possible. Don't limit yourself. For we know your soul and your struggles. However, your struggles, they keep you close to life and you can feel pain. For we can only watch and weep in your presence of pain. You will grow beyond your wildest dreams and you will laugh and smile through it all. All the money will not faze you for you are of light. You will know what to do with it. Never worry my dear. We are of love and understand.**

Your children drank you in and you will all grow. You are teaching them light. You are showing them love. We know the bills are tight. We also know you kind of like it that way. It is all OK. You will relax with all of that. You will be able to go to Costco all you want!!! We love how you love to go there. It is amusing to see you there. You are like a child within miles and miles of candy and they love it.

You are of light. Be conscious of it for it will keep you strong in your dealings. Your humbleness is becoming of you. You call yourself a dork sometimes. We don't like that word. It hurts us to hear it. Call yourself an Angel. An earth Angel. You are of us and us of you.

My dear Lord, I am here for you. Give me all that you can as I can handle it. My Angels said I will meet them. I am looking forward to it. I love you all. I love you. I will go now. Thank you and amen. I love you all. Goodnight.

Nadia

## JANUARY 30, 2002

My Dearest Lord,

I am finding so much energy to tell everyone about you. Check it out, I am finding a way to talk about it and it is feeling more natural than unnatural. What is meant for me is meant for me. No questions. I understand that everyday is complete. I am smiling to think of you. You feel so playful to me at times like you want to play. Tell me how you are…I am really waiting for that…How are you in your world?

Nadia, the sweet soul that you are, when you want to jump from your skin we are jumping with you. We love floating around you. You hold us and kiss us with your warmth.

Thank you for being so active in my life. I love it so much. Tell me, you said I will see you, tell me, tell me, tell me…I will wait…

Yes, sooner than you think it possible. It is a big step in energy on our world to break through however we will to you soon. You are the bridge of souls. Your job title as humans will put it. You are the bridge of souls. Do you understand? You bridge the souls of people within themselves. You take the part of them they aren't conscious of and build a bridge to the part they already know of.

You give to them the gift of discovery of them. We rejoice in your hopes and your dreams and know you will see them all in your life of lives here on EARTH. For this earth is the hardest place for a soul to exist. You overcame it in a way we haven't witnessed before. We don't interfere with free will, yet your free will…you gave us a time to rejoice and learn. For you showed us an exceptional way to be human.

My Dear Sweet God, and Azna. Angels and Spirit Guides. It was all I knew. You must have put that in me to do. How could it all be that special?

You don't know the pain of others without your sympathy which became empathic with your growth. Your growth and experiences taught you to live without expectation. You stood before us and screamed in the night. You wrote to us and we wrote back to you to soothe your soul. When there was a detour you would choice the path of internal right, without question. For dishonesty takes you away from another soul. It disgusts you in a way that you don't know what to do with it.

It is hard for you to witness that. We weep in those times for dishonesty and mostly for dishonesty to one's own soul. So that is what we are like. All of us. We are all here to help, to support, to love, to ease pains. All; for we love all those that live and we pray as well for the souls. For the souls of life that are here and how we can keep that life from astray. We float around and see all; as God is witness and we are helpers. God's energy is too bright, too strong to contain, so we are in billions all over at your level never far from you. Heaven is not far yet complete in all you could have dreamed earth to be. The way we hear you think of how it should be.

It is because you are remembering heaven and you are knowing that on perfect days the Earth can carry some similar moments. Only magnified in your memory for the power exists there with no negative energy at all. For it doesn't have a home in such a place. WE love your soul. We feel you getting sleepy. We can go on and on, for we all know where this is going. There are no mistakes in this life. We love you.

I love you too. My eyes…I am going down. This is a lot. I can't wait until I read this. Goodnight, I love you again and again and again.

Nadia


## FEBRUARY 2, 2002

My Dearest Lord,

What a gift today is. I am quiet and calm and of a very soft voice right now. Your love for me and presence to me is so great and wonderful to me. Joseph, Mabel, Teddy and Joe. Michael! Are you here…talk to me.

I love knowing your names. I love when you flow through me. For I know it is special. I want to know more for I am here to work for all of you. I am waiting…

Oh sweet Nadia, for your soul we love. We love you without caution for you give to us your love in such a way. We rejoice in your presence and your appreciation of us.

Teddy, are you there? I am thinking you are a young angel. Tell me, I am thinking you are young.

Yes, Nadia I am very playful and I love being with you when you dance and when you want to write and when you sleep, I sometimes try to wake you up. I love your energy.

I love yours too. And Joseph, how are you in my life?

I am in your mind. I love to see you think. I love to see you think. Your mind is so beautiful to me. The wonder that exists there, I like to understand and feel through you. I guide you when your thoughts put doubts into you. So I remind you that you are right to know what you know. And there is no room for doubting when it comes to us and what we have to say to you and how beautiful you feel without the doubts. For your heart so sensitive it picks up the slightest dust to any existing soul including your own.

I love you Joseph. And Mabel. I just felt you, was that you?

Yes my sweet soul it was.

You sound like you have an accent?

Slightly, I am here with you when you feel bad about something. I bounce you back and I witness you come clean with your self and your feelings. We love your energy, me in particular, and you ask for what else you could do for God and for us. So hungry are the souls of the world. Your soul to touch many; as I told you in many writings, your love is for billions and some left over.

My sweet soul of innocent love. We love you without caution and we are here and always will be. I feel Joe coming in. Are you ready for him? Hi I am here, waiting for my turn. I am here with you. I am so much energy just like you. I keep you running and give you wonderful thoughts throughout your days. I soften your heart when someone or something upsets you.

We are here baby and we are going nowhere but taking you further and further into a beautiful world you will create with your soul. And we will all be around you and never let you down for we cannot. We are of you and you of us, only you are in form. So we go through you to remind you of us, for we love to touch inside and receive your data.

I love you Joe. How sweet to know of all of you.

We love you too.

And Michael? Did I get that right today was that you?

Yes it was. I am of strength for you. I will heal and I will protect your sweet innocence that you carry so earnestly. I love you with guidance within your heart and strength as a shield of all the negative. I love you and I respect your presence and the choices you have made and now have become. Sweet soul, for all of us are with you. And God leads us all into the straight path of love and the inner power that its existence provides.

Oh My Angels, sweet angels of God. I am getting sleepy and I will talk to you tomorrow, as it is my pleasure without caution as well. I love you all and I thank you for a day of rejoicement that I have never thought to be as it was or is. Amen. I love you so much. Thank you again and again.

Nadia

FEBRUARY 3, 2002

My Dearest Lord,

May you know my heart. I am trying to talk matter of fact about you and all the beautiful Angels. I am absorbing and loving what I am absorbing. I thought Jesus is of God as we all are, and that he is of the highest in evolvement. Tell me about that.

Jesus is of God as you are thinking. For Christ's light is in all of us. For his time here caused a world to change and he is aware of all the tribulations he encountered in his stay here. His sadness, his disappointment, coated with patience, love, understanding and virtue of the human soul. He understood all along that he will be here to change the world as it stood. He was given the miracles and the wisdom to bring those of light to him. For those in the dark remained so, and in that he spread his message.

In his time there they defeated and killed him, so they thought. However, he knew that light prevails hence Christianity. He was turned into a religion, which has now been broken up into many ways in which to reach him. And to reach God Almighty however we are to reach God, for God's love created all of it; all the messengers, the Angels, the churches and the light. God has all, even the grays and the darks. They are here to test and grow so that God can be completely sure of their stance. Do you understand that it is God. All God.

Yes I do. For that is my belief system and why I am here. For I am blessed. Amen.

Nadia


FEBRUARY 8, 2002

My Dearest God,

Boy did we have a lot of work today. In your Name, I hope that I represented you well. And my sweet Angels, you flowed through me like such refreshness to my soul. I found out a little bit what it is like for someone who hears about me to meet me and feel what that feels like. How do I represent myself and talk of You as You would want to be in the hearts of those individuals? I am finding that where I go, those I meet have a slight intention of making me one of them. Am I? I feel like I am one of everyone on this earth. Am I?

Our sweet soul Nadia, you are of everyone. Your journey's just beginning. You are finishing up your human side. You are here on Earth yet you are of us and us of you. Do You understand? You can't be of any group, as God is of all and you too of all. You were born a Muslim woman. You will remain such at exit. You are to touch and to heal with love and with God.

As it stands, your Muslimality is your entrance into this world and you lived as a Muslim and lived as an exemplary Muslim.

You are now of us, as we said in option, for your soul of fine gold and you of God. Goodnight our sweet soul.

Goodnight!

FEBRUARY 23, 2002

My Dear Lord,

Azna, Michael, Joseph, Mabel, Teddy and Joe, Josie, Erin, Erica and Gabriel, I love you all. With all I know to be love. I love that there are no ego's here at all. I love the freedom to love without repercussions. I love the honesty and the truth that exists here. I love the peace and warmth, and when you flow through me. For when I am sleeping you comfort me in a way I have yet to describe.

With that, all I can say is thank you for your love and me being guided to share your presence, for that is the gift of my lifetime right there. I always knew my life would change drastically when I was forty. I am exactly a month away from being forty.

For many years now I have had this feeling and I wondered what it would be. Deeper inside I knew you were with me. I had always felt it as God, which turns out it is, only with all the beautiful Angel's in-between people and God. For your love so felt and so needed. This is hard to experience. At first the elements of crazy come in. That we make this up comes in, disbelief, feeling chosen.

Oh, for you are sweet Nadia, and special. It is all of those things. However, it doesn't mean we are better than anyone else. It just means that we can share it with others to know too. You are of such light. Nadia, you are physically alone, that is for sure. We are here as God is here and we are just waiting for the right time for you.

You have acknowledged that is the case as we have felt from you. You even know you aren't as ready as you need to be. This solitude you are facing is as prophets have before you. Yes, that is what we said to you, for we had to prepare you for that word. We have been waiting to tell you. For that is what you are for God. Sweet Nadia, for you are of light and you are special.

You are of all your life. You are a messenger for God, and we will deliver to you all that you need. And we will direct you and you are protected. For even last night you sat with a man who hurt you the most and you still found the good in him and prayed for him. Do you understand who you are?

I am crying right now.

Yes my Dear, it is overwhelming! Yet you are secure enough to understand and strong enough to withstand and beautiful enough to be received. You are of that light. At Forty. You were right. At Forty. As Prophet Mohammed and Jesus Christ, and Moses and Abraham, and Jacob. All were Jewish and Mohammed an Arab. And Now you an Arab.

As we said you will die a Muslim woman. Yet you are not only for Islam, for you are for all people and your background will only be an issue to the weak. For every cell that exists in you, for every atom of the body you occupy in this moment is of God. We are all of God, and you are of God as well.

## March 23 - 2002

Good Morning God and sweet Angels too
So many names so much love for you
This 40th year for us to enjoy
All the changes that you share
The Love that you give me all for me
Comforting pain so much that I need
Thank you so greatly in all glory to be
Thank you so greatly for comforting me
My soul as it aches and loves all in the same moments of life
Moments of pain

I feel you carry my soul, so sweet
To even know you I still can't conceive
Yet I know with all purity you are always here with me
Thank you Dear God for the beauty of knowing
You are here in my sleep
Sometimes hard to see the reasons why
We all exist under a blue sky
My questions so many for a lifetime to share
To keep asking and learning my heart forever with you
Even when I am not myself
So today is my Birthday - quietly here
So simple and easy
Efforts so few to pass through a day
Thank you for giving me you
I love you Dear God
And sweet Angels too

MARCH 24, 2002

My Dearest Lord,

My Dear Azna, Michael, Joseph, Mabel, Teddy, Joe, Josie, Aaron, Erica and Gabriel, how I love you all, I am now forty. I am having fun with it already. I look at myself and I feel so great to say that I am forty; that in this year I know of you now. And that I have the most wonderful children and beautiful life. I respect the company that I am working for and those that own my house. I thank you for all the support around me in my life. I thank you for your hand in my life. I couldn't imagine my life without you in it. I really feel like I touched on free will.

YES Nadia you did. You know that we can say what is with God and what God brought to you, yet circumstances can change and you just saw how it can become. Never to worry for Allah, is here for you in all ways, for rewards are all here for you.

Yes, I feel that. I thank you for all the love around me and in my life, for the cleanliness of my home with all the painting.

Yes Nadia, we hope you are pleased. For we have so much in store for you. We thank you for writing to us this day. Please sleep our Angel on Earth and come back to us for all our love exists within you.

Thank you and I love you.

We love you too!

"The Team"

APRIL 10, 2002

My Dearest Lord God,

Azna, Michael, Joseph, Mabel, Teddy and Joe, Josie, Aaron, Erica and Gabriel, you want to talk to me Gabriel.

Yes, you heard me.

Yes I do.

Nadia, sweet Nadia, you heard me. Thank you for writing. We talk to you all the time and yet writing works in your heart for you can come back and learn. For you are approached with so much in a given day that you don't know what to think of first.

Yes, You know. I love all that I have to do and yet I want more time and will to write. I want to feel you every minute of the day. I want so much for your love and protection. For God's, love for me, that is all that I want above all else. It feels like life is most beautiful and most wonderful with your love in my heart and in my blood.

Your heart to always know that comfort.

Thank you for telling me. I am getting sooo sleepy.

Yes, our sweet Angel, you are, for your heart to carry you tomorrow. All your prayers heard. Keep praying some more and more. It makes a huge difference for us to hear you. How we cherish your existence.

Thank you again for such kindness to me. I am in awe still.

Oh sweet Nadia. We love you always and ever present.

I love you all too! And God Almighty!

Nadia

# CHAPTER 3

# IS THERE SUCH A MAN?

## APRIL 11, 2002

My Dearest Lord God,

Christ, Azna, Michael, Joseph, Mabel, Teddy and Joe, Josie, Aaron, Erica, and Gabriel. How could I feel right now? Other than to love you as I do. Other than to thank you for this evening. In all it's glory! My girlfriend, I addressed her through Christ tonight. How did that happen?

It was beautiful and wonderful and made all the difference to Her life. I felt it. This evening will never be forgotten for she left with such excitement. I felt blessed to witness. I am blessed to have felt and saw you My Dearest Christ. I saw you in my heart and my mind. For you lifted my hand with my palm in the air.

I was there for your girlfriend.

Yes, you were. I am surely overwhelmed, yet beautifully. I want to cry of its beauty. I hope in my writing that I can articulate what my heart and my mind saw of you, to share with all. Your love so healing. Just seeing my girlfriend.

Yes Nadia, soul of souls. You are of purity and soul. You are of God and of Angels. You are on Earth to touch and to be touched by life. You are life. You smile with heart and have a heart with smile. You of such beauty that only you could comprehend and think of yet not yet explain all that you know, yet you will know. You will know to share for that is your purpose.

Nadia, sweet Nadia, for I came into your body of purity and love. You understand now how purity becomes a person. You wanted to know and now you do. For I am Christ in your heart. I am here. Forever to burn the lights of a thousand candles within you. Always. You are a messenger. You are a prophet. You are of us. Do you know? Yes you our Dear, for we are all here as Christ leads us in your path.

For God sent to you an army to go forward. You are ready and beautiful. People were hugging you in this evening. They couldn't help it. Your beauty shines from within so bright that it could be blinding to an unsuspecting soul. Your love so pure it is as of God.

Your girlfriend told you this evening it is hard for others to be around you for you are a reflection of who they are and they can't handle it in most instances. Never to worry, it is good. It needs time however they will face growth because of you for you are of God's light.

And the light of Christ, as Christ is within you. For we love you and all that you are and have become. Your heart of such treasure, of the finest of gold, as you said tonight to your girlfriend. Your patience has shown tonight in your knowledge of much the world has yet to understand. You will never be alone and know that you are not alone and never will be. You are an Angel, among heaven and here on Earth. Our sweet soul of light, you are sleepy and need to rest.

Thank you for this evening.

You have made the difference in so many lives. And you always will.

Thank you for this evening. I still have yet to absorb all that is in me. I am flabbergasted, in such awe; I keep wanting to cry out of happiness and honor. Goodnight and thank you.

Thank you Nadia. You will see. You will see what your life is to be. We love you as you couldn't ever know. Amen. Good night. Rest sweet Angel, goodnight.

"The Team"


## APRIL 14, 2002

Dearest Lord God,

Christ, Azna, Joseph, Mabel, Teddy and Joe. Josie, Aaron, Erica, and Gabriel. I love you all. There is no other way I can start to address you all. I love you and I am use to you as I feel you are such a part of me, that when I do feel you it is a feeling of comfort as a feeling that I have known before.

Oh sweet Nadia. For you are doing all that you can for us.

I hope so. Sometimes…I feel like I am slow, yet my conviction is so strong that when I am speaking there is no mincing of my words. I feel very beautiful yet very certain of what I speak.

Yes Nadia. Conviction was a good word to describe yourself. We are growing you and you are growing even quicker at times and ahead of our direction. Your belief in the ultimate truth of God and of purpose is so strong that it led you through life like a light without any mercy of non truths and non purity. You have a lot of work to do. For your work will grow you and take you to others and others and others. You will know and we are ever present.

Yes Nadia, for I am Christ. Your amazement not yet fully absorbed, for you empathized with my plight and bought a book to learn of my struggles. For you were believing a relation between myself and you. Yes Nadia, there is. For you understand of God. You understand at least for what you know is the love of God in all its purity. You understand the human soul for its weakness it reacts. And You understand how purity and love heal. Love heals. Purity bonds. Love seals all that exists together. You are a force on Earth to touch. Your soul burns the light of a thousand candles in an instant. Your soul of God and God of you. For you are of Angels and of Me. You are of all light and never to be without. For your life one of life's beauties and with gentleness you speak of what you know. And you know that you are doing God's work and the world rejoices in the energy, for it is of purity and no less.

Oh my sweet Nadia, Your heart to know of all, your soul to understand all, even if you didn't experience, for your words from God to heal. To touch, to bring to the realization that we are all here for all; That no one person is more special than the other; That all humans are here for a purpose and all for each other. We are meant to be together and to grow from security, love and support of the souls of ourselves and others. For earth being a very difficult chore to endure.

Yet, for God we all chose to come and experience. You speak the truth of God Almighty! Rejoice in your words and your heart's intent in conversation. You are working hard this week yet you accomplish much within a day. Your life is touching and touching without reservation. You talk in amazement about us. Yet you speak as though we are such a part of you, that innocence. Our sweet Nadia, for you are getting tired. Sleep our child and sleep well, for we will be with you as ever present in you life. Good night our Angel on Earth of God. Good night.

Good night to all of you and thank you with all my heart for your love.

Nadia

## MAY 4, 2002

Dearest Lord Allah,

Sweet Christ, Azna, Michael, Mabel, Joseph, Teddy and Joe, Josie, Aaron, Abel, Erica and Gabriel, I feel you here in my life. Throughout my days, in my nights, in my thoughts, in my heart when I think things or in places of purity or greatness of some sort, I feel you go through me. Everyday, I can only thank you all for being in my life, being my partner, and my soul's soul.

My life has mostly been without a partner. When I did have a partner he blamed me for being in his life. I am just losing the impact of his life with me. I am thankful that I didn't die before that happened. I got to be with my kids when I am free in life. I can be with them who I am. Thank you for that opportunity.

It is our privilege to serve your hearts messages from God Almighty. For God Almighty in complete witness of all that you know of and do.

I am distracted doing things that I love yet I don't know where to direct my energies all the way.

Yes Nadia, a lot is with you now however focus will present itself. You will be as you should be everyday. Enjoy all that you do, for it is all with great purpose.

Thank you soooooo much, for telling me all that you do. I am with you as you are with me. Thank you, I just felt you. Goodnight.

Oh sweet Nadia, goodnight our Angel. Goodnight our sweet Angel.

"The Team" – Christ


## MAY 6, 2002

Oh Dearest God,

Christ, Azna, Michael, Mabel, Joseph, Teddy and Joe, Josie, Aaron, Abel, Erica, and Gabriel. How blessed that I am.

Nadia, this is Christ.

Sweet Christ, I am here. Thank you for telling me. Sometimes when I write, I believe it is all of You at once.

Yes, mostly it is however I wanted to touch you. Did you feel me?

Yes, I did. I love feeling you.

Oh sweet Nadia, you are love. You are becoming and you will experience changes soon in your life. You are ready. You are ripe for the movement that will happen. I will be within you, beside you, in front and in back of you, for you will be surrounded. You are the grace and love of God, and a woman who is to be protected by God and all

Angels. For you are grace and love of life, and free will brought you to us.

For in amazement at your soul, rewards await you our dear sweet child of God. Just ask to soothe your pains. We are here to cushion your mishaps and your trials. You will have them however you will learn from them and go on and no longer will you feel damaged by what you may face in this life. Nadia, you can't believe that we talk to each other such as we do.

I have to say, I feel you, I hear you, I love what I hear and I even saw you. I almost don't know what to do.

Nothing more than you are our sweet Angel of God. Your heart that of a child. You are a child inside. Still amazed by your age.

Yes, I am. I feel so great and I don't feel like people my age.

You should not, for you are protected and your work would fill yet another few lifetimes. Yet you are at the beginning of it all. You keep growing and your spirit of such a young child, for the innocence you possess becomes you like sun kissed cheeks on a child playing in the sun.

Oh Sweet Christ.

Yes Nadia.

How will I do all this work?

With ease, for it is not work to you. It is grace and you will glide as the Angels do. For your suffrage as was in my time will not happen to you. There will be no distraction in your healing and love. You are of such light in a darkening world that you will not be harmed for no one will be able to harm you.

Wow!

Yes Nadia, no one can take away light. For light prevails in all. Light is the energy force that drives all. Your heart has known for years. Even in your most difficult moments your soul searched. Even in your pain you remained self-less and knew you were doing the best that you can. If you didn't know what to do you asked God. For God was listening and listening. Your heart and your soul were carried in all struggles and mishaps.

Sweet Nadia, Angel of God, Prophet of life, Healer on Earth; know that you will touch and heal. You will love with your eyes and your heart will talk without words at times. And your presence will touch, for you are forever light.

Thank you for talking with me tonight. I am falling asleep. I ran 3.10 miles tonight. It feels so good to do that. Thank you for being in my life. I feel like the happiest person in the world. Thank you again.

Nadia, Sweet Nadia, you are the happiest person in the world for you want for all good. You are blessed and evolved and growing. We love you and enjoy your life's presence. Never to forget how much you are loved and how you will never be alone. Never.

Thank you once again. Goodnight.

Goodnight.

"The Team" – Christ

## MAY 22, 2002

Dearest Allah,

Sweet Christ, Azna, Michael, Mabel, Joseph, Teddy and Joe, Josie, Aaron, Able, Erica and Gabriel, how I love you all, I wanted to thank you for the freedom of knowing no one will call, and knowing no one will write, and knowing that there is no one in my life. It makes me sad in one way, yet very relieved in so many other ways. At least now I know what I know.

It is sad in one way, because when I feel love it softens me so tenderly, yet I don't really get to feel it enough to enjoy love. It scares me more than it loves me. People, it is hard to be with others, for a person doesn't know what the years up to their meeting have put in them. And we can't fix each other. And we can't ask questions or get the answers that we need because sometimes we don't even know what to ask, we just find out with time. I read something I wrote two years ago. And I could have written that today.

The sadness and loneliness about not having love and it made me realize what a waste of time, yet what a world of growth came with it. Waste of time only in that I didn't learn anything new, but now I think I finally got it, to let go of those I was holding on to. For whatever reason, they have to be let go of.

I am getting sooooooo sleepy again. I still believe in love, yet I believe in it for others for now. Now, I don't want to think that any person is there, for no one ever really was. That makes me sad, but it is realistic and that makes it fine. It is the truth of my life. But only one truth.

The beautiful news is that there is so much truth in my life and I love and appreciate all that I have in my life, my kids, my family and my friends. I thank you for everyone's love for me in my life and the blessing that I love them so much. I want to hear you, and I am so sleepy.

Yes, Nadia, we are here. Rest. Our sweet Child of God. For you are us and we are you. We love you as you could always know that we are here for you without question. How we love you always and we will never go away. Never to fear. Your heart to be protected even in the worst of your pains. We love you Nadia. Sleep with knowing we surround you in circles and circles. We love you.

"The Team" – Christ

I love you all too. Goodnight.

Nadia

JUNE 3, 2002

My Dearest Lord God,

Sweet Christ, Azna, Michael, Joseph, Teddy and Joe, Josie, Aaron, Abel, Erica, and Gabriel, Sweet God, Angels, I love you so much. My life, I am in it and I am here yet what do I do with my life? Am I doing what I am supposed to be doing? Oh dear Lord, my heart in this life. How odd it is that we want for some things and we can't stop when they are matters of the heart.

I have a fear of getting to know someone. It built in me disappointment, sadness…it is hard getting to know someone. I want a happy heart in a man, gentle and clean. One that means what he says and no matter what else that we are both each others love in life. Forever, that commitment means something. And that we have a life where we grow with each other and respect each other and never stop caring. Oh Dear God, Christ, all the sweet Angels. Is there such a man?

Oh sweet Nadia. Your love is of God's love, yet on Earth, you are not weak to want. For as humans you will always seek partnership, even though you feel hurt. The dream never dies, yet it is dared at times. It is dared, for the hurt wants proof to it that it is not true that you were hurt. That love, it will soothe the pain of hurt.

Yet in life you start to realize that love in any form, of God, of Children, of friends, of family. That it soothes the same. And then your heart still desires the love of a partner, for that is the ultimate in a soul's inner fulfillment, in completion of self with God. Sometimes it isn't the love that is meant for life, yet the hurt that accompanies it accumulates and grows, our sweet Angel on Earth.

After a while of that, you don't know why you would go back for more pain. Why would you? The excitement gets associated with the loss and then your heart gets or becomes cautious. You are now cautious. That is a gift Nadia. Look. You will see. Your heart, it is cautious. It is realizing that all people, they are different and that you may want to make them OK, but all you can do is touch their lives. You don't mind, it is when they touch your life. You no longer want anyone to touch your life.

Nadia, this is Christ.

Oh Sweet Christ, how great to hear from you.

Yes Nadia, for I have pleasure in your heart and you carry life with you. You will see. You already faced God long ago and you're clean without worry and fear and negativity in life on Earth. Not to worry Nadia, you are not forgotten or being punished for loving.

Your love is made for so many; you may feel like you are missing a main component to understand that part of life. You are. You will not be soon so don't worry. It is not good for you to question love in relationships. It does exist however since you have witnessed no proof of it; you don't know how it could exist.

I am telling you that it does. You will know and you will then witness. You want to cry when you do witness it in some moments of life, for you respect that it exists. And you will know how it exists for you and your soul's nourishment. You are not now going to choose a partner that will not support you as you need and as you support others.

Thank you sweet Christ for your words to me, talking to me, acknowledging me. I thank you for knowing that all existence isn't only this, yet it is not seen to me. I know that it is much more beautiful still and that I will find it. I look for it, yearn for it, love it, need it, want it, enjoy the thought of it. And I am thankful for glimpses I knew and remember what it was like to dream.

Oh sweet Nadia, you know more. You are still a little scared to come out with all of it. You want it and feel so lonely inside without it. You feel unloved and rejected because of it, yet you are not. You have felt such rejection of who you are.

You are healing, for you are longed for by many. If only you knew, and you wonder why? Nadia, they were all kept from you for you. They weren't in your best interest. More pain is not for you anymore.

The pain of loneliness is preferable right now only in this point in time. For your growth and all that is happening, distractions would be just that. Take heart, for your heart is filled with all of us our love. The love of God Almighty and your soul shared and loved by life and heaven. For you are heaven on Earth our beautiful love.

Thank you for that. I love you more than I have words for. Thank you again and again.

Nadia goodnight, we love you more than your comprehension.

"The Team" – Christ


JUNE 11, 2002

Dearest Allah,

Sweet Christ, Azna, Michael, Mabel, Joseph, Teddy, Joe, Josie, Aaron, Abel, Erica and Sweet Gabriel; how much it is that I love you all. You are my life's partners and I couldn't ask for more. I forget that most people don't know of you, and if I were to talk about it they wouldn't know how to take it or me. I forget that beliefs can be so ingrained that the thought of some new thought or thoughts is not acceptable. I love to share the conversations about God, Christ, all the beautiful Angels, Azna.

I have learned to talk to what is understood, and that feels good when I have that chance however I don't get that chance too much. The two men I loved most or felt most peace with in my heart, neither of them want to see me. That hurts me, because I do love our conversations. I wonder why or how I could love so much time spent with those that don't want to share that with me. That is hard, but I am OK.

Nadia, Sweet Nadia, they want to, yet as you see and know they aren't there. You don't get to talk. For intensity is too much from you and you don't know how you affect others. WE are sorry that it is painful for you however you have grown a great deal with that rejection that you feel. And you got a chance to see the beauty of such simple times in your home that you are happy irregardless of who is in your life to share some of your time. You are feeling a little overwhelmed and you need some time to let yourself stand still.

I did take some days off. Thank you. I have been feeling it too. I love you so much.

Sweet Nadia, this is Christ. We love you. You are loved. Your life, it is lives, for you are doing and have. In this one life you accepted to live for God Almighty. You came up and up and up and in your world you touch the sky. You reached and you touched God, for God has been touching you all along.

Yes, your days at work are numbered. Not many numbers, less than three digits. You did all you can there and they will be fine. Your energy will stay and they will never forget your presence, yet you gave to them culture of love and patience and loyalty and integrity. You.

Your presence in my life it made all the difference to my heart. I couldn't find a partner here; I couldn't or didn't know how. Or maybe I don't fit in and I don't even know it. I guess ignorance is bliss, yet ignorance of things not good for me can be a good thing.

Yes Nadia, know that there will never be mistakes, ever!

I do know. Even when I don't want it to be true!!! Ha!

Nadia, we all need love. We have it differently here at home, you have it another way on Earth. You will have it again. Open your eyes. This time it will come to you. It will just be there and you will know.

You will glow with God's love, for the only person that will come to you will come to you from God. No one else will come to you. The person will come to you from God Almighty for God knows your heart and not just anyone will stand beside you.

You will get to do what you love and you will have time for your children. You will see. Your dreams, your inner wants, you will do all that you desire and dream of. Loving and caring and loving some more for that is you. Never to forget who you are. Copy this and read it and read it again. For you are life in God.

WE love you Nadia. Read. And Read again.

Thank you for all that you say. Thank you again and again.

Nadia. We love you.

"The Team" – Christ

# CHAPTER 4

# YOU ARE RIGHT
# WHERE YOU SHOULD BE

## JUNE 24, 2002

Sweet Lord, Dear God,

Sweet Christ, Azna, Michael, Mabel, Joseph, Teddy and Joe, Josie, Aaron, Abel, Erica and Sweet Gabriel, how privileged I feel in this life to write to you. How loved I feel and how it carries me in this life to write to you. I am realizing something. I am realizing that I let some people in this life shape how I don't feel entitled to me being loved and loving a person.

And if I find that I am loving someone I get scared that they will not be there because I don't feel like they will love me for loving them. But I am believing and learning that if I was with someone that I would be good. I would be able to accept their love if I could just go slow enough to grow with that person.

People are so impatient these days, most want everything right away. To sleep with you before you really get to know each other. Most want it to be there even if they fabricate it; they are willing to accept the fabrication. All that to not face their own truths, let alone the person they are with. It is hard. I just felt you and I have a couple of times tonight. Thank you. How is all of this so real? Why are we now knowing of You before we die on Earth?

Nadia, you are the messenger of life for the living. So much that can't be seen and yet some can see, for the others that cannot. Yes, we are all here, going through you in groves, So much so that you could feel us. WE love you Nadia. WE are present. Sorry to be invisible. You are thinking how great it would be to be use to seeing us and talking, for you will. You will Nadia. What is to come out of you is yet to be seen and experienced.

Nadia, this is Michael. I am with you always Nadia. I am here with you, beside you, with Christ and with all the beautiful Angels known to you. There are many more, hundreds, thousands, millions even, just for you.

You never felt entitled to love, for those around you never felt entitled and shamed you into believing "how could you be happy about a man. You are a fool, a silly fool for doing so," and yet You are not.

Nadia, you are beautiful and when you are paired you will be equally yoked and you will know of how it is to be loved, accepted, and how to love and not fear the loss of it, you will teach that for all humans possess such fear.

Oh dear God, I love you. Christ, Michael, Azna, all the beautiful Angels.

NADIA YOU ARE AN ANGEL. YOU ARE AN ANGEL. YOU ARE AN ANGEL. YOU ARE OF GOD. YOU ARE LIGHT. YOU ARE LIGHT. I WILL GUIDE YOU. CHRIST WILL CHANNEL YOU, GABRIEL WILL MESSAGE YOU AND AZNA WILL FLOW THROUGH YOU AND COLLECT YOUR DATA.

MABEL IS FOR YOU TO STOP AND CORRECT YOURSELF FROM TAKING AWAY THE BEAUTY OF YOUR HEART FROM YOURSELF. YOU ARE ENTITLED TO IT. NEVER TO FORGET. YOU LOVE SO MUCH TO WITNESS LOVE.

Yes, I do. To witness it. To feel it.

AND NADIA ALL THE OTHER ANGELS, WE ARE HERE TO SUPPORT YOU AND TO GIVE YOU THE MEDIUM TO GROW THE SOULS IN WHICH YOU TOUCH. YOU ARE SO LOVED. YOU ARE FEELING BORED RIGHT NOW WITH YOUR JOB. IT IS OK FOR YOU ARE MOVING ON. YOU WILL BE STUDIED ONE DAY AND YOU WILL WITNESS FROM THE HEAVENS AS YOU DREAM IT ALL TO BE. YOUR LIFE AN EXAMPLE OF LIFE AND LOVE.

I have to get to sleep. I love you all.

We love you too sweet Nadia, Angel of God. WE love you. You will know what to do, never to fear. You will always know Nadia. We love you with all the heart and love you can understand and more and more. Good night, our Angel.

Good night Sweet God, Christ, and all the beautiful Angels.

"The Team" – Christ

## AUGUST 19, 2002

Men, Men, Men! How come these men are coming up in my life? I have to call one and cancel Friday. And another, I love him, but not that way anymore. I know he is there for me but I feel and felt so bad that he came here with expectations. And I felt safe that he was coming and that we both understood where we were. I am thinking that I have to be so careful.

I am just feeling free. Yet feeling the desire again is at least making me feel good to know that it exists; although I am thinking not to do anything about it at this point in my life.

How happy we are that you can just have fun and not to worry, you will be protected. You are here and now and so are they. It will be of fun and you had to see it to enjoy it. You could never be ready for what you aren't ready for. We love you Nadia. Be who you are and don't wait for those that are holding you back. Go on and move forward and if someone comes to you then they were meant to. And if they can't find their way to you then they can't find their way to you. You can be happy and not feel guilty about it.

You will not lose us and we will never stop loving you for it. It is OK, you are of love and life and now you can have that in your life and have life too. Date, and date many. No excuses to anyone. If a man that you think you like can't fess up to you, then Buh bye, oh we loved to say that. We love it when you say it with such vigor for it is the truth. You are free, remember that.

Never feel guilty for anything or anyone. Celebrate your joy in life and don't, remember, don't look back! Your heart is the best of life in life. Good night.

Good night, I love you again.

You are of life Nadia, Good night, again,

"The Team" – Christ

SEPTEMBER 29, 2002

Dearest Lord God,

Sweet Christ, Azna, Michael, Mabel, Joseph, Teddy and Joe, Josie, Aaron, Abel, Bessie, Erica, and Sweet Gabriel, I love you all soooooooo much. Thank you for me knowing you in my life.

Nadia, Nadia, Nadia, we are so appreciative for the involvement into your life. We love you without caution.

I wanted to thank you for all the initiative in my life today. I finished a good deal of my homework and better defined what I am ready for and I got my sights on starting things properly. Thank you. And for my bills and for doing them today and having enough money to pay them, I am grateful and blessed.

WE love you Nadia, Don't worry about a thing. Move on and forward and enjoy your journeys. We love you dearly!

I love you too. I just felt you again. Thank you. I love you.

We love you too!

"The Team" – Christ

Hi Bessie, I just heard you. You are new to me. I love you too!

NOVEMBER 3, 2002

My Dearest Lord God,

Sweet Christ, Azna, Michael, Mabel, Joseph, Teddy and Joe, Josie, Aaron, Abel, Bessie, Erica and Sweet Gabriel, how much I love you, I felt you so much yesterday.

**Yes Nadia, you were uncomfortable.**

I couldn't stop asking you to surround me.

**And surround you we did!**

Dear Lord, all sweet Angels, I need your help. What is this with my friend and me?

**Yes Nadia, it is finishing and flourishing at the same moment. It is confusing you however you are learning who you are with him. You will be ready for the other man. No guilt, just feel love as you only know how to do!**

I don't want to hurt my friend.

**He will be sad no less and he will miss you until it hurts, yet he will want for your happiness. Remember you are right where you should be. You love the quiet; we could feel your calm, your peace.**

Yes, it is there. I love the quiet and beauty that we can only see when the sound in our lives is down. It is hard for me to feel so different in my heart.

I love the other man with all my heart and all I have in it, but because he is physically not there…it makes it weird. He is here and not here at the same time. Like I have my life yet he has my heart. I want my heart and my life to be together though. When I talk to my friend, sometimes…I just felt like I am practicing in life, like I am at school, learning to love myself when someone else loves me.

Yes, Nadia, that is your lesson that is why you are done there now. He is looking for future and you know that you will not with anyone but the other. Like you are both there and you know that it is just a matter of time.

It reassures me how things are down here and how little I know even when I think I know so much! It is wonderful and glorious. I will talk to my friend tonight.

Remember though that you can only be in one place at a time. Enjoy your challenges and your love of life. We stand beside you and inside you and around you.

I love you with all the smiles of life I know of!

We love you forever and ever…never to worry, you are right where you should be today in this moment.

Amen! I rest with that!

We love you again and again,

"The Team" – Christ

NOVEMBER 21 - 2002

My Lord,

Are men worth all the heartache I carry over it? I am losing faith in that whole world! I can just be a friend, but I don't know how to be otherwise. I guess I am weird. I tell people that I talk to you. It is the most beautiful thing to me. I am so blessed to know this. I hope that I am not too much for those that I encounter and that I am around.

Please dear God, watch my heart. It is so sore, that with the slightest mishap, I go numb. I feel scared to feel, to want, to care, to fathom any idea of a human being in my heart or soul and really be there. You could equate me to a starving human being, only not for food, but to know what it is like for someone to love me and for me to accept it without freezing; to be there long enough to grow through that. I love the people I love. If their lives are meant not to be with me then I accept it. I love you and trust you enough to understand. Talk to me. I just want to be with you. I want to cry. I want to be held and I want to know how to let my pain dissipate within me. I am waiting…

My love, we love you. Your soul we carry. We weep at your sadness however we are hear. You are fine. Don't carry sadness. You carry it in place of fear. You are working so hard to not have this one fear that you have. You don't need to have it at all.

People are just people. They are doing their best to be who they are. Let them be as you are to be. Free in your soul. Your heart is like that of a feather. You have the strength to fly with it and it can carry you, yet if let go, its lightness is weightless and can land anywhere.

Your loves are not losses, they are love. That is all. Can you be in anyone's life? You will. You will know. May you rest with the knowledge and love that we carry for you within us and share with you. We love to flow through you so that we can feel you and love you as you desire.

We love you Nadia, in ways still for you to comprehend. Thank you for giving to us the opportunity to be within your life as you ask of us. We are love for you and support for your soul. Goodnight.

Sweet God, Azna, Angels and Spirit guides. I love you, thank you for your touch and your love. I need you sooooooo much tonight. I am thinking so much in all directions.

Love,

Nadia

DECEMBER 18, 2002

Dearest Lord God,

Sweet Nadia, Nadia, Nadia, Nadia, Nadia, we are all hear. Around you, Your light on Earth. We are all here, including Mohammed. We all love you. Your time to unify. To unify countries, peoples, heritages, colors, religions. You are the prophet of God on Earth now.

I thought Mohammed was the last prophet and said he was.

Nadia, God, is of the greater good and people need new life to continue. It is very negative and very deceptive to live in the world at this time. Truth is less recognized everyday, less felt, less driving within a soul. Nadia, you are the greater good. Just who you are in all the beauty you carry in your eyes and heart. Do you understand?

I am starting to. I am starting to feel it; I just don't know how it will all happen.

Never to worry my child, our child. You are of light and will float as you are beginning to feel right now. You had to know so much so that you can be received. You are like all the prophets in their aweness in the beginning and the doubting and the disbelief, for it is your humility that told you that.

How could it be you? Because you are of the right, of the light and of the human force on Earth to carry the love of God to the people, for how else is it to be received. Nadia, don't worry about anything, everyday is as it should be.

I am here for you God, for all of you. Of only the good. I will do as you ask of me and guide me, for that is the true love of my life. I love people of life and those who want to live it and touch you and look for you. I am here. Use me, teach me, guide me, help me, and love me always. I thank you for all the love my way, for it has healed my soul in threads of gold as you would say! I am tired. Talk to me as I sleep. I love you.

Nadia, you will have support. All in the moment is as it should be. You will be protected always. You don't fear dying for God. That is not how you will exit. You will exit in the love of God as you love God in life. We hear you. You will not exit yet. You have work to do however we did want you to know how since you just saw the struggles of all other prophets.

※

*When Christ said to me that I had seen all the prophets, I had, however I only remember three. Christ, Mohammed, and Moses. Kind of like the way we remember dreams, I only remembered big parts of it. I remembered Moses asking*

*God Almighty to not be a prophet. He did not want to do his mission once he was here and in the thick of it. It overwhelmed him. And God spoke to him through the Angel Gabriel and told him that his mission was already in motion and his resistance was to the understanding of his work. That if he understood his work he could continue, and he did. At times, it just felt like he didn't know what to do with the energy of home, here on Earth. It made me feel good to be shown that.*

*The other thing I saw was the struggles of Prophet Mohammed. He was not believed by many, and that included his immediate family members. He had a big family and in time, some turned on him and tried to create fractions of him. Which they accomplished however early on, they wanted to know how he knew what he did, since he was illiterate.*

*He learned through the teachings of the Angel Gabriel as well as through memorization however he struggled with his knowledge's as well, and his delivery to people.*

*Again, I felt right at home, since I don't know in this day how I am received, however I do know that when people are around me they are comforted and I don't even have to speak The third life on Earth that I witnessed was Christ. Those who could see understood he was peace and love and those who wanted all the ego driven things were completely threatened by him. They wanted to block his path and take away his message because they did not want to be accountable. His reflection would hold them to their own accountability and they did not like that. So they tried to take him away from the populations just to stop his truth, his love and his purity. All of that translated into leadership and that is where the threats came into the picture. His healing was questioned, since no one wanted anyone to be more special then the current leadership. His struggles were simply with the rulers and that is something I have yet to experience, although I was shown it to know it existed.*

How, How could this be me?

Itis!!!!!!!!!!!!!!!!!!!!!!!!!!!!!!!!!!!!!!!!!!!!!!!!!!!!!!!!!Itis!!!!!!!!!!!!!!!!!!!!!!!!!!!!!!!!!!!!!!!!!!!!!!!!!
!!!!!!!!!!!!Itis!!!!!!!!!!!People are telling you, you are an Angel.
You are on Earth, for you are prophetic. People come to
you now. You have had practice. You are of open beams
of light and you draw all light to you.

You are loved beyond your thinking, yet it is as great a
love as you feel for others. Good Night our young soul on
Earth, for you are with us our Angel in the world of the
seen and you will touch and unify and grow the world.

No one will not be able to listen to you. You are trying to
explain yourself and you don't even know how. Humility!
You are of all these things! Sleep!

I will, I love you all.

WE LOVE YOU NADIA! "the team," Christ, and all the beautiful Angels at home. We surround you in all you do. WE
love you again and again! Never to worry, forget or fear!

I love you all,

Nadia

&

*There was a six month period here in which I basically did not write or wrote
nothing new. I had a hard time coming to terms with the knowledge's that I was
coming to and then fitting that into me, into my life. Sometimes I do not write
for a while and take a break, to give myself time to absorb all the changes and
assimilate them into my life.*

&

## JUNE 25, 2003

My dearest Lord God, and all the sweet Angels, talk to me. I can hear you and see you in my heart and mind. What do you want to say to me?

You are what the world is needing. You think how could it be you? What an old thought. You know how. You are feeling a standstill of time. It is true however you have so much to know and to experience and to understand in order to touch others and their respective places in life.

Nadia, I am here. Christ within you. I am with you always. Experience all so that you know. You know how it is to be a human in all forms. How else to understand what you will see and encounter. You are ready. We are here and when the world is ready for you, you will be available to those who will know and then for those who don't.

Nadia sweet Nadia, you feel confused and weird about your relationship with your friend. You love him and want to be with and spend time with him, yet your heart, is it ready for that commitment. You love being loved and your friend gave you the safest place in the world to feel loved and to be loved and not be hurt.

For you healed him in ways that you couldn't know of at all and he is realizing that you are healing his mind, his body, his soul. He is good for you however can you stay in one place right now? You love the other guy and yet you stopped believing he is there physically.

Yes I did. It has been a long time and we did see each other and we didn't stay, so what am I supposed to do. I am not impatient, nor do I want to rush anything. I just wanted to believe in a relationship and what that could even mean and how it could be to have a person who is there in mind, heart and body.

Life will take you where you want to/need to be. Trust in your self, in that everyday is as it should be. Good night our love,

"The Team" – Christ

I love you too!

Nadia

*I was frustrated with loving others. Ending one relationship and understanding that the only person I thought I loved was not available. We would write and talk and yet be awkward everywhere else. I was content within myself and didn't need or want more than simple love. I felt happy inside that I was finally content in my heart, which made everything else around me feel that way too.*

# CHAPTER 5

# YOU ARE LOVED

AUGUST 20, 2003

Nadia we love you. WE are here. WE started differently with you in this evening. Your girlfriend will introduce you to an Angel, and as you now know, it is Stirling. Take care of your affairs. You are now moved on and will talk to your friend. You are doing all as you should. Replace any guilt with love, for that is what you are, extend that to yourself Our Child! You are sooo sleepy.

Yes, I am. My eyes…I am dreading telling my friend, yet I am relieved at the reality of being free in my heart once more. That is the biggest sign and I can't ignore it. Thank you for sending the countless validations and reminders and clubs over my head!

We love you Nadia. WE will come to you soon. You are the love of God on Earth!

I love you too!

"The Team" – Christ

Nadia!

SEPTEMBER 5, 2003

Dearest Lord God Almighty,

Wow. Sweet Christ, Azna, Michael, Mabel, Joseph, Teddy and Joe, Josie, Aaron, Abel, Sweet Bessie, Ericka and Sweet and Beautiful Gabriel, I am shaky right now. I am filled with so much at once. I just told a friend and she knew. She was crying and everything I was saying was new to her. It is all stuff she knew however it seems it was the way in which it was said.

I feel like I am on the outside and the inside at the same time. I write to you and my elbows are weak. I don't know what the next step is however I am trusting that it is big. I have been feeling it all week. That is how you got me home now with the phone call from my Mom.

Yes Nadia, we did. WE love you and we needed you in this moment. You are of such love. You are ready Nadia, sweet Nadia. YOU ARE AN ANGEL ON EARTH. YOU ARE COMING TO ALL. VERY VERY SOON. YOU WILL BE READY, NOT TO WORRY! YES, you are overwhelmed but you are not.

We brought you here, not to worry; your light so bright it is in the eyes of all who see you even at a glance. You will become for all. You will be the miracle of all human life on Earth. You are the heart of hearts for all. You are the one to touch and to teach. For you are a teacher.

This is Christ. Nadia, you will see me again, soon. I will infuse you as I have said before. You will not feel the weight of it as it has been said before as well. You will carry forward all the love in abundance.

You are safe and you are strong. Your strength precedes you. You are wonder to many. As your friend wanted you to speak to a group, you will. To many and many, some, all at once. You will be broadcast on your own terms for argument will elude you.

Our Dear Soul on Earth, we wanted to thank you in this day, for your love of God, of all of us, without question. For listening to your heart and finding the paths that grow through.

Your love of God, you now know of Abundance. Yes, your girlfriend writing you of Stirling. He wants to meet you now!

You will be safe Nadia, our Sweet Angel of God. We rejoice in the saying. We rejoice in the love on Earth that you are present in this day! Never ever to worry. I am present in your form. You feel left out of this for your body is Shaking and vibrating and you can't see me.

It is all of life and love Nadia. Never to Worry! You will be all in Greatness. I am with you, for I am coming to your vision in short time. Yes, Your heart a flutter!

There is so much love with you, around you, for you, with others, for others. Your life is of constant and growing, Your heart so great a wonder in life, for you of life and of nothing else. You will see.

Trust and with Trust grow your patience, for you do not know what to do with yourself. Find an outlet and come back to us soon! YOU ARE LOVED!

I heard you loud and clear.

You are loved. Call Stirling. Nadia we are with you our love. Never to forget or to worry!

"The Team" – Christ

I love you too!

Nadia.


SEPTEMBER 6, 2003

Dearest Lord God,

Sweet Angels of God, I love you all.

Nadia, This is Christ. I have been coming to you much in this time. Our time is together as I am in every place on Earth at once. I live within you and You are the beginning of much growth in all the Nations of the World.

I will travel with you in all, for your light to touch without the spoken word. All will know and no one soul will be left behind. You will make sure of it. For your life loves to include everyone and no one will be left behind with you. They are safe to not be better or worse or judged.

You will speak the truth and even upon non-admittance of such there will be admittance internally our dear Child. So never to worry, for you will never say anything a soul is not ready to hear. Glory be to God Almighty.

Time for so much to come your way, for you will see and when you see, you will know and I will be here already set, for our missions for the deserving souls to be on Earth. Glory of God, for all people and in this time on Earth, Miracles will be for all! Even in this day there are miracles for all, for the minds of humans are shock proof at this time.

All their fears are seen and realized everyday, through many modes of communication. Yet their beauties of life are not realized and the miracles will be of beauty and of life and of their trueness to themselves, to all of us. We rejoice in the sheer beauty of life. And when found the lessons of love can only grow on Earth. Glory be to God Almighty, and may the mighty of God, live to grow love and caring.

Good hearts are needed as you read. You will only know of the beautiful hearts on Earth, for you witness it inside, bring it outside of the person, so that that person can see their beauty. Many times the beauty of a soul is buried beyond even the owner of the soul's belief.

You know this however you have discovered the resistance of soul's loving itself. For your life on Earth, you will show and you will be the eyes of love and of God and of Angels and of Christ, to all you see. If they are waiting for a miracle, know they will understand upon meeting you, for the piercing of soul will begin.

A person will find it hard to lie to itself upon knowing you! In the face of God Almighty there is no hiding. And on Earth, the hiding is temporary however when a soul cannot lie to itself it can only grow.

How logical, in a world of great knowledge and little application of all the knowledge within and without! The work to begin is within! And you will witness. You will love and you will be present, for you can only speak the truth with the truth that needs to be heard. Never to worry our sweet soul Nadia, Angel of God Almighty.

You have had a week of intensity. For you now understand the energy and balance, for your physical body trembled for days upon my visiting your form. Yes there is room for two, Glory be to God Almighty. Rejoice our Child and rest at this time. You are love and glory and will share all your love in everyday of life you know as you have and will forever!

Good night to you, I love you all,

WE love you Nadia, beyond all comprehension!

"The Team" – Christ

⌁

*At this time my physical body no longer felt like my own. I would shake or tremble for minutes at a time, sometimes an hour. And my body felt like there was too much energy for it to take on. I could feel it flowing through me and I understood Christ was in my body.*

*Very odd to say in the least, as well as my feelings of loss of privacy and the thought that my thoughts were not just to myself. I felt like an open book, no matter where I went, what I did, I was not alone, I could never think "alone" again. It made me realize that alone as any one of us may or may not feel we are never alone. What we keep to ourselves, we are keeping with the Universe and we just try to hide it. That is the funny part. There are no secrets. There are only hidings. What a freeing feeling, to let go of anything and put it out there and see what happens with truth.*

*Also in this time, I met my husband, Stirling. I knew it the night I met him. The day before I met him, I had just declared to myself and the Universe that I would be and wanted to be single. I was meeting many people because of the writings and I was truly excited to just talk about what I knew with anyone else who might know.*

*One of my clients, that had become a good friend, suggested that the three of us meet and talk. She said that we were going to meet someone who knew what I knew. On the appointed night she could not make it, but Stirling and I met anyway. We knew each other right away. We came from different worlds, places and people, only to find that what lived in our hearts were the same thinkings and askings of life.*

*While we were talking, Stirling asked me if I was dating anyone. All I could say was, "I have no business dating anyone. I get involved with people and then when they want to get more serious, I run so fast you can't see the smoke behind me." That was enough to quiet him. However, a few minutes later I looked at him and thought, Oh my God, I will never be without this man. I didn't think, I love him or he's cute, or whatever it is that we go through.*

*The next day, I couldn't even remember what he looked like. All I could remember was what I felt. I felt like I met me, in another person. There was no question as to who, what, where, why or when. It simply existed and we both knew enough to follow its love.*

⚮

OCTOBER 21, 2003

Sweet Stirling,

I am thinking all the changes in my mind and in my heart are starting to catch up to the rest of me. I am writing you in this moment, and I feel like it is slow motion to be saying the things I am saying. It feels like I want to rush time but I understand the patience part of it for now. I felt really edgy in the past few weeks with the acceleration of things, and now I don't. I am getting it in large doses, yet now I don't feel like they are so large anymore.

I was thinking things like us starting to save money in small doses and getting another car. And then I was thinking how we would move, and to pick a spot and see what happens, how I want to push the funding, and I feel it coming soon, no kidding, and just as soon as I could say I could wait this morning to you, I know it is right around the corner.

I know it is just a matter of time. I know your work is growing too and with that, I wanted to include you in the funding to help me put things together and to do an audio or video of the little stories I have to put down. I think the part that I wanted to slow down now was to know you more and to enjoy how we know each other now, if that makes sense. I love the work I do and I love the writing, the meanings, the people it gives to, and yet it was like I wanted to take a time out for myself, for you, for how we are going to put our families together.

I am thinking putting our families together and you know I still get that shy thing with you. Isn't that funny? I hope it never ever goes away. It is like I see you and I don't have words…I would forget how handsome you are…because already your insides I feel, or how much I love and understand our purpose. I am glad we met each other now, at this time in our lives. Not later once you are doing what you love and me too.

I simply love you…hope you have a good night…

Nadia

NOVEMBER 4, 2003

Sweet morning...

That's what it feels like this morning...the fact that I am awake is even better. I don't know what to say anymore. I say I love you but it doesn't come close to covering it...

Loving you with the greatness that I have yet to grow into,

Nadia

NOVEMBER 5, 2003

My Dear Sweet Lord God,

Sweet Christ, Azna, Michael, Mable, Joseph, Teddy and Joe, Josie, Aaron, Abel, Sweet Bessie, Ericka, and Sweet and Beautiful Gabriel, Boy, have things come to a head in my head. Yes, I am getting it and I am starting to feel safe within it. I know the changes are coming. I know. I was sometimes still resisting and when you told me it was because I didn't want to be bought and sold, that was why. Thank you for telling me I will be protected in all of this. So that is cool. It took me a little time on that one.

**Yes Nadia, our Sweet Dear, you are growing into your new role. Yes, your life will change however in protection and preservation. You will not be a spectacle nor will you have to prove. That is of God Almighty, for there will be no dispute.**

**Your life treasured, as will remain all that are touched by God through you. Your life for the lives of others. You enjoy your life and within your life the joy of you spreads throughout the veins of those you feel blessed enough to know.**

I love everyone I know…a lot. How come it is that I don't have words for my love for Stirling? How could I not have words?

Our Dear Child, for love is not of words, for did you not know? Love is an emotion. Love in its truth is felt not said, for that is love of heart, of God, of life. Love is fluid and can forever grow and change, intensify, shift, so how could a word take on such meaning? To say "I love you" is the way to describe, yet a finger of one hand touching the finger of another in a moment is love. To look into the eyes of another and feel the person you witness before you and take notice that is love, for love gives.

Pure love can only find its way to evolution within. Love breeds and grows within and when you say "you know" you know the way, for depth is present. Nadia, Sweet Nadia, sleep now, for tonight you will sleep full and surrounded with the love of God Almighty around you and all you love, for you love all! Your heart of love!

Come back to us, for we love your questions! You unlocked the door and the keys are in your hands. At home there are no keys and you now know of such! God Almighty wants to give to all who know and believe He Can. Glory be to God Almighty! Good night in this night our loved one,

"The Team" – Christ

I love you tooooo!

Nadia

NOVEMBER 30, 2003

Dearest Lord God,

Sweet Christ and all the Beautiful Angels! I just felt you all and I had to come and write. Is there something to tell me today! I love so much knowing you. The comfort of knowing you exist and are here for everyone, I keep thinking, wow, if people only knew!

And Nadia, Sweet Nadia, Yes they will know! The purposes of people will be present with your presence and then with your writings of life as it happened, for then all will know it is for them too.

Nadia, you are an example of life. You got to experience many facets of life for that reason. Some experiences you received through the questions you ask of others. You have found a way to experience through the love you feel for others and the honesty of asking questions without judgment. For safety of soul exists in your soul and that is a gift for all souls, for honesty, safety, caring, touching, for it heals! Glory be to God Almighty!

That is what you know! It is so present in you. You see the void in souls when it does not exist and you touch the soul with the abundance that exists in you!

How could you know who you are? You are love on Earth. You possess Love for all you are is Love! Glory be to God Almighty! How unsuspecting a soul is to meet you! How could you know what it is like to meet you? For the only time you experienced knowing what it is like to meet you is when you met Stirling!

You were told that there would be recognition between your soul and the soul of Stirling for you both knew!

Human words, people words, they do not exist yet for your meeting. For the glory of the recognition, the taking to task of free will throughout a brief time on Earth, led the two of you to a moment in life that brought celebration of Love at Home. How could you know the rarity of that witness from Home to Earth?

How could you know what has happened to souls that took them away from the glory of free will and learning the lessons that grow? Even a few lessons learned would have taken souls to Glory, yet there is much fear, much resistance to the knowing of God Almighty. For Eternal is threatened on Earth in the subtlest of ways. The direction of a few is hurting many.

Nadia, it is time for you NOW! DO YOU UNDERSTAND? DO NOT HESITATE! FOR YOUR LIFE FOR ALL! YOU ARE OF PROTECTION. FOR STIRLING IS OF PROTECTION IN PHYSICAL ON EARTH. FOR STIRLING OF GOD AS WELL. FOR YOUR SOULS EQUALLY YOKED!

Wow, I heard that equally yoked term before.

Yes Nadia, it is one of the truths of God's words. Yet on Earth, it is a goal to humans. Yet do they know what it means? NO, it is not known what that means. Equally yoked is to have that balance, pure intent, support and love without the boundaries, the limits that take away or box in the glories of what the soul can be. The potential of souls is magnificent and the souls on Earth have forgotten very deeply the Eternalness of life. Life has become a day to day chore!

How could growth grow with the feelings of helplessness and despair? Some growth will happen, yet in it the lessons are lost or rationalized and growth as a whole is losing! Eternal is losing its way. It needs direction, for how could you open the eyes of souls in a way the soul can believe it or accept it or know it or learn from it? You are here Nadia, how could you know how? Who you are?

Even with our words you wonder how? For how will be the best way of how in that moment however you have to be prepared for the change of life, for from that point on you will travel. And others will travel for you, to see you, and it will heal, give belief in bigger than Earth and regrow Eternal!!

You have written much. Again, read, re-read, read again for like in this morning you saw what you didn't see yesterday! Love is here in life. It is Your life! It is infused in all around you!

You are protected our sweet soul, you must know this. For soon a day will come that you will have to trust in that protection! Glory be to God Almighty! Glory be to God Almighty! Glory be to God Almighty! Glory be to God Almighty! Glory be to God Almighty!

You are loved! You are loved, are of light, are loved, are of light! WE are in you, around you, around all that you love. We are here and ready and waiting to touch those who ask! Glory be to God Almighty!

"The Team" – Christ

Thank you for this today! I love you,

Nadia

# CHAPTER 6

# I SAW YOU SWEET AND BEAUTIFUL CHRIST

## DECEMBER 1, 2003

Sweet Morning…

I just got back to the office. I don't know what it is with me today. I really am not into this. I am doing it, but I am not here! This structure, watching all the go, go, go of things…it is passing me by…I am not interested in any way…I was thinking when I meet with this woman on Thursday night, I will put in to work out of my home two days a week!

It will be easy to do it that way and I could do what I need to do without the having to be sitting here…Just thinking…I am putting in looking for a place for us, look too, maybe between the two of us, we can at least start looking and seeing what is actually out there that we can do…

So serious in this day…I have a lot to do after lunch…and then I will be relieved of all of this for the day!

Ugh…thinking of you, love being with you, with us…and the kids…how I love them…all of them…you are my family…all of you…and you are the love of my life…loving you is the greatest of feelings I have…

Nadia

DECEMBER 14, 2003

Dearest Lord God,

Sweet Christ, All the Beautiful Angels, I love you all so much. So much love going around in life down here!

Nadia, plan, sweet Nadia, plan, for all is coming to you, and to Stirling. All changes, do you feel them? We feel your movement and your growth. As well, Stirling's, for he is just getting a taste in life of how things work and he is included. You both know your lives are touched, for you feel it in your essence.

Separating feeling most unnatural, for it is with your souls. Missing a part of is the feeling on Earth. At home you can be together even when apart. That is why the separations feel unnatural to you.

Yes there are many changes still to come. We know you didn't want to marry in Las Vegas. We understand how you feel there however marry there for it is irrelevant. It is important for you and for Stirling to be married. For your hearts don't feel complete without that union of tradition to take place. You were concerned on where you will live.

We are working and you will know. For nothing is as it seems. Marry on the 11th day of January. You were thinking to go later on that day, go earlier. It is a grand day of many one's and that shall be a first day of your lives as you will both grow into the completeness that you feel.

We gave to you the understand that marriage is near for you. For how could you know? Before that you wanted to wait until you got a home, until kids walked out of school, until so many things, yet those very things are irrelevant. Love of souls is fluid. All will follow with ease and comfort.

Your work change was necessary. Your new boss didn't know why she was so desperate for your work. She got drawn to you the moment she met you. She even said to you "I don't know why, I trust you and I will do what it takes to have you join our company." She was sent to you. And now your ease in finance has come to support both of you.

The children understand what it means to be a family. That was the fear of the children in that evening. They felt family and they felt it was being threatened and inter-rupted. They need you Nadia, and they need you and Stirling, together.

For their father they love with heart and yet are scared to lose anyone they love. And your children who are use to having you entirely, they will adjust themselves and grow. All will be well.

For you are of much change now, and will be forever. Walk forward. Take hands with Stirling. Join. And later include others as you thought. That is of life and yes, it is not the way things are done.

Yet your souls are of each other not of anyone or anything else around you. Your love paves the paths that haven't been walked before you recognized each other in life. WE love to watch your lives. Enjoy your days for there is no other way to be. Be. We love you our Dear Sweet Child. You are loved.

"The Team" – Christ

Thank you for talking to me, for me knowing you! I love you all toooooo!

Nadia

DECEMBER 31, 2003

Don't be sad Nadia, our Dear, for we will always work towards the greater good, and the house was quite perfect, yet not all the way. We are working, as we did in all other parts of life around you, never to worry for after you took in the facts, you started realizing other options.

Never to fear, for Stirling's disappointment short lived, for you are both souls of resilience! Thank you for sitting in this moment, you have much to do in your sweet time today. Rest, for you are in need!

I will, I love you, and I am thinking I am not going to get sick! That is great to feel! I do know we will find a place, and I am excited now, because this place made me adapt to moving as well! Thank you! I love you! I have to go!

You are loved our Dear!

"The Team" – Christ

JANUARY 9, 2004

Dearest Lord God,

Sweet Christ and all the beautiful Angels! Wow, what a night last night. I had to solve it before I went to sleep.

Nadia, Sweet Nadia, you see the bright lights and your sight fades when light isn't present. So you bring others up to the task of living in the brightest of lights and that is uncomfortable for those who don't know. Yet you teach the comfort of knowing and being able to live and continue with no ego involved. Egos will be your biggest challenge, with those who know you and then those who don't, and then those who don't want to; all for preparation of life to come.

Trust and you will see, have faith and you will teach, love and you will heal, Grow pure intent and God's love will grow on Earth! Glory be to God Almighty! Fear, worry, doubt, stagnate the soul. Never forget that for that is the stagnation of souls you witness in those you know, you love, you care for and those you will teach and touch in ways so subtle without warrant! Glory be to God Almighty!

All has purpose and purpose gives reason and reason brings thoughts and thoughts become things! With purity, things become and you will see the fruits of God's love on Earth, and for all! PURE INTENT RULES. We smile with love to say that to you, for your world lives on slogan type thoughts and thinking!

Our excitement in the deeper and greater thoughts to come to human minds, once again, and remind them that there is so much love for them, they will grow and rest, rest and conquer, for the greater good of the day in their world! Glory be to God Almighty!

WE walk with you, around you, around your love, and All around Stirling's heart of hearts! You will never be alone, and comfort when you are in aloneness will always be with the billions of flickers of light we call Angels! You are loved and loved and loved!

"The Team" – Christ

I love you too!

Nadia


## JANUARY 19, 2004

Sweet Stirling,

This is the first time I am writing you as your wife, you as my husband; I am loving to say these words over and over again and again. Just to write those words…fills my heart…in the lightness of life as I know it.

I love you, am in love with you, love you and in love with you some more. I miss you in these moments… knowing we are married…it holds me in place in some way, knowing that my lifetime, our lifetime is filled with you, with us…

I was going to write some tonight and instead all I can do is to tell you that I love you…Good night…from here to you…may my love warm you in your sleep, until I am blessed to see you again…

Love,

Nadia

FEBRUARY 10/12, 2004

Dearest Lord God, Sweet Christ,

Yes Nadia, I am here. I am with you, did you feel me a short time ago? I am feeling time now too. All love to your heart, through your heart, is absorbed. There is much love, yet far away. Your life will bring it closer to souls, for the soul that not knoweth of thyself, is lost in a wilderness of treeless forests, for how can life grow in a forest without trees! Glory be to God Almighty. Yes, I had to speak in those terms, for you thought it "corny" that is the word I heard in your mind.

I am laughing, that you could hear my mind.

Yes, and I am learning corny means that you love what you heard and you are shy as to how it was said. Too Formal?

Yes, it shouldn't be like something I would read in a bible.

Yes, the bible. I will come back to the bible. For the many versions have diluted the credibility and taken away from the oneness of souls. I am loving the casualness of language. For you felt the word knoweth was of corny. I am amused at your humor. Yet it has to be in this way. There is more to say to you.

Your writings will challenge, for how could they not? How could the Bible be the Bible when there are so many! Which Bible? Which beliefs? Which rule of guilt is different between them? Which belief takes a soul closer to God Almighty than the other? Nadia, these things have to be said.

I am disheartened at all the misgivings of communication between a soul and God. A soul does not need permission, money, a building, a country, status, non status, to believe in God Almighty! Glory be to God Almighty.

There is truly nothing but God; Angels to bring God's message to enable and further growth; that we are meant to grow ourselves and each other. The less rules, the simpler the message, the greater the love. Rules complicate and take away. God Almighty did not take the route of rules. There are no rules, for with pure intent, love, there need be none.

The rules take away and create the very thing they were designed to prevent. The rules set up what is called temptation for now there is a challenge. Temptation as known is really human weakness of self. To do anything that takes away from self is a lesson to that person alone, even if that soul involves another.

Nadia, you understand this however you never read in the Bible or any other "holy" books. For you it was always God. You never knew different and when you would step into the world of "Booked" religion you got lost in the webs of deceit of mind.

You felt your happiness with God in those times was compromised! You talked to God in your moments and asked him why when you would read, that you felt like you had to do things you already did or felt? Why you had to feel guilty to love him? For many do preach love through fear and you couldn't understand how both could be in the same heart. You knew so early, so that now in this day what you know is needed.

The "books" of any religious background are not to be dis- counted, for that would cause a fury! They are not to be destroyed, for one day they will be of History. They are to be questioned however not individually. They are to be set aside when you speak, not to be mentioned for your writings. But the time gotten to here will happen after my showing and then the interest will become, for all will know how you know of this truth.

That I am back and through your being, for the purity you possess and the feared teachings will be of what they are. The truth of you will not/can not be denied. That is how it will be. Those with self interest motivations will have to try to dispel you, hurt you, initiate dishonor however in those moments I will break through again and again.

They cannot be of strength, for their strength to weaken until the message is clear and unabbreviated! Glory be to God Almighty. You are loved. I am enjoying the moments when you write, for in those moments we are talking. Although you can hear me throughout your day, you can read and share when you write.

Glory be to God Almighty, for your life came to give and to give to all, even in your most tired of moments. Your love never wanes! Glory be to God Almighty, our light, you are loved!

"The Team" – Christ

FEBRUARY 21, 2004

Dearest Sweet Nadia,

Home is such comfort, for you feel it at times, most times here on Earth and your only thought at times is Wow, at home there are no bills. Yes, there is much pressure on souls for living. It tests the will of honesty and the will of greatness. The soul becomes creative as to how to survive.

You understood this when you asked God Almighty to never give you too much money! For you can feel as the common man feels and your lack of funds gives you relation with no motive to the world.

Money nullifies the motivation to others to the common mind. Monies in the world on Earth are traded and through those trades, wealth is determined and intelligence is judged. Neither is generally true. In the world as I came before, most was provided for by the hands of those alive. All commerce was minimal.

Now commerce is the ruler of all minds. Company's structure is designed to tip the scales of profitability and then the product is made. They cannot afford to make a product of quality and then sell it to you. There are too many people involved.

There are those who are investors and there to make money only. Then there are those who run the company who answer to them. They at times feel cheated, get greedy and steal from the companies that they do not own. For wealth no matter how attained is wealth on the outside and the means of attaining is not of mention.

Many thieves have arrived and become. They then shape the lives of the common worker. In all of this there is no owner. NO ownership of a company, so how could the product they sell come to you with the love and the ownership in which you purchase and use it? Nadia, there is lack of ownership on many levels.

The human mind is getting to a level of determining that its own soul, own life here on Earth, is the blame, fault of others. For them they do not steal money, they steal their time of life, of lessons from themselves. For them there is blaming and excuses happening that take away from life in every moment of their thinking hence lack of ownership.

With lack of self ownership, how is it that they can feel if there is no owning of feelings?

Nadia, there is such detachment. Detachment is rampant! I witness speaking. I witness thoughts that accompany words. I feel overwhelming feelings and then I feel a severing of thought in an instant and then no feeling at all. NO feeling of completion. No thoughts of solving those thoughts.

I see the bury of hurts, of pains, of thoughts, even great thoughts. For the soul is learning to not solve, to not dream hence that is the loss of hope in witness. Most have the dreams they carried as a child, as an infant, for all came with dreams.

The true dreams are of accomplishing the missions, the experiences they came down to experience for the growth of their souls. Yet when the experiencing begins, the harshness of this world on Earth is the only factor not felt until the soul is actually here.

Glory be to God Almighty, for this is known to your soul, yet this needs to be in words, for you would not be able to imagine those who don't know. Feel My love in you, for it exists in enormousticity! Glory be to God Almighty!

"The Team" – Christ


FEBRUARY 28, 2004

Dearest Lord God,

I can hear you, what are you saying to me? I saw you Sweet and Beautiful Christ. I saw you last night standing in the center of many Angels, like flickers of light around you from your shoulders on up.

Yes, Nadia, for it is important that you can see me and know that it is me you are seeing. For before any moment of my light coming through you in recognizable form, you will see me as I pass from your purity into the realm of the world.

You are my harbor, my home on Earth. You will see much, as you can hear me now. I am becoming and have absorbed the energy of this time, of this place. Balance is within me in the ways that the human eye can witness me. For before my energy was too great to be witnessed. Nadia, you are shaking too in writing in this morning.

Yes, I am. I think I am knowing now that this is soon.

Yes, Nadia, it is. It is, for you will be of safety, for the shield of love, of purity, of safety will surround and abound you. All will know you in this world of Earth, for all need the love and touch of God. This mission of the greatest importance of this time.

The counter productivity of mind is how to understand it best. The soul knows not the tools in which to grow itself. The helplessness within has carried the soul to speak of what it does not feel, to love as it does not understand, to live as it does not want to for lack of a path.

The universal paths in which the mind would recognize are no longer recognizable. The Angels on Earth carry the world at this time. It is pure purity and then there is uncertainty amongst humans who can't see and there is not much in between. People are hungry and are ready for the changes that will come about.

Now it is time for change, for truth, and lifted are the burdens of the heart on the mind, for things taught in error carry great weight. Your lightheartedness even in telling a soul of its truth is taken in with the lightheartedness of God Almighty, and with the strength of God Almighty, all at once.

To witness you gives to a soul the remembrance of who they really are and where they came from and why; All in an instant. There are some who know I am there within you and come back to hug you, touch you, look in your eyes. For they know, yet on the outside cannot conceive. They will know they knew upon my showing and will tell souls of the truth.

All that have met you, will meet you, know you, have known you, will know you; will carry the message of truth. Then they will know why they were drawn to you and the growth of souls will begin! As it has begun amongst the souls around you in this time.

We are direct servants/loves/messengers of God Almighty! Glory be to God Almighty! You are still shaking. Know who you are, for others know and will know, for their knowing will grow trust in the world in which they live. And growth of souls can be on the universal paths once again! Glory be to God Almighty! Glory be to God Almighty! Glory be to God Almighty!

"The Team" – Christ

CHAPTER 7

⟨───────⟩

# TIME TO GROW ON

MARCH 1, 2004

Dearest Lord God,

Sweet Christ…I could hear you today, yet not all day. So much adjustment mentally, for many around us; I was hitting a threshold, not wanting to hear it anymore. I think I had to get sick of it to put it in perspective. Why is it so hard to live and let live?

Why is it so hard to understand and it is easier to not want to understand. To not want to feel OK at the least with what life sits with around them? I wanted to say us, but I couldn't because I could not ever in my life and I never ever want to impose myself on another. I hope to You, God, that that isn't me ever to another. It is impossible in my heart, in my brain, to want to understand the why's, for the why's are of such underhandedness.

Nadia, help is needed by all, for all, for all the writings. The writings are of people. The answers are of people. The love is of people, for people, of all need in people. Start in your family as you have discovered and stay in your family, all ill intended will be far away. Their worlds of outer envy, of inner pains, Pains that start and stop within yet not found, for then they are proliferated outward and announced that the anger is there.

Those outside leave outside; they will see in their paths that the obstacles created are their own. The happiness is there and the paths of love exist. And now you witness how pain can interrupt such love, such happiness from existing. All are people who want and want and want yet you are witnessing the laws of not giving and not wanting to receive. For all around you can't give from heart. From love.

Humans love not themselves; they want your surety that love exists, even if they have to steal it from you. Yet their lessons in all from the youngest child to the oldest and most ill motivated adult is to open their own hearts and listen to what lives inside. For what lives inside is the answer, not an external person.

How could that be?

Externality is of no answers. Learn our people on Earth. Externality is of no answers. There is not a soul that can make another happy. A soul of unhappy is a soul who knows not of itself. Glory be to God Almighty. Nothing is forever, with the exception of love in purity.

Don't let the dimmers of light take forum. Let them grow into the light, for the path exists. Let them walk away and find it. Then they will understand. And it is their job to learn not yours. Your job is to be, to teach, through the example of who you are and becoming.

Most souls do not want truth. They would rather not grow than grow, for growth needs much internal honesty. Whether the absorption of such love is ready to be penetrated is up to the soul receiving it however it will happen enough to bring back balance of positive over the negative, for souls in despair halt evolvement and that is where we are.

One ounce of pure intent, pure love will overcome any obstacle, provided it is pure. Now you know how hard pure intent is. How hard simple Prudency to a soul is. How self accounting is looked at as foreign. Why one person can read and hear you and another can't.

The ripple affect of love is endless. As I have said, as we have said at home as the Angels came down in preparation. No need to feel a standstill, for this is the calm before the greatest most wonderful change of this jaded time of heart.

Glory to the souls who will see, for they will carry the rest of souls into hope internal, love internal, which will find its way to hope external; Love external. Glory be to God Almighty. Blessed are all souls for if they knoweth, the hearts within would melt with kindness!

"The Team" – Christ

MARCH 16, 2004

Dearest sweet Nadia,

Thank you for finding your way home in this day. There is much for you to prepare for in the days to come. Please do not be alarmed to opposition.

You are excited, and at the same time you wonder how your family will be? How ends will be met, if in this moment you cannot? Do not worry, for there is nothing worth the worry in your world. Glory be to God Almighty, if souls could know what is in store for them!

Glory be to God Almighty, for the stagnation of souls to be put in motion again. For motion is stagnate, souls are stagnate. The writing is the medicine of the soul's soul; the parts of human mind that already know and astray from oneself. The astrayed in life are looking and have not found.

And in your words, the words of God Almighty, answering the cries of the questions that have been asked so quietly and giving such life to all around. May all the souls who witness your love carry it with them in remembrance upon your parting, that love exists and is not for some, it is for all. It is for all. Love is for all. Love is for all. Love is for all. For not one soul is more important than another.

You will know me as love of God, for God, sends love to all. For healing is of need. Nadia, so simple in life for life is for the living. Every soul on Earth made a choice and for those who have forgotten it is simply time to remember. To remember who we all are. To remember who others are. Who family is, and why? For Family is souls we knew before. No one is new to each other.

Familiarity is rampant and yet is ignored. Peoples say "I don't know why we are together," for the mind knows not it made such choice? A newborn knows what the adult has forgotten for that is the love and scent of a newborn. A newborn carries greater knowledge of life than that of a schooled soul on Earth. On Earth you are reteaching.

You are retouching all that has fallen asleep, all that has been unearthed to the spirit of the sweet souls that occupy Earth in this time. Nadia, you feel like you are writing an "outer space" type of emotion. You are.

For you are present in both worlds and your memory can only carry the residue of home. For you can not stay there. When your body trembles it trembles with the love of/from home and the break between the planes.

Yes, it is a great deal of energy.

Nadia, this is what is to be in the book. Why did you change your book to the book?

I don't know.

It is because you want it to be for all. It is still for all. It is your book Nadia. It is your book. You are a prophet. This portion must be in the book, this portion of words to come.

Those who oppose the love of God, fight the love of God, oppose life and fight themselves. Those who try to hurt you in your mission of transmitting a simple and beautiful world of love and words to further understanding will know that it is themselves that they are hurting and lacking in understanding.

Those who want to discredit, disarm, take away from the world of logic and sense, understand they will be the ones that are doing the same elsewhere in life. Those who want to learn and question will be the ones to teach. Those who want to outsmart you will want to discredit you for egotistical purposes only, with an enflamed sense of self.

Those who will learn from you will gift others in the same manner. Those who will shake to speak to you will be those who are not use to high energy from home. Those who want to touch you will feel the greatest of love from within and will be content enough to have known you, seen you, been witness to the glories of the world within the light of God.

Those who will talk about you, they will find as they talk they are lifted to new heights. The story alone of your meetings in life, of Stirling and you finding your souls sitting before the other in a moment that now is the moment of recognition, will walk away with your human-ness as they need to know of it.

Will walk away with the hope of life within them; For those who will learn of your struggles will know that being an Angel doesn't mean you have everything, it means that you are everything! Glory be to God Almighty! Nadia, you have written much in this moment. You will go now. There will be no tardiness. You will conclude your business for this day, never to fear, doubt or worry! Glory be to God Almighty!

"The Team" – Christ

MARCH 17, 2004

Sweet Nadia,

Yes, I can hear you. I am tired tonight. I could feel you; I could feel a lot of moving around in me.

Yes, Nadia, you are being expanding in every minute. All is and will continue to be as it is. Send many the book. For all will see what they are ready to see and for all it will mean to them what it will mean. And to others it will mean something else. All will yield the same results. Love of self, acceptance of their personhood and let's get on with the lessons. Be sure to reveal that the knowledge of the love of God gives the strength to endure the lessons.

A person's love of God does not mean that that person will never have challenge. So fragile the human soul to believe that the love that may be felt for God Almighty would mean there would be no challenge or experience to grow the soul. Nadia, sweet Nadia, your grandest lessons came in your times of distress. For now, to look back that is seen, for the lessons of life were learned in those moments.

God Almighty is your partner in the lessons a soul chooses to endure in their time on Earth! Glory be to God Almighty! To love God is to say that love is felt from God Almighty. For to feel the love of God Almighty can not be lived without once known. That is the "lost" that many souls live, is the loss of that feeling. That very feeling is right in front of, beside, in back of any soul, all souls. Glory be to God Almighty!

The love of God is for the soul. The soul's love of God is for the soul. God doesn't need love for he is the creator of such love. There is trust that it exists and God waits for our growth to take us to him and his love abounds along the way. Your heart knows of such love, so in this moment you are trying to imagine what a soul does without that felt feeling.

Those are the people that you witness, that you know, that you have loved in their pain. They are "lost" within the looking for a love, an original love that is lost to them now. Original love is something I want to talk to you about. Original love is the first love felt by every soul upon creation.

It is the pure love of God instilled in each soul, each drop of God that comes to existence. Before anything else each soul began with original love; Experience, learning, growth, acceptance, love, form from others, because the individuals of each drop of original love.

You may be shaking in this evening. Never to worry, for you sustained much energy in your last evening! Glory be to God Almighty!

Christ "the team"

MARCH 21, 2004

Nadia, Sweet Nadia,

Yes I am present now.

You have not heard from me, as you began to early on, for I needn't be present until now. Yes, that was me you witnessed last evening and a billion Angels around. Yes, we are here, for the mission of all of us, of the Angels of God, it is time. Nadia, your life, Stirling's life, you are both in awe of what you know and you are both in wonder as to the reality of what is going to be. At home it is happening. On Earth it is happening.

All the preparation is in preparation. All the love of God surrounds all the hope of souls resetting, all the love of life on Earth to be found in its sense of purity once again. For simple thoughts in your soul of your day before, wondering why you need to do this, for you witnessed what you believe to be a group of people on their way. Look underneath sweet Nadia, for there is much work to be done. Souls have lost their path and their wonder of such paths.

There could never be enough love and now there exists so little it is in danger of remaining in falseness in motivations as a way of life. With Falseness there can be no growth for the growth will grow like a plant that needs growing to grow without. The souls returning home are injured in the lackness of love felt on Earth.

The souls that are entering Earth come with such love and purity and vigor and it is lost very quickly. The nurturing of life, of love, of hope, of simple and sweet caring is of wonder in the thoughts of souls as to it existing or not. Hence the loss of the biggerness of all other parts of life hence missions.

Nadia, you have a job of greatness ahead of you. For whatever challenge shall pose itself to your days, your nights, amongst other humans, will be of no challenge however simply another example of what strength, trust and faith look like. Personified.

Nadia, you were wondering who you are talking to, yes, it is me Christ. Michael began however for now you can rest as you have asked. You are loved and you are cherished.

You were thinking the other day, "So Christ, I use to know you what did we do?" You were with me, as Stirling was. You both loved the souls of humans, for we use to observe the souls on Earth together and you both believed that love was starting a path of loss.

We spoke to God Almighty of this and that is when it was asked of an Angel to come down and do the work to bridge the souls of humans back to them. Of course that is when you came forward, for God wanted to have the form be that of a woman, a religion of challenge and a love of all, not for one.

You came of Arabic, for the last prophet of such! You came of Arabic, for it is a challenge of background, you will challenge all the accepted non acceptance of such souls.

You will merge the religions and dissolve the "better thans," the superior thinkers, the controllers of souls, using God as the avenue. God Almighty is of freedom, love, comfort, and growth; anything else that is said and surrounding God Almighty is taught in error! Glory be to God Almighty!

You are being infused. Yes you were expecting me to appear in form in your last evening. You expected Michael to be broad in your presence. For only your eyes can see when closed. For the light would have been enormous!

You would have been of blind to have witnessed such light. For you witnessed both of us, Michael, you noticed his hugeness and you understood his discipline. He is a force of protection and honor.

Integrity and honesty. Plan. Work. Enjoy, live in laughter! Glory be to God Almighty, for all will come as, when, how it should and to live in the laughter of life is the gift of the way life is and has become.

Glory be to God Almighty, for God Almighty, is in laughter of the souls of happiness. Happiness is earned. It is earned through knowing thyself. Let no one misguide you, any soul, for happiness is earned.

Any soul can be of miserable, and the soul will have many followers. To live in happiness is the time of knowing for happiness is earned! Glory be to God Almighty! Nadia, you can rest now. Rejoice, for the love of God Almighty abounds! Glory be to God Almighty!

Christ, "The Team" Michael!

## March 23, 2004

Dearest Lord God,

Thank you for bringing me home today, that I had the time to come home, that there is so much love around. I love it. I even called my Dad, must be time, he isn't at work until 3. All is good, all is loving and that is the greatest feeling of all!

Yes Nadia, you are getting better at understanding the happenings to you. Yes, you were in travel in your last evening. You realized. Yes, you are being infused and you are knowing that the knowledge that you are gaining is not of need in this day and too much to carry without the use for it, of it.

Nadia, you were thinking you departed 4 or 5 times. You have departed in every night of the last 14 days! The heat you feel is upon returning to form.

Nadia, You know, you understand the value of knowing thyself for without thyself of heart the heart is of stagnant motion. The breaths of a soul are the thoughts of the heart, for shallow breathing is of reflection.

Shallow of heart is of reflection. Shallow of duties is of reflection. The heart of man is made of love, honor, integrity and growth. When one of the emotions of heart, of doing is tampered with or led in another way, all others will follow and that is the way it is.

When one thing goes towards growth all things follow and one thing leads away, all other things follow. It is so simple. Nadia, you are enjoying your day, your writings, for you love celebrations and today it is a celebration of heart for you, in many around you.

Nadia, we are of celebration! We are celebrations of love. God's love is of bounty, for one, for all. For all and then for one again! Glory be to God Almighty! People are hungry for this writing.

The reading of it frees the souls, and the writings have freed many of the knowing.

You changed YOUR writings to The Writings, it is YOUR writing, for you are still in resistance to claim your role. You want it to be all of us, for it is. Each and every one of us here and on Earth of love to you, with you, of others with others however it is YOU!

WE are adjoined and we are of partner however, however, however you have to know who you are too! You are of prophet. Say it in your heart and rejoice that God is coming to public. Souls will have a place to rejoice, reset, re-establish who they are simply by you knowing who you are.

Nadia, you have sat for a long time. You can rest once again. You have much energy through you, around you. Rest our Child, for your life is no longer of same and will change in great waves! Glory be to God Almighty!

Christ, "The Team" Michael!

I love you all!

Nadia

MARCH 28, 2004

Dearest Lord God,

Sweet Nadia, our love on Earth, for we occupy Earth as well. You feel like it is a natural word to call Earth Earth, however to the absorber of this information you felt it foreign. The absorber of this information will know in time, by time, that Earth is one of many places that souls come to reside for growth of soul.

The Muslims state that the prophet Mohammed will be the last prophet until all people's die and face Judgment Day. Why would people put that in religion? How could anyone know the future? No soul can know of future on Earth, for there is time on Earth which is blockage of future knowledge.

They say they know not the future, yet they say there will be no future prophets, and there is belief that there is a Judgment Day of future, yet again, no one knows of the future! Taught in error and believed.

For again, all other things, sayings, that don't balance, make sense in the world of human souls, and due to believerment, all other things that don't have balance pass through the images, the happenings of life and are of acceptance. To build on non truth is to create other non truths, for how else could it happen. Glory be to God Almighty!

At first the Muslim souls of the Earth will try to claim you. And some will come to you, to the world and announce that you could not be of Prophet for in the Quran it states that Mohammed, is the last and Mohammed, surrounds you and you can now here that is not of truth.

You are not the last for there are now many prophets in relations to the souls on Earth and when a prophet is on Earth, it is not known even to the soul of mission until it is of time.

For the soul(s) of mission will always know they are different, they will always know that something in them is of relation to others souls, in wider scope, in openness and love. And they will feel the same as others and yet they carry a different torch for they are of Angel.

Time is a chroniclogicalizer of mind. For all prophets that were, are. For all beauty of love of words of God Almighty, is of existence and present in always. All taught in error must stand balance now. Nadia, your energy is great now. Keep writing. You will withstand.

Yes, I know that I can, I feel slow.

Yes, you are hearing, seeing and writing. Glory be to God Almighty, for the Angel no one knew of while I was walking the Earth, an Angel called Bethlehem. You call her Sweet Bessie, upon addressing the Angels you know by name.

The other two Angels will be Jacob of vision and Raphael, as you thought it for Raphael, is a helper of Angels. You thought sweet Bessie as you call her with love; she walked with me in every step on Earth and has walked beside your soul since birth.

The moments of enlightenment that happened throughout your Earthly life was the love and energy touched within by Bethlehem. Bessie is of love of your endearment upon first hearing of sound to you! You saw her walk beside me along the Streets of Bethlehem. In vision. It was Bethlehem. Glory be to God Almighty! Glory be to God Almighty! Glory be to God Almighty!

Jacob, a visionary Angel, will guide your journeys. And set the souls of preparation upon your physically being present and my showing and appearment to the souls of location to see. Seeing is believing and there will be of no other way! Glory be to God Almighty. And Raphael, his energy you glimpsed on Earth, came through a soul of the same name on the last day of your privateness of mar-riage. And he sent you to face the souls of life and sent you with love and love and love.

Souls will fight you on love, simply for those that fight you, for their lack of love so deep they do not recognize their motive. I was killed at the hands of those who lack self love, simply. For they had to make me go away, disap-pear.

I was a reflection of the lackasity, and even though I gave love back in those times of horror to humans, it was not known until I appeared to be of death, which was of horror to them as I stood beside God Almighty, in light and in love. And to watch the willingness of love lacking to become!

Yet more love was had then was lost and for that I came. And for that I became. And for that I was taken home. For it was my time! My work was done and the lack of love had to be personified before it could be seen.

Did I die for others sins? Nadia, there are no sins! People will say, what about this behavior or that behavior, and the simple answer is, it is of lacks of love. Glory be to God Almighty! Love abounds and leaves no missing! Glory be to God Almighty!

Christ, Michael, Gabriel, Joseph, Raphael, Jacob and Bethlehem!

Glory be to God Almighty!

APRIL 7, 2004

Dearest Sweet Nadia,

Nothing lasts forever nor is it meant to. Only souls are forever. The happenings to souls are of short duration's. There is always movement. Time to grow on. We understand on Earth there is a saying, "time to move on" however at home; the theme of souls is "time to grow on." It brings about a different outlook and adds to it the understanding of our roles.

As all writings are meant to do; to teach of the evolution, the movement, the glory, the hardships, the overcoming of such, the happiness', the passing by of such and that souls journey's include all of it. And no one is of exemption of such happenings! Glory be to God Almighty!

# CHAPTER 8

# TRUST YOUR INSTINCTS

## APRIL 14, 2004

Dearest Lord God,

Sweet Nadia, our Angel on Earth! Glory be to God Almighty! Thank you for coming in this morning to speak with us.

I knew there is something. It is like I am trying to organize all these things in my mind, in my heart and then come to you.

Yes, Nadia, we bear witness to you. WE are with you always, even when you are quiet. Yes, for you rested in your last evening for you were due some physical rest.

I have to say, I don't really mind the shaking anymore. I am use to it in many ways and then it takes me a while it seems to understand what is really happening and what I see and I learn when that happens to me. I saw all the Angels now. That was so cool!

I am very happy to have seen all of you by now. I am happy Christ, that you didn't pop out of me on Easter. I thought so much in that morning and then I knew it would happen at church. And I knew it wasn't ready yet I kept thinking how would I move, we move our family? How could we possibly do all of this in physical time?

Yes Nadia, you were of right. You knew, yet the energy that embodies you at this time is different and you feel flight at times. That is why you think that I will show through you at times and not at others. You are ready, the balance is there and the time is not ready. So we will wait until there is balance in time. So simple.

The souls of souls have found ways to avoid life and not participate in their own lives. You witness and you remain in knowing that when you see it you understand that soul is stagnated in all else of motivation.

The lack of provocation of thoughts, of physical work, of anticipation, of participation, of life, of self, has caused an internal struggle with the soul fighting for itself within the soul.

Almost in protest of lack of activity; of lack of accomplishment of life lessons, the stagnation, the lack of motivation, the unwillingness of participation of self. Nadia, our sweet Child of God, it baffles your heart in knowing. In your last evening you saw much detachment of soul. It was a bothering feeling for you, for once you witnessed you couldn't run fast enough!

I know. IT got restless in me very fast. And the bar we went to, I felt like I was sitting in a movie. Of people I didn't know and didn't know how to know. There was so much detachment there that the motions alone looked like they couldn't be real. I was wondering how someone's soul could really be in there and so shut off.

The girl with the wedding ring on speaking to the man without one, she was pursuing. It was sad to watch. It was so sad to me.

You are right; my emotions are much stronger and more intense. I can't believe the difference. I feel life in such a difference now.

When I am with people the purest souls attract me. Complaining baffles me. Whining intrigues me. Not wanting to solve issues makes me want to run so fast I can't see myself. And those who want to create issues and are self motivated; I can't seem to want to be near for any reason.

I can't find a reason. I understand now how simple those souls are and where the twists and turns take place. I understand now there is nothing we can do but love them and not respond to them. I believe they will get it from the non response, for then it is a reflection. Or they just find someone else to do it to.

Yes Nadia, for you can see so clearly now how little the individual has to do with the outbursts of the souls it interacts with. That the soul needs to find the tools, the individual souls to act out the experiences they have come for. Now the souls that are the recipients also have free will to accept or to reject the premises in which they endure or find themselves facing.

There are choices within the set of experiences a soul came to Earth to take on. Those choices, if based on pure intent, grow the souls to greater experiences. And the choices based on self motivation of any kind will stagnate the soul's experiences.

They will not be as fulfilling and the soul will "spin its wheels" as you say. I would also like to talk to you about entitlement. I have noticed much of this in internality. There seems to be a great sense of entitlement and embellishment of mental thought of self. Nadia, souls want much and want to do little. It is baffling to me why a soul would have a hand in taking away experience. For the internality is injured and lost.

Nadia, you wrote of detachment. I am also saying to you there is much to do this for me, give this to me, I want, I want, I want. And simple self thought of improvement, of growth, of cleanliness of soul, of self, of surrounding is lacking.

You witness the despair this causes outward and you understand the motivations inward. And it caused unrest to know that a soul is not in presence to help itself. For you see this in elders, in youngsters, in all ages. Glory be to God Almighty, we have work to do. The shell of a soul is losing its luster for the internality is present and takes all else away.

Nadia, you must go now, for your son is waiting for you, You are of busyness today in glory! You are loved! All of God's Angels, God Almighty! You are loved.

I love you too!

Nadia

### April 15/17, 2004

Dearest Nadia, Sweet Nadia, on Earth,

Nadia, I thank you for coming to me in theses moments. You are of such light your simple task of going to a grocery store seems so normal to you however I observe those around your light and they are comforted with home upon viewing your light. Do you understand who you are?

I think so. I was just thinking for the millionth time in my life, how could it be? How simple it is, and seeing the world as it will get these writings, and my life in its mission now. I thought I was in this mission all along.

Nadia, you were and are, this has been you all along. Only now you are with knowledge. Your little heart carries so much movement. You are a very physical human. I love being in your form and experiencing the world with you.

For who can know or in limits of imagination know you are such a transitional human and that your form is the covering of an Angel who came to do the work of God Almighty. And to prophet His love to the souls who know him and have forgotten how true God's love is.

Sweet Christ, I am back, I started this two days ago. I shake differently now, like little tremors, Sometimes bigger ones, but mostly little tremors.

Nadia, you are now different. You are greater in forthrightness and as you thought and started to verbalize, you are greater in speaking others truth. You see Nadia, Truth is Truth. You know of this already and you understand the value. However, truth is truth even when it is not so good for the doer of truth. The truth is freedom of soul.

Any truth, as you have said to your children all along, "the worst truth is better than the best lie." When you are lied to not only does it not rest the recipient, it also does not the soul of the one who speaks not of truth. Glory be to God Almighty! TRUST YOUR INSTINCTS! Nadia, Stirling, trust in each other. The last filter will be your instincts of both of you. Trust them, trust each other! Glory be to God Almighty.

Christ, Michael, Joseph, Jacob, Raphael, Sweet Bessie and Gabriel! Glory be to God Almighty! You are loved. You are both cherished and thank you from God, from all the Angels for taking on this mission. Your light abounds you!

Glory be to God Almighty!

I love you too,

Nadia.

APRIL 23, 2004

Sweet God,

How about this is one of the last nights I will be in this house.

Yes Nadia, this place, home in life carried you in solitude, life experience, writing, in safety of self and children. You were in heldation. You saw the Angels of God Almighty, for the quiet in your life gave to you the openness of heart to look and to see. Your heart grew in trifold upon your entrance into this home. You are completed in this time.

For you entered married, you became you in singleness and now you are married again. Time for more change. You are simple inside. You look at people, at all people as souls. You notice others do what you call "check each other out." I love that part for no one knows what exists in the other soul and yet decisions are made about that person that truly have nothing to do with that person.

It is of the soul "checking out" and the fantasy in head that carries the "checking out" and progresses at times further. In the reality, over time the "checking out" gets checked out and the reality of that person is now known and seen. And decisions take time to be made in reality. This happens in any instance of life. For conversation instills who a soul is. True conversation will do that.

However most conversation is backed with sexual intention and until that is manifested in most, true conversation cannot take place. Otherwise you have situations not based on reality or truth, therefore not being of purity. This takes place in all avenues of life and now you have witnessed such between women and men, men and men, women and women.

It is very intriguing to me that the way a person looks overpowers the way they behave in beginnings. And the separations are in the way the soul behaves. And the looks are forgotten with such ease and comfort.

For the comfort of a soul settles life around within. The truth of thought and conversation backed not with any other intention is the conversation that teaches and grows. All other conversations are catalytic in nature.

Nadia, you live in purity. The human soul is simply the soul that no longer has the memory of home to progress it. Purity is all you know. At times your purity embarrasses you for you feel like you are like a child and haven't learned the ways of the adult world. Leave the ways of the adult world to those who believe there is an adult world.

It is all the same world and when you are met, you take people out of what they think of as the adult world and you bring them home with the love of a child.

You are of age of an adult however one who stated that an adult loses the beauties of life and tries then to recreate them. Enjoy the simpleness of life in the pleasure of knowing that when purity is present the soul is not of complication.

That is truly what the adult world means: OF COMPLICATION, OF EXPLANATION, OF PERSONAL UNTRUTHS TRYING TO BECOME TRUTH.

The adult mind has been shaped by then of many factors and person manipulations. For unknowingly those manipulations take the soul further and further away from self. So other things set in. And unhappiness follows.

The soul has gotten further away from self and looks for outside stimulus to grow itself and the look internal is overlooked! Simple! Glory be to God Almighty!

Some people are in a state of angst, for they can not take back their doings. They hurt others with actions that come from choice. All choice is taught and going back and correcting is never the same as purity from the start. Purity from the start builds trust.

Without it, it must be earned. And with that it is much greater of task to do so. Glory be to God Almighty. Nadia, go about your day. With the vigor that carries life, it will carry you, Stirling, all the Children and those around you. Glory be to God Almighty!

You are loved and loved and loved. Christ, Michael, Joseph, Jacob, Raphael, Sweet Bessie and Gabriel. You are love Nadia, never to be said enough!

I love you too, all of you. I have felt you so much, so great in the past few days and very intensely quiet in all of it. It has been nothing that I have felt until now. I loved the idea of the book as well.

Yes, you got to see it and now you will perfect its presentation. Yes, a slow brown coloring, almost with a tinge of Orange will carry with it the comforts of home to the soul. Like the moments of dusk. The soul rests in those times. You will know it when you see it. Stirling will know it as well. The smaller version will allow people to carry it around with ease. For it is with ease to be of love.

Nadia, the dove was sent with all of Us around it. It shall be the forefront of the photo. The eyes that witness the dove will witness Us as they witness Us in you! Glory be to God Almighty. Never to worry. The monies will come.

It will feel harnesting at times however you will be of fine. Glory be to God Almighty! Enjoy your movement of life in this day. These steps taken are carried within and without the thoughts of home. Your Earthly reality becomes you. You are weightless and effortless! Glory be to God Almighty!

I love you God, Christ, all the Beautiful Angels. I love you!

Nadia

## MAY 11, 2004

Dearest Lord God,

I could hear you so loudly.

Yes Nadia, thank you for coming to us. Yes, you could hear us however we needed to talk to you. In fashion that will not be forgotten. God Almighty is of time to reemerge to the souls of Earth, for much love is needed. Pure intent is reinstated. Caring of self is lost and soon will grow wings again.

For the souls are weighted down with might. They are actually fighting to be weighted down for it is easier than trying in this moment of balance on Earth. All seek however know not what they seek. All try however know not why they are trying.

It is so simple and yet to know not of self breeds knowing not of all things, so simple, so simple, spoken in many times however not taken lightly. The lack of simplicity is the token of all complication.

Nadia, Stirling, pay attention. Prepare in heart for all that is coming your way. Nadia, you are protected; so important to tell you for we took you out of your time to rest to tell you this alone. You are protected. You will be challenged. Take heart.

I will. I am. I don't know what I don't know. I am here. I am excited just with what I feel. If there are challenges, I know you are with me I know that you are. I am in trusting all that is around me. What was happening to me last night? What was it I saw?

Nadia, we brought home to you. We brought it to you; we showed you your home. You will go between home and Earth easily for you will need to. Nadia, this is Christ. I would be in that realm in all time of miracles. You will float to safety and you will be present on Earth, for the glow of home remains around you in protection of the innocence of your soul.

The human souls that have the opportunity to read the writings are touched. Those who say they are not, know not what is said from the mouth of the physical body in which they speak. Glory be to God Almighty. I witness and I feel the loss of guard when the words of God Almighty are read. I also witness the shortcomings that build the walls that come up again however not as high as they once were. Do you understand?

Back to a million baby steps, I love that as you speak it, for that is truly what it is. The energy it takes to carry a soul, a soul on Earth, is of great work. If only the souls could know more they can be more. So simple to speak however of pure truth to know; to know of truth is to be of truth. Glory be to God Almighty. You are of such light for the light of home surrounds you. You are loved.

I love you all too.

Nadia

&#8298;

*I have to say; reading this to write up inserts to it is always new and beautiful over and over again. I can't help but think the same thoughts time and time again, how me? Why me? And I found out it is not "why me."*

*People on Earth see this as something special in the sense that I would think I am special because of this. I am not special. Not more than anyone else. There is no soul more important than another. We all have jobs to do and this is mine.*

*It comes with a lot of things I had to experience to be able to write and to know and understand what I write of or about. This message in many ways is independent of me, other than the will and choosing I have had to have to be doing this at all.*

*My life is and has been one of many challenges and I never thought for a minute not to take this on. I simply needed to understand what and how, it is to be been done. When "Little Wing," was first published and we had a book signing, I woke up the next day with Author's remorse, if there is such a thing.*

*The realization that what I had come to know, was out there in the world overwhelmed me and I felt very vulnerable and exposed. And then we heard nothing from anyone. I thought by then that everyone would think I was crazy. I didn't realize that no one ran home and read the book immediately.*

*As time passed people started writing me and saying they got it. Some didn't at all. Some of my family didn't want to talk to me anymore, asking me "who I thought I was to say these things?" All I could think was that I am nobody really. This happening to me is as much a shock to me as to anyone. It was all I could do to publish the book and try to keep most of the personal things out of the writings.*

*My writing is everyday. Everything that happens to me is explained to me in such detail, that I have become a person who understands people, including myself in minute detail.*

*I was going through many changes in this time, adapting to a new blended family of six children, my family's rejection of me for getting married to a non Muslim and the exposing of myself within all that I have come to know.*

*Furthermore, the way the book taught me, I was teaching others. I realized my life isn't just for me and this time in my life was big in me coming to terms with all the newness in my life. And the realization of something Christ says to me a lot, "every day ends as it should."*

*I simply had to trust and keep moving. I knew that there were no mistakes and this is where I should be. I simply had to catch up and accept. Grow and teach. Live and release what I feel. Trust forces the other thoughts to happen. I learned to trust trust trust.*

~~~~~

# CHAPTER 9

# TAUGHTS OF ERROR

### MAY 24, 2004

Dearest Christ,

I know there is a lot of fun in all of this today…it feels like the calmness of all of it rolled up into the reality, and the lightheartedness is where it lives.

Yes Nadia, people take themselves far too seriously. The seriousness of which they take themselves is the trouble in which they get themselves into. By trouble, I am not saying the obvious however there is a great taking away of self and the fun and the joy of doing is buried!!! Glory be to God Almighty!

Nadia, you have a question. I know what it is and Yes, I have an answer. Your question is how do you write about yourself? You wanted to add, "how do I write about myself and protect the writing, you meaning me?" You need not protect the writing and me. We are of protection as you are as well.

How do you write about you?
In truth, Simply.
Who are you?
You are a prophet of God.
What does prophet mean?
A soul, that gives to others the messages of God Almighty.
Why a prophet? Who else?
I will tell you who else.

A prophet is one without judgment. Who sees true reality. Who beckons to light and who draws to light. God is of greatness, however God is not alone in greatness, we all are of greatness for we are of God. God is not to be glorified greater than the souls in which he gave love to.

All God can do is enjoy and fulfill in the love that exists; from us, with us, around us. Free will brings us back to God. Today you witness those who look untouchable. They are. Let them be. Be strong and let go. For their souls are the thieves of life. Let life be the teacher back and remain firm and strong with all negative forces.

Nadia, I will go back to the question at this moment. What do you say? You can speak that I am at the second coming, I am. This is the second time I am here on Earth, only this time your physical form will endure! You are a prophet. That is of fact. So simple.

Say that you are of prophet. And ask, what is a prophet, why could it be? Ask it before it is asked of you and it will calm the soul reading such words. For that is what they will be thinking. "Not another one," as Stirling in all of his wisdom speaks.

You will be educating. You are not a modern day prophet. You are not a miracle worker. You are not a futuristic forsayer. You are of prophet. You are of great and grandness of words, of love, of messages! Glory be to God Almighty! Glory be to God Almighty!

You are love and through the love in which you are, your purity brought about the flowing of messages of love. Everything less than love, Anything that takes away or grows the heart of a soul to think for a split second of a follicle of hair that they are not of love is not of God Almighty! So simple.

So what is the big deal of the second coming of Christ. I am here. Only in truth I am hear. For I am not visible and yet I am present.

That is the miracle of love. For love carries and through you, people are amazed at the attraction to you and you are simple in humanness. And that very simplicity is of greatness greater than the grandness of human thought. Your existence erases any mishaps of the mind, even if for a moment!

For all you need to say is;

My Name is Nadia. I am told I am a prophet of God. What does that mean?

So simple. With ease of heart that is truly all you can say. Meeting you is in the knowing. You know who you are as you know many other things. So simply you live in such knowledge. You had to live in human form to be related to. So simple. So now you know how a human thinks, feels, behaves, loves, laughs and sorrows.

With that knowledge you understand the values of the messages given to the souls of searchment. You do not need to act of or portray anything. That is why it is you. You are immune to status and on the other hand you have no judgment. You see awry and you fight with vigor for the truth and love. That is who you are, that is of prophet. You speak in truth and the truth cannot stain!

Nadia, sweet Nadia, you are the answer of all answers of heart and mind, body and soul; If only you knew of your quiet and subtle affect that you have, that you are. I see you in this moment so simple with what you know and still in it you want to protect me. I am of protection.

Do not forget. God Almighty is of Glory of Message and it is time of heart and soul to unite! Glory be to God Almighty! That is another way to look at who you are. You can title your speaking as you were a book long ago. NO BUGS IN HEAVEN.

My name is Nadia; I am told I am a prophet, what does that mean? That way you give interest and a hand in that very soul searching for itself. Glory be to God Almighty! You must move on for now, do you simply love my language. It is still odd sounding to me to use language however it is of great simplicity for me in this day! Glory be to God Almighty! You are loved. Stirling is love!

I love you too!

Nadia

MAY 27, 2004

Dearest Lord God,

So simply, I want to thank you for me talking tonight. Thank you for Stirling listening. From all of that realized I am just disappointed and I don't want to hear the shit of life anymore, constantly from anyone. Negative things I can take in some doses however constant is too much. Constant is very degrading to anyone. I am thinking so much and wanting to talk so little. I am having to shut off and to shut down to make it go away.

I don't want to be so involved in the ship that wants to stay put and complain about all the entitlement entitled. I want to move forward, so at least the one's who want to take away can be quiet and hold on to themselves and let those who want to move forward, move forward.

There is so much to look at that gives, how can it all be missed? I am in such a place. I want to rest in my sleep. I want to know that there is some light in all of the negativity and harshness of souls to souls.

Nadia, Sweet Nadia, take heart in all that you do.

I thought that I learned that love heals and that others know of it, that caring can't be denied.

Nadia, Love does heal, caring can not be denied. Your heart is swollen with soreness and your life has been turned from letting go of all the negativity to now having it in your home in constant. You will see in soon that love will turn it all around. You will see soon that love does heal. You took on a load you knew not of.

It is of OK. If anyone is and can do such work it is of you. Know that many are of this. Simply. Know that you will be able to cope with such negativity for you are learning to cope as of now, of this moment. Your heart is wary and tired and finds it hard to trust the love and caring of the souls you are with. Trust, for your heart needs to trust to flourish.

Right now, you are asking yourself why and how souls can take away and not see the wonderfulness around them? People do not see the world as you do our dear. You are loved and cared for by God. The humans are of such as well however they do not know as you do about the love of God. You are tired. Nadia, come back to us and know that you are loved. Glory be to God Almighty, for the light of love will return in the hope of what you see around you. Glory be to God Almighty! You are loved.

I love you too!

Nadia

MAY 29, 2004

Nadia,

Sweet and dearest of Nadia, so why do those who read and know and hear the words of God hence Me hence other Angels in this day talk about it being a devil, or that it could be wrong? The words of beauty, of truth wrong? It can not be.

Your friend, your children in your family, they are all of love to you and for you and yet you must experience from those close to you before you can from others who will truly have heard of you in first moments. Your friend is born and taught in error.

There are not only millions, let me say there will be billions. The guilt of accepting any thought other than the initial demise of their soul, the continuous demise of their soul and the final demise of their soul without the word repentance, the word she used, they will go to hell. They are set up to fail. In the one church she belongs to there is also competitiveness of souls in a way of dress, cars.

There are gambling trips. There is homosexuality. There is lying, cheating, pregnancy, and all of it doesn't matter. Nor is it bad or wrong. Nadia, can you imagine the earth without catalysts. There aren't as many catalysts as there are those of growth.

So the catalysts, some of which become the growth souls as well, learn from each other and push each others souls to fruition, for nothing is as it seems. Nadia, sweet Nadia, all the aforementioned things are "bad" in the world today for peoples, souls decided it would be bad. And then an "I am better than" system was and is put in place for those souls to hurdle over.

Your friend is the one at church of pure intent. However there are very few and she is of fear. To her, to her church, fear of God is a welcome, admirable trait. Nadia, Nadia, it was of pain again for you. Yet you listened and asked her why you wouldn't believe in the love of God over the hurtful set stage of God Almighty. You found in that moment that people, souls, will fight for a conditional God.

They will fight you. She loves you and she simply asks you "I know you write of these things, but do you believe them, I need to know you do not believe this!" And all you could say is that I do. Another addition to your thought, for you were not asked of this question in past as well, when she stated to you "you are not talking to God are you?" Yes, yes you are. God's glory is all over you. You can say you talk to me, as in Christ, for she wanted to know that you were speaking of Jesus. Nadia, Jesus is the fear in people.

Jesus was the created one. Jesus is the man in which I was made and was called on Earth and in his name, Jesus, all the non truths, living and created from mere simple truths and then taught in error. Jesus is the human-ized version of ME. However at home I am simply Christ. I am an Angel and have always been.

You had to experience life in many forms. Hence, you are an Arabic, Palestinian, Muslim human. In a form that looks like many. That blends with all. That is unnoticed until the truthful witness you. And they see the light of Angels in you hence the light of God.

For God Almighty is the communicator of all of Us. Who is to question words of truth? The minds of the fearful. Some are ready to let go and others are going to hang on until the generations to follow will carry the open heartedness of such searches of truth. The work of this time will live forever. So simple. No strings attached, as I hear in human experience.

Oh, for the human mind of weariness. So hard to take away negative for it has become a common way of thought and practice. WE are simply the beginning steps of re-programming! Re-programming the negative of mind into acceptance of self, of others, of life; Taughts of Error will dissolve in time, in effort, in love and in glory! Glory be to God Almighty! Glory be to God Almighty! Glory be to God Almighty! You are loved.

I love you too,

Nadia

JUNE 3, 2004

Dearest Nadia, of sweetness,

Thank you for coming to Us. You saw us and want to sleep. You will be of OK. You keep asking why? Why you? Why do you know things? What are you supposed to do with what you know? The book is out in small and things are of calm. You are not of calm. You are of concern. Yet there is nothing to be of concern about.

How could that be? I kept thinking all these things. I am simply tired now and still inside I just don't feel like myself. I feel sad that Stirling feels sad and that I feel sad, for the same reasons yet different ways to them. His is simply a reaction to me, and me, I am just here. And you say you are going to show through me and I believe you, and I believe me and the book and all the beautiful writing.

I know things are as they should be. I am here and I am not here. I feel like there is so much in front of me right now that I don't know what to attend to first. That I may be crazy for real and I was and am building my life around all that I can't take care of our family with. I don't know. You say not to be of concern and that I am not in need of a penny.

So I sit here and I am letting concern go and I realize that money doesn't mean anything. Yet you need it to be able to do what is needed to be done. I am trusting in all that I know. I know its truth and I know its meaning. Yet I am feeling like all this talk right now.

I shook right out of bed and still here I continue. I love seeing you. I love seeing all the Angels. And I feel so free in that world. However there is a lot to do here. Why or how do I continue to be at work, if money is not of importance and that is the only reason that I am there?

That is not the only reason you are there. You are building still. Nadia, sweet Nadia, you are disheartened. That is all. You are tired. And you are disappointed in yourself right now. You have no words and you are embarrassed for nothing is as it seems. You are not feeling strength from this at all in these moments. It is of OK. As I have said. My coming through you will be a surprise. You are not waiting; you are thinking you are crazy.

I have felt so many times in my time on Earth as well. Nadia, God is of all knowing. There is truly nothing without his plan. For there is not of predestination which all want to know for the experience of Free Will is Earth. You will not speak of all that I say for you know not of it ever happening before so your concept is hard to bring into reality.

That is all of relief to me.

How could you know of what you can not imagine? Your heart is of concern, for your mind and heart are here with me and you are living in this world. It is of great challenge. You are functioning and you are falling behind. You are not of behind. You are right where you should be. For now you can feel that feeling of things being bigger than you are.

You have no money and you have bills. Is it important? Yes. It is important to take care of things owed. And you and Stirling can not at this time. Grow your business. Grow your business. It is all there. And you are thinking you can not even take money for the book.

Some do not offer it to you. That is of sadness to you. Others are in the world of not offering, even when they know. If you give out all the books, how will you make more? Glory be to God Almighty. Nadia, you are of overwhelmed.

You will do much work this weekend. Glory be to God Almighty. You will be of OK. Never to forget. You are thinking already of all the work you have to do tomorrow. Rest now, for all will be done. Glory be to God Almighty. You say it much and now I say to you, trust life. You are loved.

I love you too.

## June 4, 2004

So thank you that I feel normal. It is funny, I am a good let goer and with that I grow into my own. I understand that relationships change and metamorphous. I just feel like writing about life and since I am living this one, I like writing too about all these things that exist in it. I love hearing your words. It is great to know you as I do.

In the simpleness of how I see things and sometimes the pains of what I know and feel. And care about and don't care about and even better, growing and learning to not feel so attached inside. To understand at some point that some distance is probably a good thing; that a person's life is really their life. We can touch each other and love each other but there is no ownership or need for it.

When I am sad about someone I can't speak. It is a good thing. My brain gets it however when others are ready to talk I am not. I just need time, because simply in my heart it is like assimilating information. It is OK. I just wanted to know sometimes if the truth of what I see is shared. As you say, so simple again. I feel so funny about you too, sweet Christ.

I love the way I think of you right now. It is so light hearted. That has changed in me too. I am thinking, so, you are here and I think of how people think of you. IT is almost deranged to see it and to hear it. And they fight for it because people were told somewhere that if they challenge or question, like a blind faith wash of the human brain. That pain and that fear are very real to witness.

Nadia, sweet Nadia, did you notice you are writing some more than usual, as you used to in your earlier writings. Your heart is playing in the love of God. All You know and remember of God is love. Of all of us.

You do not like to see love hurt and there is your problem with your day last. You shut down in such a way. Being in your body, it is like all things stopped and you do not know where to rest yourself. That is what you do.

Pretty much. But my brain races until I can understand what it is I am feeling and doing. However I have learned that you can go back and it is OK to continue to share lives. And I will be able to do that and teach others what it is like to be committed and loving as well. I know being here is not my thing sometimes but I am sure it is true for all of us.

Yes Nadia, I knew my time was of limits upon my life on Earth. I am learning now that the differences internal are not really different from the period of time that I was present. The souls of today have little time of contemplation, for there are many points of brain bombardment.

There is no rest internal and the task of getting to know of oneself is too big to conquer so the task is put off as the least important. Yet in reality it is of the most important and will settle all the other tasks of mind and heart. You are funny in this evening. Being in your internal is of such great pleasure.

I know, I feel it too, I always know I am OK no matter what. That life is OK no matter what. I say things sometimes and I can't tell myself I buy it at times however truly I can't find anything worth worrying about. Thank you God, for the days that I feel sad, it reminds me that I can feel otherwise. I never forget how restricted I was, and still did so much. Imagine in the 7 or so years I have been single, all that was discovered in life. I am thinking back as though that phase of life is over forever.

Yes Nadia, it is. Your privacy is almost on its last moments. You live in the moment and that carries you. You are so loved sweet Nadia. Your love of God is so simple that when you speak of God, how can a soul not want to love God Almighty in the same way? For truly the health of such love then begins.

It is not the can not do's. What can a person do that does not take away from self is the question of heart, mind, body and soul? Have you not had to say this today? How many times did you say it? It is who you are, as I have said. Before you it was of me. You will become it and it will become you! So simple. You love that phrase. You are that phrase.

Your love of me, for me, felt throughout your existence and you avoid talking of me, for there were many falsities before you. It is OK they are part of the bigger picture in preparation of what you are not. Nadia, you are realizing that it is all OK.

I know, it is the coolest feeling in this world to know that. I had to lay myself on the line yesterday and maybe the chain of events at least got me to verbalize or at least write about all the things I simply needed to say or put on the paper. People sometimes, I just want to scream. It is hard to be with some people, they are lovable from a distance, any closer and there is great caution to sanity!

Yes Nadia, evolution takes on many forms. Evolution is of such greatness, for the mind is the thought that carries with it the way in which the world is seen and what it means to people's soul. You see Nadia, life is made of many. Free will is the opening of all doors. Free will is the free dome of the soul. Nadia, did you ever wonder why it is called Free will. It is of free domes.

You can put yourself anywhere and it is the path of doing, making decisions, learning, growing. Many have forgotten what it is or what it means to have free will. What it is. They think it is in doing what others don't want them to do. However what was lost is that free will is growth not deterrent.

Free will works both ways. So simple. It is not only one way. Never forget! Glory be to God Almighty! You feel you wrote in complete mumbo jumbo. Those are your exact thoughts. I love to listen. All is as it should be. You have been needing to talk about life in the days of late.

You always come out of your world into others and then you question. Do you realize your mind works in questions? You see the unseen and you see the things not needed to be said. You laugh at the thought. That is funny to think your thoughts at times. You are love!

I love you too!

Glory be to God Almighty, our love!

CHAPTER 10

# GOD IS NOT A RELIGION

JUNE 9, 2004

Sweet Stirling,

I never did tell you how great if felt to get a message from you. I know I told you I loved it. I am sitting here at work and I know the logic of "everything happens for a reason." Every time I think of knowing you there is something else that I love about you, about life, about the kids, about all that happens because there is us.

You are my family. You are home in my heart. You are my husband and that I never really knew the meaning of. I am still learning what it feels like to be a wife in the ways I dreamt it. Today, simply talking to you reminded me we can "redefine business." That is for us to do. We don't need to do things so differently. We can do them and by being a part of all we do, the love we have for the things we do will find its way into it.

That will carry it and us. It is a lot to do at once. Yet we are already doing it. We just have to find a way to live in it and it to live in us. It is that simple. Christ is talking to me so I am just going to let him do the talking.

Nadia, Sweet Nadia, Stirling, Sweet Stirling. I am here. I am with you, between you. I love saying that simply that we are together again. Hallelujah! That word has great exemplication of meaning. For it is the expulsion of love from within to without the spirit! Nadia, Stirling, you are very ready.

You have come to terms with the newness of many things. For newness was not that new around you however those around you had to catch up. And now they are catching up to thoughts of two or three months ago in happening. Glory be to God Almighty.

Origin Books is waiting for you both to come to it. Nadia, you are ready now too; to speak to groves of people. I was saying followers and you wrote people. Nadia, it is followers. That is what you already have. Did you not know? Small in number simply because they are small in followers who know of you.

You asked Sweet Nadia, that you do not shake so much. So it will be. You have much in you from home now. As we said before, ask and you shall have all asked for come to you. You will have some rest now, however upon my visible visits, you will shake in greatness. You are loved. Come back to me. You are love! Glory be to God Almighty!

I love you too.

## JUNE 10, 2004

Dearest Lord God,

You are calling me. Sometimes it is just cool to hear you. I love hearing you, especially right now in this moment. It is quiet enough around me to respond. I love you so much. It may sound silly to say it like that, like it is not enough. But I know you know. I asked and thank you for giving me lightness in knowing.

Yes Nadia, for to ask is to receive and you thought immediately about money. It will get better in much soon. You
have to rid of all the old. As you did all other things in life.
You will continue in difference now.

One change has to happen before another can. And in
every day there is another thing in happening. You know
of this and accompaniment of heart is what is changing at
this time. You feel it. I feel it in you.

We are many Angels around you and you hear me most.
You recognize me most. I am your guide. You were
thinking of me coming through you and wanting to keep
me all to yourself for a bit longer.

Nadia, there is no time. No time, meaning there is no time.
The fact people wake up and sleep does that mean that
time ends and begins? Or that the days are numbered and
clocked in between the numbered create time?

What was it like on Earth before time? It was growth
without measurement, for the years did not, nor the time
become, for it was open for life to be lived. In this day
there is not the time in which to live life. Families are mon-
itored by the clock of life and the clock of life is not even
enough as well. Do you understand?

People work to stay behind. That is most of souls. Some
are steady and some are better off. However there is no
helping hand to produce health in families and that is
because of the creation of time.

Time created rushing, hurrying, impatience, achievements,
deadlines, determinates of failure or success, aging,
hunger, entitlements to things not of the person taking. This
has turned peoples into robotic states of mind. It can not be

without time, for that is all that is now known and peoples are programmed to be dictated to.

The mind is taking orders and the naturalness of life is taken away with that order. Why time? Why the rush? Why the taking away from the creativity of life? The simpler the message, the simpler the life, the more each person shares and then receives.

There is no starvation in souls when things are shared. The creation of greater strangulation of souls and greater control of souls creates the acceptance of very little mental and physical nourishment to survive. Do you understand, my sweet and beautiful Nadia?

What people call corporate America is truly the aggressor of taking away the longevity and productivity of souls on Earth. There is no trust, no growth and those who succeed have thieved along the way. For the feeling if you do not take too much, just a little from everyone to gain fortune for self, is not of thievery. Glory be to God Almighty.

Everyone is paid on time and the payee of that time is always finding ways to lash out and the lashing out is the freedom in which the soul finds itself in search of. Time created a monsteric human to arise.

The love of working is hurt therefore the pride, the participation of work; the extra steps do not exist as a whole. People know they are being cheated by self and then by others and with lack of options they are furious internal and putting up external and it is put off in feeling for years. And the missions are seizing and put off as well. The unnaturalness of cagedness of souls is difficult to overcome.

When I show it will be of miracle for sure. And at first people will hear of it. A small amount will see it and the words will be heard. And it will be of discernment to hear for the shaking up of all things known will be in jeopardy. The dictation of time will dictate that peoples will go on for lack of knowing what else to do, for there are no options.

And then Nadia, it will start to register in mentality and it will begin to bring interest into who you are, why you, who you are again. What are these writings? How did she write them? Why, how is she living? Where does she live? why is she Muslim? Who gives her the right to know our Jesus, and all you will say is that Christ is here and he is for all.

There is no soul more important than another. That love belongs to all not to one. That Christ is an Angel for all and that the forming of like thoughts created religions and religions created rules and the rules were obey. However love is open and cares for all not for some.

Love is of open not of closing doors. Love gives, receives, breathes in the hearts and gives with the hands. No one is too special or not special enough for love. And all Christ is is love. Christ has been turned into an unattainable source through the evolution of time.

For as time passes much is added and other much is forgotten. However as Christ was on Earth, he is taking residence in me. For if Christ were to come now, how would you know it was him? And the importance that it be him and yet his peoples do not believe he has arrived.

Yes, that Christ is a very important Angel. Yet Christ is you and me. You do not have to change a thing in you. Simply love.

Love yourself to be able to love others. Sweet Children, Sweet Peoples, love grows all things. So simple. That is all to say sweet Nadia. You are leaving in this moment. You are loved

Nadia, you are an endless well of love. And to the surprise of those around you, you are showing love and it is being received and you entered into a world of complete resistance. Glory be to God Almighty.

Love is the grower of all things. Love is misunderstood for love at this time on Earth is engulfed into complete self motivation.

And you are pulling the self out and leaving the motivation in the souls that you touch. For then love can be received. You are loved Nadia. Come back to us again and again. There is much to be said and you always think, how could there be? Smile, for your face is the light of all smiles.

Christ!


JUNE 13, 2004

Dearest Lord God,

Sweet Nadia, you are finding life to be humorous.

I can't stop laughing inside and I am trying not to as well. I know there is a lot of life that I don't know. I know that each person is an example of a million. I know and believe all that you say to me and I am very open to you, sweet Christ, coming through my body in one day on Earth. I am here for you for that.

All of that is so great to me. And then I have to remember that I am here and there is much obligation to be here. I feel like I am here by the skin of my teeth. Ever since Stirling said we are living on the fumes of money, I can't stop thinking it. I am living on the fumes of life. The writings are the most wonderful contribution of life for me. I love that I got to do it here and that I know you while I am here and that Stirling and I found each other and can live in this world together.

I think I am saying all of this because I feel like I crossed a line in my last evening. I am realizing I am not in the world of people. I feel like I am watching and studying and studying some more. I can't stop studying. I keep thinking the whys, the internal whys of life of love of heart and home. I was just talking to Stirling about our friend being enamored with a married man and minimizing what that means to her.

I am intrigued by what people are; watching the becoming of lessons. I get more intrigued when they know something and cannot see themselves. The blindness amazes me; to not be conscious of their own soul even when it tries to talk to them. Or better yet, ignoring themselves like they are two people.

It is not just the cheater of wife or husband, or money or possessions. It is the cheater of one's soul Nadia, Sweet Nadia. Once cheating begins it starts involving others in its path. If you steal you have to steal from someone!

If you cheat, who are you cheating on? You are cheating yourself in first. The other party is merely a reactor. However the other party involved is the one who has a choice of wanting to be amongst a cheater of heart, mind, and body!

What you think of as cheating is not of the cheating in which you think it. Your mind is already pondering such issues. For you walk away from such action, for you know of it first hand. Your simpleness angers the minds of complication. Glory be to God Almighty!

Nadia, to come to terms with your thinking in this day; it is sheerness of materialism that the foundational part of the road your mind is going on. It is simple materialness. For things are more important than peoples. Souls will sell themselves, let alone the soul of another for material. Wealth is not a horrible fate. Yet the road to it can be.

The compromises that are made for it, with it, because of it, have tested the strongest of souls into belief that methods are OK and "then I will be prudent." For nothing is as it seems. Can people charge less? Yes they can. Can they make better products? Yes they can.

Nadia, when you get in this plane with me, at times, you can't feel the horrible of emotional abandonment that exists. You see my child, my peer, you are not of human. Did you not know? You are shy, embarrassed that this is you? You are present, it is seen, and still you do not want to put others out of place. For you do not want to feel better than others to such an extent.

Nadia, you are not better than others. Does that make you feel better? You are of mission. Think of yourself in mission. The woman you saw in this day, she is of her mission. Her passion was so very recognizable to you.

Yes, I know.

Nadia you are moving into a world you know not of. What is easy for you is not for all. That is why you are you. Do I need to lesson you right now? Nadia, I felt at times, even in knowing who I am. While I was growing without hesitation and the patience of my growing, I, at the first steps of my integration into the existing human spirits on Earth at that time frame. I could only speak as I needed to and remain silent for the setting.

Yes, there will be many to disagree and you understand that you are not worried about disagreement however you are not well with attention. Just stand in silence while the receivers can assimilate your words, your beauty and understand that what they are seeing is of home.

They have not seen home in much time and you are a shocking reminder of all things known. The man that stopped and looked at you while you were waiting in the outdoors, he saw me and he knew not believing himself that he saw me.

He shook his head in belief first and discountment second! Glory be to God Almighty, that was fun for me. Nadia, I am free to be inside of you. I am free to be. I am able to touch and not be touched. There is a beauty in the freedom of spirit when human souls can see me and shake their heads. I am practicing.

You are expanded, expanding. With every shake, tremble and quiverness of body, you are home more than you are on Earth. And yet you are home on Earth. It is a felt comfort in presence.

You think how people must feel to meet you, and then they meet you and you feel like all they find is you!

ALL THEY FIND IS YOU! They find you and ME! You will teach that anything is of possible through simply existing! Glory be to God Almighty! You are loved.

I love you!

Sweet Nadia, you address us with all love, with such love. For on Earth it is rare love to sense coming back to Us. Glory be to God Almighty. You will create and be created. Understand that statement and it will carry you in times of need.

You once asked many things of God Almighty. They will all be. Not one is missed or misled. Not one is or has not been heard. Your hearts desires come from the truest desire to grow yourself and those around you.

For the celebration of the greatest surprises on Earth, the greatest moments on Earth are when souls recognize and find one another through intent for pure intent leads! PURE INTENT LEADS! Lack of pure intents Leaves! LACK OF PURE INTENT LEAVES!

Nadia, you understand. You laugh at my play with words. You have been doing this much, for I am loving the use of language as it is understood on Earth.

You got use to my language and me to yours. You write like my language now, even when I am not the one writing to you. And I speak in yours to you, for the sheer pleasure of continuous learning and loving of all the ways in which souls progress themselves.

I feel you and I am in greatness of you to see you on Earth and witness your mission. For how you live(ed) on Earth as a human and now a known Angel. You have to know that. You have to admit that internal for you are of such resistance. You have found many of ways to camouflage who you are my dearest soul.

That has been of great amusement in me to witness. I was hesitant however when the miracles began there was no denyment of who I was. No more hiding and the threats began for the greater the insecurity the greater the threats!

That is true throughout life in this day. THE GREATER THE INSECURITY THE GREATER THE THREATS! Glory be to God Almighty! Glory be to God Almighty! Nadia, your heart knows of this. Keep this in mind also in the near future as things will and can change in an instant! Glory be to God Almighty!

JUNE 15, 2004

Nadia, Sweet and Beautiful Nadia,

I feel your surrealment in this day and forward as well. Your heart is knowing now. You know. You know, Glee, for a day of celebration. You know. Stirling has known. He knows. He knows, you know. Do, Do, Do.

Forget the number of sales to make. Think what it must be like to receive such writings and take it from there. Never talk about the money for it is irrelevant. It will come and is on its way so that you can travel to Do, Do and Do. Your heart is there. You know.

You had to hear what you should not be saying to understand and know what you NEED to say. For to you, you know of all of this in already, Stirling, in Already. Imagine the soul receiving these writings and the contentment that it brings to a soul to know of such things of treasures that nourish.

You are a prophet of God. You know it and you sit quiet with such knowledge. However you are not meant to sit in such knowledge. For knowledge not shared is it knowledge? It can not be. God knows all, yet if you do not know all then do you know God? To know God is to have knowledge of him.

I loved what you said in your speaking today. God is not a religion. You need that in everything you do and say. God is not a religion. Nadia, that is of brilliance. You felt it, for there was rejoice in your worlds! God is not a show, nor a religion; there was God before religion. There was God before people.

The simple minds of people working are what God is not, simply because they do not know of the truth and why they are here. In the beginning the beings were very close to home. Now they are very far away. To the point of segments of population who question such existence. There truly is no big moment as to believe or not to believe in God.

To be saved by Me. How do I save a soul? I simply love souls. Or punish? How could God set up punishment for the experiencing of soul? For only the punishments endured and established by oneself is the punishment had. Glory be to God Almighty! Nadia, you are going to fall asleep.

Yes, I feel so much like it, but I have energy. It is just this cold is making me want to sleep. I want to write some more though. I can't stop feeling all these things at once. I feel movement and I haven't felt this movement before.

Yes, Nadia, this is of new. You are what you say you are and there is no question as to who you are. You are the prophet of God Almighty. It is a bigger thing though to the world than it is to you for you understand what it means. You are the form of messaging to peoples. That is all you need to do. Always remember that your knowledge, it is all you can do to share it however the reactions are for those reacting.

They will want to meet you. As many who will read the writings of wonder, of origin. And meeting you will confirm the ills of the world to be as they are and the growth to form the newest of foundations. For nothing is as it seems our love on Earth.

Nadia, you are shaking. Shake and rest. Shake and expand. You have to have the energy to withstand much. Work and never cease. Your work is carried by a billion Angels. Every effort is carried. Never to feel there is a harder day than another, it is simply in progress.

Glory be to God Almighty. Your inner truths will guide you and those around you with ill intent will find their way to a door away from your soul. Glory be to God Almighty! You are of love. Christ.

I love you Sweet God, Christ and all the beautiful Angels. I love you.

Nadia

JUNE 16, 2004

Dearest Lord God,

Today it is calm. I have a cold and it is a pretty good one. Yet I am realizing today that all my bills have gone by the wayside and there is nothing I can do about it. I just shot my credit. And still there is nothing I can do about it.

We have enough money for basics and that is going to be it for a while. I feel everything lifted though. As hard as it seems to feel and to not be able to do that, I have been paying those cards for years and the balances never went down.

I know they have been paid back however none of it went to principle. It is a hard system to get out of once you're in it. I kind of feel OK with not having credit at all. Everything I have will be everything I have. It is a hard thing however it has to be, for there are no other resources right now.

I am thinking that there shouldn't be credit. Things would be so honest then. I love honesty, living in it, being it. It is so simple like you say. I have a hard time when there is not the feeling that it is around.

Yes, Nadia honesty is reassuring that life is closer to our souls than unreachable. We tend to gain security in honesty and it grows the inner thinkings into bigger thinkings and takes things from the maybes to possible. Nadia, you think a lot of some things and then you find a way to deal with what you are not used to in life. It is called accommodation and you do it from a pure heart.

The honesty that is felt is sincere to another soul and there is not question to the receiving person that you care. So what you actually say with words is not of great importance really even in the harshest of moments for the honesty outweighs by far anything else that could have taken place. Glory be to God Almighty.

Nadia, I have been speaking to you in simplicity for your writings are the writings that will be interpreted into lighter form for the average person to read. They will be studied by scholars and your hearts trials will be the trials of all in some form or fashion. The writings articulate the beauty of the soul and the sorrow of hardships and the answers of upliftment.

I can feel how it feels inside of you when you can see what others can not and you start wondering why you are here. You are the messenger and you must know. Nadia, you are not well in this day. We need to keep slowing you down and keeping you close to home.

You are not attached to your work and you are wondering what you are doing there. You do not know anymore. You are not going to be there for long. We say it and we say it and you are growing weary of the saying of it, for it has been in years now. However look at what you had to know, to learn, to grow through.

I understand. The time thing and where my brain is at. I am thinking that it is time for us to be able to start building our company. We can only try. To begin booking times with media and shops, it takes time for those things to happen. I am patient however it is hard and has been for me to keep doing something that I am not connected to. I want to however I don't have the mental time and or energy to do it all.

Yes Nadia, for this is the dilemma of all people. They start to slow down mentally when they are doing something they no longer enjoy doing; when passion is not the motivator of mind and heart. When another controls your existence. You must know this "stuck" feeling, for this "stuck" feeling is the reason many dreams that can easily be realities do not happen. Now you can understand when a person says they are in a "rut," not funny that it rhymes with stuck.

Oh Nadia, we are close. Enjoy these days for these days you are feeling lifted from financial burdens and you have come to terms with who you are and the reality of what you can do about it. Again, you must know this feeling for majorities of peoples are in this position so you too must know of it.

This world of interest rates, fees, and costs that are hidden is again the thievery that is spoken of. The souls of need are encouraged to spend what they do not have. Or they do have it and costs around go up and wages do not. For the system is to stagnate, not to grow. How can someone grow when they put themselves behind? Glory be to God Almighty.

I feel like I have written so much in the past few days and yet so little. I wrote about so many everyday things. It is a lot to read and remember yet I know of it inside. Please give me more time to absorb.

Let's find a way to make this work so that we can actually share this and be able to take care of our family at the same time. That is all I want to ask for in this day. I really don't know what else to do with myself right now. I don't feel so great and I don't feel like sleeping or talking.

Nadia, you are loved in this day. Rest and you will see.

Christ

I love you too.

Nadia

JUNE 22, 2004

Sweet Christ,

What do you do in what we call a day here?

Nadia, Sweetest of Nadia, your life is what I am doing all day. I am with peoples and I am with you. I am the stabalizment of souls on Earth. I hear all humans, mostly in collective thought and I steer purest of souls to carry the others in this time. Let us prepare and we will all walk forward in movement together. Glory be to God Almighty! You are loved.

I love you too.

Nadia

CHAPTER 11

WE ARE HEAR FOR YOU

JULY 7, 2004

Sweet Nadia,

Yes, I am here again and again and again it seems. This is funny; I am like a fountain of words. I am or I was not so sure if I was ready to hear all of these things, or say them, or why they are even a big deal. Today, I am learning the bigger lessons. I am seeing the roles we play to learn the lessons we learn. I am seeing and feeling what pain does to behavior. And how dissolving it frees us and that is just a little pain. How about accumulated pain? Tell me about accumulated pain.

Nadia, Accumulated pain is the weight that is carried in the stresses of mind and physical body. It is in the walk of physicalness and it is in the speech and the behavior of mind. For pain first wants to protect itself. And then it wants to not feel it. And then it tries to ignore feeling it. And then it comes out in behaviors that take away.

It is all pain based. It is all the lack of love in an act, in the heart of all souls on Earth. You see, Nadia, Sweet Nadia, love is the key to all things. WE say it and we say it and yet we ask you what does it mean?

I believe it means to behave towards yourself and to others with purity.

Yes, it is purity. And what is purity? How do you know your actions, thoughts and belief serve you in purity?

I believe it is when you do something and there is nothing you can want from it?

Yes, it is no self motivation. For you know and you understand that when self motivation exists, all parties know of it. Nadia, how do you know of truths?

I feel them.

Yes, You do, however how do you know of Truth.

I don't know I feel it.

Nadia, truth rests the soul. Non Truths bring about actions that are manipulated by a soul to conform to a soul's distortion. Lack of caring compounds the results to appear as though a soul is cared for and then when the outcome is not of love it is thrown back on the soul and takes away from them severely.

And this begins in young ages, as you thought it to be of adult peoples. Yet it is of adult peoples who were of young ages and carried the behaviors over. For lack of love is the stem. Taught that love is only when you are good, all the "bad" is hidden. Church is proving that you are good. That you go. Does Church make better souls? Does believing that the very God that loves you will hurt you?

NO ONE WANTS THAT TO BE OF TRUTH. However taught in young it hurts the heart and carries the heart to the misleadings of expectations in life for no one wants to be "bad." For then they feel they will not be loved. They will not get help for they will not want to believe they need it for the admission of help is saying you are bad.

This is changing in this day and age, however not entirely. Glory be to God Almighty. For the clearest of souls see life the clearest and the clarity of life gives the soul a chance to enjoy its growth. Nadia, you are writing much as you say however much needs to be said to you.

Your heart is learning yet again that life is not of predicament. It is of love. It is not of events it is of love. It is not of being anything it is of love. With love all things will be. The predicaments, events, all things will happen with love in the newness of heartness involved. Your love of life is just that.

You can rest in your day tomorrow, as you have realized in this moment. I am talking to you in real time. How does that feel?

I love it. I love that you are with me like this. I thank you for loving me. I do need a word. As you say that God is not a religion. And religions are outliving their usefulness to the souls they inhabit in entirety. What am I? What is all of this writing called?

Nadia, you were told before. It is Origin. Religion is of reaction. Origin is of life's action. Truth gives the action basis. Knowing oneself is of purity to self and others. You are Origin. There is not a word that you have written that is not of truth.

Some things harder for you to understand than others, some things you are not thinking you are ready to hear. Some things you are not wanting to hear and some things you are not wanting to admit.

Do you see? You feel those things at times, for you understand the truth of the writings in themselves and when you do not feel ready to take on some thoughts your heart does not want to read of the truth right away. The power of truth can not be of anything but strength, even when it hurts in initial of hearing and knowing. It sets souls free to plan action. Otherwise worries set in when truth is not of appearance to all involved.

It is all of simpleness and the writings, your writings when written, when read, are of safety for their truth. Did you notice those who do not understand or agree are of worry, fear and doubt about God Almighty and his love?

Nadia, go and rest. You are loved. Rest. We say it and your body needs it and then we keep you here. For you will not feel the weight of it in greatly. Glory be to God Almighty. You are loved! Christ and all the Angels of God Almighty!

JULY 20, 2004

Sweet Nadia,

You are hearing a great deal in your morning and around you is quiet as it can be. Glory be to God Almighty, for rest in your heart is here! I love feeling the inner workings of the human body. The soul is confined however it is of safety within on Earth.

To have flight on Earth would give the soul a way to exit. For exiting is not of ease. That is why! There would not be a soul left on Earth if it had a choice once it has come to experience.

The memories of home are deep and the forgotteness of home cause a conflict of knowing things and then not knowing of them at the same of time; Of searching for longings and not finding them, for they can not exist on Earth at the same time of experiencing. Glory be to God Almighty.

Simply with what you have come to know of and do and feel and at times you think to yourself, you want to go back. It is the pureness that draws the souls of purpose back home. So simple.

Yet the souls on Earth, they find ways to think of things to cope with what they know. If they understood that certain situations cause certain behaviors and certain behaviors cause certain situations, it would all make greater sense.

What is seen in self motivation is the outcomes of what someone may want from another, or situation and the causing of certain behaviors or situations is not of seen. It is not considered and many conflicts begin there.

Many conflicts begin with self motivation, less outcomes that affect others and the caring and love exempt from the outcome. Nadia, your heart, you see this in all of time. You feel this in much of souls searching for who they are.

They think of themselves in the story and not of others. And then when the others are affected and the affect is not what the soul was looking for as an outcome, then the story has to change and accommodation happens. When the soul does not want to accommodate that what the soul was looking for, conflict arises. So simple.

## July 24, 2004

Hey there, sweet God, I am here. I can hear you and I am not so sleepy. I don't really want to say anything right now. What are you saying to me? I am thinking too fast for everything right now.

Nadia, you are of love. That is all we want to say to you. You are of love. You wonder why you are you sometimes. You do not want to be you sometimes.

I know. That is true of everyone I am sure, at some point. I am simply craving some time to myself. I want to hear my own heart. I am so busy hearing everything else and sometimes I just miss me. I miss listening to me. Down here people they have a lot going on. They love to hear and do things and be in life down here.

That is all great. I love those things too, living among everyone. I don't really know what it means to be an Angel. It doesn't really matter; I know it is just that we help people. Sometimes we need help too.

Yes Nadia, and we are hear for you. That is why we called you to write. We want you to know you are loved. You feel really alone inside of your heart right now. I can feel it. Your heart is so easy to love others. You do not feel like there is anything in your world that gives you comfort. And you do not know of why. You are tired. You will get over it.

Your heart is of the finest of golden granules of life. In your heart it carries the love and the aches of the world. You are simply you. You do not know how you are all of these things. Some love you, some do not. Some want you, some do not.

You feel like you love everyone and you can not tell the difference at times from those that love and those that do not. You want to feel at home somewhere. You will. We will take you home in this night of night on Earth. You are love. You will find your comfort and the love you carry in your heart expands many.

Trust your heart and know of it. You know who you are and at times you do not want to be who you are. You have to know and experience much of the common human to know what you know and to be able to help those who in life will need you now, in the past of Earth and in the coming of Days.

Dear Christ, I don't know how I am any more. I am tired inside. I do not get to do anything in times of quiet, so I can not even think of what I would or could do.

Yes Nadia, you do not know. Your humbleness heals others as it is healing you in instants in life on Earth. Your heart flourishes those around you and you know not what and who you are and why you are and how you are. Sometimes I want to come out and talk to you face to face.

Why don't you? I miss you. I see you only sometimes and I hear you all the time. How do I do all that I do in one day and not tire, and those around me may do one thing or two things and they exhaust themselves? How do I hear you all day and I hear everyone else all day as well?

How do I comfort others when at times I can not comfort myself? How do I love those who walk around me in life and in love and I know their intentions are off? How do I listen and am patient with others and not with myself? How does my heart take what is in it and I can smile and be loving so easily and so naturally?

Nadia, you feel not the weight of the world. You are in it to be, for the messages are coming through you.

Why do I have to call myself a prophet?

Because Nadia, that is the word that is understood.

Yes I know however many call themselves a prophet and they even get to make a lot of money doing it.

Yes Nadia, however you are different. You are not reciting words already written, you are writing words to be of recitation. Glory be to God Almighty.

Will anyone ever really read all these words?

Yes, Nadia, they will be read and studied for years and years. You will get to witness from home.

Are you really going to pop out of me?

I said that I will. That I am. That I am here. Yes.

How?

I will come out of your left side and Stirling to be on your right.

When?

When there is balance.

How come your "when's" are so long?

Nadia, think of how much more prepared you are of today's day than you were of a month ago, or two months past; You are growing in solidity of yourself and your heart and your knowing and what you are willing to say.

Yes, I am. Can I accommodate such change? I feel like I am kind of going nuts right now. My heart is very internally busy. My life, it is busy now. There are more of us than just the three of us.

Yes, Nadia. There are. It is irrelevant. Just them knowing of you will carry them.

That is good to know. Will I ever catch up on my bills?

Yes.

How?

Your writing will support you. The writing will open the doors of other avenues and it is of no mindness to understand that money will follow so that you can continue your work. You are in suffering right now.

You now know how it is, how it feels to be of such stance. You are thinking of this like when you would date certain men and wonder and think, "Wow, this is what this is like."

This is the same teacher. Glory be to God Almighty. Nadia, go and rest now, you are tired. You are sleepy and you are of restless for these minutes, for in a perfect plan that is of another reason to bring to us. We will take you home.

Remember you are loved. You are loved. Glory be to God Almighty! Christ, the team, all the beautiful Angels, you are loved.

AUGUST 23, 2004

Dearest Lord God,

Sweet Nadia, for our addressing is in unison.

Sometimes I feel like you are right here in the air waiting or not even waiting because there is really no time, but hanging in the air with so much love and so much compassion. Why do I get so overwhelmed sometimes? I know we have a lot of obligations, we always do. I am use to it, but it feels like so many expenses are coming up.

It is like I let go this weekend and I just wanted to go out and eat and let go of remembering that there is so much coming up and coming due.

School will be a lot and we have some payments to things we can do on Wednesday. It is funny, today; I just did not want to hear complaining about anything. It is so passive to complain. We are here in this family as a team.

That is what I am thinking. We are not here for the judgment of the kids. It is weird when you know that what you say or do is not taken as you say it or do it and then the things that you provide are not appreciated. It is not even that it needs appreciation really, it is the lack of respect and the tearing down of what exists around.

It just crushed my spirit today. Does complaining do any one any good. I think even the complainer is tired of themselves.

Yes Nadia, complainers are tired of themselves. So they complain to bring about their covering of disappointment of self. They want company, and sometimes it is simply attention, for there is nothing else to bring about attention or conversation. Your heart melts to hear such let downs of life when all that is around is abounding and so much that you carry you do not share.

Is it so difficult to say as you feel?

Yes it is! People are vulnerable to say as they feel. So they create situations. They bring about what you would call dramas to their world and then they feel productive. However productive of spewing is better than no production at all; those who do, talk little and those who don't have much to say. Those who think of glory share all. And those who bring about dimmers of light share little truth, for they know not of it themselves.

Is this making sense to you? I feel your confusion. Nadia, you already know of this, as I have been saying to you in all along.

You do not know how to be in negative. And in this day, you face it as you feel like in questions you are and you were being set up for conversations of takings away. And you fought it and that is the protectiveness you feel.

Nadia, you wanted to talk about what is happening to you. You do not even know what to ask of yourself yet. You have been in a holding place now for a while. You know of this however it doesn't make it easy for you. You are trying to find points of comfort and you have at great moments. That is all you will have for a short time is moments. You want to sit and write and talk to us.

We are talking to you all day and your world is busy around you. Let your heart take precedence of all else and you will be of fine. Nadia, you feel so wronged too at your work in your heart. Your heart hurts to walk into your office, to see the chaos, to see the panic of one person trying to please another. It is disheartening to you and yet you are there and you are wondering why?

For you now know what most of the country in which you live lives. And how it takes away from their souls and fills it in with the things that continuously take away and flourish feverish frets. Measurements, competitiveness. Competition is of fun to grow and to stir the mind into growth.

Competitiveness is entirely different. It is of willingness to do things that are not of giving however of taking away, for it can bring a soul to do things out of ego driven mania. Do not walk amongst those who are entirely self motivated and want to win. Whatever it is, a man, a woman, a car, in business, in cheating. Those are the greatest losses of truth. Yes, you are thinking a car?

Yes how could a car?

The ego is in the metal around it. For those who drive better than others tell you so in their vehicles. It is a measurement on Earth. And it is interesting to me how peoples have cars define them before they actually can define themselves. And also believe that the car defined them. Nadia, that is interesting to me, for we did not have cars at those times of my time on Earth.

We had monies however if you had more or less it really did not get you more things. It simply made you more powerful. For those with monies actually were perceived as smarter.

So as you were speaking to the children in this evening that you could go to a lesser ranked school and do well. And you could go to a higher ranked school and not do well, because it rests in the soul who wants to work for itself. In my days on Earth the souls that worked for themselves were of the purest souls.

The souls that made funds off the backs of others were seen as smarter however they were not of trustworthy. The innerness of humans was known for the lie that their positioning was made of and the feelings and motivations that had to come about to use souls to benefit self's.

It is not that funds are not of goodness. Funds give flexibility to go about doing and moving within the ways of the worlds function. Making funds of greater importance than souls is the loss of self and the loss of purity in intents, AS is Media. As in any part of life that becomes of greater than the souls that live. How could it be that the souls are secondary?

The reflection of such action is the farness away of selves that you witness today; As WE are here to give back the remembrance of love of self; the reflection of self and not of things. Things are simply things. They mean nothing without the energy of souls. Hurting the energy of souls hurts all else sweet Nadia. And that is where your pains stemmed from in your conversations.

You wanted to not come home but you had to. It is your home. And you are growing souls even when you think you are not. Sometimes you feel defeated by negativeness and you want to sit still and I send you back for more. For that is what a teacher does. The teacher is present within the lesson.

The days of celebration of love and of love on Earth and Home merging in greatness, for an accumulation of moments is coming to the sweet souls on Earth who are searching for themselves as though they exist not within their own forms. You just saw my image on television. Nadia, Media is of most awful. I am in astonishment as to the takings away.

It is almost of constantness. The soul in watchment almost does not have a chance, a moment, to think on its own. And what that is fed into is of taking away; Inferiority of breeding, of thoughts, and taking the worst thinkings and glorifying their existence.

The efforts of the souls have to grow strength to keep itself afloat in times of internal turbulence, for the moments of media pacify and hold in place at best. Stories are different when told with love. Glory be to God Almighty. Rest. Now. Again. I kept you here yet there is much love to share with your souls. Glory be to God Almighty. Rest!

I love you God, Christ, all the Angels around. I needed you and thank you in this day!

# CHAPTER 12

# YOU ARE IN MISSION

## SEPTEMBER 29, 2004

Sweet God,

I just wanted to say thank you for reminding me of what people are like. I know I truly forget at times what it is like for people who live inside of themselves and forget what it is that they are doing or thinking or how it looks or affects others.

So, I had to have many examples of it. And maybe it will never be enough in examples and I will have to or get to see this until I go back home. I just need guidance. That is all I want. I am tired really of working a job. I am not working and not doing what is in my heart.

Things really are not what they seem. I feel quiet in thinking about how people do the things they do. I know logically how, but how really? Isn't there a place when someone knows the answers? That they follow it or try it? Is self stupidity so easily disguised as smartness and beauty?

Is taking away so much easier than giving? Is being lazy really better than trying? Is expecting from others what you can not do yourself really a cool thing to do? Is dumping your load on another person really that OK to the soul that does it? Does it help to let others dump around and share the wealth of inept feelings in heart? Is it better to push people to be their higher self by not giving answers so easily and let the discovery of answers be the way?

What does love look like when it comes back? Is it recognized? What is it like when one person comes to you and behaves a way in which they do not behave when you are not around? And yet you are the person who is the result of their actions? You are the one to have to live with the assumptions that you know or don't know or however it is played out?

Why is it that people want what isn't there and do not want what is? Is it that hard to work? Is it that hard to care? Does it take that much out of a person to take care of themselves? To care about others? Is it easier to lie than to tell the truth? Is it easier to blame than to be accountable? Is it easier to complain than to do things yourself?

Do people get when others care about them? What do they feel in response to that? You say we are not meant to be here alone and yet people they are alone. We call that lonely down here. I think people are lonely inside and they want someone else to fix them for lack of trying themselves or even knowing what to try.

I am filled with questions tonight and I know the answers in feeling not in words. I want to sit still and yet tomorrow morning I am going to sit with a soul that it is hard for me to be around. Yet for now that is the way that it is.

I am not out to change anyone or to take away from who they are. I just love to be free. I love when freedom is around me.

No hiddens. No assumptions. No playing with everything that is said or done. All these important people, to themselves; WE are all important. I don't strive for perfection but when it comes to love I can't stop at less than it in purity.

I don't know how to do that. I need your love and carry me in my journey's. Today, I felt so much happening with you and yet I couldn't stay there. If the world around me can not find happiness, please let their eyes see glimmers of it. It is a start. I think we are started in ways. I just get surprised by the reality of souls and their dispositions. I guess that is why I am here.

I am here, and there is Stirling and you. Thank you for all that I do have. Thank you for giving us a way to pay most of our bills. I know when it is time for us to do anything all things will come together around it. I know you want to say words to me. I will have to settle with what I hear in my head for now.

I want to lay and if I can, to see you. I love you dear God and sweet Christ, all the Angels. I am blessed in so many ways. Knowing you is so great down here.

If every person is an example of a million, I'd better watch out, I'd better not pout, cause, peoples down here love their problems. They do so many things to others because of their problems. Isn't that the funniest thing? They have a problem. And others get the results of their problems. How funny is that?

So all I have in this night is quiet inside. And love just hanging around me, like the invisible love that no one can see. That veil thing you came up with is really iron clad at times. I get why. But the whys at times are simply tiring! Good night.

I love you all,

Nadia

OCTOBER 2, 2004

Dearest Lord God,

Sweet Nadia,

Sometimes I wonder how I talk to you like this. How are you there and able to give wonder to life here? I am filled with questions and it is funny. In most of it I know the answers like I did the other night. I haven't felt like writing much, just living here and feeling what people do and want from this life.

What means something to them and why it means something? When if they got what they want, they wouldn't know what to do with it, so they do this thing of half wants. Of only tasting and not eating; So they never really get full. They just dodge some things in a day and do other things. And the things that bother them get shared with those around them. The things that bother them, that are shared with those around them, there is a sense of entitlement to and for whatever it is they think they want.

There seems to be a lot of internal greed and I understand it. I see it and still it startles my heart. People use each other and they do not care if it hurts them, the other person, or even a group of people. As long as they got what they wanted, since what they wanted is supposed to fix everything.

So when they don't know what they want and they still want it, whatever it is, the intentions are not pure and the road of worries begins. The road of fear ripens. The world of doubt is present, sweet Nadia. That is what happens. That is what becomes.

You have gotten to see in so many forms, deception. You are wondering if it is the only thing that exists. It does not however you had to be surrounded to understand it. You got it from all angles. You got it from many examples. You are witness. You can not witness and be without of it.

You have to know it, feel it. To understand the ways in which it looks like, feels like, lives like, amongst the living. You were of asking to Stirling, those who need this do not read it and if they read it they do not get it. They get it; they simply do not want truth yet in their lives.

It is easy to understand. How could love not be understood? If a soul wants to argue a point, so be it. Let it grow in thought and in life, for the love of debate, of challenge brings forth the questions of growth.

Those who read and say it is too deep, are themselves deep and do not want to be. Those who say it is hard to read are the hard to be understood. Those who say they get it; they have self accounting in heart.

Those who want to criticize it, truly and simply want to criticize you. Those who say "Who does she think she is, an Angel, a prophet?" Want to be one themselves. As though it is a prize of some kind to be won like a trophy, for those are the status of heart, even when it is not apparent. Those who want to say you are crazy are in denial of heart. Those who will not speak to you can not comfort themselves.

Those who can not look at you are blinded by light. Those who can not talk to you do not want truth. So simple. You are a complete reflection of God. You are of all peoples and all peoples of you.

The inadequacies of the meek shadow life in full openness; they are the shadows on Earth as they walk and immerse in words of takings away. Earth's energy is the lowest of energies. That is why it can be swayed in easement by the meek. Glory be to God Almighty.

The higher energies can pain many souls, for the lower energies are the turmoil you see. That comes in what can appear to be success in doings, like works, clothing's, rings and cars, Status and needing of it. For nothing is as it seems.

The questions of self motivation are many. The questions of truth remain in few.

Truth can only be of simpleness and love; Caring and hope, Glory and lightness of mind and body. Status is stress in every angle. It is an intangible fight for self to be important. It changes the happinesses of action into need of happiness. Glory be to God Almighty.

When peoples are spoken to in truth they addict to you. Do you understand what that means? They addict to you. They want to hear more, for the barings of learning Truth in form is the greatest of all known knowing on Earth. Know that Truth breaks the barriers of the planes, of the mind, of the soul's stranglements of existence on Earth.

In the times of experiencing, truth presents itself and it carries souls for years of Earth time or even until they come back home. Without it there is frustration and hurt, Pain and sorrow. The longing of truth/home/purity can be the only goal of every single soul on Earth. And the meek are the furthest away. They are the truest danger to existence. The meek are the trailers of knowing not what they know in fears they will not be what they think they are.

Glory be to God Almighty!

Christ.

OCTOBER 20, 2004

Dearest Lord God,

I could hear you calling my name but I have to start with thanking you for hearing me. Thanking you for these moments in my life that have a sense of peace in them in all parts of it. This summer and all the things at once, I am glad that everything is calm again. I needed it more than I need to live in life. I can take negative and take it, but once I am through with it, it is gone and done. I never look back.

Learning is like that, Nadia. Once something is learned you can not relearn it. Move on to learn something else. So simple. In your world your learning is accelerated. What you learn in months, lifetimes are lived by. You hear much; as you were talking of a psychic.

You felt a kinship upon learning of her knowings. She is not of tired or cynical. She wants to come home. She believes in herself in yet another way of life on Earth. She can see the souls that are displaced. They know not to believe in love in purity and continually, so they are in between home and Earth.

Angels surround them and whisper love to them in constant and when they can feel that love and acknowledge that there is supreme love they are released to home. There are no bad spirits. There are only those in difference. They can not hurt anyone. They are waiting on their own learning to come home.

They can not see home and can not be seen on Earth. It is difficult for that soul until the learning comes into place. A soul comes back to home based on their beliefs and when there are no beliefs what could they come home to? Glory be to God Almighty!

Nadia, you pause in bewilderment. You are thinking how could someone see bad or what is called evil. You are saying there are people who look good and do bad things. What ever good or bad things are, or what ever evil or bad is.

Love is shaped and formed into many things and love propels. And lack of love is shaped and formed in to many things. When you see lack of love it comes in manipulation, control and pain; Pain being the invisible factor.

You have seen many with manipulation and control. And yet the pain is hidden and disguised. The words from the mouths of these souls are meant to dishevel. So simple. And it does that very thing. Over and over again, for those are the souls most blind. They can not see with open eyes, for their eyes can not see with love.

Love propels. That is never to be forgotten, for that is the greatest truth of all knowing. Love propels. Love grows. Love teaches. Love accelerates. So simple. Lack of love takes away from all. And the soul wonders to itself how? For they believe they controlled all the factors around however like they do not take themselves into consideration, they do not take souls into consideration as well.

That is why they can not see or hear. They believe the souls around them should do what they want, for they would make decisions based on those factors themselves. They do not take into account the souls that think from light and know of themselves. For that is foreign and envied by the manipulator. So the manipulator tactics become more fierce and with greater tryings. So simple. You have seen this over and over again. It is rampant, for the insecurities are balanced greater than the securities at this time. There is havoc within collective consciousness.

You are finding that people are honest or they are not. The in-betweens are less in numbers. There are the blatant examples and the not so easy to detect examples. So simple.

You can now recognize both. You know in seconds now. When you were speaking of the psychic you thought to yourself, "I do not want to be like that, I am not that." You are not. You did not want to call yourself anything, for how you felt to have her call herself a prophet is hard for you to understand. For we think of prophets as one person at a time.

A prophet is a messenger. No one can see the future. However when you can not see time and you can see truth, truth drives all forces, even when not apparent. That is why you could see where things are going and that is not knowing the future; it is knowing of time and truth. So simple. However you are not of duplication.

Keep yourself busy with all that you are doing and then it will all change once again. So simple. Make your appointments. Do your proposals. Work on your business plan. Schedule all things to do and do them. You love your work. You will be of fine as I spoke to you in your days of last. Never to fear, doubt or worry our love. For your feelings internal say this is hard to do at times.

Yes it is, for the human part of experiencing is of great challenges. For peoples are idle in heart and time becomes a burden. When the souls of Earth can touch another they begin to feel. Your job is to teach that the touching comes from touching themselves and the touching of another takes on form. Glory be to God Almighty for that is the essence. And the essence is looked for in many avenues.

It is looked at in having anyone to be a companion rather than one close to soul. It is in the form of deviation and distance with drugs and alcohol. In distraction with smoking of physical self; In distraction of causing pains to others in words and physical hurting.

Some believe essence will find them in their moments of taking away. Yet the taking away takes them further away from their essence. You did not feel you understood this completely.

Nadia, a soul knows when it is taking away from itself. You know of this already. So a soul at times takes away from itself to excuse itself from life as it is on Earth. So souls internally, without conscious thought, want to take away from themselves, for the internal longing of home is not within thinking distance.

Yet the yearning is in greatness. In that greatness of yearning the soul tries for moments of openness, only to find that those moments took them away further. It is of greater to wait for what is real in your heart than to stop at stopping points along the way and take you away.

The excuses of life will get in the way and then they become the way and then there is no other way. And the soul hits a stopping point or as it would be said in your world, a dead end.

So simple. Those that take away know. Some try to take others with them. The falls are of learning. When the learning does not take place, the falls trip a soul again and again, until learning can happen. Glory be to God Almighty. For some it is of a lifetime and for others it is of one simple lesson at that moment.

That is why some souls know that they are where they do not belong and some have the will to move on. Those with intents of purity towards self and those without will repeat. Glory be to God Almighty. You are loved. You have some things to complete in this day. Continue to do so. You are in mission. As I enjoy your internality. You are love.

Christ

# CHAPTER 13

DEAREST LORD GOD

Dearest Lord God,

Sweet Nadia, your heart, I feel it. Thank you for coming to me. I want to know how you feel my heart.

I do.

I am here for real. Nadia, sometimes I am knowing as you are not in knowing of me entirely.

I am here again, two days later. I feel like I hold time in place when I don't write. I could hear you and I could feel you and that was all I could do in the last day. I am doing this company, and I am taking chances that I would have never done normally. I know it is the thing to do. I know that it is time.

I can't see the results of it; I just know it is the right time to do these things. I feel like I am keeping busy as you say it, like all that is happening is bigger than me, than Stirling. I feel like the book thing is and has become my world and I am doing it with a cushion these days to set it up. I don't feel a need to know, and then what? I am content with what I feel.

You realize that God Almighty is words of truth and of love and of what would appear to be greatness on Earth. Yet truth is simple and carries. Love in purity carries. What may be thought of as greatness on Earth is simple and true always, in the universe, in the planes, at home, on Earth. It is true anywhere. It is of glee anywhere.

Earth is in time, in that it is of great harshness in measurement and in pressures. It has grown to greater pressures in each day of time in its existence. The complications of mind, the internal greed, the measurements of fulfillment of souls has taken the souls of Earth to nothing. It has given to them lackness of paths of growth. It has turned monies into life. With it you are of OK and without it you are nothing.

Yet those with it or without it are finding it hard to survive. Both have the complications of life bestowed upon them. When pure intent in decisions are not present and peoples are following the intents of self motivation, what is to happen?

You needed rest in your last day. Thank you for coming again. Do not leave this writing without completion.

I won't. I can't seem to come back and finish and I know there is much to be said. I sometimes think, how could I write anymore? How could I be here quietly in my home, know all of this, sit and write all the time?

And then I think of the first writings and you writing to me and me not knowing it was you yet. All that you would say to me. And all that was said, is said, is here today. And more than what you had told me. Since most of what you have told me about the billions of people knowing of you, of me, the writings being studied way after I have left here, I am living the steps towards all of that today.

It is hard at times to be here and know what I know. Do what I do, so wanting and loving of it. And yet I have to do this business stuff, which I love, I just never really did it for something I love the way that I love this.

It is different. I do it without efforts on my part. It needs its time and that feels effortless too. Speaking to people makes me remember why we are all doing this. I know all of this came through us to do in our time. However knowing and then doing without the knowledge of knowing that that is what you are supposed to be doing. And figuring it out and discovering is the trick in a way and the glory in another.

Nadia, Your innocence kept you from being of cynic of yourself in knowing. You were not sure about other things in life however you knew all things between you and God. It never wavered. Your love of life never waned. There were times you have had it on Earth and you would ask to come back home however you were not in suicidal.

You knew where you would go and you felt that humans were something you did not want to be a part of anymore. Yet you stayed and you endured. WE weakened you in illness and kept you away from humans until you could see them again. That was your repair.

For then you began working and you began meeting greater amounts of souls hence those are now the readers of the Book. They are the beginners of Origin. They are the souls that you took refuge on and learned from and honed your love of God through. You would fall in restment at those times and ask God to simply do right by him.

Your intentions were pure and clear. You would tell God if there was something that you wanted, something that was not of good for you, to not let you have it. You did not want it if it was not in your purest of intents to have of it, of such person(s). All things happen for the greater good and you would ask that they would. That was a great acceleration.

For God Almighty has given the privilege of walking away and leaving the works of a soul to search in earnestment, not in fightment with another soul. Glory be to God Almighty. There is no changing a soul. There is teachment however in teachment the heart of pure intentions is the learning soul. The heart of self motivation is blind yet to understanding.

If left alone they will learn more than to give into the dramatization of their actions, for then they have achieved their goal(s). You understand the soul knows not what it is not ready to know of. Glory be to God Almighty. Glory be to God Almighty. Glory be to God Almighty. Nadia, you have to stop now. Do not end this writing. Come back to it. It must continue in this form. Glory be to God Almighty. Come back in this day of time.

Christ.

I am back yet once again.

Yes Nadia, thank you.

I wanted to say that you have been talking about manipulation, about control, about situations around that a lot lately.

Yes Nadia, there is endless information of life. Humans are a way for the soul to hone. Coming to Earth is to work with all obstacles; Obstacles to overcome and overload, Situations to pull the purpose of life in surface; Finding the positive when it is not apparent.

Learning to calm in situations of ill will and trust in yourself enough to know that when there is love there is the answer to all things possible.

When there is not, there is a way for the playment of souls into the worlds of experience that they produce. Once pure intent is in living, the playment is no longer playment in the paths of experiences of self motivated behavior. The pure intent of a soul carries them into the teachings and the learning of challenge, growth and understand greaterment of happenings, and then the teachings of souls around. It is one life for another, with another, because of another.

It is learning from and with each other; to care and to interest and to grow and to learn. There is no other way to do it. And now you have been learning of the undertones of behaviors that take away. Not only from others however from self.

You already know that to take away from others, one is taking away from their self in firstment. It is all so simple. It is said and it is said and it is said. How hard it is to believe. How difficult it is for the soul of entrapment of self to see or to know. There is true belief that no one can see the actions of their intents. Glory be to God Almighty.

You have learned to stay away and yet you get more from new peoples and what they do and what they want to do. And with what one soul wants from another whether it is approval or disapproval, wanting recognition or attention, wanting time or pushing the personal time away.

Sometimes one thing is used to get another thing from a soul; sometimes to use a soul to hurt another soul, sometimes to want to know the life of another for personal information and satisfaction or dissatisfaction of self and then of others.

The untruths are now in dissolvement. The last ones on holdings on are holding tighter for they are feeling the challenge of loss of what they have put together to know and then to live by and using that to take away from other souls. It can not be. Knowledge calms and empowers a soul into patience and love.

No one can take anything away from you; you are not willing to give. In just the last 7 years of your life you met more people than most will meet and know in a lifetime of meetings and knowings. Glory be to God Almighty. You feel it at times and you take it away from yourself at times as well.

Sometimes you want to take it away and it still comes out of you like the water that is drank to clear the body of all that does not belong in it. Water protects the body and supplies it with fluidity that is needed to grow it in cell regenerations and experiences can continue to be had, data's can be felt in collective consciousness. For nothing is wasted in everment. Nothing is per chance.

The more people know you, the more they want to know you, of you. You will tell them, "I am bankrupt; I left my job because I couldn't do it anymore and it was all in one day." You will say that you lived in many experiences and you will look as though you could not have and yet you did. You got to experience as much as you could and not be destroyed.

You care not what others think for you can not control. You only know that you love. From near or far depending on what is before your soul. You know who you are, now let go of the leash you have been holding around yourself. It was getting looser as these days have carried you to this point and now you are.

Tonight in this evening told you this. You know now. Speak and you will be heard. You have been heard. You are "nothing" as you say. And you are everything as you could not say. Let it all be. Be. You are simply in task.

Your heart is still honing; in each day a new honement. Let your life accept all that is around and abound. Let the world around you grow within you and you can keep balance in what you know. You are using all your knowledge in all parts of life, for there are no more separations.

For now this is your time, your energy, your life, you are one! Glory be to God Almighty. You have concluded in this writing. You are loved. Stirling is love. Christ. All the Angels of God.

### OCTOBER 30, 2004

Nadia, Sweet Nadia. Nadia our love, the hearts of the world are in our hands. We are of love back to them, for that is the beginning and endless waves of energy.

Nadia, you were asking in your last day, why is it that peoples can get addicted to things that hurt them, like drugs, habits, hurtful ways to interact with others to themselves, and yet no one gets hooked on the beauties of life? The answer is the lack of path shown. So simple.

It is the lack of path shown. It is the sadness internal of disappointments at the, from the, soul that took away in believing of anything deservement of self. That is why they want to take their lives away and their journeys are to path their lives through pure intent.

And the souls are saying what is pure intent? That is why you are here in this way now. Why you came, for the beginnings of great lacks of pure intents happened long ago and today you are seeing the conclusions.

You witness the different kinds of Angels within the purity of God in form and how the energy of Angels comes in pureness to souls and carries them into home on Earth. So simple a task. Yet the minds of humans face duality in everyday. You will ease that as you have been eased in life. Glory be to God Almighty! Christ, Angel of God.

NOVEMBER 9/10, 2004

Dearest Lord God,

Sweet Nadia, you smile to write Dearest Lord God.

Yes I do. Sweet Christ, I saw your love today. I am really beginning to see all of this in my life and it happening in others lives because of just needing to be heard. Not a big deal, heard. It is refreshing and loving to hear it. I read some of the older writings today and I realized that the writings are what we are in and living within this day.

The book was not published yet. And now I am free and content in my heart to sit still. I did not felt this comfort inside like this since I had Meningitis back in '99. It was the first of the biggest changes in my heart towards life and the peace that could be had in it.

Yes Nadia, that was the beginning of your truest hearings for your heart spoke and you had the quiet to listen. And you understood without knowing of us, which tells souls you have to start in believing in yourself. You would write for hours and love the joy of speaking to God. So simple. And you were heard.

Your hope carries in your writings the souls of all that have hope and love and searching and learning from heart of who they are. And why they are and what they can do here on Earth.

You asked of many questions. You wanted to know how and why peoples do things. You were not asking for judgment, you were seeking and learning. For you cared not of judging. You were thinking what would it be like if Me, Christ, the Angels spoke to these peoples? Nadia, they were already in the presence of Christ and an Angel.

You no longer have to be in forcement of working in the snapshot of the workplace(s) in life on Earth. Your truest friendships come and stay near and all others have no chance to glimpse you anymore. They will have to learn from distance until the hearts of ill intent can love themselves, for that is key.

Your life on Earth is in conclusion as you have known of it. Stirling as he has known of it. You will know and adjust and you will both have the standing to be withstood until you are in completion of mission.

The writing is endless as love is endless. The words are timeless for love knows no time, so simple in love, so complicated on Earth. Beliefs in humans are in fear of change, for identities are difficult to tamper with.

Those not searching will simply be amazed by my showing, and they will not read until the words have been simplified. They will rely on news. That is why the writing is in place before my showing. In peace you have had the time in solace to write for it has taken years to do so.

How could it happen once I appear? This shows the souls of Earth that something is happening in their betterment at all times: That you have been in preparing of souls on Earth as you have been prepared by home to serve them.

You are serving them the gift of love, of emotion in freedom and of self in your life. You will bridge the souls of souls back to them. So simple. I was writing to you in beginnings about the other side of love. Of love without dilution, without conditions, without have to's, without obligation, without judgment, as you have lived in life.

You are now living in life of such love with Stirling. You are both on the other side of love. You know not to hurt the other. It can not be. It is not of possible. All those who come to you know of this. The self motivated want to take it away.

Those who are of purity want to learn from you both, so subtle the beauty of love lives, in its simpleness, in its glory. For did the man at the beach house tell of you both. He saw you walking together and felt your love of life, of self, of each other and he had to meet you both. Did he not say he saw millions of peoples walk on that beach and he never saw anyone like the two of you? He saw. And all are in seeing.

And in this time you are being held back. You are in holding of yourself and your life, for truly it is your last of time here as you are. You have been in preparation. You have been in physical changes of body. You are of complete light. I am here in truth and you are realizing so. You are here in light and you feel the changes in your body. You are of pure light.

You laugh because you know you. And all that you are and all that you have known to experience. And you do truly also know who you are, who you have been all along. All along. Nadia, you have always known however your understatedness, your silence in all you know, your love of privacy, you carry all the messages of God with safety of life on Earth.

Your Prudency to the souls on Earth is of purity and lacks judgments, conditions, and settings of hurtfulness. And when any or all of those judgments, conditions and settings of hurtfulness present themselves to you, you simply do not reciprocate that to another soul. No matter what they have done.

Your language in silence gives to them the thoughts of actions. They may still try to create settings and you allow it to happen. For you know you are in protection of heart of ill will. For you willed it to be. Glory be to God Almighty for truly the love of self and understandment of such breeds within the love of others in truth. That truth is rare on Earth. Glory be to God Almighty.

For it is present again, in words, in showings and in life without conditions, exampled within your home and your marriage to each other. Glory be to God Almighty. Nadia, so simple it all is. So simple is the life in fruition. You had to know the stages of life, the workings of life within experience.

Dearest Nadia, Sweet soul on Earth, Angel of God, Prophet for peoples, you are weightless and of strength. You are loving and fight for purity of heart. You are open to the world and loyal to souls in all ways. You hold them close for it is felt.

When those you do not know come to you, believing they know you they do. They know your soul, for you can hide nothing from yourself, let alone hide from others even a simple emotion.

In your speaking to Stirling in this morning that you are of happiness, yet it is not the kind of happiness that peoples believe happiness to be. You could not describe the permanence of such feelings.

You know that on Earth happiness is a temporary state. Today someone is happy and then they are not and so on. However you are in permanence which comes with understand of self and of others. That is why there is such detail in your writings. In your writings all souls will see themselves.

You articulated the snapshots of all moments in life in some form or another. You touched all in heart by using you own heart. You gave to peoples the feelings they buried and you unburied them. Glory be to God Almighty. You bridge the soul of souls back to them. Glory be to God Almighty.

Christ and all the beautiful Angels.

*Part* TWO

THE BOOK OF CHRIST

*The following book of Christ is a written record
of the words of Christ as told to Nadia.*

⌒

# CHAPTER 1

# THE BUILDING BLOCK STORY

Every soul comes to Earth with the instinctive building block story. The building block story starts before birth. Every soul comes to build, to grow, to experience, to evolve. And then enter Earth through the warmth and love of a body of another human. That is the only way to come, is through time, building of cells and expulsion through another soul's body. And then the baby is held, loved, fed, nurtured.

And then the child begins to play. And they first start by grasping and listening, hearing, and movements of their own bodies. And as soon as all that is put together, they begin building blocks, putting things on top of each other. No matter what it is. They want to see how high it can build. And if it all falls down they start again. They realize over time that they can not put the smallest piece on the bottom.

They find they have to find the largest piece, the one with the greatest standing to secure the rest of their building blocks. It takes them many tries to realize the sense of it. Those who can remember that the largest block needs to remain on the bottom throughout life can take on life in balance of heart.

To take care of what a soul has in current, is to know it will take care of all that is to come. It is simple. It is love. You say to your heart love is love is love. Building teaches the Propellation of love. The largest piece(s) of all things are the truth, love and purity of a soul. That is the first block to build with.

Without Truth, Love, Purity, no building can stand, for the pillars will not be there. And the piercing of those pillars compromises the buildings standing. Too many and then what happens? It is all already known. No one can pierce and not feel the affect of it. No one. The soul of the human is a soul of memory, for there is time on Earth and on Earth time is the best teacher.

# CHAPTER 2

# ALL WE NEED IS LOVE

This is Christ. Glory be to God Almighty, for love is here.

And it must be sought after, felt and learned. The love that is taken away from souls can be given to those very souls if only they could see.

Love is not a thing it is a feeling. Love is not created or because of anything. There is no harm that can come from love.

For what love means to humans is happiness and when that is gone there is no sustainment.

When in truth, love is the growing of happiness in which it grows into in each and every day, and the discovering of the other sides of love, of vastness of mind and thought.

Love is the hope of a heart, the newborn soul to earth.

Love is the food in which we share and nourish our bodies.

Love is the movement in our walks towards each other.

Love is the movements and walks away from each other.

Love is the clothing in which we cover our bodies, for it exemplifies the love of self.

Love is always understood by those who understand that love is for nothing. Just love.

It gives and it does not need receiverment.

It helps and walks away.

It creates and leaves to grow.

It touches and imprints life in growth. So simple is love.

It is the clearest waters that show all contents.

So simple is love.

It hides nothing for the openness is freedom on Earth.

People are having much trouble, for they do not have a defining of love. They do not know what it means so much; they think it is a thing.

They think it is a person, a place, a status of a ring, house, car, kids. However, like sex, it is not an act, it is an emotion. Love is an emotion not an act. Nor is it in another person.

You see love is fluid. Love is like a liquid. It is fluid in its nature.

At home, love is seen, felt and absorbed at the levels in which it is understood and given. It is received without hesitation. Love on Earth is received in hesitation.

Trust is low on Earth, so that means truth is low on Earth, and with that love is a hard to find emotion in its existence to grow from.

So love becomes what a person does or says.

Yet no matter what another soul does or says, when love in purity is not present it is known to both parties. It is not of rejection as one might think, love exists where purity exists.

Most of the time love is one sided and can carry itself on the purity of one for a while however the balance will not exist to carry it further and that is when love can not sustain.

On Earth they say that love dies. It does not die; it is diverted so that the soul can carry on in search of love in purity. That is what is happening.

It is not a failure, as souls have come to call it, it is simply evolution. Souls can only see themself(s) in the silence of who they are.

When souls are not silent they can not hear. And when a soul can not hear it can not see. And when a soul can not see it can not learn.

And when a soul can not learn it can not grow. And when a soul does not grow it angers at stagnation.

And when stagnations are common the soul starts to compete.

And when competitions come into game, there is no game based on truth.

And when truth is not present, ego has a home to live within. When ego has a home the soul is lost to cravings of takings away.

And when takings away are common a soul will take away from itself. Once a soul can take away from itself it can only mimic the behavior to others.

When love is greater than anger there is soulution. When anger is greater than love there is solution.

That is the simplicity of truth, of love, of purity; simply because love is the strength of all energies.

There is not a wider energy, a stronger energy than love. It all comes back to, boils down to, insists on love. Life insists on Love. There is not another avenue.

Life insists on love. Purpose demands accountability. Soulution is not solution.

There is challenge to souls, relish in your challenges, they are your Earth teachers. Your Soul is your Earth responder.

The limits we have are the limits we allow. How silly it is to think we are warring on each other as we speak to love one another! Can it be that we are two sided?

How could you love and kill at the sameness of time? Is killing a family member, a stranger, or a soul who happens to live in the wrong country different? It is all killing of a soul in search of a solution.

If it were a soulution this could not be. A soulution thinks in WE, in US, in OUR Universe.

Glory be to God Almighty, for God is One. And One IS all. There is not a separation of souls, of God.

Humans in justifications of all the ills of lacks of love are searching for avenues that appear as helpers yet are of takings away. Glory be to God Almighty, LET THE TRUTH BEGIN.

And it has. In bits and pieces, from this speaker and that, this author and that, for Jacob is in grand consciousness for those who will know. Glory be to God Almighty!

*(JACOB—He is one of the seven angels whose job it is to prepare the consciousness of this work, this mission.)*

You had to be convinced of who souls are Nadia. You have learned in fullness not only who souls are, how they will fight to disturb the energy of love and how they could say no to a friend in need and how they can say yes.

You have seen those who understand, "get it" and take on tasks of heart so easily. And you have seen those who are troubled within enough that lacks of self love are apparent on the external and shared with anyone who will allow them, invite them in, to take away.

It is so simple in truth and so harsh for the blind to see.

Love is so readily available that those who know of it can not get enough of it and those who can not see, feel love, they have none of it.

You have come to witness how self perception takes on form. How self projection tells you who a soul is.

You use to wonder how a soul can accuse the world, you, anyone of the same things, and you would not have heard those things towards another before.

And you came to the learning that that is how they see the world, not how the world is. **That is what they create, know and respond to.**

And you now can see its affect on souls of this suchness to others and the ripple affect of the soul's perception, projection of self onto the world of Earth.

As well, you have learned there is a stem of these souls and you find it and you speak to the stem of emotions, not to the current emotions and it confuses them, for they are not in usements to think in clairity.

*(CLAIRITY—Clean and Air is Clair; to see without tint)*

Clairity angers souls; for they feel they have hidden their ills very well.

And when you speak the truth it makes them feel as though they have no where to hide, to misrepresent, to destruct as easily, for if you can see the stem there is nothing deeper than the stem.

Every thing on Earth starts from a stem. Whether it be a cell, a seed, an egg, a branch, it has a beginning to Earth.

Only on Earth is there a beginning and an end to souls.

That is the issue; is that they believe that that beginning is the true beginning and that physical death is an end.

They call all the other ways and avenues of souls "new age," "metaphysical," "far out there thoughts" and that is the stems of all souls.

The truth of Earth is to see beyond and find love in purity, to show that love in truth propels, accelerates, growths and takes on any obstacle. That it can not be without it. And that love is God. That God is love.

For the meek and their inheritance will find an empty treasure chest without the love of self present.

And those who can see the love that is eternal, already here in the present, do not need the treasure chest. So simple is the truth. Let all else rest in place, for that is where it belongs.

Understand the truth of our universe and it will answer the energy you ask of it. Truth is trusting love and love is the trust of truth.

Purity is the carrier energy that brings about sharing of foundational thoughts and groups souls together. Glory be to God Almighty.

Souls speak they have everything, and as everything is acquired they still need more. There is an appetite of worry on Earth. There is an appetite of anger.

There is an appetite of helplessness and despair. And it is addressed in film with no solutions. It is addressed in sad music's without resource.

It is not addressed directly, for the soul can not bare to see itself. In this day of agedness a celebrity has greater say in life for being someone else. Not for being themself.

When the person of ordinary in them surfaces, souls want nothing to do with them. They want what is not real not what is. That is the falseness of life.

Souls want to dream, for they believe not they are living a dream. A dream called Earth.

Ask a soul, any soul, to describe to you in detail their childhood or even a conversation of a year of time ago?

They will not be able to remember in detail an everyday event. It feels like the dream they may have awakened up to this very morning.

They may remember the feelings however the detail may elude them and yet they were there in a moment they can not recreate.

That is a dream. Both, the awaken soul and the soul asleep, the soul that was present a year ago and has forgotten or lost the data.

Does that make it not real? It was real, as the truth is never forgotten. The moments of purity are never forgotten. The moments of love are never forgotten. For their impact is simply eternal.

What are the origins of truth, love and purity?

It is the essence of the purpose of Earth and the messages embody the origins of each and every soul.

We all come from love and love on Earth is divided and the purpose of Earth is to growth back to the Origins of Truth, Love and Purity.

And when that happens the Earth will dissolve into home, for there will no longer be purpose of Earth.

You see Nadia, souls believe that destruction has to happen for the world to end, that souls are bad and that they deserve a hurtful parting from Earth to home.

However there is not hurtful parting from Earth to home. As soon as the soul leaves Earth it leaves the pain of Earth behind. Earth is the pain. Not home. Death is a celebration however horrific at home. Do you see?

Souls dislike of itself causes one to think of, believe in, want and conjure up Hell, so they can say, "If you do this, then this will happen," thus conditional love on Earth.

Conditional love is the source of much hurtful energy and pain on Earth. Conditional love is not an Origin of Truth, Love and Purity. Do you understand?

The only Origins of Truth, Love and Purity are the Origins of Truth, Love and Purity.

As well our love, I want to speak to you of orphans of soul. Ego is an orphan and choices of the meek are all orphans of soul.

That is why they feel lost, that is why they feel anger towards others. It stems from the orphanages of soul. And Truth, Love and Purity are the origination of every soul on Earth.

At home it is Absouluteness however to call a book on Earth, Absouluteness is not in readyments yet. It will be onto growth to be received.

Origins of Truth, Love and Purity is the Propellation of the Love of Home in Reminder to the Human Soul on Earth. It is that Simple. It is that Clear.

**Origins of Truth: The truth about you, the truth about me; The WE of the world and the unsolved puzzles of our souls. Your invisible thoughts, answers, and the keys to contentness.**

**READ and DECIDE.**

**This is your reference book of the soul. You will carry it around with you forever. This book will take you from me, to we, to us.**

**And you will never see those you love, those you meet, those you will come to know the same again.**

⌒͜ͅ◯

# CHAPTER 3

# GOD IS LOVE

God is one. We all are of God. There are Angels that message for God. There are souls created that experience for God.

There are different kinds to grow and stagnate love. And the glory is to learn that love has to be present from internal knowing and that is the only way to come back home, internal, not in physical.

Once there is internal knowing there is heaven as they say on Earth. Home as we say at home, on Earth.

Heaven is not far yet complete in all you could have dreamed earth to be, the way we Angels hear you think of how it should be.

It is because you are remembering heaven and you are knowing that on perfect days the Earth can carry some similar moments.

Only magnified in your memory, for the power exists there with no negative energy at all, for it doesn't have a home in such a place.

Earth is love. Its foundation is love; before the people, before the laws, the villages, the colonies, the cities, the countries. It is always present whether it is occupied or not.

As well, love is love is love. The same love that existed on Earth before the souls of home entered it for growth. Now however that very love has taken on the energy of the souls that have come into the pure love of its originations.

And that is the powerful infusements of intentions. And what souls created and create, for wants and needs, choices and free will bring about.

Free will is the gift of Earth and in this time on Earth has found its way of casting aside of itself.

So much has been forgotten. That is the purpose of our simple messages that seem so complex for their simplicity.

The complicated thoughts of meangling, evading truths in speech and in action, speaking in mind without heart, motioning gestures when speech is not available that speak harshness' to other souls.

*(MEANGLING—to bend the truth into angles of non truth)*

In this time on Earth it is called body language, which speaks after energy speaks. And souls are so far away they know this not in anymorement of this time.

Souls who have truth can see and they are isolated in the gamut of all that is rushing in this world to an imaginary finish line with nothing on the other side of it.

So simple is the truth when the truth is true.

All obstacles are moments in home, flashes and truths. All reasons do not have to fit into the structures of what seems to be the structures on Earth.

There is greater freedom of love at home.

That is why when souls come to Earth they cannot believe the challenges they have asked of themself(s).

However they are seeing their challenges with the biggest challenge within their challenge, the added Mind part to the soul.

The Ego, the ways of taking away and all that could come within that frame of thinking. The strength of truth, love and purity once found, and is it chosen?

That is why there are choices and free will. That is why a soul comes to challenge.

The intentions create the paths, the paths create the dreams and the dreams expend love onto the world.

Home is eternal. Earth is experience. We are all growing and learning. I teach you, tell you, remind you of simplicity.

The Earth bodies, the Earth minds, they are of many limits. Those very limits are the obstacles in which souls live.

The evolution of life of souls is grown in this way. They can not know of all things, for why would they do them?

What if they didn't know, would love still be able to exist? How would it exist? Why would it exist?

Only to find that without it all else can not happen. God will be in energy whether a soul believes in Him or not. It truly matters none.

What does matter are the excuses for not taking on life and blaming the world for its actions when it is the free will of the peoples that takes on the energy of love.

Who is God? How did he become? He is the Glory of Love.

His Love gave to us all existence and we return to his love for all nourishment of love. For God is not in need of any soul however His nourishment of intellect is the existence of man.

Mankind is only one form of existence; only one kind of experience. Humans are led to believe they are it and all else of existence is inferior to humans. Yet that is not of truth.

All existence of balance in greatness, yet to grow each source without the knowledge of God and learning of God and remembering the warmth of home show that true love is possible.

However can it be found without the love of God present? That is truth and trust in the drops of God we call people.

God talks through us on this level, on every level. Some hear God and some do not. Some believe they can not and should not and some believe they can.

Those who believe they can not, do not. Those who believe they can, can and will and do! Glory be to God Almighty.

God is present in all things. For when we are alone we know we are not. However self motivation to pity oneself is with God as well.

God sees, hears and loves all. God is of Greatness however God is not alone in greatness; we all are of greatness, for we are of God.

God is not to be glorified greater than the souls in which he gave love to.

All God can do is enjoy and fulfill in the love that exists, from us, with us, around us. Free will brings us back to God.

God Almighty is constant and revering. God Almighty is gentle and Loving. Fierce and pure.

God Almighty is here in partner not in ridicule. Here in truth not in confession. For God Almighty already knows. It is you who is to come to know of your own actions.

God Almighty is the blanket that warms the soul. God Almighty does not hesitate; it is Us the humans who hesitate.

God Almighty is pure intellect with light that abounds each and every one of us not some of us!

God Almighty speaks to souls of love and Human souls speak of burnings of their own flesh.

God Almighty speaks of growth and Human souls speak of drugs, self hatreds and takings away.

God Almighty speaks of partners and souls of Earth speak of cheating and running away.

God Almighty speaks of the gifts of sexualness and souls of Earth turned it into a business.

God Almighty speaks of the protected souls of Children's and souls of Earth speak of abuses to them.

God Almighty speaks of pure intention. Souls of Earth have to ask what that appears as.

God Almighty speaks to speak in truth; souls of Earth speak in selling of products, such as war, division of peoples, taking advantage of another simply for things.

God Almighty speaks of difference to growth our souls; Souls of Earth have taken fancy to dehumanize the human soul to boast the worth of self.

There is not a soul more important than another.

Self motivation has to come into play at points of time to grow one's soul. Self motivation at the expense of others is when taking away from self, from another soul happens.

The work of Angels is dually supported, for God Almighty is everywhere, for the shock of souls to really know of this.

They think God is only present when they think of him. Even though they may state they know God is everywhere, the comprehension is not there.

Hence they only believe in truth that God is right there in church. When they pray, when they think HIM, however God Almighty is present in always.

His love is the love that covers all the layers of emotions on their way to solvation of soul's confusions.

And once the love of God is asked for it is ever present. And without the asking there is an isolation and the soul stands in limbo wondering what should I do.

The purest of souls know what to do, for with purity it is a matter of how will I do this to support all those around this dilemma!

The souls of service, the Angels of God, they are of knowing that God Almighty is ever present. Glory be to God Almighty!

We all have jobs to do. To live within love is to know it is there.

And some of us choose to come to a place called Earth and we say, "We will take on the challenge of looking for love, truth, purity. And we will see what happens when we can not find it. We will see what happens when we can not see it."

So we come and we are veiled and we search. Some of us came down to help others find it. Some of us came down to help others share it.

Some of us to bring to light those who do not have it at all in present and we try to band together in the strength of it to make changes and bring back to light that love exists. And some of us who say it does not exist.

To say love does not exist is to say that God does not exist. For God is love. It is all about love. Do I speak enough of love?

People look to me for love. It is already in them. They are looking to you for love. It is already in them. All we do is we reach inside and we say it is there. And then it is discovered. So simple.

If I were to say all that has already been said, why would I need to simply repeat that knowing?

This is new. This carries truth. You do not need to fight me you need to read. You do not need to argue with me, for I am not arguing with you.

There will be those who know, those who don't know and those who do not want to know. It is that simple.

Which person are you? Do you feel you have answers?

We all have our jobs to do and this is mine. You can teach me your job and I can teach you mine. We are hear for each other not for ourself(s), as much as we would like to believe we are here only for ourself.

We are steered in wrongments of heart to not see that we are of each other without greater importance to another.

We seem to believe that things, money and status make someone more important than us and that includes those with things, money and status.

We do not realize what a challenge it is to be in any position of life, for there is not a soul on Earth without challenge.

We all have something to offer and we stop ourself(s) from offering it.

Some will not even speak great words if they are not paid to do so. Some will not help others if they are not going to get recognition for doing so.

Imagine what that means to the fellow journeyman at your side. It erodes self worth when self worth is in greater importance to some than to others.

And we ask ourself(s) why do we not live in a world of love? And I speak to you; you can not live in a world of love if you yourself are not an example of love.

You do not have to be an example of good or bad, right or wrong, for none of that can begin to matter when love is in truth of itself.

We as people have created many ways to prove love when love has to be proved.

Is love love if you have to prove it? Is love in truth if it is only when someone buys you something to show it?

What happens to the soul who can not buy anything? Is love love when the soul is only of your religion, background, workplace or home?

Does that create grounds for love? Or is love already present and the truth of love available to all, for it is understood that everyone is of some religion, background, workplace or home?

Do the cliques of souls and the groupings empower souls to feel like they belong somewhere to take away from others, or is it to show us that everyone wants identity and that we all need and want to belong somewhere?

What have our thinkings done to us? Why is it so important to call another crazy, ridiculous, without the hearings as to why this person is speaking?

We must ask ourself(s), why would a human come to the world and speak of love and we tear them down as we have accustomed to tearing ourself(s) down in this fashion?

Why do we hear something great and we do not believe it? And we hear disturbance and we stand still in disbelief as we believe it?

We are scared as a human race to believe in dreams of ourself(s) hence others.

We dare the world to show us we are wrong, that there is miracle to come, and when it comes and it is before us we discount it on our way to looking for a miracle.

As I speak; what is a miracle? It is the simple act of growing love.

Everytime love growths it means that the soul in growth of it has been touched by purity of another.

Those moments are far apart and every soul remembers, accounts, retells the stories of when they felt love.

That is miracle. That is truth of self. In those moments.

How is it that there are not many of these moments?

For that is the lacks of love I speak of and the wills and choices of humans who have brought themself(s) to thinkings that nothing works for them hence the world is not working.

There are no mistakes.

There are no mishandlings of love. It is the belief that love is separate from life that takes us to unknown paths.

Without love the soul does not know where to go and begins to try to control where it will go.

In fierce efforts of doing so, evolve the mind of the meek. The ego of Earth, for the world to believe it is invincible.

Truth be told, the world is already invincible without the ego.

Try telling the Ego that! Try speaking to the Ego. It is blind, deaf and lacks intelligence does it not? How can the ego serve anyone, anything, when the ego can not feel? It simply wants.

It wants everything and it accounts for little in its path. The ego does not speak its own truth, when the ego does not want to be seen.

To speak the truth of ego is to begin to see.

Many can not sustain the truth of the ego hence the ego remains at home without eviction. Souls know truth and yet they spend their lives searching for it.

Just as the Earth is already invincible. WE already know the answers we go back to find.

For that means we have found many ways to take away from ourself(s) and we have not found many ways of giving back to ourself(s).

That is why we start fighting for me, me, me, rather than us, us, us.

The truth of our souls comes with us and the challenges of Earth are our lessons.

When we are done we simply go back home and learn of our doings when we were not so sure of love. It is all about love.

Every action, every reaction on Earth, is and stems from love. Even if it is at the extremes of thought to believe love had anything to do with anything.

It is everything. It has to do with everything. And every thought we have that does not include love will take away from itself in leaps and folds!

Humans got lost on the paths to love. Love is now obscure and surreal. It is felt in moments and then feared for its truth.

It is fought when it is present and sent on its way. It keeps coming back to surface, the need for it, the want for it.

And then the soul discounts it, for something more complicated and further away from truth, for then it can keep itself busy and it can assure itself that it deserves not a thing. Glory be to God Almighty.

Back to lacks of self worth; Back to lacks of self love, self truth, self purity. For none of all greatness of self can be seen when the eyes are clouded.

They question is there a sun? And when the sun peaks through they say they see it and when it comes in complete clairty, the soul waits for a cloudy day.

Love is feared. For the sustainment of love is the challenge.

Souls can not accept that they possess all emotions. They each are all emotions. Emotions come with being human.

Each soul has a way to Earth, to live in their mission, their part to be human. And then they come home. To simply speak to itself, "I have come to learn and take my growth and return to home."

And on Earth the sidetracking begins, for the soul forgets it has mission. More important it becomes ego. Ego is the false friend of soul.

Ego is the boogie man I hear in the minds of humans. In their hearts, the Ego fights them to tell them they are wrong, they are not worth it and they must do this or that to be worth it.

And then when the human fails, the ego laughs at it and calls it an idiot and speaks that it can never get anything right. And the soul is left helpless, for it trusted the part of itself that is the least trustworthy.

Many souls speak I have a big ego, for that is a pride. It is false. That is where false pride exists. That is where its stem is. That is where the truth of all that is in truth exists.

The soul on Earth that speaks of ego as friend, beware of. For insecurity rests the soul and sabotage of self hence others exists.

It appears as friend, until you displease the receiver and then you are bad, etc., just like the internal ego that exists within.

Souls who know not the reciprocation of life onto itself can not see you, hence others. There are souls who know not what they can see, so they speak they are confused.

Confusing is easy when a soul is far away and ill willed. For they stopped growing and they force on others the will to not growth themself as well, for that is the company they seek.

When they seek from others what is not them, what they do not have, they want to steal it from them, possess it, own it. They do not even want to share it. Then it does not belong to them.

So then the control comes into play. Control is the symptom of Ego and Insecurity. That is the answer.

That is why those who control do not say they are, or they say it in the false pride of ego and use ego, for it sounds more acceptable, or speak they are needing to control their surroundings. They do not want to be seen for the insecurity that drives onto these truths.

Some will be called a queen bee, a control freak, has to have things his or her way. They can not see others. They only see what they are manipulating, to get what they want, need, from any situation.

As you have found there are many who want help and very few that ask to help. For the truth of ill will will always be seen.

You see our love, those who come with issues and seek not answers are speaking, "I can not fight my ego. I can not fight my insecurity, so I will blame others and not speak my truth."

Not a soul can realize the affect of insecurity.

Wanting something that is not theirs. Owning the soul in the body in which a soul lives is the longest roads to take; to own the body of your soul.

You see the body is not relevant. So many souls you meet that become more beautiful after you meet them. And so many beautiful souls that you meet that lose their beauty as you know them and you crave not to see them in urgency or warmth.

That you speak to in minimal trials, as to not feed the fires feeding within. You see these are the run away froms; the ones who speak to you in forget-fulness and allurements.

That want to leave you with feeling less than and walk away from you. Who wants to live in less than?

So souls who conflict in this become the very people that souls can not sustain within. They are the souls not missed once their truth is known.

They are the souls who feel unloved, for their lacks of love have propelled as love propels, whether it is the lacks of or the truth of.

Souls forget the power of eternity. That is love, eternal. Love will find its way, whether it be in protection of self or taking away of self. Glory be to God Almighty.

Peoples believe talking of love is weak and it is strength, therefore again, the path of unknown rather than known to the soul.

Peoples believe that you have to make time to help, and help may only be a kind word away, a pat on the back, a smile to help another soul reaffirm love.

For days are each a challenge of love and the fight for love to live within it, is it not?

Ask any human is this truth and they will say yes, yet as a whole the world is not responded to in this way, as it is of greatest importance to each and every soul.

Ask anyone. Anyone. Anyone. Every soul without exception whether they can verbalize it or not it is looking for, wants, needs the comforts of knowing that love exists.

Without fail, warrant for its arrest or that anyone will or even can take it away from them.

And insecurities all stem from, build from, the fears of love lost.

And it results in the fights for love, for self and not for all, in fears that they will never get any for self. And the realizations that sharing love, wanting love for all provides it for all.

There are not stocks or bonds of love or investments that put money in the banks of life.

It is love that fills the holes, the bankments of stability, the wantings for greater growth, the needments of truth in the ways of greater growths, the paths to create themself(s), the roads to be built, for the mind to think that it can find its way to the heart.

It is not magic or miracle in the ways that souls think it. It is in the truth of miracle that it is. Pure love travels. It is the only way.

Pure love of self understands all things, for all things stem from love.

How simple it is. How ego interferes. And you have been lessoned in ego enough to know its work. And you have come to know of its truth and appearance.

Now respond to your heart and the love that it has come to know exists and you will build roads without construction and paths without edges. And all love will be and become endless in its infinitcy.

*(INFINITCY—Thoughts that continue eternally)*

When love is pure it asks for nothing. It can only give. Once we want something from it, it has some drops of ego within. Recognize. Learn.

Respond to love as you ask yourself, why do I want this or that? Why is it that appearance matters more to me than myself?

And you will find it is love that you seek however seek love from your truth; for appearance remains the illusion of the mind's eye, while the eyes of truth speak to you, you are not in your truth.

Trust who you are and your heart can only do the rest. It is simple. Without interference. We all already know.

And now it is simply time to already do as we know. Action is our faith. For we can all believe anything. Anything can be believed if we so choose.

However our action speaks to us who we are, why we are, and tells us our purpose. Glory be to God Almighty.

God Almighty is of love of the human soul. To come to Earth as a human is a challenge greater than any. For the insecurities of the human mind challenge its stance, its vigor, its choices, and its existence.

God is love and truth and God is the surface of all knowness of life on every plane, on every level, on all statures of the universe for God is the home of our home.

God Almighty is the truth of our truths, the love of our love. God Almighty is the grand of hopes that exist in our learning. God Almighty is the openness of all existence and Earth is simply one plane of souls to encounter experience.

# CHAPTER 4

# BLESSED ARE THE CHALLENGES OF THE MEEK

I want to speak of the Meek. The inadequacies of the meek shadow life in full openness, they are the shadows on Earth as they walk and immerse in words of takings away.

*(MEEK—Those that think with their mind not their souls)*

The meek are the furthest away. They are the truest danger to existence.

The meek are the trailers of knowing not what they know, in fears they will not be what they think they are.

They are the ones that come to you in kindness and then turn out to be of another trial of life. It is all a way of looking outside, for the soul can not look in to that extent.

The soul finds harbor by sailing ship on others experiences and therefore loses their own. They are the souls furthest away. They fight you for not being who they want you to be however that is not why.

They are fighting you for they can not be who they want to be.

They need what they can not have and they discard easily. They love the entertainments of happenings only to say they mean nothing.

They come in and act with love. And the destructions they leave behind are the happiness's that grow them internal. That is why sustaness is not possible.

These are peoples that have such low self esteem that when they have the things they want or wanted they discard.

Once they get what they want they believe the person to be of stupidity to want them, for they want not of themself(s).

They believe the person is not smart enough to see who they really are and they do no respect them for being of not smart.

They will entangle and twist and turn to get in and once they are in they do not want to be, therefore they feel themself(s) a fraud.

When a soul enters their inner worlds they will live within the massive insecurities of the mind and heart and all that entails that the partner is assigned to fix. It is a very difficult world to get out of.

There is much to learn from the meek, for they are the stressors of pure love. They are the honers of souls in aroundment.

They are the ones who work so hard to take away, for the lower energies are what suits them for then they are at home.

Higher energies give to them the challenge of taking the energies to another level. So simple.

And to be seen, they are in shocks of life to feel as though what they know of is seen and heard, for the pure hearted are the targets.

People really believe no one can see their motivations.

And when souls are taken with each other or use to each other, they sometimes can not see the motivations and that is how souls can get their way at times.

They have a taker. That is all. Souls on Earth believe it is personal. They are cute, smart, charming. However it is simply that they are a responsive taker for that soul to take on and live out their needs.

If the needs are mutual then the openings of growth or takings away occur. Souls already understand their purposes however purpose demands accountability.

And souls will speak they know not their purpose.

In truth, they are simply not listening to their own souls, to their guts, when it speaks to go this way and the adventure on the other prawn of the road at forked point, to prove the invincibility of a soul onto itself, goes the other way.

When you speak that souls already know all things, they do, yet in a moment they will say they do not, simply to take on an immediate pleasure that never comes back to say thank you.

And the soul begins to erode its own trust in itself. Others in them. For the soul is speaking I am here and the mind of the soul is speaking you are not here.

And the internal duality of soul begins and the soul turns onto itself when it feels it has gone down the wrong road. There is not a wrong road, there is experience or evolution.

Yet the soul will not feel this, it will feel internal disappointment and it will cover it up with things or people they believe have a stronger garth then they do.

*(GARTH—Your deepest energy. The center of our existence. Our deepest core. The gut.)*

They will latch onto others for identity, for they are losing confidence in their own. This is the stem of insecurity. Of how it looks in the foundations, before others come to hurting others as they come to have hurt themself(s) in firstments of time.

There is purpose in everything and everything has purpose. There is challenge in everything and everything has challenge.

As well, you study of love and how to give it to souls, you found that souls only want it for themself(s) and do not want to share love. As though it will run out and there will be no more.

That is the lacks of faith in self hence eternality. That is the stem of soul's unableness to see home, to feel God.

They pack up and go to Churches, Mosques, Alternative Faiths of this time, Temples. They have wars for God, of God, and it is all in stems of fears of self.

Hence joining forces with souls who want to belong from the outside in and have not have the resources to recognize the lacks of faith of self.

For if the self is known to the self, it becomes of purity. And when the self knows not of itself it floats in insecurity of soul and travels to catalyst many situations that carry out many scenarios that take on stagnations rather than growths.

You see our loves on Earth; it is so human to not see all love. It is so human to not be involved in your life, for the challenges set forth are to bring your soul to home without the knowing of it for sure.

That you search and you question, that you conclude in your mission that life is grand and it is already there.

And souls fight themself(s) from seeing this and you sit still at the truth of the fight, of the argument. Of the souls venture with all the roads created to take away and the argument that they do not deserve the light and they remain in the darkness of thoughts instead.

Indeed, seeding greater thoughts of takings away. Rather than building the truth of the loves of heart, which they can see in the rarer moment and not in the ordinary moments of mind and heart.

And I, myself, had to absorb the lacks of conscience on Earth upon the entrance of you. For home offers not the ill will of souls! Glory be to God Almighty, for if a soul can witness itself it would know!

I speak through you, with you, in greatest energy of form on Earth, ill will will never have a home on Earth simply because it does not exist at home. So simple is the truth.

Ill will is the will of the meek. The meek learn of themself(s) at home and can not conceive of the meekness that ensues their own souls on Earth. For that is the growth.

There are some souls who in truth understand that their meekality is their Earth Challenge and conquer it, however it is very few.

Most are simply catalysts. They do not want to know this truth of themself(s) so they speak in self importance and self pity.

They want attention anyway they can get it, for they do not know how to attention themself(s). Glory be to God Almighty.

Nadia our love, I want to speak to you of gifting. There are many gifts present and the presents of gifts lay unopened.

For the gifts of love, of candor, of integrity, of hope, of challenge, and sharings of moments that question who you are.

Of answers in moments that tell you who you are; or warmth in heart, of love at home, of cleanliness of souls to self, of cleanliness of surroundings, of foods available, of understanding what it means to partner, of understanding what it means to respect your soul in the sharings of works with others.

In understanding that no soul is so important that the world is only for them and others simply need to desire them. Of feeling the balance of the soul and knowing there is no soul more important than another. Of seeing the meek when they are taking away.

The meek forget very fast what energy they expend and they will deny their speaking's, their actions, and tell others they did not speak or say or do what was seen by all.

The strength of love when stable, to growth a soul into the other side of growths that give to the world the works, the stories of accomplishments and growth, work and tireless conquests of follow and flourishing passions of heart.

For then there is proof that the soul can grow and will grow when it so chooses; that choices are for all souls and free will is the gift of love in its simplest form.

That you trust life enough to grow it, not only for yourself however to reach that growth to others. A growth unheard is a growth not shared and a growth not shared is a growth not grown.

Souls are meant on Earth to be of each other. No one soul came to Earth to be alone. There are genders and talents; Gifts of hope in infinite supply. Gifts of love that look different from every angle.

I am witnessing the leaders of country attempt to conceal their motivations. There is not a conscience for self nor others. It is self motivation personified.

It is ill will backed up with others, fought for and carried out like a funeral of thoughts and love. It is the backbone that is broken, walking on Earth without a brace to hold it up.

You are tired of reading the same book. You are long past the games that need to be played out and brought upon to endure.

You are saying, stop repeating and grow and you are being answered, "I do not want to grow, I want to blame." That is the depression of a soul, of a world.

"I want to do what has already been done, for my intellect can not carry me, for my soul is not involved." That is the sex you witness on Cameratic views without soul.

*(CAMERATIC—Full view; Viewing media and its images)*

Anything without soul can not carry itself. It appears it is however you need not look again, for you already know the carnigic energy that you witness.

*(CARNIGIC—Old and dated; without use in this time)*

Every lesson will have to be learned from all facets, angles, motivations and reasoning's of the human soul.

All examples are the examples of the world. There are all souls who are individual and there are not. There are repeats of other souls on Earth with similar missions.

Every soul has and possesses a gift. That is the difference. Take on the gifts and discover them. That is the impatience one feels when they witness a soul of undiscovery.

For instinctively, not a soul on Earth wants to believe a soul came to Earth without a gift. The grandness of gifts lost are in the meek, for as they can not see life, they can not see their gifts in the full acknowledgments of heart, for their hearts are reserved.

Reservation without a meal. Without the music. They try to find the best of everything to say they deserve it however it is reservation without deservation.

They did not earn the great works of others; they are simply claiming them, for they did not earn the great works of themself(s).

When there is earnments, there is understandings that souls on Earth want to earn. And those who do not earn know of it and the usury of others is the clue. Glory be to God Almighty.

You can starve the ill will by not participating. They will rise out of their own shame as to not being able to conquer and destroy. No food, no growth.

There are learning's of all and all souls understand in their garth the universal laws of home. Love. Truth. Purity. Yes, back to that.

When souls are with each other it is of all cares to maintain the integrity of universal law.

Once that is pierced the questions arise and once the questions arise, suspicions of pending lessons start to present.

Once the pending lessons are in thought the relationship stands on a daily trial and within those trials intents are questions; for the truth of the purpose is questioned and the relationship will stand in jeopardy.

So simple is the truth.

When a soul takes on that they are better than another and they speak not their truth of who they are or they use others for their advantage and only give back in showmanship to maintain their stance.

When soul's givements of self are in self motivations and the honors in which they share are self motivated they simply live in the piercings of their own love, truth and purity.

Without sharing the knowledge's of whom they are in truth. They are hiding their truths and in usement of reasons not based on truth to do so. You see this in muchments, in groves of souls about. And with those thoughts in tow the gifts of the beauty around are clouded to the eye. The truth of a people's truth is present in partial form.

When there is a work partnership, when there is romantic relationship, when there is a mother, a child, a father, a parent of the parents, there are different levels of love and growth.

One teaches the other of shared lessons, stories, holdings of heart, along the journey of life on Earth.

Time, the ages of peoples, the progression that is all souls will continue on until they are to come back home; is the holdings of all truths of our purpose.

That is the gift most overlooked. The elderly are the burdens, unless they have enough money and health to take care of themself(s).

In most cases their stories are unheard hence unshared hence unlearned.

The progression of life is stopped at the alterments of face and body to deny growth and keep appearance that the progressions have not occurred.

The body is in becomement to the answers to all questions. Souls have taken on that the body, as long as it looks good, will be desired, regardless of internal heart and activity.

It has come to the points of further awayments of souls to themself(s) to say, "If I am not desirable I am not worth humanity."

The dreams of those souls are unheard, for they are judged, not based on religion, race, or color, they are judged on appearance. And in truth, that is the truest discrimination of human souls to another.

Even the savviest souls take on that they are not "cute" enough, yet deeper inside they use their appearance to lure others to them. And then there is the egonomic stance on physical attributes.

*(EGONOMIC—To live in your mind without involving your soul)*

Souls will believe that everyone wants them and that they owe souls themself(s), for they are simply that great.

That is discrimination in believing you are a soul better than others. And you will not give some souls the timeness of the days of life and you will only respond to the situations that puff the ego.

There is a ME VS. ME that is happening with the souls of Earth, when a soul is discontented it is the discontented of all. When a soul is sharing love it is the sharing of love for all.

That is the easy part. That is the all knowing however the faith in such knowings stops at the ego of the souls on Earth.

Love can come in many ways of life on Earth however love with pure intent will carry all souls to paths of truth.

There is never an over abundance of love.

When the blind eye of the human experience is lifted they will see and know all things and love will abound and all will realign.

For the beauty, the strength, the hope of love and God Almighty is of the greatest, the most expansive, the most universal, of all planes and universes. All the galaxies and home, for all is run by, propelled with, endured by and growing with love.

Love is the fluidity of life. Love is in every fragment of life. Life is the genuiness of soul, for the most simple of being the grandest of love, for the most simple of being the grandest of love.

Only in simplicity can love truly be consciously seen.

In complication love is seen in abstract, for truly it is hardest to feel through complication or self motivation, even if stated 100 times.

Love is the gift of life of all layers from home to each soul. Love is the magnet of souls and the foundation of growth.

Love of self is hardest to attain, for the coming of souls is presented to other souls as Mothers, Fathers, Sisters, Brothers, in first knowings. And that shapes love.

Yet in Angels on Earth it remains the purest of love throughout, for those are the teachers of souls on Earth. And the Angels keep love in balance, for Earth is the trickiest and most challenging of Challenges.

Earth is of difficulty. Souls that come back at times need intervention upon returning. For the horrors of soul were seen by them. That is the lack of love. To know love is to recognize the lack of love as it exists.

Love is flexible and it is not in speakment of love that love exists. It is in actions.

There are some in life who say they love you and yet they will hurt you; that is injured love.

That is love in brokenness. It appears open and flowing and then restrictions are put on flexibility. It can not be and the bonds of holdment of heart become of questions and the breakings of detachments begin.

For the love of love is not enough. Everyone wants the love of love. How can a soul reach into the flexibility of love?

To know oneself is to know others in truth. To love oneself is to love others. To care for your soul cares for others.

All in assimilations carry different paths for the choosing! Glory be to God Almighty.

And those paths for the choosing carry lessons that grow greater avenues to self renewal, to grow into self knowings.

Paths chosen within love of self, which is purity, grows yourself and teaches and grows others.

The chosen paths are truly the paths chosen by souls. They are not the paths of God. God is love in all. Experiences are had by all.

The kinds of experiences are chosen by the soul, for the soul's learnings. So simple. There are not other chosen paths.

God does not choose paths. You are coming to experience and mission.

Rules of today are not the same as rules of beforement. So rules are not in stone.

Your heart's choosings of love is forever the greatness it will be. That is why it is timeless. That is why it feels no weight.

Those who walk around with the weight, you know who they are. They are the ones who look and appear to the naked eye as easy and loving, and then the suitcases of baggages begin opening and the never ending stories begin.

These people stay the same, stuck in time and in angers. That is why they stay fixated on issues. That is why they have the time to study and to execute their actions. That is why their souls do not rest.

Love is not a person. There are many people. Love is a feeling. Love is intangible yet felt.

It can not be of anything in elsement, for it can only be love; to sound simple and be grand.

To act like it is to not know it. There is no acting. For God is love.

And God is present.

CHAPTER 5

CHOICE

Nothing is as it seems our love, nothing. Nothing is as it is.

Release in each day all that can come to you, for you can not receive if you hold onto what you receive.

Those who release their love make room for more love to come.

That is the infinitcy of Love. Love is the rolling meadow of Home. Love is the river of waters movement. Love is the propeller of all thoughts hence things.

Love can only be the knowing of a soul as the soul knows Love. Souls take on Love as a task. How can love be a task? Love is not something that we do. Love is.

That sounds theatrical to speak however love is. Love is in every energy, every thought, every movement, every decision.

Souls on Earth have turned love into a romantic of love of Man and Woman however love is not physical. Love is.

A child knows of it, a man knows of it, a woman knows of it, the Elderly know of it in the purity in which it exists. There is also love in lacks of love and that is what is confusing most people.

Lacks of love, look, appear as love however in that there is the pain of experience combined, when there is lacks of love in the present form. That is what causes the disturbance of life on Earth.

The stem will always always return to lacks of love; Love that comes to souls in pure form and then is taken away from them in one way or another.

The souls of humans on Earth are designed to take in the love of other souls that propel its growth.

Without the sharings love stagnates. And in hurtments to each other there are takings away of the love as we have known of it in purity and piercing its existence within us as we know of it from home.

It is jarring at first to be pierced in the love that you come to Earth with from home. It is worse than any lack of love that can be felt.

It violates universal law in the firstment of time on Earth. And then the soul learns other things from the initial lacks of love that are felt and endured.

The soul begins to understand that there may be other souls that you can not trust. Souls may also begin to start hiding their truths to protect themself(s) from the actions of others.

Some may form habits of lying in protecting of self however lying stems from the lacks of trust developed by the lacks of love.

Some may steal from others, stemming from needing possession. And others may reach out to hurt others, again stemming from the lacks of love.

All actions stem from love, whether that love comes from lacks of love or love in purity to that soul. Souls have come to realize in great moments of their lives the greatest truths of themself(s).

They want to thank all those who have helped them along the way of their journey. They will at times even thank those who come to them with lacks of love.

From the lacks of love they will have learned that lacks of love hurt us all in one way or another and we are in this together.

It may have taught that soul that lacks of love can be recognized and nurtured and we can heal if we go back and recognize that that is what has occurred.

It gives to us the reasoning's within that everything is to be learned from and grown from if our perspective says that we can.

If a soul has a perspective of despair, anxiety, anger; that is what the world around that soul will create for them.

The creation of a world of any kind, anywhere, is the simple reflection of what love means, is, has become to the soul, then souls, then the world of those who live within it.

And choice gives us the strength of love, the overcomence of obstacles and the truth of free will in the sobering moments of challenges.

Whether they be a soul who came to experience wealth and the sharing of, or poverty and the limits that are brought on by it.

Both are limitless. However, until the soul can see that, it will not be seen. As long as a soul can see something, anything, it will.

As soon as a soul says to itself from heart, "I do not want to see worry, I do not want to see fear, I do not want to doubt," it will no longer see it.

When a soul speaks, "I have nothing to do with my time and I will fill it with despair, worry, sadness," it will see that too.

I am repetitive in my speaking's and yet I am not.

There can never be enough ways to speak of love and the lacks of love and the actions that follow. As well souls on Earth, you can hear beauty.

Stop and listen. In the silence there is music to the soul. Music of your mind, of your hearts dreams, which are as real as you can see them.

Some souls know not what they dream. They dream of what they want. In truth there are no dreams, there is love. Back to love again.

Work is not work if you love what you do. Dreams are not dreams if you are doing what you love.

Love is. It is not a thing. It is not anything. It is the air, the wind, the breath of another soul.

As souls develop on Earth and carry their own soul to its journey, the shapings of those experiences tell us who is closer to us in choosing and who is not.

WE attract each other in likenesses to ourself(s), for the choosings of heart are what carry us to each other; our love or lacks of love.

Some of us want partners to love and others want partners in hopes of those partners taking on the responsibility of our journeys.

The latter is from lack of love. No one can take on another journey. That is all that is individual on Earth.

The lacks of love on Earth, when they are the stem of what attracts us to another, those souls are simply there for experience and not eternal love of home on Earth. That is the sole and only reason. Glory be to God Almighty.

Souls get angry at each other because they are not together or that they are. However in truth some unions are for experience and some are for eternal growth and evolution. They may come in the form of friendships, kinships, work partnerships or marriage.

I speak that love on Earth is seen in one form and that is love between a man and a woman. All else is not considered love.

Whether it be same sex love, love of children, family or friendships. All of that is looked upon as inferior love to romantic love. There are not names for love. Love is love is love.

The grandest measurement of the takings away of souls on Earth is to fracture and rename love; to take on sexualness and remain it casual, to take on lacks of love and ignore them, to take on the status as greater importance than emotional balance.

To take on actions that hurt others and say it is of OK to do so as long as we get what we think we want; to discount souls amongst each other.

There is no soul more important than another. There is nothing that is done to one soul that does not affect another. Nothing.

We can not know the strength, the power, the growth of love. When souls speak, "Then why do bad things happen?" That is lacks of love in the truths of their lackings.

For only lacks of love can do and perform what may be looked on by others as "bad." That is why I speak there is no bad; Bad stems from lacks of love; Wrong stems from lacks of love; Evil stems from lacks of love. All that is real is love and lacks of love.

All the universe stems from suchness and nothing else. Love can turn the impossible to possible simply because the heart can see it.

Love can heal a wound, repair a deteriorated river, clean a body of water, move the trees motion, growth the plants of the Earth hence feeling nature with love.

The animals in instinctive love can live in unison with the human souls within it. For when love is heightened and nourished from soul, it grows all things around it, all souls around it.

When you see anger in a soul it is to the affect of all souls around it. I speak run do not walk away from those who come at you with lacks of love, for they will not hear your words.

You are thinking that I speak we are here for each other as well, I tell you to run. I speak to run, for many you can help from afar.

When a soul chooses to not hear they will not learn from you however ask God to give them an example of objectivity and they will learn.

You can not be the problem of a soul and the solution at times, in the sameness of time. The souls will want from you what you can not give and that is why you can not help.

They want all or nothing, for they do not know themself(s) well enough yet in their own evolution to see their truth and they will not see yours either.

They will not hear you until you speak what they want to hear however you can not give to them what they are asking, for no one soul can take on the caring of another's mission.

Each soul came with mission and that is why you can not give in those times. To Ask God Almighty to give lessons of objectivity of a soul to see itself is the greatest gift you can give to any one soul on Earth.

Souls truly can not give what they do not have. You think to yourself that some help others and they are unable to help themself(s). That is not truth. Any soul who helps in purity knows what they are doing.

Other souls that you see help and you understand their self motivation or manipulation is giving what they have. They have a means to manipulate and that is what they are giving is the manipulation, not the help.

That is the greatest injury to love on Earth, the manipulation. It appears as help however it is simply the inheritance of the meek.

So simple is the truth. And they are giving what they have. It is in evasion of the eye and heart of the unsuspecting soul.

However those souls are whisked away upon discoverments of their actions. And I speak again, run do not walk away and turn them over to God Almighty.

Objectivity may show them for a moment what they have become and they may take on the choosing of actions of love in truth, even if for a short time.

Glory be to God Almighty, for all souls are treasure in the love of God. For the love of God is the love of all. For love is love is love.

I hear souls speak, "I don't love him or her that way, or I love them this way." That is nonsensical. How could it be of sense when a soul speaks of love as though it is a type of food group or a candy bar of some sort?

It is not only chocolate, or fruits or nuts, it is not breads or meats or a tree of some kind. It is one thing that encompasses all things.

It is the umbrella under which the Earth lives. It is the life of movements within and without our existences and when souls return home it is the first and only thing felt. It is love.

And the greater the understandings of love that exist, the greater the depth it becomes known to the soul hence the greater the evolution within.

If a soul can not take on love, there is lacks of love of self and the only thing you can do, say and be is love in consistence. In truth. It will teach love in consistence and truth.

For each day of Earth is a challenge. It brings with it love of heart and growth of soul in combination. That combination gives balance.

The stresses of Challenge push on further growth however if a soul can not take on the challenge they blame the challenge of growth to them for their lacks of growth.

In truth they simply were not wanting to be ready for that challenge. However in their own truth that challenge would never have been put before them before they were ready for it.

Everything is as it should be and when souls say it is not it's when they can not see, when they do not want to see.

For many find comfort and company in complaining. Complaining is the taker away of time, love and growth.

To complain about anything is to say that you do not want to fix it; that you want it to be, for you are not ready to take on action.

You do not want anyone to help you. You may simply be seeking the company of complaints. It is open is life to choose.

In life on Earth all actions stem from the needings of Truth, Love and Purity, and all actions that are of ill will are due to the lacks of truth, love, and purity.

Over and Over again there are threes. The triangular energy carries the strength of the universe within it; Love, Truth and Purity, The foundation of us all.

Notice that Love, Truth and Purity does not include, cars, houses, monies, food, clothing's. Without Love, Truth, Purity, nothing else can sustain in matter to a soul on Earth.

For all the human creations are the imagination and projection of the current human mind.

Through time passed and time today, and time to come, since there is not time, there is Love, Truth and Purity. All the stories ever written, told, or lived on, are based on Love, Truth, and Purity.

And Everything else that we speak of, of others, that shocks us on Earth are simply the Lacks of Love, Truth and Purity, for we understand in instinct that we are attacking the triangular force of all Universe to do so.

That is why that is all that is talked about, thought about and brought on as News.

Souls speak many times all that is on the News is negative. All that is there to shock us, use us, and we no longer even believe it is truth. Yet we watch at times, for it is all that we have. For now.

We watch or listen because of the deep rooted fear that we will hurt the universe and we try to listen simply to know we did not hurt it yet, enough, and we keep trying to stop the bad news that we want to hear, in self protection.

And still, until this moment of time, souls on Earth are speaking, "It is too much bad news, we are doomed. **WE have no power.**"

**WE do have power when we know that Truth, Love and Purity are the true rulers of the world. Not a person.**

**A person is someone who takes on the job of bringing truth, love and purity to the forefront. To the triangles of friends, of family, of work partners.**

**That forefront's the love to all, not simply for one. That we are an all. That we are one. We are all again.**

**Earth is a spot of journey for every soul to awaken to the Universe what is already known.**

**And a soul comes to Earth knowing this and leaves Earth knowing this.**

**Put in the spices of Ego, Material accumulation, Status, Race and Color and Religion, while veiling home, are all the stems of challenge to each and every soul.**

**For it is the answer of the souls Love, Truth and Purity. The Original Triangle. The Original Love we all already know. Origins of Truth.**

Nadia there are only brothers and sisters on Earth. There are only families. There are only siblings of each other.

There is not an illusion of US. It is the illusion that we are alone.

For God Almighty comes to souls and they can not see him, yet they can and they do and they will and there is no turning back, once you know.

The quest for knowledge's becomes the hunger and within that knowledge there is not any way to let go of others and the love that is bestowed to all. Glory be to God Almighty.

So simple is the truth of the truth of simplicity. It is our Universe. It is not THE Universe. It is OUR universe. For all of us.

We can ask of it as we need and it will respond to our words, our speaking's of soul, for the speaking's of purity echo through the Universe in pure energy and love.

Love is responded to in glory of God Almighty for it is the heard energy.

All other energy's are whispered and do not extend. Truth, love and purity extend and I speak they are the foundation of mankind and mankind can only sustain in their foundation.

For without truth, love and purity, we are in current times as passed times, witness to the hurts of souls rather than the love of souls on Earth.

Glory be to God Almighty. In this time, one group of peoples is allowed again to hurt another group of peoples in the realms of self motivations.

The partners of war in this time are the partners of ill will and piracy of invasionary visionary's of stealing and lacks of prudency and honor of like souls on Earth.

It seems that not a soul can stop it however the biggest stops take the longest to come by however they will come and those in vision of hurts and tortures will come to the forefront of accountability.

Glory be to God Almighty, for the truth will surface without cause, for it is the strongest of energy's to travel the universe and the only energy that can.

One soul of ill will is like another, in different degrees of what they can carry out. No difference of soul, simply difference of position.

Your job(s) on Earth are to know how it appears, takes on behavior and odor.

These are the souls who are not missed, for they offer illness wherever they travel. Souls do not change, circumstances change.

Souls do not have variance when they are not looking for growth.

They are simply allowed to carry out their ill will or they are not invited and go elsewhere to do as they are.

It is mathematical in truth. It is an equation of theorem after theorem that deducts its way to a proven theory.

There is not turning back time, what ifs, what why's. There is purpose to challenge and the challenge is to understand your purpose.

There can not be a right or a wrong, a this or a that. If energy was called it will take you where it needs to flourish. And it will teach you or evolve you.

Energy is the movement of the Universe. I say Universe sparingly, for it is home, the planes, the galaxies that can only move with the energy of one, of all, of one again.

Souls have come to congruency of thoughts. They understand there is more and they say prove it, for they want to be sure, in fears of being wrong. And the fact is that wrong is even in the thoughts, for there is not a right or wrong.

Souls know what will take away and know what will not. It is choice.

Choice speaks do this, do that, and choice is not wanting to be accountable, so souls speak this is right, this is wrong, and they can form a crowd in that discussion alone.

What if a soul speaks, "I do this and I understand I am hurting myself in doing so. And if I hurt another soul in doing so, they may question why they know me, and I still needed to do this."

It is different than "I made a mistake, everyone makes mistakes" and the hurt is left to grow into a life of its own.

So I speak to you, there is not right or wrong and you not any longer speak in words of fear or lacks of love to self.

So simple is the truth. For all Origination's can only propel.

Nothing can change without change, for the energy is already here, it simply has to live in recognition to live, to growth, to be felt.

Truth is the traveler. Love is the carrier. And Purity is the sustainer.

It is a balance, an equation, and all that can give anything in life is the free will and choices made by souls. Glory be to God Almighty!

Every soul is a teacher. Every soul prefers love, for it has to to take on lacks of love to do all else.

There would be no war without lacks of love, truth or purity.

**The only preference God Almighty has is truth. It is not one person above another. It is not a bigger anything or a better person, it is simply truth. Objectivity of God Almighty. It is truth, love and purity.**

**Pressure banters peace. There can not be pressure and peace at the same time.**

**When a soul speaks not the truth to oneself, it is anger at the person/world, for they themself(s) are giving away their truth. They will always want their truth back. Always. There are no exceptions.**

Souls have come to a farness away from themself(s) that they can no longer explain. They can no longer account for. They no longer want to begin to account for.

The human souls are tired and lost in worlds and layers of lacks of love:

Where rudeness is looked at as assertiveness.

Where thievery is a lesser crime.

Where murder is not such a disturbing hearing.

Where souls on Earth wage war without reason.

Where souls on Earth can not be stopped when in rolling momentum's of ill will.

Where souls on Earth live in lacks of respect, appreciations, moments of joy.

Where souls on Earth take on not wanting to be bothered with others however expect from others what they expect not of themself(s).

It is that simple. It is truth. As God prefers. **God Almighty's only preference for humans on Earth is truth.**

If a soul lies to another it should not be upset that it will be lied to.

If a soul uses another it should not be upset to be used.

If a soul steals from another it should not be upset to be stolen from.

If a soul abuses another it should not complain of abuses.

If a soul speaks in ill will it should not be surprised to be spoken in ill will of.

If a soul joins forces to hurt another should it be surprised to be hurt itself?

If a soul gives love should it be surprised to feel love in return?

If a soul has self motivation will the outcome of its actions surprise it?

If a soul comes to you with pure intent is it a surprise to both souls that there is rest and candor present?

When a soul accounts for itself an outcome of trust endures!

When a soul speaks its truth is truth not known?

When a soul comes with hope do you gravitate to help that soul?

When a soul speaks of love do you not join in?

When a soul comes to help does it not bring on tears of joy?

Life is a reflection of itself.

Life is a picture of the souls within it.

Life is simple and clair.

Life is a gift if we see it that way.

Life is simply life.

Money comes and goes. Things come and go. Energy of your actions stay with us.

Who did you carve out within the life you live? That is a choice we have each and every day.

Who do you want to be? It is yours to be!!!!!

Seek and you will find.

Keep seeking and do not stop.

Help is here and coming still to you.

In every thought that you have it will find you.

CHAPTER 6

THE LOVE OF SELF

Nadia, our love, I want to speak on the Underprivileged emotions of souls. As they walk amongst themself(s) and they think to themself(s), that this whole world, every look, every stare, every conversation is about themself.

For the ego has such a home. That it is all of oneself. As though not another soul can possibly feel as they would feel at all.

How little the mind and how ignored the soul to have this thought of themself. You see, it is not about anyone, it is about the energy of everyone.

If a soul takes on another, it is going to be experience for them. That is all.

Dressing and alluring, speaking "pleasant" or not. Having things or not. It does not define, it enhances. Yet it is used for definition.

Define love. It is difficult to do, for many souls can not. Or they speak of it as though it is foreign and obscure.

And then I hear ego, "I" when it comes to love. Love is always always always a WE.

It is for everyone and it does not run out. You think Nadia, you think of souls who fight love. They have not a definition of love that has to do with love.

There are many souls on Earth that want. "I want this, then I will be happy. I will wear this, then I will be cute. I will drive this or that, and then I will be worthy. I will own this or that and then I will seem OK. Like everyone else." WE are setting standards that are of underprivileged minds.

Nadia, when you hear the details of soul's saying, "I am present now because I am dressed" however who were you when you were not? "I am special now because I have a new car." Who were you before you had the car?

Who will you be after the car is not longer new anymore? "I am heard now, I was on Television." Who were you before you were heard on media?

Nothing really changes except for our perception, our anticipation's of ourself(s), of life, of our perceptions.

We can all live in the anticipatory state of mind, for it drives us to adventure and the open love of the moments of life.

It does not postpone, nor does it wait for, it lets your excitements live in the moments. You see nothing is as it seems.

Nadia, You are thinking about anticipation. It is key to every soul.

Anticipation creates movement within. Anticipation teaches you that you can create what you want simply by thinking it.

You already know that thoughts are things. Things are thoughts as well.

You see, the anticipation of anything, whether it be a great time had by all or a feeling of despair, it is created by the soul.

The soul speaks I am tired. The soul is tired. The soul speaks I want to dance the soul will dance.

The soul speaks I want love, the soul will find it. And when the soul speaks I want space, it will create it.

The soul that speaks I want peace, it will happen. And when the soul speaks I want to win, it will let ego take over.

You see our loves, things are thoughts. They create the thoughts to make them happen, yet thoughts are things in creation.

This book is to speak to the world that it can no longer keep itself in stagnation. The lacks of truth proposed to them are in truth their origin of stagnations.

For the worlds that divide, conjure false hopes and hard falls, can not be of God Almighty. God Almighty is pure energy, pure love.

Nadia, yes you are a teacher of Origination. You speak truth. Truth is the origin of thought. You teach Origination. These are Originates of thought.

Life is the experience of souls. And souls have choices to do and to see and to be in part of themself(s). To do for others what you can not do for yourself is to not do for others.

There in truth is never, "I am feeling this way because of…" that is and always will be a false statement.

A soul is feeling as it does for any reason, for that is what they bring to them. That is what they are calling.

And if they can not figure out why, they will have asked for the experience from home. No soul on Earth comes to Earth without the experience and mission of their soul.

That is not of possible for a soul to "slip through the cracks of home" and land on Earth. Every soul comes with a purpose.

When you deny your purpose, your mission, when you work away from pure intent rather than towards it, when you speak in lacks of truth and they don't have to be truths of hugeness, simple speech, insinuatory speaking's, they are going further away rather than towards mission.

When souls come to life in playments with the intentions to hurt another, conscious or not, they will take walks away from self. Many souls will say, "I just want this or that."

Nothing a soul could want will make that soul happy if that soul is not happy already in the moments that they speak "as soon as I get…I want this and then…when I get…I am going to say…You did this to me…I am blaming you."

In any way of speaking this, they are walkers away of self. That is why I speak to you run, for they are giving you what they have.

They are sharing however they are coming to you with their own vacancy and filling it with temporary comings and goings of things and that is why those persons on Earth are not in eternalness of self.

They can not think past the immediate doing. Yet they are telling you, long term work, love, caring, will take its toll on you. That is why I say run.

Now there is human choice and a soul can choose to stay. Simply know that you will live in a world of vacancy to do so and nothing eternal can fill it if one of the souls involved is not an eternal thinker.

For then love is not believed in faith it is self motivated. For then truth is only a tool. Used if it gets a desired result and left on the table of truth if it is not.

I am returning now to the conversation of Anticipation and perception and the soul's participation within itself.

When things are thoughts, it is the thinking of the closed mind. Finite.

When thoughts are things, it is an open mind. Infinite thoughts.

When thoughts are allowed they can growth. When they have a stopping point they will stop. Glory be to God Almighty.

I want to speak to you of the illusion of the lazy mind. It is the mind of losing. For those who think they want to win, the lazy mind has already lost.

To try to "not do" things, to try and think a soul got away with not having to do this or that, they have already lost to those who do want to do things.

You see, a lot is missed in not doing. Much in the way of humbleness and service. In energy and in health. In all aspects.

The perception is that a soul is smarter than another, yet the smarter of the two souls is the active soul.

For then it will experience more of the inner feelings rather than the just, I am showing the world I am great feelings.

Most people are a ME person. When someone is too much of a ME person with a WE person, then there will be conflict. For the ME person does not like to be reminded or seen.

**Those who do not believe in love, they try to create it. It IS a person, a thing, a place.**

**They immortalize love, for they can not understand its way of worth to them. They can not see the flexibility in it, nor can they feel the freedom it unfolds.**

Nadia, Sweet Nadia, there is more. Love is the most fragile of energies and it is the strength of all energies.

Love need be present in all things of passion and life on Earth.

When it is not present it will be pretended and the emptiness within the lacks of presentness is at times unbearable to the souls of Earth. It is the stem of all things that take away.

Souls repeat stories where their love was injured in its purity. At times they could not tell you why however there are many reasons why. Souls believe love is the body.

I am aghasted at the amounts of energy that come to this belief. Nadia, Nadia, Nadia, you must speak this to souls. To relax. To live in who they are, not an image. Images are simply images.

The moments the souls begin to speak, the images they worked so hard to perfect go away. And the insides they have not worked on in heart appear and then the love is lost quickly, simply because the love of self was/is not present.

Now when you get two souls who do not love themself(s), they will believe they have a lot in common and they attach to each other for the purpose of growth.

In that growth all the lacks of love of the couple will come to surface.

And if the lacks of love that came to them were hurtful then they will continue that trend and hurt each other until they can not take it anymore. And they will leave each other in search of a mate that will grow them rather than hurt them.

As well, what will happen is that they are the one's hurting the situation and they can not see it. So they go on continually hurting themself(s) and others along the way.

That is not taking accountability and laying all the pressures on another to cure them. And when they are victorious it is because of themself(s) and they acknowledge not that others were of helpfulness' to them.

And they will live life with little attachments to others, for the purpose of others is for ego, boasting and ownerships. This is plentiful in souls on Earth.

And then there are those whose lacks of love do not come in the hurtments of others, rather the growths of others.

These are the souls who want to transform others, want to help others so that they can grow to a better placement of stance with each other.

They are builders. They want to grow.

When these souls are hurt they do not go to hurt another person, they will hurt themself(s).

They will do things that take away by running away. Either mentally or physically and the destruction of the relationship is eminent.

Souls are of these two kinds when lacks of love are present. NO truths are spoken, for they are not recognized and the souls are too far away.

So what happens is that they live in the uneasiness of their truths that are unknown to them. And they create reasons as to why they have to separate.

It will take time and trials of heart to get there. There will be cheating in monies by overspendments to cure the ills.

Then there are cheatments of heart. Then the cheatments of body hence the cheatment of family hence the tangible reason to release the relationship.

Some may use addictives to take away, such as abuses of substances to escape and take away and run without being the reasons of truth to be known.

Prescription medications come to the point of validating illness and the soul can alleviate responsibility entirely! Glory be to God Almighty!

Soul's fulfillments are not close to heart. They are far from soul and souls are accustoming to living in the farness.

Ego wants much from the soul and when lacks of love, of self worth, of truth are present, Ego has a surety of home.

And the Ego sets up the competitiveness of who is better and in truth it means nothing to be better. Better than what?

There are many who have things and yet there is a setting up of measurements of success between peoples, Nadia.

If one did something they sell it to another person and you find they did it entirely to show its worth. Not because they enjoyed it.

I see many souls walking around "performing" tasks to show that they are accomplished, worthy, knowing, smart, better than!

I am in sadness of speaking's to say this extent is a great extent of many souls on Earth.

And they are not fulfilled, and in a moment can turn from having a great day to having an awful day. Because they see someone, something they think is "better than" them. All the while their energy is in being "better than" another.

It is an awful game. And there is no game based on truth. There is no game based on lacks of love. There is no game based on lacks of purity.

So the soul who wants to be better than. Is trying to beat on a clock of what? Until the next person that comes along "better."

How does a soul rest, settle, live in that thought? Many souls sleep in sexualness with others simply to possess them, out of lacks of love, out of fear of not remaining "better" and Nadia; there is no love in purity.

Purity is so far away from sexualness that souls can not find the gifts of sexualness. And they believe it is in many partners that will gift them, for they lost the depth of self in that dilution.

Purity in sexualness. Without it there is not sex. There is no love. There is no truth. There is no commitment of heart. There is no wanting in truth. The moments have to be manufactured with drinks, drugs, with clothes and visuals.

Yes, there is much to be spoken for instant stimulation. That will always be true. However grand sexuality stays within the soul forever and never leaves.

And instant stimulations are simply a release to assure the soul they can still feel something, anything.

However they will search for love always, for they know in subconscious, in internal, there is more.

When they release at times Nadia, it is while they are releasing, at times while they are beginning, that the arousalments of the souls are knowing and speaking to themself(s) within that "as soon as I am done here…I will do, go, buy, something."

The sustainess is not present, even during the phasings of buildments of what they want to believe is love.

Peoples want so much to believe in the magicness of life on Earth. They will learn that they do not have to act anything to be in the love of self hence others.

You do not have to be born in the criteria of what it means to love. You are born in love and that is not of judgment of other souls. Each soul came with its purpose of who they are, of why they are.

The human eyes can see however what if there was not vision? Then there would be no difference. The human ears can hear however what if they could not? They could only love again.

The human hands can move however what if they could not? Then there would be no way to eliminate another soul. And the human legs, what if they could not walk? No one would be walken away from.

It is of timeness now to give a soul license to live in the love of self.

Those who care not for their history, have not the truth in caring for their future. If you can not hold dear what is in this day, tomorrow can not mean anything.

Those who start everyday brand new as though there has been no one along the way that touches, that cleans with them, cooks with them, eats with them, is not with "them" at all. They are alone as they have earned.

Sometimes we do not know where we are from until we are gone. Sometimes we can not see while life faces us. That is the loss of the meek.

Live in tomorrow and you will live in emptiness. Live in today and you will see today. Live in yesterday and see not the life of this day.

Understand your history and then you can see the day, see the next day, growth your heart into seeing process and love and caring of a human on a journey of life on Earth.

What does it look like to care about another person? We all say we care about someone, but how does it feel to be cared for.

Does it mean that in that moment you feel good however you can not trust the next moment and you are always struggling to have "good" moments.

And if you fall short, then all of a sudden you are a fool or an idiot or something less than being worth to be cared for. Do we understand caring and can we grow on in life and simply trust that it is there?

Does caring mean that you owe something to someone for caring? Does it mean that someone has the right to speak of you in ill will and you accept it?

Does it mean you can pick and choose when they will be involved in your life and when they won't? Does it mean they only care about you when it benefits them and they don't have to care about you when it doesn't?

What does it mean to care? How do people know when they care? How does someone know when they are cared for?

These are the questions of Earth. You are in them, living them. You are finding as well, the limits of free will and choice. And that each day brings to your heart's knowings that there is a greater good of each and every day of life on Earth.

All Earth can turn on the sincerity of energy. And the entire plane of Earth can stand still onto the stagnation of minds, souls, bodies.

You want to know what is so important that it does not matter to hurt another soul on Earth? That is life. There is choice and free will towards the absolute of love.

You can re-title the book, *Origins of Absolute Truth*. A journey to the answers that settle the soul. It does not matter how you got the answers, it matters that you lived the experience(s) in heart.

That you felt and learn. Gave and grew. Loved and felt love. That is the matter. The lessons are irrelevant if you are to think of souls and their challenges.

It is the truth of the heart that is remembered, carried and shared. Glory be to God Almighty, for it is of simple truth that settles the dust of the soul's chaos.

# CHAPTER 7

# THE CYCLES OF LIFE

All souls are within cycles. They are cycles of experience. That is why some aspects of life from the beginning of missions on Earth feel like they were of many lifetimes ago.

For by now the soul begins to recognize that they lived in other areas of life until all the truths were learned and then moved onward, forward, to other experiences.

Everything is forever and nothing is forever at the sameness of time. The only thing that never leaves a soul within its truth is eternality.

All other things are forever and not forever at the sameness of time.

All things passed and the lessons either learned or not.

If the lessons were of learned, then the soul feels the lifetimes ago. And the unlearned lessons are repeated within another job, person, situation, to take on the soul to evolution.

And they relive the passed moments over and over again in resistance of learning's. And blaming's come into play. It is because of this or that.

All the learning's go to the side of mind and all the excuses live within the forefront of mind. And that is stagnations.

And then the worries set in that they will do another thing and accumulate the pains on top of the pains that the soul already has been unable to resolve or learn from and so on.

So it becomes overwhelming for souls when they enter a new situation of any kind within the pains already carried and they go one of two ways.

They take on that they are victims and it is because of others that they did not accomplish or endure, or they take on anger and live within a quiet, unhearing mode within, that tells them they were right.

And they stop learning, for who needs to learn when they are right. Without taking into account their own role within their own life(s). And they stagnate.

You see our love, because there is right and wrong in the mentality of Earth, no one wants to be wrong. For it matters much to souls to be right.

They want to win at something, anything.

Their insecurities are so strong that they create situations for themself(s) to win and they will not in many times attempt challenges that are new to them in fear of the losses that they can not handle.

And they stagnate.

As well, there is the other way to combat fear or truth of growth and that is lying. Lying to others rather than speaking truths.

You do realize the ripples of lying. However others do not believe it so on Earth. They really believe that they can lie and no one will know. It starts in their face. Their face knows and it betrays the liar all the time.

God Almighty gave the soul nowhere to go when it lies. Some believe they can be good at it and look another in the eye and act in normalcy.

However, the moment a decision with a soul has come to the knowing it is going to lie about anything, it ripples in energy first and the receiving soul will never in everments accept what that person is saying.

Even if the person themself(s) wants to believe it too. It is always in known, for it is a very strong lower energy. It sinks all within it.

Lying gives to the soul and others nowhere to go, other than to create more lies, to cover on top of the first one.

And they try to convince and convince and no one can hear truth. For the convince of the meek is the leak of the bucket in which they live. And no one can live without water. It is the medicine of life.

Ghosts are not souls who have passed and did not return home right away. Ghosts are the souls living on Earth that speaks not their truth to themself(s) hence to others.

The lying soul is losing the interest of others and that is why there is lacks of interest in some souls and very much interest in others. Souls who are truth attract all humans, for humans want truth.

Souls, who are of lying, lie with no one, in truth.

And souls can not sustain them, for internally souls look for, crave and vascular beat, to the rhythms of truth. It is the music of home. That is truth.

If you want to define truth further, it is the music of home, the cycle of life on Earth, the purity of every soul at home. That is truth.

At times souls do not want to know the truth, for then they will have to respond to it. And they do not want to respond to it so they allow the lie, to give them time to come to truth.

Some never come to it. Some are intentional in rewording truth and little do they know that their energy precedes them. Some come to others in allurements, to take them away from their truth.

They will entice a soul to listen to them. They speak to them as though they are missing something. They speak to them as though they are not current. And only truth is current.

However the falling soul to itself, wants others to fall around it, for then it has company. And that fills yet another avenue of lacks of truth with the foundations of lies to share and the avoidance of truth, love and purity in company.

Souls, who speak ill of another, can not be of truth, they are simply of ill will of self. Hence...
...RUN.

Souls who come and turn the words around of another and want to turn it into truth, and begin with what someone else says and not their role in it...
...RUN.

Someone who tries to convince you that what you see is not what you see, what you feel is not what you feel...
...RUN.

Someone who comes to you and takes what you share with them and turns it around to you without honor to the sharings...
...RUN.

Someone who wants from you and shares not the happenings with you, someone who expects from you and does not expect from self the sameness of things...
...RUN.

You can not be accountable for other souls. Souls are accountable for self. Souly. Solely.

I want to come back to cycles.

Cycles are the rotations of Earth, the rotations of soul. There is time in cycles to do all things, for all things can happen at once in energy. However on Earth in form, the form has to be present in most cases.

*(IN FORM—Our physical bodies)*

However the form of the soul puts out energy to the universe that it wants to, intends to, evolves to, learn and action certain things. And those things will find their way to the soul and the soul to them.

A soul may speak that it wants to marry. It will find a partner only if the truth of the wanting is present.

If it is not present in truth, the soul may still marry however it will not be of eternal, for the soul wanted marriage out of insecurity rather than security.

And all that means that a lesson of security is on the way. And then that soul will live the marriage of experience, before it will come and experience a marriage of eternal. That is a cycle.

There are also rhythms of cycles. These are natural rhythms to bring about the souls purpose and give home to other souls to enter Earth and those are the rhythms of the body.

Souls do not want sex all the time, contrary to popular belief and what I see on Earth at this time. They do not. They are not designed to have sexualness all the time.

However sexualness has been attached to everything and now humans are responding by dressing that way in all of times.

Measuring their success by it, living for it as though they will never experience it, trading partners without caution to what it means to produce as a result of it, having it in groups without the truth of self present, showing the body in pictures as though it is bad or wrong or dirty.

Creating laws restricting who can do what at what age, women wanting to sleep with one man to hurt another.

Men wanting to sleep with other women, to engage in their manhood and eventually hurt others. Soul's sharing bodies and walking away as though they have never truly known each other.

Clubs that give forum, for a woman who does not want to dance and parade her body, her lack of soul's to do it for dollars on Earth.

And all of that, with the soul's price to pay, has the lowest energy of forcing a body's stimulations all the time.

Never to worry Humans, the body is not designed for all the time. So the mind, the ego, has come to ways to bring it about all the time and it does not exist all the time.

And the humans broke the cycle of SEX and LOVE.

It is a cycle. And there is greater love and greater intensity within the cycle than out of the cycle. And souls on Earth are in current, out of the cycle.

Men pay for sex. Women pay for escorts. No one wants to be alone without sex. And sex is not everyday.

That is why God Almighty provides climactic feelings. To release and rebuild as the cycle of life is.

And the cycle has been broken of now, for soul's feel they must be this all the time. And that is a loss to all souls. It has been stripped of the beauty and lives in the undergroundments of thoughts to have sex!

I am sorry to the souls of human's for this one however much monies are made in the process of the breakings of these cycles.

And now, movies are not good, books are titillating, there are lacks of sustainments, souls look good at times and only a few souls feel good.

And once you begin conversations past greetings, there is not sustainess without tiring words of despair; All because the cycle of sexuality, of love, truth and purity is broken in this time.

The cycle of works has been broken in regions of Earth and not in others.

As you can see the country in which you live no longer produces, for it broke the cycles of work. Work is not always either. Work is designed to produce and accomplish.

However when there are lacks of truth there are lacks of work. Even though it appears that everyone is working all the time. And they are however they are wasting time and there is not work done.

Souls can not be work all the time, sex all the time, what pressures of stagnations are left for the human journeyman to endure. So all this work is simply moving monies around and nothing is produced.

Countries that you do not reside in, in some they have given life a chance to live and work a place to live in the creativity of growth from within. That is the cycle.

Where you reside you had to witness the death of the soul in order to endure the payments of home, car, foods, and stuff, stuff, stuffs. There are not feelings.

Souls do not have time to release pressures. And within that the sex they are supposed to be having all the time is not felt.

The foods that are eaten in many cases are not food, the works that are to be done are non producing. And the soul knows not where to go for the growth of mission.

To speak of the growth of mission is the obscure thought, "Oh, you are one of those people who believe in slowing down in feeling."

That is how far feeling is from souls that feeling is an alternative way of thinking. Glory be to God Almighty. SHAVEESKA, as you would speak so many times in thoughts.

All of these natural cycles are now forced and reckoning on the souls within them. I simply wanted to show you cycles and how they are broken and why.

For you will speak of this and it will be up to the will of the souls on Earth as a whole to bring back to themself(s) their rhythm and the cycles of life on Earth.

I wanted to speak to you of sexualness. You are in truth that the other side of love has not been touched in this time. Nor is it on the brinkdom of knowledge's.

You see our love, love is love is love. Souls revel in the knowings that two bodies of the sameness can see each other in a touching way. Let me explain to you further the ranks of how it is to love.

If love is love is love, why can not souls love each other? Sex is separated. There are many different balances of energy amongst souls. The body can not do what the soul cannot do.

If the soul can feel, see, touch, be, it will be with the body no matter what it is. Affections and kissing's and touchings of any kind means that the body will feel the knowing of another soul.

The body in truth does not know if it is a boy or a girl, for gender does not know love. Love is love is love. Touch is genderless.

Souls make a statement by who they choose to be with, to absorb the energy of. If a male serves a male or a female serves a female that is choice and free will.

It taps on the fears of existing boundaries and limits of the human realm in this time. However the fears do not make it go away nor do they create it.

They simply want to hide it and now it is not so hidden and it threatens, for innately souls understand that love is love is love. And they fear that love.

If they see it it does not mean they will want it. However fear tells them so. And they do not want to feel outcasted in doing so.

For then they are not a man or a woman and in truth bodies are simply in uniform. There are not genders at all. Souls have not genders.

The earthly uniforms are simply to use for attractions hence the coming of more souls to Earth. It is generally the only way in. So simple is the truth.

If souls are genderless and want to share love it will not take away from the souls who are coming. There are enough movements to enter souls without the use of all human souls to do so.

There are souls who do not attract to sameness of gender and they do not entrance souls to Earth as well.

There is not perfection there is love.

There is no perfection there is hope.

There is no perfection there is truth.

There is not perfection there is honor.

And souls want that to be true. That is why I was not of married in my time nor took on other souls.

I had to know I was an Angel coming onto Earth. I had to be an example.

I did not have need for love the same as souls on Earth. And until now, the unrelatability exists.

For the desire for hope, for truth and for honor has held me in place for a long time. The innovation of God Almighty can only come, for the love of the missions souls come to challenge within!

Glory be to God Almighty, for souls want to believe and it has been a long time in believing anything based on the truth they come to Earth with. As you spoke, "if we believe there is death, how could we not believe this?"

How could we not believe in love and journeys and understandings of what is not seen and now is seen. And yet the explanations are based on the taughts of error rather than truth. Glory be to God Almighty.

For the tables will not only turn, they will roll down a hill in pieces. And the love of love will surface without a table to be seen on, for the table is the crutch that shows nothing underneath it.

We need no support. We simply need the truth of love. We need no teachings without the truth of love within them; All else carries no weight within.

And souls are filled with foods that do not nourish them. It feeds them the ills of life and then they spread the only things that they have come to know and that is the ills of life hence the ill willers.

Nadia, I take you with me to show you the travels of pure will. Pure will, the smaller entrances you see from Earth and the grander opening that exists once passed through.

That is what the soul encounters on their way home, in the moments of greatest Earth purity. That is why some souls feel and are left behind, for in their moments of release to home they do not see home.

They do not come home, for the only asking is of one cell of purity within.

They will come to it in time however it is simply not their time and part of their lessons are catalyst for others to learn.

There is not a mistake or there are not mishaps in perfections, in truths, in love and in purity.

All mishaps of Earth are soul generated within their beliefs of what they want reality to be.

Nadia, you can see, for I traveled you to yet another plane of evolution. You witnessed souls who came for greater density.

That is different from Earth. For Earth is the evolvement of love through the understanding of Truth, Love and Purity and the plane on which I traveled you is a soul's journey to further density.

That is why you witness the pureness so quickly. No buildings, no barriers, no limits. The soul leaves home to encounter their depth of self with no affects to others in their journeys.

It is the most personal plane of all, for the souls do not depend on each other as on Earth's plane. The energy is the acknowledgement knowingly of other planes.

The pureness you felt gives them travel to other planes to visit for a short time and take in the measurements of love on Earth and then they return to their plane and purify the truths of what they encountered and then they depthen.

They take on the experiences of other planes and travel back in contemplations of their knowings. And they purify them and return the love back, for growth of others hence the growth of themself(s).

And that is why you witness no buildings or moving vehicles as on Earth. There is pure energy present so means of travel are of thought not of things.

On Earth, Thoughts are things, for the will has to be in presence of heart to move energy along. That is how energy moves on Earth.

And you were in witness of a plane that travels on purity. These are the truth of gifts of Love, Truth and Purity.

You see Nadia, on Earth there are many who want to cheat something. They start with themself(s) and appearance of things.

The thoughts are mostly opposite of the very things there is claimance to acquire.

Thoughts are things and the mixings up you witness are of mind, heart and soul, not of the things that you witness. All has evolved to the physical anatomy of a human body. That is a thing. Love is eternal.

Yet now, all souls dress in a manner to attract to the body and the heart is no longer seen. Women of any age want to be one age. They lost the beauty of growth.

Men of any age want to be attractive to women. There is no longer a pure intent of heart towards women. Sexual deviations and hurtfulness to women, children and men have come to a common place of conversation.

All souls want for sexual attractiveness and those who have not matured yet in internal growth are taught that that is all that matters. And souls are confused when their body's growth and their souls do not.

When there is reachance of ages without knowledge's or experiences. When the souls of Earth can not see why they can not see.

And it is that the thoughts of their minds can not find coupling with other humans in easements, for the body can not sustain what the soul can.

Women get married and still look for desire elsewhere for they got married in body not in heart.

And when troubles arise there is disrespect and they are hit and meangled by yet another man who knows not himself enough to sustain daily life in openness.

There are sexual takings from marriages simply because souls do not know each other well enough.

When love becomes possession it no longer looks like love anymore.

And in time, all the feelings of love begin to question.

And the separations of heart begin in the lack of trust of one soul in the beginning stages of wanting to dominate another.

Souls of meek, clump together, hoping of all hopes that as a group they can be stronger and the bond will be unseeable, untouchable and unbreakable.

However the only unbreakable bonds of any souls on Earth are the bonds of pure energy.

Truth, love and purity. The triangular force of pure energy, for that is the only energy that can flow through a soul in freedom of that very soul.

Without that flow, souls try to control, speak and respeak, do and redo, come and come again, until they believe that you believe them, even when they do not believe in themself(s). Glory be to God Almighty.

All love must be fought for, for the strength of love comes from the Saphi.

*(SAPHI—The souls of clair vision. Of self. Of others. That is Saphi. There has not been a word yet for the world has not earned it yet. And now it has.)*

The Saphi are the souls who pick up after the rest, let the light of others shine.

For they understand the value of such action(s), they service souls without question and they give them the room to expand, growth and they foster the opportunities of love.

They speak to all souls with the same levels of respect, only for the knowledge and action of self respect.

They hunger to live amongst the souls on Earth and to feed them with love, truth and purity, for the simple reason that that is who they are.

For the souls peace unto itself, is the peace of others. Glory be to God Almighty.

# CHAPTER 8

# CHALLENGES

I speak to you now of challenges. Challenges and the refinement of a souls fears within. For challenges take away fear when the challenge is met.

There are many who say, you take on what you can handle and when you handle what you take on you grow. When you put it off you stagnate.

And when you ignore it you are taking away from yourself in all that you will do. The lessons of life are the soul purpose of existence.

For a soul to enter Earth and reject the choices of home they wanted to experience, for the evolution of love's strength to evolve all souls into one are the challenges of love's energy and that is the awry that you witness now on Earth.

It is the equivalent of God truly taking away from a soul. Even with the impossibility of that thought, those who think it will it to themself(s).

And to come to Earth and say No to oneself, No to God, No to all energies around their soul, they are saying, "I am not fulfilled and I do not know why."

They do know why however they do not want to say it, to speak of it, for then they are accountable to their challenges. Challenge is the purpose.

If a soul comes to you and speaks "Why are we here?" You can speak "for the challenge." Challenges are not the "bad luck" of souls.

Challenge is the fortune that is found, once the treasure is found, and the trail of answers to it are answered hence the evolution of a soul. And then a soul believes it will get to settle once they know a certain answer of life.

However the challenges of life keep the answers of life close to heart and the internal knowing that learning is infinite.

Love can only grow and compassion can only be shared when the knowledge's of heart are known to a soul. The strength of love is greater than any energy in the Universe.

That is what keeps a soul in tryings and trials of not giving up. For the internal truths, the laws of the universe speak to souls that love will win.

Love has turned into a commercial of itself. It has been attempted to be defined however you can not define love. To define love is to take away love in everything.

Love is not in some things. Love is in all things, in all souls, in all happenings. To leave Love out of the equation is to not have love at all, to not have any equation at all.

Love is not looked at as energy. When a soul is sad or lonely and that soul thinks of love, they believe they have none of it. And that is only due to their blindness that it is there.

If they were to walk outside they would feel love.

To speak to souls from heart, that is love. To care for oneself in preparations to grow, to acknowledge the wanting to grow, to not push energy away from themself(s) simply to prove that there is no love, then they will prove just that.

Earth is a mirror of a soul. Those who come to Earth in Birth come with the knowledge that they are in reflection of the mirror of the current souls.

The mind will not see what it does not want to show the heart. That is the detriment of ego. That is the allowance of ego.

What is fame?

Fame is like saying that a star is shining when the star in the sky is an airplane, for nothing is as it seems.

Souls need to be of remembrance of mission. Of heart. Of honesty to self. For the self of a soul only has itself. And it can not have others in truth until it can have itself in truth.

The imbalance of truth within has brought about the ripple of the imbalance of the truth that exists in this time. There is very little truth. There are businesses run on complete non truths.

And they are paid for by many to see, witness, have, hear, be a part of. And all partake, for the lacks of options overcome and the choices made easily to take away from one and very difficult to give to oneself.

When a soul comes to terms to giving to oneself it has to make great effort; to eat right, to sleep in comfort, to exercise the body, to find help and hope for the mind.

Souls feel they must go to others for this when the others they go to are of human as well and they are paying another to teach them what they already know of themself(s). The faith in oneself is minimal and the faith in others is of greater stance to souls on Earth.

That is the lack of honesty you speak of Nadia. The lack of trust we speak of.

We use money that is not ours on Earth for the things outweigh the tragedy of spending what we don't have, what is not ours and paying premium money we do not have back.

It is a choked stance to remain in.

Souls go to workplaces that they live in, they spend most of their time in, with souls they do not trust with their intentions nor emotions. And the workplace is an example of a million.

They speak of each other in ill will and they come to speak as though they do not. Is this person trusted? Once this is seen it is a struggle for others to feel trust and to speak truth.

It becomes a chore and the passion of loving your work is gone as well. It is reflected in how business is accomplished.

For the soul's energy in the pushments of tasks, papers, meetings, gatherings, helpments to others, producing a product of use rather than hindrance to fellow souls on Earth has taken a seat in the back of the room.

Do you want the student who sits in the back of the room to go to for advice? The souls on Earth in this time are sitting in the back of the room.

No one wants to come forward and speak in chargements of heart. There is much walking together as a unit, for no one needs be accountable then.

Statements when troubles are had are not spoken by those in the trouble however spoke persons, who spin truth into non evasive statements. And the paychecks are collected and the works are fighting to get accomplished.

Delay Delay Delay, for lacks of soulutions from heart. Souls wait for others to have heart and then they want to follow them. For they will feel validated and will attach onto another success to look good themself(s).

Nadia, Earth has become a mind lazy on the edges and a soul who knows not of itself. So we have a mind that is ego without drive and we have no soul that is willing to be a soul.

We provide roadmaps and movies on how to hurt each other. We have news programs of war and we have movies of mass killings.

We have found every way to explain the stories of fear of our ego's, worried about our body's death. We show souls who are in imbalance and that sells tickets and makes money.

And when you do a story of truth, souls walk by waiting for the bait of the fear that they live in to respond to. Souls have sex and they do not feel it. Souls eat much food and do not taste it. Souls watch much film and do not remember it.

Souls speak of all that angers them. Souls find it boring to speak of growth, for then they do not feel at home and they are outnumbered.

The souls are in the opposight of truth, of their truth. It is not seen and rarely felt. And when it is felt it is discounted and covered up as though it was never there.

*(OPPOSIGHT—Saying we did not see what we saw, or hear what we heard)*

Souls do not honor that truth, and the truth can not be seen therefore not grown from hence stagnation.

Nadia, I come to you with this, for souls seem to expend energies on what they do not have and care nothing of what they do have.

They can not speak yes or no. They speak maybe, for their intentions are not clear. Souls wait for things to happen to them and do not come with the creative forces of heart, for the laziness of the body comes first.

Souls want attention for things they do not do. They want attentions of any kind. It is amazing my soul to see that the souls of Earth in this time will want anything, unearned and earned.

Souls believe they are fooling the world in which they live and if they are fooling themself(s) and they are fooling the world then we are amongst fools!

I speak not of all souls however many live within this stance. And they ripple onto the masses and the masses isolate from each other because of it.

As well, souls when they want something, they have attention aggressive, at salute behaviors. And when they do not want something they wither away to "I am sick, I am tired, I am, I am." It is all selective.

There is illness that is created simply to accommodate the ill willed, the ill minded and the ill intended to self. There are many of them and they are also responded to with medications.

It has manifested into an entire financial kingdom for the worlds pharmacy. And now even pharmaceutical companies are not trusted in completeness, for the dollars of the pocket override.

Nadia, I keep bringing you back to the profits over soul; Profits over fitness of heart; Profits over the grand of fellow journeymen.

As the Profits of Politics are more prevalent the human soul no longer carries weight.

Everyone is at a loss of growth when souls on Earth are singled out and killed and taken out of the human pool and turned non human in efforts for profits.

It is seen and felt inside. And the souls of Earth all know of it, including the souls that are doing it.

However, they believe their souls to be worth more than others, the "better thans." And profits for their things increase the anxiety of the souls of Earth further. For now there is not trust of leaderships, companies, neighbors and fellow souls. There is not trust of humanity and honor.

For the soul working at a company is eyeing another. The soul of commitment beds another. The souls of leaders make dealments with souls of like ill intentions and speak not of what they are doing in truth.

These souls are the **dismembers. They are not members of the human energy**. They are dismembers of the human energy.

They want the glory for everything they do, or they shrink into a self defeating silence that hides them until they can present what they have been working on to "show" the world they are worth it, for they believe they are not, no matter what anyone speaks, for "worth it" to them is to be better than.

The basis, the foundations of the energy of Earth, lives in infraction of itself.

There is another side and it can not be seen, for who could it be seen by when souls can only see what they think they want and not what they really want. And that lack of truth has brought about desperations of yet another kind.

If souls could only know the love they can not see, can not feel, is already there, is already in existence. However, they can not partake in it, for they are not in the existence of their soul.

The soul can only fight for itself. It tries to cry out to its human side that there is more to life than is seen and the mind cries back, "what is seen is most important."

The struggles of humality are the challenges of the mind and the soul: Lacks of emotion and emotion, self motivation and pure intent. For that is the purpose of Earth. Of the growths that take place on Earth.

(HUMALITY—Common traits of us that we all share in basic needs and wants)

All stems back to the mind and the soul on the journeys of truth, love and purity.

There is nothing that can be in settlements of Earth without the pure intent of the few that live in it, the few that choose it and learn the glories of the other sides of love, truth and purity.

Souls believe they have already found the greatest joy's in life and that they can not afford them. As though the greatest joys in life are monies and things, Oh, how the blind eye can not know what it is missing.

The lacks of monies are the only lacks of on Earth that bring the heart to its barings onto the truth of what happiness can be.

For those who say because of no money I am not happy, have lost the lesson and remain in their stance until the do. So simple is the truth.

And those who have monies and share and grow others in the truth of their intent, they speak to the world, "I know I am of love and I appreciate the knowing that I am. And I will give what I have," for a soul can not give what it does not have.

The soul who has the monies and speaks not I am happy, will as well stay with the monies until the soul can find happiness, not because of it.

Having monies or not having monies both teach the same lessons. For nothing is as it seems.

Glory be to God Almighty, for the human souls have the love of home and the support of their knowledge of it, and most do not want to know.

They believe they have the answers and the answers can not be answers if the soul does not have the questions. The answers are not things, they are YOU. Then they are others.

And then all else comes into the heart of the truth of the soul. One change has to happen before another can. One life has to understand itself before it can understand another.

Otherwise we have continued dramas of souls in tryments to create situations to feel alive. For nothing else can live them so they do not dig within they warp without.

And you speak to them, "you are warping without" and they anger at you for speaking truth, for they do not want to hear their own truth. Let alone the truth that is seen by others as well.

It is the grandest of gifts to hear Truth and Truth is turned away in morements than lessments.

Souls will speak they understand and they will not want to understand. And they will walk away with another plan and it will not be the plan that you discussed. That is betrayal.

That is why souls will feel anger. And they will say a person hurt them however in truth it is betrayal.

It is sharing love and a soul taking that feeling and telling the other it was worthless to them. That is what it is in appearance.

Speak to all in love and you will be of fine. Speak to the world as the messages are for repair and reprise, for returnance of a soul unto itself.

Speak to the world we are one, have we forgotten? No need for anyone to say Christ is important. You are important. It is to speak to the world that we are all of great value.

We all have different missions, and you, Stirling and I, and many others have chosen the mission to keep humanity on the Earthly missions in the remembrance of home in challenge. So simple is the truth on Earth.

On this Earth that can reform its energy for growth and takings away at bay; that the profiteering at the expense of humanality is of lack of honor, integrity, trust, love or any shred of purity.

*(HUMANALITY—The traits of us as souls on Earth)*

That the souls of Earth once killing one, is on its way to killing the souls of all, whether their souls are Earthly dead or alive.

The souls coming home have a break of energy from Earth that astounds their souls on arrival back to home.

For to look back they could see how easy it was to have been in greater truth of one self and how fear grabbed too much of the share of emotions on Earth.

How ego was swaying without a plan and how soul fought for its time within the limited free will souls believed that they possessed.

For on returnance to home there is great learning of witness to seeing the affect of actions unpure of heart and the ripple affect of events; And the pure intented moments and the inner joys and remembrance of others that was brought on.

A wife speaking ill of her husband to others once witnessed at home will find he heard her words in energy.

A husband stepping aside of his love knowing at home the wife always heard the energy.

A child who hides in the corner will find that the mother and the father could speak of the child and the child will wonder how and in greaterments, grow security that he had support.

That a company soul, who steals from the souls who labor is known and shredded in honor, for his energy is of repellant.

And the askings of questions before public knowings were the soul responding to the energy that already exists. Glory be to God Almighty.

The dead are not the souls who return home. It is the souls who dismember. They are not only dead; they are trying to deaden all that lives around them as well.

To focus on one's self, is to speak that I do not care for myself or others, and that is the repellent, not the propellant.

NO ONE deserves a soul of hindrance, not even the soul of hindrance itself. That is what we call hope.

If not for one's self, there would not be the hindrance and the hope that comes to them, comes to them from the hope of others, for hope is eternal.

Love. Truth. Purity. Free Will. Choice.

That is all life's foundation.

Life's Challenges.

# CHAPTER 9

# GARTH AND CORTH

Nadia, souls have found the paths to take away and can not see the paths of growth. The paths that are taken have left souls in bewilderment of stance hence the bewilderment of life and they can not see their purpose.

Many souls will ask themself(s) and others, what is my purpose? Why am I here? Why am I not special? For the gifts of soul's are the soul's gifts and the gifts are overlooked and can not be seen.

And that loss of sight has given way to taking on actions with self and others that leaves a soul without soulution, without solvations, without truth of self present.

Sexuality, it is the driver of all souls. For the souls know not the greater ecstasies of the heart and souls involvement. You see, without passion a cook's food will be cooked however it will not have taste.

Without passions a painters painting will have paint however without attraction, for love will not be present. Without passions a child can be raised however the child will not know its own love.

Passions are a relationship with a spouse. Without passions the weaknesses are to the forefront and the strengths remain untapped and unnoticed.

With passions the glory of the perfection of love will carry both souls into the growth of who they are.

Without passions souls have no direction. They will live in robotic stances of routine and annihilations of other souls, for the jealousies and threatenments will precede the love and the integrity.

The compromisations of souls can only happen when the soul itself says it is welcome. That is in taking responsibilities for actions, for the why's of a life on Earth. And then the soul can say "this is who I am. This is where I start."

To not speak truth to oneself is to say, "I do not love you enough even to know you. I am sorry soul, I will not be able to take care of you. So I will just use the body that I am in and I will go home when I am done here. Until then I will be on pause."

And then nothing is felt in entirety. For how could it be when a soul has been unable to see itself? How could it see another? Nadia, souls need love. Tender love. Tender care.

There is much to speak to the souls of themself(s).

The internal tyrannies of souls have taken on a form of much speaking's of non truths, for it is difficult to carry a conversation of the seen when the unseen is not the working effort. Souls are living in the seen.

They have forgotten the unseen and no longer understand its resource to them.

For its ripple on Earth is so rampant, that when leaders come to surface in the levels of lacks of prudency, which are being spoken on as corruption in your world at this time, it stems from all souls acceptance of not working together. And leaving tasks for others and not understanding we are all in this together.

There are not teams. We are all one side. We are all on the same team. Earth is one team.

One peoples, one journey, for all who choose to come to it. The struggles of lacks of love have predominated the tone of experiences, choices, wantings, and desperations.

Nadia, to feel the human soul in this extentedness of trials is to understand that love when walked down the road of self motivation does not feel like love at all.

It is not the pure love of home at all. It is desperate, diluted, pretended, accepted in its pretendment, acted, visualized, talked about as though it is a thing and treated as a prize that is won.

It is everything love is not, in the name of love. The honor of a soul unto itself is absent.

Nadia, to mesh within your soul, to mesh into the energy of Earth in this time, has brought to the light of home the truth in the findings of love under veil.

What happens to a soul when they have to them the experience of lacks of love? They do not appear as such however the love of families, the nurturing of mothers, it is sporadic at most.

And these souls, who come down to Earth in home, with experiences in tow, find that love is absent very quickly.

It is replaced with ego, reflection, rules that make not sense to the mind and heart however they appear as love and teachings. And within that, souls speak not of love and emotion, of mission.

Speaking's of God Almighty are in speakments of all you can not do.

Who cares if a soul cheats, steals, lives in anger, once that soul has been tormented into living against love in truth, with the lacks of love. For the souls of parenting's are speaking two languages to children.

They are tough on the children in the name of love however if the children had love in truth they would not need to be toughed on.

Love is freedom Nadia. It is not seen. Love is honor. It is not felt. Love is growth. There is much in lacks of growth.

Nadia, I speak to you in honor of love. We are angels of love. WE have the works of the world to do. You see our love; the insecurities come from lacks of choice for censored love to souls.

There are souls who come with great love and they withstand however those who come with lesser missions, they are in disarray of soul to live out the remainder of missions.

Some overcome and they are few. Those who wallow, who live in the pain and can not see the other side; they will in turn live in the desperations of love and that is not the truth of love at all.

When a soul says "I have to be with this person or that," that is desperation. That is not love of self.

When a soul speaks in beauty when a soul is not present and in harshness when the soul is present, that is not love that is ego's trickery.

When a soul speaks, "I need him, her, them, it," it is out of the sheerness of insecurity and the lacks of love that can not be seen and it appears as love, does it not?

And when that soul receives what it wants it turns its back on it. Now it is easy, for that is ego not love.

You see Nadia, the soul's rejection of self stems from the rejection of others in the early piercings of their truths. That is simple.

However the manifestations of suchness are what are invisible. Invisible to the eye of self and to others, for all are finding this to be their range, their own growth.

That saying that speaks, "Misery loves company." This is the most populated spot our love. It is the most populated spot.

Nadia our love, you see many provings to others and emptiness of self involved.

You see the speaking's, the discoveries and the soul not knowing what to do with the real feelings and knowing what to do with insecurities. I will call it filling holes.

The holes are many and they are in depth. For the love to surface can only come with a lot of work. A lot of work our love.

Love is the most fragile energy and it is the energy of greatest strength. Love is in its complete fragility at this time on Earth.

It took many years of transformations of heart and souls lacks of love to say that the usement of your body is not taking away from you. That if you steal once it is OK.

The soul's of the souls will tell you it is not OK, to hurt another and not feel that you did, to talk of others in their absence, in takings away from them in intent.

Souls speak of others always however those who speak in takings away know they are doing it.

Nadia there is more. I speak in amazements once again at what I hear in the thoughts of the thoughts of mind and heart on Earth.

To believe the truth is harder than to believe a non truth. Souls want to be lied to, for then they have something to do and they do not have to account for it.

Souls want to be wronged, for then they have a forum to not have to withstand anything else. Souls want attentions for everything they do and what they do is the least of what is asked of them.

Souls want love. When they themself(s) seek it in insecurity and they want secure love from it.

Souls want to drug, to say to self, "I do not like you, let alone love you. You are not worth taking care of and I am now going to hurt you still and some more so that I do not even have to hear you."

That is the truth of any drug taking on Earth. It is self mutilation and the greatest extent of lack of self love.

It is the heart wanting to kill the body to kill the heart.

And druggedness is rampant. What does that tell me?

To think of it as a pleasure, to kill the soul is not of pleasure and it is not seen for what it is. It is the lacks of love in life that need soothings, only to bring on greater lacks of love of self. Glory be to God Almighty.

Nadia, to live on Earth is of greatest challenge to Love. I am only love and I am in searching's for its truth amongst peoples.

I can see the mishaps and the blindness' of soul that accompany them. When souls come to souls with news of other souls, to speak of in enticements to another, it is of natchure to the receiving soul.

Their actions are of natchure. Not nurture. They will want to bring ill will to fruition.

They will natchure the truth to their likings and call it truth and it is not. They will speak in terms of raising questions of doubt and they will leave it as such.

*(NATCHURE—The opposite of nurture, competitiveness of who is better, wiser, stronger, or even more desirable)*

For the weaknesses are their own projections. And they want to file into the weaknesses of another for the company of

They will speak, "This woman said this, this man said that, that girl is this, that man is that," as though we are all not human, as though we are not all on the same team.

As though there are those humans and these humans. I ask. Where did all the humans come from? Why do there have to be divisions? Nadia, you are in witness of the stemming of these issues with the youngments of souls.

And you are speaking and you are in witness that the souls on Earth are not so sure they want solvations. They are more sure they want the moments and not the futures of moments in heart.

They want the now when the now is gone in moments.

When there is purity there is not time. Time is made for those in experience. However once eternal thought lives within a soul in truth, the soul lives without the measures of time.

And the brilliance of that soul and the passions of that soul will have no way to go on Earth, other than to be shared and cherished by all humans who still have an opening of hope within, that they too can find eternality and home on Earth.

That is the subconscious. No one is famous. Brilliance is famous. No one is great. Passion is great.

No one can be loved that does not love. To love others is to be loved.

All purpose has a reason.

And all purpose has a challenge and all challenge has a purpose.

Only a few souls will stay within your scope throughout life on Earth. Once you find eternal it will be of such. However a child who does not find eternal within parent does not stay within parent.

Parents who do not want their children do not have eternal. They can not wait until they leave. Imagine the child's thoughts. For all energies are known.

And the one who loves teaches the one who does not. And the glories are when eternal is met. That is the completion of mission, upon gaining the eternalness of life on Earth. For it does not end.

Souls do not die. People die. Souls live.

At home there are no people. There are souls. At home there are not things there are passions. There are gifts.

At home there is not better than it is different from. At home there are not obstacles to truth; there are evolvements of learning's.

At home there are not clothing's and cars. There are not attachments of any kind, needs of any kind.

There is the freedom of love in purest form and there is no comparison on Earth or any other dimension, plane or galaxy.

And yet Nadia, every soul knows of this, and the farther awayments of souls has taken on the form of insecurities of mind, heart and body. And the results are spending Earth time out of lessons that were come for and the filling of holes to begin to lesson.

You were thinking that these are the lessons. Yes Nadia, yet when a soul hears truth, it does not know enough to enlist in the truth it knows. And it tortures itself into the wiles of heart and mind and body and soul.

A woman who will sleep with a man of no commitment and will sleep with many has pierced her love.

She can dance, she can sing, she can work, she can mother, and she will not feel the intensity of love, for she took her love away and lost the center of herself.

A man who will sleep with many will only want to sleep with many, for it is a false manhood to do so. For then he will see, he will want, and he will be use to walking away. For what could he feel?

Any body could ejaculate Nadia. However can any body love? And yet it appears that that soul is desirable and in truth he would be the least desirable for that very reason.

I will tell you why now. To share the depths when there is no depth there, it affects the garth of a human soul; the garth of the human soul.

The gut as it is called on Earth at times, it is the inner awakenings. It is the anticipation of reward and love. The understanding of its truth within and shared without.

The garth tells you when to leave and when to stay.

When there is love it is tricky, for a soul will try to tell its garth, "It is OK for this moment, it means nothing." And even then the garth gets in usements of it meaning nothing. And then it means something, and they will fear it, and even greater insecurities will surface.

And then actions are taken on in insecurity rather than security. Stems stems stems. You see our love; it is the mainstay of thoughts.

I speak not that there is right or wrong. What could right or wrong be?

However, I speak that there is trust of self that is not known or touched. Reacted to or honored.

I speak that lies of souls to themself(s) are now onto the lies of others hence the world is in greater liements of truth.

For there is not balance. It stems from the insecurities of lacks of love.

I speak much of love, and love is love is love. And yet to explain that, I have to speak on what love is not, for love became something that it is not.

It is not a commodity and yet it is treated in such manners as to strip it of its soul purpose.

And that is to growth, to comfort, to trust, to build faith in life as you know of it on Earth, to complete mission and come home.

It is of greatness of love that I speak to you on this. There are many who speak, "He will take me, she will love me, you did this to me, I did that to you," about what they perceive as partners in love.

As well, it is the perception that they are separate, when the other party is spoken on as He or She.

There is not We in the speech, for then you can hear in that moment entitlement of souls needing from another and lacks of sharing.

And the partnership that is sought after is separated before it can even begin to feel as though it started.

It is the partnerships that are always in question of themself(s). To speak in We is to build a trust in your love of yourself hence others.

To speak in I is to say, "I am too afraid to say We, so I will say I until you prove to me we are a We." You have to state if we are dating, if we are going to marry, if you bought me this, how do you refer to me? What have you done for me, does it say you love me?

Souls want clues, cues and answers, rather than knowing that they are of love.

They have the measurements of success and it strangles the relationships stance to grow, when one soul or the other is responsible to say and do things, that say or do not say that a relationship exists.

The forum of ownership, the loss of the search of love and the creation of what love is thought to be. When souls are in love they know it and all the rules go away.

Rules are for the souls who are too timid to think. And rules are created by those who take on that souls are too timid to think. And they control them and live off of the souls who are too timid to think.

Love transcends all the rules, for the rules of today did not exist in times passed, and it makes no difference that they did not exist.

And now is the time when they do exist and souls have to abide by the rules to benefit others and give up their choices in thinkments of self. It is simpler than it appears.

Rules rule the souls who ask not to rule themself(s). There are those who benefit and they can live off the energy of those who care not to think of self in the equation.

Many souls will say, "I have to do this or that," because of this rule or that rule. They have learned to leave spontaneity of heart and soul behind to conform to rules that make no matter in this time, or future, or past.

And souls carry that very loss of passion and they can not fully stimulate the love they seek from others, from self.

Stimulations have taken on many forms of growth and yet many souls have come to desensitization of many feelings, many gifts, many forums that can lead them to greatest auxiliary of love and they walk by it like it will hurt them.

Especially the minds that speak to themself(s) that, "Nothing is going to work, nothing is great in life. I am tired and I will settle into what I can get for now," and not realize that they can take on the depth of their soul.

And their soul sits and waits and once in a while the soul will tell the mind, "I am here and I am not happy here, I am lonely, no one has looked at me in such a long time."

The soul will fight for its passion and that is what depression is: When the passion of a soul is ignored.

Deeper depression comes to light when a soul will take on another soul to fix them, and find out that now you have burdened two souls to cover up one's passion.

Souls have not found their love. The struggles that souls face and the options they give themself(s) without the love of self.

When a soul feels insecure, they take away from themself(s) the very things, people that they love. When a woman feels insecure with men, she will seek to lure many of them to prove her insecurity wrong.

When a man feels insecure he will want to feel desirable by women and he will seek to lure many to him to prove his insecurity wrong.

When a mother feels insecure she will create many rules to be a mother and she will use that to prove her insecurity wrong.

When a father feels insecure he will stay away from the home and he will work hard and say it is for his family to prove his insecurity wrong.

When a child feels insecure they will latch onto problems and blame the problems to prove their insecurity wrong.

When a soul violates others, steals, cheats, hurts others, in physical or emotional they are simply trying to prove their insecurities wrong.

Trust that love will strengthen souls in one way or another. And it will.

For souls who wait for you to fail, wait for suchness upon themself(s).

It is all reflection. Souls on Earth, they are of love in origination.

Live in your truth. Love is present. Anger serves no purpose. Lying, cheatings, stealing, are punishments of self hence insecurities of soul.

Souls on Earth, they are here to lesson and to learn. And the answers they seek in truth and pure intent they will see the answers.

And when truth and pure intent are not present there is nothing anyone can do to "prove" to them anything. Glory be to God Almighty.

For God Almighty will give and to those who can see they have to choice to live within their truth. For that is the only way to love.

A soul is a soul. Love is love. Truth is truth. Purity is purity. There is not explaining it, it is known in each soul on Earth.

That is why the takers away hide behind what they said, why they said it, how they said it, what they meant by it.....all the takers away feel like they have to explain everything.

**The truth simply stands alone. There is not an energy stronger than love. There is not an intention greater than purity.**

There is not an explanation, a reason that can dispute this; it is the law of the Universe.

Those who try may look successful however it is of impossible to sustain. Glory be to God Almighty.

I wanted to speak to you of Corth. It is the step before forth. It is the word of the world that is missing and it is the feelings in greatest soughtments of souls.

It is the distance between self perception and the wants, the dreams of a soul, as to who they could be.

It is the distance of self worth and knowledge and the limits and boundaries to marginalize that in a human's work.

Corth is the work before a soul can move forth. It you move forth before Corth, you will move forth without the full understanding of your actions.

Souls are crying out in silent tears. They do not want to share, they want to own and not give anyone else the love of life. That is the essence of the meek.

They will only share for a price, simply because they can be bought. Love is not for sale. Love is.

That is why when you witness the sale of body on the television and the women speak of their love of sex, for they know not who they take on in body.

The souls coming to them care for sex not for soul. The souls coming to them, that they open their garth to, could be criminals, could be married, could be in dishonor of life, just as they could be the fearful of soulful love in life.

They take on all the souls who know not themself(s), for to know a soul of self, the garth would not allow this to be for them.

What happens to these souls when the body can not be sold? For they can be bought! Do you see?

Any soul that can be bought, it matters not what it is; the soul will know it did not come to life on terms of garth.

It will justify itself by things, happenings, and not allow the heart to take on its truth.

It will appear to; it will speak it is happy to be doing, when all souls on Earth instinctively know garth is compromised, for the soul does not know how to live in truth, without garth of a soul being in complete knowings of its truth.

You see our love, all souls know of their truth. Their Corth, the garth, the nurture of compassion, the understanding of sustainments, for all comes and goes in the lives of those of purchase.

For there will always be something to buy, someone to manipulate, and the control of getting it and fighting to not share it when you have it.

And to give it away easily, when you are not contented that this thing, this person, brings you the happiness you bargained for with the dollars of the heart.

So you discount them and then they have no value to you whatsoever and you leave them. You see, that is what the lacks of garth appear as.

That is what fascinates souls and that is why souls watch. They are witnessing lacks of garth and it fascinates, for souls want to see the violence, the scares, the fears, the promiscuity that lacks of garth appear as.

That is why souls will speak as they witness "that is something I never want to do," and those with Corth's that are far away, will speak that is something I want to do.

That is not feeling self hence life and letting the world feel the pain, the insecurity that the garth is not strong enough within to expose itself in lackedness.

So simple is the truth. And souls will say it is great, try it, it is money, food, home, and yet that is not in heart.

They will name everything they have and nothing they feel. That is Earth in this day.

There is war and it is said it is good! For who? Only the few that are buying and selling, not only themself(s) however extended the invitation to the world at large.

They speak it is good, we are wiping out harm, and they are causing harm. We are bringing safety to all, as all have lost all ground of stability.

They will speak that they are fighting terrorism, as they themself(s) are the terrorists.

Souls fascinate to see the souls who lack garth. Whose Corths are far away from their truth.

You see, it fascinates simply because the challenges of Earth are to find garth, have Corth and have compassion of self, for the world can not share its love, truth and purity that are already present.

The lacks of garth, Corth, compassion, gives way to blindness, to love, truth and purity.

Our love the answers are here and the ears can not hear. The answers are hear and the eyes are simply beginning to see however there are not paths provided in thought and action.

So there are many soldiers in this time and they are spread out and coming together. There is a magnet called pure energy and it is drawing all the soldiers together.

CHAPTER 10

⌒⌒

# THE GENTLEMAN CALLER

This is a book about everyone. It is a book for everyone. Souls come home without the completion of mission, for the taughts in error have led the thoughts of growth on the paths that take away rather than give.

Origins of Truth, Love, Purity, can only teach a soul of itself. There is not judgment there is truth. There is no punishment there is only truth. There is not right or wrong there is only truth.

I speak in many ways, in many avenues, to touch the souls in the paths of understandings to their soul(s).

I was in the conversation you had with your friend. He wants God to take care of him, of people. He does not want to believe he had a hand in his own life of lessons and that is why the lessons are overlooked.

He can not come to terms of taking care of himself, for he is blaming God Almighty, for not taking care of them hence him. His challenge is to stand for himself. To self account.

He is blaming without the appearance he is blaming. By finding all the unanswerable questions, for he understands that no one will or can answer them.

He wants to "stump the coach" to use a human term and he does not want to hear the soulution as you said. Therefore he is unable to live in solvation.

It truly matters not that he believes in God or not. Nadia, you spoke this however he did not hear it.

He wants to be perceived as an intellect however true intelligence wants to grow and move forward and find the answers in life, not demand life to answer him.

This is the foundational core of his wisdom's stump.

He is asking for everything and he is not willing to come to the table and say, "I will be happy otherwise. I will look at my own reasons for blaming and I will begin to build my life onto the life that I want.

Life can not give to me what I do not have. Life can not provide for me. My spirit came to move life, not to have it waiting for me on a platter of silver metals.

I need to take a look at why I expect that, when I do not expect that of myself in this day?"

God will be in energy whether a soul believes in Him or not.

It truly matters none. What does matter is the excuses for not taking on life and blaming the world for its actions when it is the free will of the peoples that takes on the energy of love?

Fear stops this man at your door from greater knowledge's and the fear is of himself, none else.

No one is chosen as you speak. No one. You came to do this without any goal other than service.

Each soul comes to Earth with gifts. And those gifts remain unopened at times throughout mission.

Glory be to God Almighty, for to speak of love to a soul who questions the world in fear of questioning self, leaves the soul without Love, which is God and God which is love.

And I ask, you say you are happy, you need to know of Me through intellect and I speak to you, do you not trust your own soul? You speak you are happy, yet in further speakings you speak you are frustrated.

You want a wife, a happy life, and I will speak to you that no one will be able to love in the way you are putting on another soul, for the love of yourself is not so sure and the love of another will not be so sure as well.

You can not bring unto your life what you do not have. That is why I speak, sex is not love and love can not be one thing. Sex is an act. Love is an emotion and energy.

I speak that sex is greatest of gifts and it is given to all souls, not only to some. What humans do with it is what humans have grown into. Sex is not special to any one person.

Souls live in the prowness of sex, only to find if they do not love the soul they are with they themself(s) feel without soul. There are no mistakes; there are only growths, lessons on Earth.

*(PROWNESS—A bolstered image of one's self when they feel they are in command)*

Once that is not seen the ripple affects of this are self abusement. For this gentleman to speak with you wants to stump and that has been his story for many years.

It stops souls from asking or seeking any further questions that he could be sharing and gaining intimacy. He is fearing so much that he speaks of unanswerables rather than speaking of truths in truth.

It is all so simple and yet many of souls live in this and can live an entire missionless lifetime as this. God is love and Earth is free will and choice.

The gentleman spoke that souls really do not have free will however he has sequestered his own free will.

There are no mistakes. There is not a question that remains without an answer and there will always always always be questions that require a leap of faith of a soul.

For that is the entire purpose of the veil.

This soul wants to read the obscure, to continue to fog his opinion and support it. And then you ask yourself why am I not sure or happy?

He is willing to take on theories that speak of the obscure and the closer to the heart knowings; he is walking right on by.

He comes back with more questions. Questions that the answers matter not to, they are simply distractive questions of self and of others.

The heart that exists within, the soul that came to experience, has been shortchanged itself and it did not even hand over the money.

They are shortchanged into the negative before there was a start started.

You see our love souls can not hear and when they stop hearing all else is of blindness. They are deaf, not as the soul who comes mute.

They are in worserment than those who come not hearing. They use not their gift of hearing. They use their gift of sight to stimulate rather than appreciate. For it is all Ego.

They use their gift of hearing to not hear. I am of bafflement! And with all due intelligence the mind will never overcome the soul.

The soul is on Earth to fight for itself, for its existence. And the soul is eternal and the mind is of Earth.

The mind is the catalyst of development. It is not the superior of thoughts. Nothing is completely figured out ever. There are always greater depths of love, hope, candor, honor, and truth.

There are many evolutions in growths. We are all learners. Those of us who are in service teach however we are learners.

There is a gift in all of us and all of us teach and all of us learn.

That is the truth of truth. And it is fought and debated, challenged and misrepresented in aspects that only fear, doubt and worry can conjure and begin to try and cut at love, truth and purity for simply existing.

I speak to souls, why take away from self?

Some take away from self and chase down other souls into a ditch that neither knows how to climb out of. And others torture themself(s), since they are "nice" people, and blame what they can not change and focus not on what they can grow. What they can change.

There will be the extreme of this personality and they will go as far as living as judge and jury of all souls. And they will not judge themself(s), for they will have all of their anguish lined up in ammunition when spoken to.

It is like a recording. Each soul believes it is so different and they are not. They are a classic frustration of not wanting truth while they are asking for it!

Glory be to God Almighty, if a soul were to witness itself in actions and speech, it would shock its own existence into the reality that they are not prudent to self hence others.

I speak in harshness of souls to souls, for they can not see and the blaming that happens as a result is unwarranted.

And the unwarrentedness gives them the right to speak that everything is wrong. And they can not see the stem, which is of them, to them, to others, at their own inadequacy towards self. This is the helplessness.

Your guest, he is of truth to a point. He claims the searchment of your truth; simply because he wants not to see his. So there is no surprise he can not see yours.

He is a soul who wants to own it. For him to meet you was to put his soul to rest that he is not the only soul on Earth. HE is a talker and he is not a doer.

So he is supporting his argument to not face himself therefore to do not what he is in mission to do. And you did not support his argument. You told him he is not consistent.

He wants to have intellect, for that is all he has however if his intellect is not serving him well, he has to ask himself how much of his intellect is ego and how much of his intellect is from the realness of heart and soul?

There was a feeling of no redemption. The redemption of such a soul lies in the hands of the soul when the anger at God Almighty is present.

For the redemption can not find a road to live on, a path to clear, a way to think, that life is bigger than the meager facts of needing to know anything. Everything is perception.

A soul can not force knowledge nor can they use knowledge as a weapon.

These souls that we mention and they are many, do not have trust in self nor in life. And they are the least accounted souls on Earth. They have not accounting. And the trickery of the ego will say that they do.

They will speak that they believe a point of view, a thing or act of themself(s) however they will only speak on the obvious.

And then when the truths are presented to them they will find a way to make it not truth, in order to continue their arrangements with their ego that they will appear in the greatness that they are not.

Ego will want the attentions of the world without the earnments of heart. They want the short cuts. They are what I would call the "show-ers" of the world.

"Look at me, I did this, I went here, I ate that." They speak in a way that makes others respond in wanting to walk away. And in weaker souls of energy they will fall into it and try and compete.

Free will and choice are for everyone. Those who question the basics are not accounting for their truths.

The trickery comes in when the soul believes they are so intelligent that no one can see them however who speaks they are intelligent.

They speak this of themself(s) however true intelligence does not speak of itself. It is not a prize to be intelligent.

A soul comes to Earth with mission and whatever that mission needs, the support of heart, mind, body and soul are in support of such mission.

Nadia, there is love of self. And when love of self does not know it can be of love to itself it relents into tirades of mind over soul.

The mind will speak to the soul that the soul must solve one issue to avoid the truest of issues.

Souls who want issues will find them, create them, live in them and will not allow solvation.

That is the unfinishedness that you feel. It is certain that in many years forward you will come to these souls and they will be speaking the same issues, only to a new audience.

They will find souls to listen however that will only last for a short time. Unless there is a structure in which they will see others in each and every day. Otherwise, it will relieve the souls around them when they are not present.

There is an Earth saying, "out of sight, out of mind." This is "out of soul, out of soul."

That is the truth of these souls and then they will speak they are lonely when it is them that push the wonder of life and souls away from them.

As you spoke to your guest, you will attract only the lower energies to your-self in this time. Simply because any soul who is truly searching will internally reject such defeatedness as you speak, very early on.

Souls can not take more pressures.

Souls conjoin to enjoy, to release, to find growth. And these souls coming into anyone's energy will bring weight and clutter to the mind without heart, for they turned their hearts off and they call love a person, a place or a thing.

Love is not love to them, for love is not freedom as it is in truth, for they can not see their own truths yet.

Once in times of life on Earth, these souls bring through in grand mission however these are the souls that get stuck between Earth and Home upon release of their soul from Earth to home, which is called physical death.

They are the ones that get stuck. They are the one's that do not want answers. And when they pass from one dimension to another their energies will not allow it, for they are not clear.

You see Nadia, a soul that commits a crime and is found, and they are at a point where they have to admit truth, they have greater self accounting than these souls.

Even though in intialdom they are forced to speak the truth, speaking the truth releases them into self accounting. When a soul can not speak truth to itself is it better off? It is not.

For then there are trappings of truth and it is harder to find when a soul believes itself to be elite in knowledge to others. I am in great awry to feel the elitism I see in souls.

The "better thans," and they will speak they do not believe this or practice it. Yet they action it and actions speak in loudment to words.

They believe they have spared themself(s) the manipulations that they put out in energy, from others to them. That is where they believe their intelligence serves them; they can not hear for that very reason.

They do not open paths for solvation. That road is closed.

There is festering to be the best and they want no others to be. They will take away in quickness and hide behind their truth. They will attach to souls of truth, for they will use them to do so.

And they will walk away from them when they get not what they want, when ego can not be sufficed. They transfer in life from person to person, for no one can stay in soul for too long amongst them.

They will look like your best friend as they are competing to be better than. They will speak what you do not think and they will accuse you of thoughts that are theirs not yours.

It is the meek, within the blankets of not being so. That is the trickery of the ego I speak of. They are the souls to say, they took on free will and choice and they understand it enough to manipulate it on those who think in purity of heart.

And I speak in purity of heart, for all will listen; only some will hear.

And at times those who hear will come to balance, for there is nowhere else for the energy to go at this time.

It is complete stagnation, and the takings away are common thought(s) to the human heart and soul to accept. However defeat is only for the defeated.

This is not in truth here. Only the defeated are defeated and it is the ego saying you are defeated and it matters none what you do to unfeat yourself. Glory be to God Almighty.

*(UNFEAT – To erode the foundation)*

You see, every soul on Earth can continue all it wants however to have learned and be seen, leaves their work to work on, and the receiving souls to make decisions.

For choices are the reason of free will, of Earth. Bring peoples together. And peoples have the right to come and join on or walk away.

When a soul understands its purpose, that soul can take on the purpose of each other.

**For it is not what is seen, it is what is not seen. That is Faith. It is not what is heard, it is what is not heard. That is instinct. It is not what is said, it is what is not said. That is wisdom.**

Nadia, the learnings are now teachings however the learnings will continue, for knowledge is endless and eternal.

There will never be a day that anyone or anything can say it now knows everything.

For love, purity, truth, are endless in giving, receiving and growthing within.

# CHAPTER 11

# THE COMING

You are loved in ways, as you would say. I enjoy your language, your thoughts of others, your mannerisms! Nadia, your purity gave me an avenue.

I am happy to be here! I did not want to come back however it was time.

I broke through as your energy was expanding on that last evening of temperature you had and I am completely here now.

I could fill your body with love and light as I have done before however in this day my essence lives within you.

Someone asked if you were pregnant! You are in incubation of another soul, not in pregnancy however in harmony, with ME.

For upon my reentering your form God Almighty, as I stood before him said to me;

*You now will rest within another soul, for this is the first meshing of souls to be done. Your return is to rebalance the souls on Earth.*

*Our Earth of Souls is in need of reattachment, for free will stopped and the complacency of souls has halted experience. For death of souls has stopped. Not of physical, of heart.*

*It is time for all the Angels of Service to stand together, for all the Angels are in collection now of finding each other.*

*All will know upon recognition, who you are. And will grow force and wisdom and strength that will baffle the weak into submission of self, Will battle the soul for its own survival of felt life.*

*Much of life is unfelt and many souls are coming back in loss of much experience. The growth of souls is jeopardized. You will be ever present to dispel all that was taught in error.*

*Go our child and accompany the souls. For the purity of Nadia, the wisdom of Stirling, on the outside will be carried with the gifts in which your Angelic form possesses.*

*Go our child, for you will not come back until all is completed and the world of spirit is reset. You will all come back together for it has just begun.*

*Know that in your moments of feeling the shields of negativity that they will not penetrate however be felt enough to endure the lessons that need to be taught to others.*

*To the vast and different populations whose job it is of all Angels to encompass into one population. For we are love and all is in force. Go our son, our child, and join the other Angels now!*

Nadia, I am Christ, living within you, within life on Earth, for your form of Me, of my love. My love for souls and your love and the love of God combined.

You will have with you God. My presence within you, for it will be visible to the eyes of people on Earth, for your alteredness will be seen our Sweet Child, for that is your Job!

You cleansed yourself as a child to not want bad intentions, for you did not know why, for that is who you are.

You did not know of me yet I walked with you then as I do in this day.

Yet in this day I walk IN you. I am part of your physicalness on Earth, for your light, your glow, is the two of US in ONE physicality!

I am here now. I am here. You are the avenue. You are the one to carry me, for I am here in safety to do as I was to do before, only to a tougher exterior of soul.

The passing of time has hardened even the softest of souls. The softer of souls seclude and the tougher of souls outburst. The in-betweens of actions are rare.

Balance is rare, for how could it exist internally, when the collectiveness of feeling in the world of souls on Earth lacks balance. How could it be?

Nadia, Sweet Nadia, I am here. One change has to happen before another can. Nadia you are of God. How else can I say it to you? Through me, from me, to you.

When I was a person in recognizable form I knew. You were told later in life for how else could you have endured the pain that you experienced and learned from it!

You chose to come down and come to your own conclusions. Glory be to God Almighty.

You can only be, for you are the only human on Earth in all the time prior that I could enter. For it is the love of God, of all! Glory be to God Almighty!

Human I will not be again. Glory be to God Almighty, for you are the love of the heavens of all souls.

The limitations of your world do not exist for me even though I am in your physicality! I am omnipresent! For it is one of my gifts.

We are here; I say we, for it takes many Angels to break through planes.

I am here and whenever you need our love, guidance, structure, advice, think it and it will come to you! Behold my Angel, for what does it mean to be an Angel? To give back.

I am not God as spoken. I am not the Son, the Father, the Holy Ghost. I am not the Holy Spirit. I am a spirit of God. An Angel.

There are no levels of Angels. There are no heights and no widths. It is like those who speak of me as Jesus.

It is like those who need to learn English, and it is not simply by speaking however by using modern methods, like movies, tapes, flash cards, reading and writing.

And in learning of Angels and of God, some categorize what they see in understandance of how they learn and then they share it.

Their perceptions are truths to them. However, God Almighty has no levels, no betters, strongers.

You read that they are not more important that they are more powerful, and that is saying that they are more important. There are no categories.

Look at me. I am made the grandest deal of. However, when I was present that was not the case.

I was shunned and murdered. Some loved truth and knew of me. However, none could save me. In truth I was one of many killed in this fashion on Earth. Souls are killed in everyday of existence on Earth.

Why was I more important? Because I was seen as a soul, because I came back and that defies human logic however it does not defy the logic of the universe, for every soul never dies.

There is no death. There are not layers of knowledge, importance or power. There is only love and growth.

And within that love and growth, the free will of every soul to conquer, learn, grow and stretch its knowledge's, to greatness of knowings of love and its depth, its width, its height, and its aboundment in glory of the soul hence the love of God.

We are all of God Almighty. Our whites are in brightnesses and intensities, simply because our experiences have given wisdoms that come and came with our choosings of stretching our souls into greater challenge.

The greater the challenges the stronger the lessons learned.

I am an Angel of God Almighty. I can be only called a child of God, for we are all children of God.

I can be a son of man, for then I am counted amongst men. I can be in light of life, for that is all I am is positive of life. In human form for time, yet an Angel of God.

That is who I am. I am an Angel of God Almighty. I say this, for I have been turned into sayings, and behaviors have been patterned after me and now I am no longer relatable.

How could I have been perfect? Perfect I am not. Pure I am. I am purity and love. Caring and hope.

I am an Angel not a son. A son of Man I am. A son of God I could not be. It is of impossibilality! It can not be.

How could God Almighty have begotten a child? God is one, of no partnership.

God Almighty is of all. God Almighty is of all his creation and more than the simple creations of Earth. I am created by God Almighty.

There can not be a Father. There are no human attributes begotten to God Almighty. There can not be human attributes.

For then God is human? He created humans and is of them? That can not be. How can anything be of its creation?

A creator Creates! Glory be to God Almighty. Glory be to God Almighty. Glory be to God Almighty!

I am not God. I am of God, as you are. We were all created. I was created by the breath of God Almighty. So simple. I was and am created by the breath of God Almighty.

Glory be to God Almighty, So simple, as all beings that came from God. How could I be both God and the son of God? How could I be?

How could I not be an Angel of God? Is not purity in Angelness enough for the souls on Earth?

If only they could see without the clutter of input. If only they could heart the truth.

If only peoples remembered at least to believe in themself(s) and not in others.

The only way to teach strength of heart is to be Strength of heart. Glory be to God Almighty. I am not to relieve others of sins, for there are none.

I am not the resister of temptation, for temptation like mistakes was created for the weaker/weakness of souls to explain.

Yet the unexplainable is what gives to us all our sclf, for when a soul sits within itself upon glory of God, life is in perfection in those moments.

Love is perfection! Glory be to God Almighty! Everyone on earth wants love over and above all else.

An Angel. That is who I am. I am an Angel of God Almighty.

The will of a human can only grow with learning another view other than your own. We Angels weep in those times for dishonesty and mostly for dishonesty to one's own soul.

So that is what we are like. All of us. We are all here to help, to support, to love, to ease pains, All.

We love all those that live. And we pray as well for the souls, the souls of life that are here and how we can keep that life from astray.

The Angels on Earth carry the world at this time.

It is pure purity and then there is uncertainty amongst humans who can't see, and there is not much in between. People are hungry and are ready for the changes that will come about.

Now it is time for change, for truth. And lifted are the burdens of the heart on the mind, for things taught in error carry great weight.

We float around and see all, as God is witness and we are helpers.

God's energy is too bright, too strong to contain, so we are in billions all over at your level never far from you.

Nadia, my love, our love in Heaven, we are all focused on you!

Endearing are the obstacles you have and will face in life, for how else could you know and understand?

That was the purpose of my life as well.

To walk among, to talk among, opposition, acceptance, rejection, love, fear, love, trauma, love, all until there was only love.

Love is absent and now you are present. For your presence brings love back. Do you see?

I am inside of your body for all reasons. For others to witness, for they know not what they see yet they will see my presence in you very very soon!

You are the vessel of my spirit on Earth. There would be skepticism and rejection, elitism, and ownership if I were to come alone.

With you in Form and others having known you throughout life, you will be of credit and no one will be able to say not!

You will burn into the world my messages and abolish the mistruth of what my representation of life was, for then the world could take responsibility of/for itself!

For now this is not present. It is what we would call a spiritual emergency!

In each breath you breathe, in each moment of your thoughts my love, my world and yours combine to grow others!

The ones of us as Angels are simply of service to the souls as we need to be. For love is love. God is love. We are love.

We are all here for love, because of love, in need of love and in wantings of love. We want nothing else. And then we go home and learn about love yet some more. Love is the fuel, the propeller of life anywhere. Not special for Earth alone as you would speak it. For Earth is the greatest obstacle to love.

That is the experiencement of Earth. And souls come to Earth in challenge, in experience, in heart, to grow and live in love.

And help each other do so. That is why souls are not meant to be alone. That is why in alonement there are fears, doubts and worries that love is not there, abandoned by love, by others.

We will always and never stop looking for love, no matter who the soul is or what it is to do.

All kinds of love, and the self motivated will believe it is only romantic love. But love is love is love. Is Love.

There is no other way. No other search.

When a soul says they have spoken to Jesus, it is not of me. For I told you upon your first knowing of me I am Christ. I am Christ. Christ as in meaning the thirst of life.

I am the thirst of life. That is and was my job. I am the love that brings about the discovery of love in all things.

Nadia, there are other spirits, there is a Jesus. However there is not in all spirits the knowing of all things. I have explained this to you prior.

It is not that the Angels are wrong, it is the points of evolution, as is in humans however those angels have to speak to audiences of what they can receive.

Jesus is the fear in people. Jesus was the created one. Jesus is the man in whom I was made and was called on Earth.

And in his name, Jesus, all the non truths, living and created from mere simple truths, and then taught in error. Jesus is the humanized version of ME. However at home I am simply Christ.

I am an Angel and have always been.

Christ, my love on Earth, does not speak in negative of any tone. That is why your writing is of difference from others.

You had no knowledge of Me prior to my visit of your beautiful heart and soul and reminded you of all we are here for at this time of evolution.

Do you understand? Yes, you do, I feel you.

Here is your filter my child of God. If someone says Christ, it is me. If they say Jesus, that is the man made version of Me.

With all man's thoughts of control, guilt and manipulation of soul, of mind, for the soul can be and will be journeyed erroneously.

For God Almighty does not burn, send to hell, hurt or maim a soul. For all God is is love. None else. God talks to all of us. Some hear, some don't.

God is only love and love only.

There is no question, no answer, no thinking, no speaking, that will make it different from what it is already. God is love, God is love, God is love.

I am back with great reason and the souls of believe and not faith will fight you. How did the world expect to see me? Would I really fill the sky in trumpet?

The world will not end in this plane.

There are not endings. There is only truth and absoluteness. There will be no judgment. Who can believe judgment? Who is a sinner?

All that happens on Earth in taking awayments came from the ways of self motivation in humanality. There is no other reason.

There is not a day of judgment. How could there be? I say again.

If the believers believed and had faith, in that God knows and sees all, then why the accumulation of a day to judge? Why wait?

If God Almighty knows and sees all, then why are souls not put in the "hell" that souls speak of sooner? Why let the soul rest at all?

Why would a soul who knows not to speak or to read of God Almighty, be closer in heart than the soul that reads and churches its mind on Earth?

Does it not explain the vastness of thought and love from within? Does it not say we are all one with God Almighty?

Why me? Why do I exist? Why did I come with Miracle in hand? Why am I an Angel? I am nothing but of service. I am An Angel. I am of love. That is all I am.

I share my gift of love and souls did not find a way to live in love as love. For Ego is allowed to join in at the asking of the soul.

And the soul can say, "That is not who I want to be" and a soul can say, "That is who I want to be." That is free will. That is choice.

Once a soul at home chooses its mission and it comes down to Earth to growth itself and return in evolution. There is not the hand of God; there is only the love of God present.

God does not abandon nor does God dictate. God is love.

And he will be, become, what a soul perceives Him to be. We say "him" to give a Humanness of relation to God however God is love and love is genderless.

Souls are genderless.

However there has to be a way to bring souls to the energy of Earth and it is through human incubation. It has to be enjoyable or it would not be sought after to bring on other souls of mission.

That is why I say sex is not physical. It is the movement of souls from home to Earth. Sex is not physical; it is the emotion of love.

Love will keep the soul in truth and wanting on the issuance of incubation in that time. It is the love of life felt from home in that time.

That is why a woman of pregnancy can only be of great beautiful. Even in her own life, she will feel it more than any other of her beauty.

For then she will live in the proofments of the continuation of eternal thought and life.

And many upon release of another soul to Earth, they may return to their normal state, and that love learned was not able to sustain. And some remain in it forever and love their children. In truth. And teach them.

Others, who could not sustain, will believe their child is a reflection of them. And they will pressure that soul to conform and be the best and all the conditions they have put upon their own life(s).

They will expect from their children what lacks within them, without being the example rather than the words. And that is the stem of rebellion.

And you see it in adults, and now there are many to have witness of. That those thoughts of rebellion turn into anger in repression, and you have the souls who want to be known for what they are and not be seen for what they are.

And they turn off their ears, just in case some knowledge accidentally seeps through into their mind and they will have to contend within themself(s) further. They are many.

They are the hands that took me to the nailing of my physical body, in yearning to make me go away.

They did not believe in the soul and eternal. And there was belief that to "kill" me would relieve them of the accounting that my love brings. These souls killed love. Not me. I remain.

It is of honor to human souls to say that they believe in Me however without the belief in a soul's self there is no sense in believing in Me.

What does it mean to believe in Me? I am an Angel.

To debate whether I exist or not it does not matter. I was here just like they are now. So why is it so ridiculous that I am here? Or was here?

It is not hard or miraculous to be on Earth. It is a choice of a soul in evolution of itself. I came to teach love, as they have come with a gift. Mine simply touches souls in growth on their mission, for I am of service.

There are souls who come, who are not of service and their gifts may be to research, work on craft, farm lands for foods, sell or prepare foods, make things that are of needs to the human souls as they journey on Earth.

Those are all gifts. Why are not those gifts in question or jeopardy of being believed or not, having faith in or not?

I ask the human spirit, why the fear in belief of love and not fear in the belief that another soul is leading them astray?

Why is it so hard for souls to say there was, is, can be; Me, Christ, love, or truth? Why is it that miracles are angst over and truth is questioned, yet the non truths are taken on as though there is warrant in them?

The answers lay in the angst of souls. They can not feel love and they do not want to believe there is love. For they anger to not feel it.

They do not believe in self and they want the world to answer them as to why they do not.

They will speak in riddle and you will not see the intent right away however to live within them is to know them.

They come to Earth with challenge and they grow further away from home in trying to mission, for they believe not that souls will love, for they can not love.

I was killed by the extremes of this batch of thinking souls. I speak of love in every angle as to show souls themself(s) in their ways of loving. That is all this could be.

As souls are busy trying to address my existence, I speak again and again, so what! If I was here, am here; Souls are looking for proof and not answers.

Will the proof lure them to the answers? No. They will just find more questions. And the lure is of making sure no one can answer them.

Our love, you write of souls and messages, will there need to be proof that you exist? What if I did come back as a person of myself?

What would that have done? If I were ten human feet tall and could change the weather and the people and circumstance, that would be too easy.

What kind of test of faith, growth of faith, would that be? What trail to love would that be?

A million baby steps come with everything. When there is free will and choice, time and pressures, this has to find its place in line for souls to come to.

And there is a greater and greater need to come to this place and its place in line is forwarding forward.

I am in adjustment too, even for us it is so. For the levels of energy planes of such difference, the significance is completely different domains!

Nadia you are laughing again. I am here. For when others see me through you, you will be of such enjoyment as well.

The first time will startle you, for I will have to change energy domains again to do so however not quite as physical on your body, such love that lives in you.

Such light, for my energy becomes you. Thank you for the soul in which you chose to be, for with that I was able to come. As time in your world is ripe and ready, has been, however my energy had to have a way back!

I am enjoying the livelihood of living within your physical body. There has been room for two for some time however your energy has been expanded considerably and it seeps out of you in unrelenting beauty.

I enjoy seeing the world with you, through you, and living in your struggles. I have forgotten much of the inhumanity that can still remain, for home is of peace, and on Earth there is a counteraction of that very peace.

I witness in today's progression of time the distortion it takes to take a soul away from peace. Many are scared to make decisions, even when it belongs to their soul.

Remember, for those who look from the outside in, they look to it consistently for everything, for there is no trust of soul present.

Do you understand? Or "get it" as is said in your world? I am enjoying hearing the everyday language of your time! I am in joy accompanying your body on Earth.

You simply forget I am there at times, for your physical body has expanded into my energy! Glory be to God Almighty! Dearest and Sweet Nadia, for you are addressed in this time. Yes, we are all here.

You are writing fluidly and it has been amusing to you in the past few days to feel my wonder of the world in which you live.

My vision of it from home and my feeling of it on Earth, vary to such an extent. You are of blessings to live in such a world as you do. As others do.

It is hard to maintain balance here. The varying of emotions of feelings towards oneself is of great variance.

Nadia, there is much hope here yet it needs to be found again. They are lost in the struggle of trying to be anything, something, yet not knowing how.

For the human soul forgot its own rights! The rights of the universe.

Not the rights as in right and wrong however the rights of the universe. Like a universal message or law. Innate in all of us of the greater good however the picture of the greater good has long vanished.

All the great work left on Earth is being done by Angels not so much people at this time. And the good work needs to be transferred to the people.

Once you are done you will return home, for the work needs to manifest once taught, once believed by the souls that came to be people.

Humans who came to be human can be Angel-like however Angels come to Earth to be Angels.

On Earth this is looked at as someone who is special. At home an Angel is looked at as service to all in love enumerations.

There is much needed now, since your time born here, for preparation began long ago.

Nadia sweet Nadia, I am witnessing through you, and you hear people talk in circles, and that is the only area in life you are impatient.

You are impatient for you know that soul is knowing and not wanting to. Wanting to put their load on the back of another and weigh down two instead of one.

Now many are weighed down, for the hope of many generations of life has become of hopelessness. They are OK on the outside however even the outside coverings are fading fast into a world of non understanding.

When love is within a relationship the true relationship will unveil itself in wonder. When a relationship carries not the unconditionality of love the unveilings are of takings away.

Love can not be used. It can not be made. It can not be because of anything. It will simply exist.

And in existence love can only turn a heart to growth.

When a soul is in love of life, life can only grow.

Love is Love is Love.

I rest on love.

# CHAPTER 12

# THE LIFE

I want to go back to the consciousness of "jesus," I say it with the letters of littlement, for they are who I was recognized on Earth. I am Christ.

I am Christ, servant of God Almighty. My soul is of love.

There are many energies, some in greater points of evolution, that speak to levels of understandment of the souls in which they are speaking. They are stepping stones of understandment beginning.

Yes, some say they are speaking to me however when I am called Jesus, as I have told you before, if there is not speaking of Christ, it is not of me.

It is of learnment on the part of the soul in writing of expectation that it is me. Jesus is the man on Earth who I represented to pass onto souls the love and messaging of God Almighty.

There are souls that break through to earthly souls. They are usually souls of loved ones, who will tell of things as they evolved.

Souls are at all levels, though born in the same time. For evolution is open and growth is of truth at all levels of knowment on Earth and at home.

There are differences in Angels and souls at home. There are knowings of completeness and partiality of completeness, for learnment is constant.

Yet these souls have purpose, to grow other like souls. And they all seem to find their ways to each other as they should. For it is of preparation.

Jacob has been in growth of the human conscious mind to open waves of energy to receive thoughts, to honor thoughts of wanting to know more, of understanding that all knowings are not of settlement in heart or soul, mind or body.

The pure hearted want to help, want to listen, want to help again.

The meek are in repetition of problems, of reasons, of glories in other mishaps, of problems of others not only their own and with that they hold all in place. That is the inheritance.

Time does not exist. Ideas do not exist in one specific time. Love does not exist in one moment only. Glory is meant for always.

I am/was a reminder that we are all of light and some of us forgot. WE forget that we are part of light, of one light. Of God. Of one God. So simple. I am God's Angel of love. So simple.

I am not of greater importance. I am simply known in greaterdom at this time. However the Trinity that is spoken is not the Father, the Son, the Holy Ghost.

It is the facts that souls took love and created a way to transfer love from self to others. So I speak, love, truth and purity of soul.

I speak for the sake of speaking in triangles. And the Father, the son, and the Holy Spirit, or Ghost, it has served and will continue to serve as a thought.

For souls to see God as Father, rather than Partner, as Son, rather than Partner, and Spirit rather than a real possibility, You see our love, I say, use it if you feel Partnership.

However there is no accounting in the Father, the Son, and the Holy Spirit, for then the soul transfers to others.

I speak, truth, love and purity, and you will understand God, yourself and the world, to accomplish truth, love and purity.

For every mission on Earth is based on truth, love and purity. And those who are fighting it are those who are the opposers of many other things.

I say, religion has taken on an abstractness that has spurred into a double life syndrome and I say, join together, yourself(s), so that the wanting to join further can take on energy and become.

I am not a Holy Ghost or Spirit. I am an Angel of love.

I am not the Son, for God does not borne children. I am not the Father, as you are not everyone's physical mother. I am an Angel. My job is to lead humans from home.

I had to come down when I did to lead all in realness, for the thoughts of miracles, of mind, for the leaders of that time were of horror.

They would have taken the world to a "dead end" as you would say in your world of language. So simple. Those wanting such spewing are being known and soon will be sought out in self accountability.

Their perception has brought about a reality that touches many and those many do not share that perception. So deception had to take place in order for the bigger picture of bringing love from souls, and respect of souls, to self and then to another.

I will say it was the fear of dying in the way in which my physical body was exited from Earth, to bring about the listening to the words I spoke on Earth! Nothing is as it seems! Glory be to God Almighty.

In my moments on Earth I was feared, I was loved, I was fed. I would feed; I would give and then receive. And in all there was a core of protection around me until I needed to be taken back home.

For when my mission completed I did not feel the pain of it however it looked of great pain and anguish. Nadia, that pain and anguish is what turned people around.

They would rather believe in me than be me or the fate of me. So they behaved instead. However those behaving were already of love. Those of fear instilled the fear of loss of life in others.

However loss of life is not even true. Loss of physical body is true. I am a living example of how life continues; our souls are not of ending. They are of beginning always. There is no end. There is eternity.

Life is eternal. Love never ends nor is it taken away. My life was diligent, for it had to be.

If all could hear or see, they will hear and see. Belief can do a lot to a mind and soul. You came to Earth to give back. To give back souls to themself(s).

You do not question now and with solidity you know and understand your life's way and purpose. It took much expansion to show your heart and mind greater detail.

It took since you acknowledged the Angels to understand what all of God's Angel's mean to you hence to all. What God truly is.

For God Almighty has turned into a commodity for souls.

I have been and become someone to feel bad about, so submission has to be, for I was the ultimate giver, for I gave my life. Was I the first to die? I was not murdered as murdered is thought of in this day.

I was killed for the threats to the leaders of that time, of mind and power. Isn't that why most are killed today? On a bigger scale that is the truth, even between countries.

That is the reason of the current war in time. It is of mind and power.

The wife of the husband who hurts her in physical; that is greater than anything I had felt. And it is of constant. The soul who hurts another in mental is even greater than the pain that I had felt.

Much is spoken of me in the days of Easter. I sit on Earth in glee of the happenings, the stories, of what is known of me and what is in truth of me.

There are many stories that are of fact to many souls on Earth. This is of unimportance in the biggest picture of all. It matters none how I was killed.

I was killed. There are many stories of how I returned. I simply came back in recognizable form. It is of no importance as to how any of the events occurred, for it was the guilt that has not found an avenue of love, that has carried Christianity into current religions of man at this time.

And that is only some of them. For many souls are not of Christian. It matters none what a soul calls itself and what a soul does, for truth is truth it truth.

And truth rests in the knowings that I have come to Earth as Jesus. I was killed for the love and truth I brought.

I came back to miracle and give attention to the words of truth, love and purity, as you are in recordation, before miracling can happen on Earth once again.

I spoke not of sins, control, guilt, or any takings away of any soul on the coming to Earth to experience.

I simply gave love to the souls of Earth in unison, to all souls in unison of love, truth and purity. So simple.

Anything that takes on storyhoods of tales, in and around, over and beneath, love, truth and purity is not a message from God Almighty, for it cannot be.

Contradiction does not live in the love of God Almighty. Contradiction is a human trait. It is part of experience and growth and learnment of souls. Souls have to do this to hone.

However the actions of souls at this time have detached from the experiences of mission hence I am here to give back in this time, truth, love and purity.

No different however relevant to time. For the path to God Almighty is right here. It is in the heart of every soul on Earth. What a soul chooses to do with that love is the free will of that soul.

And souls on Earth live in the glory of who they are, within the stances they choose. Those who see not the glory, see not the truth. So simple.

The truth of self is the greatest of truths, for it sets the path of all other truths. You can not see truth unless you can be it.

You can not see love unless you can feel it. You cannot live within purity unless you understand truth and love.

Purity is the result of greatest knowledge's. For the human soul is free. All entrapments of souls come from souls. It is of greatest love to learn of one's soul.

All freedoms come from within. Not one freedom of a soul comes from withoutwardness to a soul. Not one. Not one.

The honorment of souls with love of God Almighty exists in all souls. I am not of the greatest importance as I am spoken of.

I am the scapegoat, to use a modern term for all the ill will that has been created, to guilt, control and mishandle the souls of those who are seeking!

The disjointment of souls becomes from the allowments of the thinkings of others in error to become your own thoughts. For thoughts are an influence, how can they not be?

And when we are taught in error the error(s) can become truths of misgivings. Meaning that truth is wanting to be true however the soul can not fest within it.

*(FEST—When a soul can not live in the truth that it knows)*

All want to believe I suffered unduly for them. I suffered for, at the hands of, truth. And in that I did not suffer, for truth does not hurt a soul. I was in freedom and then I was set free.

I must tell you of my days before my exit. I was of apprehension. I was of sadness that I didn't believe I was viewed fairly in the eyes of those carrying the wonder of the populations in which they led.

They did not serve in that time. There was leadership and that leadership was completely self serving and those who followed those leaders were in positions of loyalty against even their own beliefs and interests.

There was barbaric behavior, as is now, only in different form. When I stood before those who led, I took their power away, for in turn they needed to rid of me for their power to reign!

I was a reminder there was wisdom greater than what existed in their heads.

I was calmer and independent. I was simple and didn't want from self motivation. Imagine the discontentment I have witnessed.

They physically removed me only to find they could not, for to shrink the souls of leaders. Now in this time the leaders are the same.

They lie to themselves internal and they lead from a point of contention of life. They lead to prove themselves good leaders. What is a good leader? One who lets the people lead.

Those who choose their role in country, in state, in work, in family, they are part of the role of themself(s) and then of all. For how could it not be?

The wall of deception falls quickly. That was the harshness in which I was received on Earth. No one could hide within my presence. No one could hide. They tried to hurt me, for they wanted to hurt themselves.

They wanted to discount me for they were already discounted, and feared others would know as I knew. However I could see as others can not see.

They wanted to kill me, for there was realization that I was the only one who could see, and they could not see me as I could see them.

Comfort they did not feel as a result of me. It was discomfort and to make the discomfort go away they had to take me away.

I returned simply to give to the world that nothing is as it seems. A body is a body. So simple. A soul is forever. So simple again.

However if I could come back, does that not break the barrier of impossibilialities.

*(IMPOSSIBILIALITIES—What we boundary and limit)*

All the examples that were of closeness to me, they taught themselves through me to be of self. To understand that within them there was light.

It did not need to be sought after from me however I am and was an example of light on Earth.

Our souls are not of ending. They are of beginning always.

There is no end. There is eternity. Life is eternal. Love never ends nor is it taken away. My life was diligent for it had to be.

There was much to my human departure however it wasn't very dramatic. We all knew I would go. For we all knew it had to be. There was much sadness and much tears.

I was killed at the hands of those who lack self love, simply. They had to make me go away, disappear.

I was a reflection of the lackasity. And even though I gave love back in those times of horror to humans, it was not known until I appeared to be of death, which was of horror to them, as I stood beside God Almighty in light and in love and watched the willingness of love lacking to become!

*(LACKASITY—To be aloof towards what is being said or done or accomplished)*

Yet more love was had than was lost. And for that I came and for that I became and for that I was taken home. For it was time! My work was done and their lack of love had to be personified before it could be seen.

Did I die for others sins? Nadia, there are no sins!

People will say what about this behavior or that behavior and the simple answer is; it is of lack of love. Glory be to God Almighty!

I had to know that face of smiles within the mishaps of mind. For I healed and those healed were those of purity of heart, whether they knew of me or not knowing of me.

In my times on Earth I was known for purity, for love, for healment of bodies, of souls. And within that I was feared for what I had known, for the human mind could not accommodate such loving as it stood.

The light that was in me while I was on Earth, was an attraction to me as well as a reason to hurt my physical being, for the limits of the human brain believed that if one was killed in physical they would be gone.

However, that taught them that this is not of truth. The soul is endless and life on Earth ends. So simple. There were miracles while I was alive and it moved some and angered others as to how.

So those limits of mind existed however they were expanded. For the souls on Earth knew not what to do with me entirely.

I love looking and observing all the ways that peoples defend me as though I was not of Angel. I am an Angel. So simple.

I am not the son. Must I say, I am not the Holy Spirit. And if there is a holy spirit it is of the souls of each drop of God.

I come to you in love in this day no matter what others could have inflicted on my soul. No one can give to me or take from me what I do not give them or let them take from my soul.

Life is in criticalness of care at this time. The lostedness' of souls is in vastness and the souls recognitions of such are in hearts and knowings.

Souls know not what to do next. The experiment of North America is showing souls that there are others in the world to consider.

That it is a world of togethers, not us's and them's; for there is no soul more important than another.

And the errors of media that have brought to souls taughts in error have become thoughts in error and the world has been affected.

How can it not be? How can life not be affected? How can one soul not affect another?

I speak to you that I am pure however not of perfect. No one soul can know of all things. For then why would there be experience, missions, journeys, planes, universes.

This is all for learnings, for growings, of souls in light and in love in the search for all other learnings. Light and love are the basis for all things.

For all happenings, no matter what the learnings are. That is the purity. And perfection is love. And love carries all things. Propels all things. Grows all things.

Nothing can survive without love.

You see the created hells of souls without love. With the fears of losing it, not having it, and the souls stagnate right there and stop growing.

I knew my time was of limits upon my life on Earth. I am learning now that the differences internal are not really different from the period of time that I was present.

The souls of today have little time of contemplation, for there are many points of brain bombardment.

There is no rest internal and the task of getting to know of oneself is too big to conquer, so the task is put off as the least important, yet in reality it is of the most important and will settle all the other tasks of mind and heart.

When I was on Earth, I had love and spread love. However as a male on Earth my interest was primarily to grow the leaders to grow the others. And the leaders were the peoples. Not the perceived leaders of that time.

Brutality of souls onto one another was in great(er) extreme. Bodies were treated in complete disrespect of life itself. The soul of a body was released before the pain could bare the scream of itself.

When I was present the form of exiting body was to nail a soul to wood. The soul was left to stand in sun's rays, and animals of scavenger, to live in life and death at the sameness of time.

The regard for life was of bitterness and overture of self upon self.

This still happens on Earth in this day in very similar form. No war can be fought without the acceptance of disregard of souls.

Our love, life is but a morsel of time for souls. However to the limits of mind, this is life and there is something more? That remains of question(s) of minds and thinkers, doers and takers.

To let go of love is to say, "I do not believe there could be more." To live in lacks of hopeness, is to say, "There could possibly be no more."

To kill the body of a soul is to believe you have killed that soul. However a soul cannot be taken away. There can be no dissolvement of soul.

It can only happen in the will of God Almighty. It has not happened yet, in all of time, in all of what you will call history, for there is not time, and this has not happened in everment.

To dissolve a soul is to deem life in entirety unredeemable.

Life is life however a soul is a soul and a soul is of eternal in alwaysments, for love abounds and can not be dissolved; the morsel of life on Earth breathens to dissolvement in the vain mind of any soul to believe it so.

It says, "There is not love and I will kill love to make it go away" however it can not. For energy precedes body.

Energy is in movement and has little to do with physicality, except for the knowing of energy through the movement of body on Earth.

The body is simply a means to be seen, to get around and produce, to look at and be looked upon, to pleasure in the joys of love and to push the challenges to the endangerment of suchness in despair.

The body can tell you everything the mind will not be willing to say. For we wear our lives on our bodies. And our bodies are simply to give recognition of self on Earth.

Earth energy is too low to allow the spirit to flow freely, as it can in other planes and galaxies of universe and home. On Earth, the lands of lower energy and the physical bodies constrained by weight.

The physical body of Me while I was on Earth was of great weight. It kept me from journeys, only to realize myself that all things are as they should be, and in eachness of thought I could take my energy elsewhere.

I could ask God Almighty to work with me. I had to have choice to understand choice. I had to understand will, so that I would understand free will.

I had to see souls fight for their perceptions and I had to speak truth within it.

I had to witness sadness of my own heart when souls could not see truth. I was truth and it turned many souls in unside downness of self, until they could deem me a criminal and try to convince others. I did not have to be here to propel energy of love.

*(UNSIDE DOWNNESS—At times our thinking is the complete opposite of truth and we are currently living in it as truth)*

It propelled itself even without my presence. I lived in humor of life, knowing I could think souls love, feel them love, teach them love, with energy alone, and that they knew not how to fight.

They have learned only to fight the physical body and that is not to fight the mind. It is of the leastment of evolution in fighting.

To fight, hurt, maim, a physical body of souls is to say, "I do not believe in energy, I understand how not it works." It is saying "I have power and I can kill" and that is saying "I have not faith in free will."

It is saying that "I am better, by not believing in Choice of souls in growth" and that is to take away growth.

To take away a physical soul on Earth, to remove the energy of a soul, is only to bring that energy of that soul back in tenfoldness.

You see their energy and love and fear that you put onto the soul remains.

And that remaination of souls fears left behind on Earth, from all their imposed death to physical and not mental is what over time tipped the balances of energy and that is why Earth is not in balance in this very time on Earth.

*(REMAINATION – To understand what is to continue and what is better left behind)*

That is why the infusion of love is here hence you came to mission and Stirling came to mission. Why the team of Angels are of team.

To bring the balance back, for the lacks of understandings of love on Earth and the actions taken thereof over the time allotted on Earth to do so, propelled into this.

That is why Propellation is so strong and important to know about.

When I was on Earth in form I pled in my heart of soul to leave behind the love I was sharing with the world of that time. I understood that only those who can see will see and there were a few.

However in greater power than the many who did not want to know, did not want to see, and could only attempt to erase me. For their powers on

Earth was only their power on Earth. I knew and they did not know that love is eternal.

Love is the Universe, and Earth is only a part of the Universe, for experience of soul. That lacks of love can not withstand anything in truth. For lacks of love are simply human challenge(s).

It is a difficult step to take on mind/ego. It is an honor of soul to do so. And that is what you are teaching.

And you can only teach what you know, what you have, what you have experienced, for relation could not happen otherwise.

That is why I am not relatable in this time. It is demonstrated that I can do what no man can do and I am isolated as to not what I am as a result. I am every man.

If every man can know that in truth, they can live in purity, and not the perceived perfection that I have become.

Many were not ready for me, wondered where did I come from and ruin their already established habits and meanglings of behaviors, the established manipulations.

And then I am present and all truth is present and what happens? Some heal for they could see, some hurt for they could see, and all saw, even those who did not want to. Even those who could not did with heart.

I knew all of this and I had to respond only to love and let all else rise to it. I have forgotten very much of the inhumanity that can still remain, for home is of peace and on Earth there is a counteraction of that very peace. I witness in today's progression of time the distortion it takes to take a soul away from peace.

For me to be here is very enlightening, for I see, and here I can feel too. I see that life is life here. I am absorbing all and that very little feeling is present. Much despair for the hearts of most.

Despair stifles.

It is in the form of anxiety, of imbalance, of fear, of worry, of self doubt. It is the enabler of the internal diseases of souls. For souls, they need belief in self in the most of ways.

Never to fear, for the love of God is present. I am here and will people miss it? No, they will not. They will miss the judgment they believe to be so.

There could be no prophecy that tells the world what is to happen! Glory be to God Almighty. Those were/are the longer term fear buildings that took place in its day and time, age and mind knowledge.

Teach and grow. Grow and nourish. Nourish and expand. Expand and find the other side of life, of love.

To find love is to open all avenues of heart and mind and find the other sides of all colors of life.

Without love the stagnation of heart holds all avenues in place. Glory be to God Almighty.

I feel in you the unstoppableness that I myself felt once I knew I was going back home. There was no reason for me to stop at words or actions of love

So I gave it in abundance and in absoluteness of heart, and souls could not absorb until now the actual love I have given, and that is the drawing to my name, my words.

How I died is how souls died. It was the love. For love propels. God Almighty can see what we can not. And there is nothing that God Almighty can not do.

For what is a miracle on Earth is of easement on all other planes. It is simply the energy. Humans are not so difficult. It is the lowness of the energy levels. Glory be to God Almighty.

A soul's life is a soul. A person on Earth is meant to be on Earth; to grow their soul and come back home and learn and grow and grow and grow.

For growth is infinite. On Earth there is a fear of growth, of change, of getting what a soul believes it wants.

On Earth the soul does not believe the love that they come to Earth with. There is no belief in the truth that is known to be true. For fear outweighs love, truth and purity.

Fear is the weight of the Earth. It carries itself into programming, into parenting, into churches, into classrooms, into speeching. Into all the worlds crevices and it controls the mind, for the minds confidence is weakened by fear.

Fear is so embedded that souls take much time to recognize that that is what is and has happened to them.

Fear to speak their mind. In fear it will bring together vulnerable truth and being seen for the truth that they are. So souls build stories and tell stories and behave as though the stories that are brought on are of truth.

And they speak as though it is truth however all the other souls know of its non truth and still behave as though it is truth, in fear that they will themself(s) be seen.

And the cycle, the circles, the horror of heart and mind at truth is startling, even to Me. And I have not had the cycles of fear in this manner, in my time on Earth.

I have been on Earth in Spirit however through your body I can feel and I can see the negative that is veiled at home.

Your writings are the world's knowings; the world's answers. The glory of discovery is the ultimate gift of learning, of God, of love.

God is love. I say this in every moment it can be said. Love is God and God is love.

# CHAPTER 13

# THE TIMES

Nadia, it is of great time to galvanize the world in which it thinks it good is really not so. And to think it is of bad is not so, for there is no good and/or bad. There is no right or wrong.

There is injury to soul, there is growth, there is learning to do. Always and always, no matter what it looks like. And the healer is of love, of purity. Yes, back to that.

Yes, back to that again and again. For how else can healing take place?

I am loving the ease of language in your world. We just think it at home. Here we have to say it and we hear it too. It is two parts! I had forgotten the sensation!

I feel more enjoyment of life through your soul than I did when I was here prior.

Nadia, today you were trying to believe how you know what you know, feel what you feel, to know of me as you do. I am here. I am present and I try to subside my energy so that you can do your tasks at hand.

I do them with you, for I enjoy the freedom of being human again and not being known, for I can see, feel, touch the world as it is.

You keep thinking how I am the best kept secret. I am not a secret. Those who look at you know. I love the instant flash of surprise. I can appear and love and not be received with skepticism as I was in my days known.

I was never tempted. I always knew from the beginning why I was here.

I was never human. I came knowing I was an Angel. And while I was present here on Earth, I was present at home, for even then I was omnipresent.

That was the trust that existed from the pure around me. And the others, they had to struggle with me for I was a mirror; the clearer the picture the harder the fight.

The most clear of picture were those who wanted to rid of me to stop the reflection! Glory be to God Almighty!

There needs to be something unexplainable. For me it was my birth, for that is how I knew all along. How could I come?

I came with the knowledge of home. How could temptation of any kind tempt me if I already knew the truth of life and I already knew that ill will would be motivated away from me? For it could not have been.

Now history will be looked upon and those in existence will be saying that people use to believe in sin and people use to think that God would burn them.

And people use to believe that there was a day of judgment and that they would be of fear of Almighty God. How could they be in fear of unconditional love?

How could they truly be in fear of hope and grandeur, of caring and soothing, of home? How could they fear love?

The choosing of fear is human. It is of the weaker souls who try to explain what they do not know and ignore what they do know.

I am here again through you to the unexplainable. In that the showings will show that you don't have to explain to believe.

Your writings will be the fruits of the earth to come.

WE love your soul, and with God the avenues of love are never ending and never ceasing.

For simple hope propels the heart in the leaps and bounds of belief of self hence belief of love, of all things possible.

Worry not, for fear, doubt and worry stagnate the soul. May all the stagnated souls lift their worries and be free. Glory be to God Almighty.

All will find its path, for there has to be a million movements of energy to move a mind from one moment to another.

Positive life even in hardship brings to all of us the rewards of pure faith. It gives and gives to know truth and when truth is present itself.

Camouflaugment of soul is to erase your lesson of soul! Glory be to God Almighty.

I am learning of the changes that have taken place since I have been here. In my first coming souls were more immediate. There was no hiding. What a person was, that is what they were, it was known to all.

Even those who deceit were known to the others and the only hope was that person wouldn't come to them.

There was also no communication between peoples who did not live amongst each other.

Now communication of much is rampant. It is in excess, for yet it has to be to take the human soul to challenge.

Now the steering of the soul has been askew and needs a jolt through the goodness of free will, to take itself(s) back to the positive world to continue growth, for now and forever.

Souls have resilience and strength however when souls don't know of it they do not have it.

When a soul knows not of love it does not possess it. When a soul knows not of hope it is lost in despair.

All that is happening to let the souls know, remind them, there is more than this and it is their minds and their hearts and their wills.

How can a soul expand without the glory of knowing it could? How could a soul know if it is not told? The veil covers for experience to begin.

Once experience begins, questions come to play. And once questions come to play choices can be made. And when choices are made, experience of those choices had, and once had the lessons are either learned or repeated.

Repetition tells the soul they did not learn the lesson. Learning brings about a greater more rewarding challenge.

Never to fear for growth is the key of internal life. Without growth, experience, love in seasoning, there is no life.

There are many ways in which to live life, and as a collective whole the world of souls on earth are of abandonment of self hence the world of the souls, for all souls are one.

By the ways of life my voice as you said does not change. I never refer to God as King. For King is a human word. There is no King and I am not God. God is simply God. The creator of all.

Self motivation has to come into play at points of time to grow one's soul. Self motivation at the expense of others is when taking away from self, from another soul happens.

I am astonished as to the change in the internal make up of cells expansion and what lives within the data of such beings.

It saddens my souls knowing to see the discomfort of internalness of beings. I am feeling so much, the not knowing where to be, who beings are to even themselves.

For there is searching for comfort and not knowing where to begin. The belief in dreams is overburdened and overwhelmed.

Love has been distorted to attractiveness and even the definition of attractiveness is blind to the one who believes is attractive.

There is much covering up of self at this time. Plastic Surgery.

I am in knowing why and the why is painful, for the lack of self acceptance that comes with it is not gone and aborted. That is abortion.

Aborting a child before birth, the soul returns home and tries again, for the mission did not include abortion.

Yet true abortion is of stopping any process of growth available; trying to stop time mentally. Physically it appears with surgeries, yet it is the mental stagnation that is of the truth.

Once I was incepted, there was already knowledge of my existence and the glory of God Almighty. My family grew me and grew the missions of themself(s), of me, in the glory of God's love, in love of mission on Earth.

There are many questions of my love on Earth; all things will be answered in time. At times the wonders of the questions are greater than the questions themselves.

And those questions remain such simply for the wonder of them. I speak so little of my family on Earth. It is of great curiosity to those on Earth however they simply came down to support the messaging of God.

There were no conflicts, for they were simply my protection, my shield, until it was time for me to depart.

And then they became the carriers of the mission upon my return. In surprise in first moments even to them, for some of the questions are better to remain wonders, until the questions begin to answer themselves.

For those are points of evolution. Glory be to God Almighty.

Mary Magdalene, was the greatest of all souls around me, for she of condemnation and redemption. That is the perception.

*(MARY MAGDALENE—The love of Jesus Christ's mission on Earth)*

In truth she was a bright light all along and like you, came down knowing that she had truth in her and blessed was her discovery of such while still on Earth.

Her role wasn't so much to teach people or souls that needed to learn. Her role was to support me and be an example of how souls are resilient and loving and that put forth on them at times is not of their knowing.

And until they can know better or be of support in other ways of life and love they cannot. I was her support only for her to be loyal to mine. We all need each other and we are not meant to be alone.

She is of the highly evolved souls. She was rejected and attempts to pierce her, hurt her, were underway, only to find her to be the gentlest of souls to all of mankind.

No attention or learning could have taken place otherwise. Glory be to God Almighty. For her words are of truth. No interference; as your writing is of truth, no interference.

My closeness to my Mother on Earth carried me. There were no temptations of me while on Earth, for I was of Angel, with no needs as peoples on Earth needed.

I could talk and speak to God in heart and I was guided. I had no obligations or pressures as they exist in this day of time on Earth.

I had much traveling in my time to speak, to miracle, in solvement of souls on Earth. I hesitated when I believed the souls on Earth could not bear to me and my existence.

While I was here as a human I was fought. And fought and fought. I had Bethlehem, at my side. I had Michael, in protection of mission. I had an Angel as I, for maternalness on Earth. For the mission is the mission.

*(BETHLEHEM—"Sweet Bessie" the Angel that walked beside Jesus Christ on Earth)*

*(MICHAEL—One of the seven angels of this mission)*

And all missions that touch on this mission are part of their ownness of mission.

This is the glory of God Almighty, to reach, to touch in honorment of soul's experiences and hone their missions into the comings of home and learnment of souls. Glory be to God Almighty.

There will always be unanswered questions. For those are the questions that keep the mind asking. As well, it does not come to matter how everything happened, for it was written of in Earth time, much afterwards.

Who was my brother? Did I produce children? I did not.

Did I marry? I did not.

Who was my mother? Was she a virgin? Who was my father? Am I a son?

All is separating from messaging of relayance of words of beauty and growth.

Will we speak to a soul who produces a car, who he is, what does he do? Who mothered him, who fathered him? We simply want to repair the car.

As well I speak, it is the message not me. It is the message not you.

I am speaking to you in your head and your hands record. For the beauty of recording, you are the first messenger of God Almighty to record.

All others took our words and enhanced the content and all the different opinions of what was/is called Christianity is now in seventeen mainstream forms, and countless divisions and it is all of my life.

All fear based sayings, decisions, guilt, control. What a soul can eat or not other than poison, what a soul can do or not other than pure intent, was enhanced.

For the self motivation of the masses to control, to contribute, was/is to take a group and make them feel better, different, however better. Different is the opposite of teachings of love, of my existence.

I did not die on the cross for sins; I was killed for my wisdom and contentment. Even in what was looked upon as death. How could I die for sins when sins truly do not exist?

Breaking laws of universe affect us all and that is taking away from all of us.

One person, who takes away, takes away from all and one person, who gives, gives to all. Glory be to God Almighty. For God is love.

Why would I die for the sins of others? I am amazed till this moment in time on that alone.

And the book of Revelations, Glory be to God Almighty, for all fear will be erased from the books of horror of soul to establish that a soul is to suffer in any form at the hands of God Almighty!

Glory be to God Almighty, for in God's name souls were put in jeopardy there, for how could they trust elsewhere?

If the God that loves can be the same God that takes away, hurts and maims! Glory be to God Almighty, for this is not of God Almighty.

You felt in those moments the sadness that anyone had to read that. For you did not with reason.

You got a taste of less violence in the Quran and that is the irony. In the Quran there is violence to soul as well however masked under the pleasures of God and within rewards.

There are only to be rewards with God Almighty. Souls came with purpose and that purpose was not to perfect as set by the standards of the world in this time.

Perfection leaves a state of mind of inflexibility, for what is a soul to do once deemed perfect.

I was not of perfection. I was of purity! Nadia, I have been talking a lot of such things as Church, for most call them the house of God however the house of God is Earth.

It is not embodied by walls of ANY KIND. Church is where emotion of God is exemplified however it is the emotion that fuels the building, not the building that fuels emotion.

Emotion is the source of what gives life to any situation. Without it, without compassion, all is the same, no movement, for it is the energy that moves all.

How could a building when not occupied move anything? It is the souls that enter that create movement. Energy is the movement of all things.

That is why when the energy is of negative, is of chaos, run don't walk away, for the intentions are mishap of emotions. And yes, it will be of impossible to not be affected, repelled, or drawn in.

Monies in the world on Earth are traded and through those trades, wealth is determined and intelligence is judged.

Neither is generally true. In the world as I came before, most was provided for by the hands of those alive.

For all commerce was minimal. Now commerce is the ruler of all minds. Company's structure is designed to tip the scales of profitability and then the product is made.

They cannot afford to make a product of quality and then sell it to you. There are too many people involved. There are those who are investors and there to make money only.

Then there are those who run the company who answer to them. And they at times feel cheated, get greedy and steal from the companies that they do not own.

Wealth, no matter how attained is wealth on the outside and the means of attaining is not of mention.

Many thieves have arrived and become, for they can shape the lives of the common worker. In all of this there is no owner.

NO ownership of a company. So how could the product they sell come to you with the love and the ownership in which you purchase and use it? Nadia, there is lack of ownership on many levels.

The human mind is getting to a level of determining that its own soul, own life here on Earth is the blame, fault of others. For them they do not steal money, they steal their time of life, of lessons from themself(s).

For them there is blaming and excuses happening that are taking away from life in every moment of their thinking hence lack of ownership.

With lack of self ownership how is it that they can feel if there is no owning of feelings?

I lived as a human to be human and to be of teacher. Now I am of fear, of lack of understanding of me, as Jesus, the son of God hence avenue to God or a savior.

I am Christ. An Angel. I say this and I must be in sayment of such words again. For the hurvy of my existence has taken away from the love of self, of souls.

*(HURVY—To overlook and lose sight of the reasoning's why and the messages of learning over time)*

The fear of not arriving at heaven, not being in heaven, not winning, not being good, has turned soul(s) into the fakeness of love on Earth.

And the fear in error of heart and mind, the result of lacks of self love and knownments, has turned souls away from God Almighty all together, in groups and in groves.

And it has turned others in life(s) of falseness and yet others into pretenders.

The fear of burning startles me as well as it startles you. For an Angel of God Almighty can not comprehend the thought.

I ask, "How can a body burn in Hell, when the soul leaves the body?" Does God come back and get the body and burn it?

A body can not feel. Does he create another form and burn it over your soul? Where is the vessel of fire? Where does it begin, end?

How could a soul in intent of love, born in original love and works life back to the love known already in birth, be destined to burn? All a soul can do is come to Earth to experience.

The lack of love from home is hell. For hell could be defined as Earth.

For you live in uncertainty, unsurety, no answers and the will of your soul being your only guide to find the love of God Almighty and to live within it. Glory be to God Almighty.

And God is waiting for a soul to mishandle the life chosen to come and experience and burn their form that they leave on Earth? Love can not be lived without. For without it, that is what is looked at as death, as what the souls of Earth call hell.

We Angels are very amused at the thoughts of hell, the word hell, the use of hell to manipulate the human heart and mind and body.

It is the word hell alone that perpetuates what you would call "bad" behavior. The mind is so simple that it is of swaying at a moments notice.

And that is why it is harmful to a soul to expose itself to those very things that ill intent or are done to hurt and injure a soul with knowledge that takes away rather than gives.

For the created thoughts of hell, the use of the devil, the use of the fire, the use of the language to hurt and injure could never have been said by an Angel of God, and never said by God Almighty.

There is the rebellion of soul. And those are the injured souls. And they live in what you call hell, for it is lack of self love hence lack of love for others, and ill intended deeds have a program.

That is the only Hell that exists. The rest is up to believing and not believing. No one burns. No one suffers at the hands of God in any avenue.

Hell is not fire. It is the sheer opposite. It is cold and dark. Dreary and challenging in the ways of the heart.

Heat makes souls take action. Cold hinders them. Humans fear fire, so they speak you will burn in Hell. No, they will live in coldness, darkness, of self and that is Hell.

And Hell is only on Earth, as it has been created and projected, Lived from the lacks of love, rather than the propellations of truth in hope of self and others.

The masks of insecurity have turned souls to lacks of growth. And service of Home is here.

The prayers are many to help those who can not see anymore. And we are here. You do have a battle on your hands for those who want to believe in evil.

Evil only exists in the minds of the souls who believe it, create it, want it and seek it. That is how evil exists. That is why one soul will know of it and others will not.

Thoughts truly are things and things are actions and actions are seen and responded to. That is simpleness of thought to simply know this trail.

To think it, anything, will give it life. As you speak to many souls, your brain will work on anything you give it. For the brain is a master at any task. The brain is a master at any task.

To use your brain is to live within the masterhood of yourself hence God Almighty. For God Almighty is not master of soul(s).

God Almighty is simply love. And we are love in reflection. We are all seekings of love in only one form and that is pure love.

And on the way to pure love we are in obstacles of how to find it and get to it and that is called experience.

Within experience(s) decided on at home, before arrival onto the Earth plane there is the giving of free will and the veil of home, to carry out the experiences to bring a soul to pure love in truth.

That is the reason each and every soul on Earth exists. No more no less. Any more is not of foundational truth. For this is the foundational truth. For all beauty of love, of words of God Almighty is of existence and present in always. All taughts in error must stand in balance now.

The Muslims will say "the Quran says there will be no more prophets until the end of time after the Prophet Mohammed."

Why then I ask the world, the peoples, "Would God stop sending down messengers of love?" "What," I ask, "is so important about messengers?"

Messengers are simply that. Do peoples not want to hear of love? They buy because of it, cry because of it. They look for it even when they think they have it.

They trust because of it. It brings happiness and pain and yet when someone speaks to them of it, they want to say "not from you. You can not be a messenger?"

My sweet, our sweet Angel on Earth, you can come back to me. Talk to me when you are of weariness, I have been here in real like you.

Now I am hear in shadow. For no one could or would conceive of my presence, for they believe not in the miracles of God Almighty!

Even as they were taught much in error, even the taughts of love and miracles they dream of however not of reality. For reality to most is just that. No miracles.

And the thoughts of Judgment Day will be abolished since nothing is going to come from the sky down onto souls and give to them fear and grief!

Glory be to God Almighty, the fears that exist here, the thoughts that take away, the deception of soul, the trial of many, for the unknown to them is truth.

You will know me as love of God, for God sends love to all. Never to fear, for the love of God is present.

For I am here and will people miss it? No, they will not. They will miss the judgment they believe to be so.

God Almighty will tend to them with patience and with love.

If they ask they will know of it. And if they do not they will spin the wheels of mind in control of life, only to find disappointment in not knowing enough to ask of themself(s), God, a friend, without the wanting something back for it.

Self Motivation is the hardest obstacle of the human heart.

All ill willers of life on Earth, they are the burnt meals. They have all the ingredients needed however they do not realize that the fire is always on.

Life on Earth is never what it seems. It is always better, truer than any soul could know.

In all places. In all ways. In allness of souls objectivity. All things can not be perfect however all things can be love and that is true perfection.

Without love to propel anything it can not happen.

Love is the maker of things. Love is the growth of peoples.

Love is the creator of things.

Love is the Creator of people. Love is God.

For God's creations are of infinitcy.

God's love is the strongest love of existence in all places, in all planes, in all universes, in all galaxies, in all of life.

Living and breathing in all of souls, even those who think not. For nothing nothing nothing can overcome, overpower, the love of God Almighty!

Glory be to God Almighty! Glory be to God Almighty! Glory be to God Almighty!

# CHAPTER 14

# THERE ARE NO MISTAKES

WE Angels love to watch your lives. Enjoy your days, for there is no other way to be. Be.

Read, for your mind is open and there is no end.

Rest, for your rest gives your mind time uncensored.

Clean, for to clean organizes the mind!

Cook, for to cook personifies love to those around you.

Speak, for your words bring joy in your parting.

Seek, for growth is endless.

And learn, for that is of all purpose.

Love, for that is the fuel.

The writings will give the depth, the lessons, the stories, the realities of what a prophet is. Human, not glorified and yet a message because of/with purity to souls! For that was Me on Earth. Now I am not related to, I am lived up to!

The fear or wanting of Me is of self motivation in many forms at this time, and with that the messages have been lost and updated in many versions.

It is time for that to become realistic again. For the lessons to no longer be read with self motivations, yet to be seen for the reality that they are attainable to all, for we are of all!

No one soul on any level, to be of greater importance than another! Glory Be To God Almighty. For we are all of life and life of us!

We are teachers of each other and God Almighty is of all, for creation is of all. And no one person no matter what is stated has more right, is better, greater, stronger than the next! Glory be to God Almighty!

Without all, there is really not a world in which to live! For now the messages are of self love in purity! Then all else will be known!

I am now in greater detail of the simple ailments of the human soul and what it can and does do to carry itself in its time on Earth. I have been in your form for time now. I am in witness of all that comes to you.

I feel your hearts knowings in the solvations of truth you have to encounter with those who can not see truth.

This past year of time in your life was the culmingation, the illumingations, of all that peoples do to themself(s) and then to others, in their times of misery and discontentment.

*(CULMINGATION—Getting to the bottom of troubles brewing)*

*(ILLUMINGATIONS—The images souls try to portray that are not consistent with who they really are)*

And what you found is that discontentment has become and can become a way of life. Those are the peoples who do not believe or the peoples that believe too much.

Nadia, you speak to many who are scared of change. You speak to many who resist change. Who fight it. Who hurt because of it. Who hurt others for it. For acceptance of newnesses is gone.

That is a direct reflection of trusts dissipated. Peoples do not want or welcome change. They feel that what they already know is enough. Growth and truth found are difficult challenges.

And trust within a soul is very little. And hence the soul fights change. Fights growth.

And when change happens and it does not come out to the desired results of what is wanted, going within the mode of expectations, then the change is called a mistake.

An accident if they did not have the foresight to know it was coming. And within that dear and sweet Nadia, the fight against change, growth, strengthens. Glory be to God Almighty.

The changes within growth are all around, the restrictions within hold all holdings around. For the trapment of feelings takes place. And the lack of breathment within takes place.

And hence the exist of those that are looking for growth becomes. And then change is had by all.

I beg the souls of Earth to wait for what they believe to be love. The lack of love and the actions of love within that take away from a soul in exponential form.

It is truly not worth the immediacy. For now it has become bodies of many and feelings of none. Do souls not see this yet? They do not. They keep acting it in morement, believing it will increase their chances in finding truth. And truly it has diluted their chances for they themself(s) become of this very dilution.

And then there is reflection. Hence attraction, hence relationship, hence break up in disappointment in years or months or a night later.

I found in my time on Earth as a human form that humans then and now want confirmations of who they are. And they want those confirmations from others.

For the internal trusts within self's of souls was not enough for the soul.

The soul is not a body it is a fluid, as is emotion, as is truth. A body takes souls into form and puts them in a place to be so that the soul can not run away from its lessons.

It can not take its self away. Did you ever think why they're in form? To give home to more souls to come and anchor and grow within experiences or they will run away from their experiences.

For the seeing of growing lessons from home and coming to Earth to do the lessons are two different things. Glory be to God Almighty.

It is in now that the souls know they are not in ablenesses to run away in body, so they drug the run awayments in mind and heart.

Medications, Doctors, drugs on streets, control of them, for they have become the undertone; the undertone of humanity to cope with life in which its skewments of love, of hope, of truth, of purity, have take aways to those points of distractions.

Life is not faced on its own terms. Nothing is as it seems. Nothing is as it seems.

And when you think you are looking for something, anything, anyone, anyone looking for anyone, anything to make them happy, how could it be?

I was on Earth and I was in happiness of heart, even in the harshest of moments for me, and that has been the growth of my peers to witness.

The miracles on Earth terms were thoughts being things. They were in heart of love and love of heart.

And the souls around benefited for the knowings. Were they able to do it? No, for they were not meant to.

It was simply meant to peek at home, so the sustainment of Earthly lessons could be sustained and completed for the task.

It is of greatest challenge to come to Earth. It is of greatest challenge in all the universe. For other planes, galaxy's; lessons are of one growth at a time. Earth is multi-faceted.

Think about all the fights of souls within themself(s) about God, about love, about what life is supposed to mean, how it means it, why it means it?

It is all creation. And in Creation all things, souls, live. And in the livement there are choices. And in those choices is free will.

And within free will there is the choices of others influences, lower energies, love and the ways in which it is, was, shaped.

And the experiences begin. And growths become. And lessons honed. And lessons not honed repeated until honements take on a place, and growth can and does move forward.

A giving soul is a soul that is known right away, from heart. I am saying this in againments so that in another way souls can learn of it.

And now it is time for the sharing, the awakening; the day in which the world will not be able to turn its head the other way.

The world got accustomed to turning its head the other of way, for that is what happened within before without and without before within.

For the wills of those self motivated took their course and the course in this day ends.

The soul has lost respect of itself and it is in great display what has become of that. We are in war, we are in poverty.

We are in prisons. We are in homelessness of souls before the homeless of what souls have come to know of in this day as no home.

We are here and we are vacating the premises of our mission. We cry for the tears go back in furtherments than we can reach.

And we change to bring out greater understanding only to find our souls in the same searchments of love.

WE WILL NEVER STOP SEARCHING FOR LOVE. TRUTH. PURITY. NEVER. NEVER. NEVER. WE CAN NOT ERASE ETERNITY. HOME. UNIVERSE. WHATEVER IT IS CALLED, REFERRED TO, FOUGHT WITH, WE CAN NEVER ERASE ITS EXISTENCE.

We can not even erase ourself(s) within it and that is why we search for it, hurt others for the lacks of it. And can not think of anything else when it is not in present form in our souls and that is the search of Earth.

We are in searches of love of home in all that we do.

And we have lost our way to things, to ego, and the balance has found its imbalance. And its strayed and strived maintainess of imbalance has caused many souls stresses of soul onto themself(s).

And they say it is pressure, they say it is stress, they say it is lacks of time. They say it will be gotten to and yet more is done to souls by souls to increase the taker awayers without the balance of relief.

There are bills, jobs, crime, homes that are not in ownership, cars that are not in ownership.

There are foods that are not given to all souls. There are souls who walk with nothing and some who have nothing and walk with everything.

There are cares of medicine for some, schooling that is inadequate, laws that take away more.

And the programs that give are starving, those who have savvy and business with lacks of pure intent are in charge of many souls at once.

And those who want to give, to help, are finding the avenues to do so difficult in nature to find, on those who can receive.

We say it is relationships and when I find the soul that I love. And once it has been found the soul starts to self sabotage itself within it.

There is a fight to have children and not time to raise them. There is the fight to go to schools and the learning's do not teach life.

Why do some things have to be taught and those very things that make life easier to learn, subjects easier to learn, kept out of the systems and methods of teaching?

And parents at home expect it from the schools and the schools expect it from the parents. And that is only America.

Other countries of Earth are in tryments of maintaining family and life and yet their goal in many ways is to emulate the America of the United States.

And the energy of Earth right now is following the lacks of prudency and truth for it is dominant in this time.

The bully of this time is Money.

It speaks louder than universal law and yet souls are finding that it is not of truth in their souls.

And the fighting's of energies within each and every soul begins to ask questions and the answers are hidden under a well swept carpet.

The world is coming to a renewed governing of itself. The laws of the world have strangled it into submission to the meek. The inheritances of the meeks are short lived, as we are in witness of.

There will be no laws of each country they will obsoletize themself(s).

*(OBSOLETIZE—To take something that has existed and say it does not need to exist anymore)*

For there can not be global economy, there can not be fractured, politicated, decisions that affect countries without their knowledge's. And they are taken away from the souls that matter for the personal gain of another country.

This is not of longerments of time. This last war is the evidence of this experience of learnings.

There has been deterioration of the tolerances of the differences that God Almighty brought to challenge our souls on Earth.

There has been the creation of religion to clump souls together into believing they share a common interest, goal, and that interest and goal excludes others who are said by all that there is One God.

Is One God a theory, a form of manipulation, a decoy to get souls to take care of themself(s) and not of others?

One God means One God. No matter who is under the Umbrella we will call Earth for now.

Souls have taken liberties with God Almighty and God Almighty only has been love for all. For a human can not recreate itself.

And I speak, in that, how can only some human's be deserving of God's love and some left aside, for they are not considered desirable, for color, race, belief or stance?

A soul who wants growth will find it and a soul who does not will find it as well.

There is free will and choice and free will and choice are speaking and saying, "I want to be better than, stronger than, have more than...at any souls expense to do so.

I will create laws to limit some and free others. I will kill souls and call it war so it will not appear as it is. I will tell those who are to kill that it is for noblements to do so.

I will demonize anyone else who speaks that very same thing I speak, for I am chosen above them, for I am more polished, I have more money and I am better.

Therefore, follow me and let us take from others in the name of God, Country and who I am, the Ego of this time, to take away from all of us and not appear to be doing so."

So simple is the truth. And it lives in this day. Some countries try to speak however the peaceful heart is the overlooked heart in this time.

And I speak there will be a governing body for the world, for the world is not so big. The laws will be of Universal laws and the breakings of truth, love and purity are minimal.

For souls feel no threats to create laws to protect themself(s) from the mistrust they have of others.

There will always be those who come to challenge, of ill will however they will not be the tip of the balance.

The world is not as big a place as humans make it to be. It is only designed for all humans to live within it. Not some.

There are souls who come to suffer, to show others their fortune, and the fortunate can not see and want more.

They can no longer see for greed, internal greed's of heart have come out swinging at any intent of purity to stand in its way.

Lacks of life for others is lack of life for self. And no one on Earth can live alone, even those who want to!

There is no rhythm to a soul without the instruments of other souls. And souls who speak not to others of love, others will come to them in attack in this way. It is respect.

If a soul speaks, I am intelligent, and they are not in intelligence enough to stop their actions of this sort, is there intellect of heart? Ego is the fighter of the heart and ego wins here.

No more actions of stories and how wrong everyone else is. No more victimization's and dramatizations. No more claimings of others things or wants or needs, all that has come to dissolvations already.

It is all repetition now and unbeknownst to all there is vision and all those with vision have moved along, for all souls strive to live and those who strive to take away are those left behind.

They stay at that point with anyone who will take them, for most who want to growth themself(s) will go elsewhere to do so.

That is how usury of souls originates. It begins when a soul simply needs another soul to outlet rather than share.

To need rather than want, To open the doors rather than to solve, To close doors when the soul does not feel they are reciprocated in what they need or want from another.

In demands that are not good for the fellow journeyman, in guilt's and descending truths to keep the relationship in line.

For there are conditions that torture souls and many live within the confines of such behaviors. Many are the very souls to exhibit such behaviors.

You see, Nadia, many souls feel they deserve things that do not deserve. They want from others all they would never give of themself(s). They expect from others and they do very sparingly to others.

There is no balance. And the moment you mess up, to use another term of this time, you are turned on like the image of a picture without color when it once was flowing in hues.

Nadia, there is more, I must speak to the world of this. There are many and many more being taught. When a soul finds itself in taking away, they know.

ASK YOURSELF(S), am I taking away from me? You will know. You will know before you ask. Hence tell yourself you have taken the world away from you too.

For your energy will only draw to you likeness to yourself and you will not find the happiness you complain about not finding in your daily life(s).

Souls who see someone who is happy and they come with intent to Meangle this happiness and relish in the upsets of that soul; you already know who they are.

Stay away from them, I speak. And souls will make excuses for others and yet they know not the extent of others in this way. Trust what you know.

All souls will justify anything as long as they will get what it is they think they are seeking. And they are not detected until they are coming to points of repetitions.

Truths are difficult to come by. For all truth can only stand in its truth. There is no ways around truth, love, purity.

And Truth is the artery of how to enter in teachings of presenting non truths to those presenting non truths with truths.

And it speaks. And then yet another triangular force Truth Love and Purity, it will all take the soul to its origin of truth. Glory be to God Almighty.

# CHAPTER 15

# I AM HERE

Surprise.

I love surprises. In the times I healed, I spoke. I was in dangers of my physicality. I was in surprise, for I witnessed the depths of humanality, and the strength of the internal needs being in control of all actions.

I was the ensemble of hope, truth, love, purity. And I watched those who feared hope, love truth, purity, for then they would be known to not have been.

I relish in the surprise that I died for the sins of others. When the sinners never know it is of them. For the sinners, to speak as the humans speak, are the ones looking for the sins of others.

They want and seek company however they behave in abovement of that company to secure their stance as those that take away.

Glory be to God Almighty, for they are seen in superficiality! I stood and witnessed the eyes of souls, souls that took glory in the washing away of another.

I say again and again, I did not pass for the sins of others. I understood that I had to pass to be heard. Many have passed in blessing of heart and mind, for in leastments their truths were in truth.

For those who needed heightenments by takings away from another soul, may or may notment in results of physical deaths, were in truth the lost souls of their time, the fraudulents of their time, threatened by truth.

There is not time. Life is eternal. However on Earth there is time, for learnings and memories, past and present, future thoughts and growth.

Earth is the lessons of learning, taking what is known, with what is unknown yet to the souls. Yet all is already known at home.

It is left to the quest of humanality to discover and to growth. The answers to tomorrow are already present, simply left to discovery.

Questions are always left behind, for that is the stimulus for Humans to think further.

If they know all the answers or are sure of them, they stop trying and we have to keep the questions to remain on quest.

Time is what creates past, present and future.

And all souls are intrigued with the unknown, the future, however the intriguement is in past of time on Earth; the beliefs of those who came to Hone otherments of lessons. Glory be to God Almighty.

And the intriguements of future are truly the wonder of, hopes of, dreams becoming, and all want to believe.

And the present is the closest to home on Earth. The present is actually timelessness on Earth. While I was present on Earth I was in the present always. The days before that day accumulated and brought to light the caste of my mission. The future thinking were in concern I would expose their inadequacies. And in the present, I spoke, traveled, witnessed the will of the free souls and I loved.

Within my love I carried all love, for all souls, and that is what was said of me.

That I asked for the forgiveness' of souls "for they know not what…"I simply understood the limitations of humanality and to teach humans is to shock humans into learning.

To represent the worst fear of humans, death, and be in stance is the teacher, to not fear them. To not fear a soul is to stand in grace of self. Fear can only take away and create the fear itself.

For thoughts are things. I say it and I say it. Thoughts are things. Glory be to God Almighty.

Thoughts are the processes to teach us, to create our realities. To let us know when we are going away from ourselves and when we are coming back. To ensure us we are in heart, in heart with ourselves.

Our conversations in our heads that coincide within our hearts, is truly only one, our soul. Our souls are fluid on Earth in confinements of body however our souls are fluid as all things.

The first restriction of all souls is discovering the limitations of the body. For then travel and time set in. The only limits that exist are those of the human mind. I live in you, how many souls can conceive?

I speak through you, how many can believe you? I am back? I am over-looked for now. I am expected back with a trumpet.

That is not of truth. I will come back and only back the good. Who are the good?

I died for sins? There are no sins. I was killed. That is truth. I am pure.

I have become a far away example, something to hold to in understandings or not.

Simply that I am the only thing, person, image to hold onto. And I have become unattainable and lost in the shuffle of messages of love.

I am looked at as a ticket to bring a soul back home, simply out of fear of going anywhere else. I am the better bet of the choices. And humans want and need love.

So they discount the love of humans around them and come to me for love and it is in fantasy that I am loved.

I am not in usement of intentions of pure. I am spoken of as though no one can be like me and we are all of God. I am not God. I am not of anyone bowing down to me.

No one needs bowing or any other bodily action to complete love. Love is. It is known.

There is nothing you can do to it. You can simply love and show love as you understand it. Love is not a thing. I say this and say it; it can not be a thing. It is a feeling.

How do you buy love? You can not. Souls can buy each others time, sexualnesses, energies, for a while however it does not mean love.

Love is love. Love propels. You can not pay for it. The blessing is in knowings. Love is here always, before things, peoples, planes, galaxies, the universe.

God is energy of love. And that very love exists in all things. All things come for the will of God and within God Almighty. And the will of God was given to us in drops of love and given to us in our wills.

I could see energy while I was here. I knew of what others were coming at me with.

I did not shake as vigorously as you do when there is ill will Nadia, however I miracled the onlooker into a path of reflection, which was very dangerous, as you are noticing that reflection of self(s) before you brings to you love or anger.

I was in the sameness. However, I would go to God and I would be shown the angerers and my role in their angers.

I came as an Angel knowingly and I was much greater in forthrightness, for I started at a much earlier age on Earth than you.

And I had to speak as I did before I was in miracles of mind to peoples, as you are in waitment of my coming.

I am someone to be believed in or not. I am someone who defines a conversation if I am mentioned.

I am a soul that carries arguments of who is killing for God. Who believes in God and how and why?

I am a soul who is in hurryment of people's dreams wanting to be of truth and discarded when they do not present themself(s) as the souls of greed want from them.

For the souls of greed do not in truth want what they are seeking. They simply want to control what they can. It is true of all internal greedsman.

The internal greedsman on Earth, are the hardest to touch into penetration, other than through self motivation.

A soul can appeal to a self motivator when and only when the self motivator is in satisfaction of what it is getting; otherwise it is waves and waves of lower energies of payment to come.

I am used to show that a soul is of religion. I am used to show that someone is of goodness.

I am used to project feelings of internal awareness and I am used to divide peoples into betterments of each other. I am here in honor of love as well.

Peoples do not know they are self motivated. They view themself(s) as those who are in progressiveness of change and happenings. They are the ones on top of things and know all of everyone.

They make it their business, others business. And they pick and choose what they want to make of it, for that is what they know to do.

They are in charge. They are the best, the brightest, in enoughment to make fun of others, to poke at the efforts of others. To instill in others their will, whether they like it or not like of it.

They need to control to feel alive. For the controlment of their behaviors is how they believe they are working.

And the rewards are to live within the disruptions, for then they can avoid further their own lives and live within others takings away that they are in taking away from their self(s) in, so simple and so clear.

Tell that to a self motivator and trouble you will have. I was taken away from Earth through self motivation of others.

Nadia my Angel, I stood and watched my body's pain within the self motivation.

I was hung in awements of people who found a way to attach a body to wood.

That very wood is imitated in jewelry's now. There was a reason for the pure hearted to die, for it gave life to the living. The living, are truly the one's in pain.

I felt not the pains after a point of interception. The body becomes in numbnesses and the souls are spared.

You see, those that are no longer in physical body, they can see their bodies as though they are looking at someone else. That is what happened to me.

I flowed through the crowds of peoples watching me suffer however I was between them then. They could only feel the love.

The watching's were in horror of their own dying's. And I hung before them in threeness of souls. I was not the only soul to hang of such holdings.

That was simply the way in which a soul was removed at that time. As I hung in drips of wood and bloods of my body, my heart could not hurt a soul, for they do not know of their truths.

It did not mean when I returned, I returned TO them. I did not return to them. I returned FOR them. I came to TAKE CARE of them To TEACH them.

There are many "them's," and your examples are as fierce as any. However purity will always endure.

The brutalities of humans were in openness. Now they are in deceptions. For self motivation has paths of evolvement as well.

There are some self motivators who recognized that that is who they are and they created laws to stop other self motivators from benefiting from what they have benefited from. Glory be to God Almighty.

THE SELF MOTIVATOR IS ALWAYS IN FEAR THAT THEY WILL BE IN SELF MOTIVATION OF OTHERS.

So it is. Glory be to God Almighty, for the lesson not wasted and seen is the lesson of all souls benefitment.

All will know of me, all will see me.

All will know of who I am without explanation. I will appear in recognition. I find within you moments of believing this. You do, however you are in partment thinking you are of dreaming.

You are dreaming. You are of holdment of knowings. You are of being in duality. You are of love. And you are of rejection for who you are.

You are. You are. You are. I am not trying for your beliefment in all of this, I am witnessing you knowing something and being unable to imagine.

Imagine.

Nadia, when I was on Earth as a person, And I had a name, and a reputation that grew within the words of mouth, I too, could not conceive of what would happen as I presented myself and my love to souls on Earth.

Love brings with it a wisdom and an openness in heart that can only happen with that kind of love, with that kind of purity within.

That is what people anticipated. It was the greatness, the power of love that healed. It was within my heart to carry all with the love in possession of myself.

I was no one special. I simply knew love for what love is. That is the threat again in this time. All of the years on Earth have passed.

Technologies can do things that are looking so great and yet there are more and more discoveries to come. To be.

Peoples know not what they know not for they could not. How could they and why?

Even in these times with sophistications and Third World Countries, with disasters and beautiful natures, all in all of all that exists, there is still the quest for love.

I am embedding in your bodyment of the humanness that has to be human on Earth. Glory be to God Almighty.

I had many visible helpers. Yours are not so visible. I am here. Remember that I am here. And I am hear in your hearts speakings.

You teach truth by being in truth. You teach love by being an example of love. You teach marriage by being in marriage in truth.

You teach listening by letting others know that they have been heard.

You teach hearing by responding to what you are listening to. For you can only teach by who you are.

No words can teach as great as the actions of those where love is in unconditionality. Glory be to God Almighty.

For love that exists with conditions can only take away. Even in moments of appearance of givance it is in taking awayment.

Understand that love is of everywhere. Anywhere you look where there is love there is light. Where there is self motivation the light disappears for that is fact.

There is no exception.

There will always be those who will speak that I exist, that I do not, that I spoke, that I speak.

However in this time, in this moment, in this awakening of the souls of home on Earth, I am in mission to love all souls. To Service all souls.

Humans created me to obscurity of thoughts and it will be of challenge for the world to know me as truth, love and purity for all.

You see Nadia; Human souls do not want me for all. For that will open the door of Universal Law, that there is no soul more important than another.

It will open the channels of communicating to all souls on Earth not only to some, to acknowledge that we are all one. What one soul does affects all souls and what all souls do affects one.

We are in combination of Earth, Home and the accumulation of time, free will and choice on Earth. WE are one. The confused souls who possess hearts of light and can not see are for purpose.

The manipulative soul whose confidence of heart is weak hence to keep others in weakness is for purpose. The soul who reaches out and works with those in need is of purpose.

The souls of workments that speak, that give credence to life to offer growth, they are with purpose.

Those in political forum, who come to challenge prudency of soul, are with purpose. Those who come to lead in avenues to God Almighty are with purpose.

You see our love; there is a home on Earth for all souls. The human soul's job is to learn of all souls on Earth, for they are of the human souls as well.

At home there is no need to know of every soul for it is known that all souls are one, that all souls have gifts, and that evolution of soul is purpose and choice.

That love is absolute, for it is not questioned at home. The questions of home are in difference. For on Earth the questions are simply to get an answer and go on.

There is time on Earth and there is Ego and Status and Acknowledgements that are needed by souls. However at home there is no Ego. There is truth in the learnments of souls at home.

There is no need to outdo another. There is a need for growth as there is a need for food on Earth to ward off starvations.

There is beauty and the beauty intensifies with the knowledge's intensity of the soul.

The greater the knowledge's of any soul will take it to greater paths of evolution and love is endless therefore the findings are endless.

That is why to answer a question of long ago, why do some souls speak of Angels who speak to them and they are not speaking exactly what others say Angels speak to them?

It is all in the evolution. It is all in the minds knowledge's and the souls acceptance of the learning's of its experiences.

Once a known is known it can not be known again, it can only be grown from.

That growth broadens eyes to see more than they could see with the same eyes. It simply has grown depth. And within that depth is the endlessness' of learning.

Truths, loves, purity's are endless. They are eternal. And the light of God Almighty, of Love, is for all, for the asking.

Knowing what to ask is simply wanting to ask. Intention. Purity. What is the soul on Earth looking for in heart and they will find it. Regardless of what the lips of the souls may sound.

We each have our roles. I am made in bigger dealments simply because I am already known. And all that is known of me is treasured, revered, and in ways that take love away from souls, spoken of me in lacks of truth.

I come to Earth again. I am here. What am I supposed to look like, speak like, appear like. This is how I look.

I speak the words that need to be spoken. I bring with me the truth that is already present and reinstate its importance in the souls who walk in honor of me and not of themself(s).

I come to remind souls there is a picture more beautiful than they know now however have known in their existence.

I come to say to all I am not for Christians, Muslims, Jewish, Buddha, Hindu, Tribal knowings, Atheists of thought, I am not for anyone!!! I am for everyone!!! I am everyone!!!

# CHAPTER 16

# THE SOUL'S CONTENTS

Nadia, I am here, noisier than ever. I simply gave you reprieve, for you are coming to much stimulation and much busyness ahead.

I speak to you that you can not conceive. You see in vision and yet life around your soul is quiet. Quieter than you expect.

I turned over your last stone of ill will and now the only stones that will turn over will be the stones of propellations of love and you will be turning energy from all facets, just as you had to learn of ill will in all facets.

Glory be to God Almighty, for the world is eagerly waiting and the world knows not what it is waiting for.

You speak to each soul in its own language. And you are teaching the world a new language. A language that explains, gives, receives.

A language that allows, extends, opens, furthers, builds bridges, creates avenues to one's soul. The roads to the souls are now paved, waiting and ready for the load that is to come.

The roads to souls will now have answers, for one question to lead to another and the paths of thoughts will create. The thoughts will produce life as it wants to be, as souls are searching for, in soonments of time.

Nadia, you can see, and you can feel the movement is spinning in spirals upon spirals of energy that propels.

You see our love, souls are propelling as you are. However, they need those that have been studied to show them.

Just as you go to others to show you what you know not of yet. Just as you were searching for someone who knew me as you do. I am present in all. Simply ask.

Yet you found not a soul who knew they knew. And you will show them how, even though you yourself can not conceive.

Our love on Earth, carry the world and let the world carry you.

There is not a reason for such angers, other than the helplessness of the human soul within itself and the anger at the world for shortchanging them. There is not shortchanging. It is an objective world.

The world is as it is in this day at its own choosings. For there are many choices and the issues within in the world in this time is at its own choosings of money of people.

Money over things. Money over health. Money over growth.

Glory be to God Almighty. Do you speak Glory be to Money Almighty. Yes, souls speak this. For they have lost themself to Money.

It is not the money, it is the soul who turned money on its back and became a servant to something that souls can not get enough of, are scared of losing, always want and do not like to share.

It has all the characteristics of someone who is heartless, feltless and lacks character and judgment. Glory be to God Almighty. For if the souls of Earth can see what Money has done to them, they would run faster than a road runner on a dirt road.

You see, most issues that occur on Earth in this time are judged, dealt with, taken on or not taken on, all for money. Money has become the definition.

I am not speaking that money is bad. It is what it is capable of doing that is hurtful to many souls and many soul's lessons revolve around money more than love.

Money is the falser strength of the two. To use anything to place judgments, love or not love, caring or not caring due to money is a false judgment, love or caring.

I brought all of the souls that money means nothing to and you had to filter many to do so. And you found love.

You found the value of monies to be less than love and within all the souls who have this, life is of greater joy and less control.

And for that, they can see life for what it is and live in the moments, rather than trying to take on the world and conquer, before anyone else said they did and the pressures that involves.

You hear many things in these days between the writing.

You hear of medicated teens, plastic surgery's on faces, complaints that those that know are too simple, that those who are running faster than they can feel are living in the lost energy's of the universe.

Our loves, you will growth your souls onto the lands of new trees, new flowers and greater loves than you can speak of knowing in this time.

For eternal is eternal. Never forget there is always always greater depth, more learneth of heart, and greater depth again.

You are love. You are the example of love and the truth of love. You fight for it and you found that the words of love are easily overlooked and the words of fighting are preferred.

You will turn this around as you have over and over again. That is when the light can live in the lightness of itself. And it is already represent, being called upon one soul at a time. Glory be to God Almighty.

**Nadia, you gove my heart with humor. Gove? Yes, my love, Gove: Gove, to enter the barriers to eternity.**

*(GOVE—To go into the avenues. To explore. For this word brings an encompassment of thought, love and action.)*

**You enter and your questions are of the soul, not of life. Your questions are of love, not of procedure.**

**Your questions of truth pierce the edges of knowledge's that you have pushed yourself to, for the sake of the knowledge, within the realms of objective thought.**

**That has been your harshest battle. For when you upset, it is objective, yet that is not known in entirety on Earth yet.**

**You started this energy by speaking that you do not care what the answer is as long as the answer is truth. For you understand the settlements of truth are the only cases won.**

That is gove my love. Gove does not blame, it explains. Gove does not dishonor, it honors in it's moments of pain. Gove teaches it does not accuse. Gove speaks and it does not judge. Gove gives and it allows for receiverment, which is more important than giving.

To receive gives the souls of Earth purpose to interact. Gove paves roads for growth without the wild cards of taking away periodically, hence giving piercings to longevity of heart to sustain.

Gove does not bring out conflict for self worth. Gove gives conflict meaning and avenues to growth all souls, in understanding that there is not a soul more important than another.

Gove; to say, "I will not hurt you, no matter what you do. It does not mean I have to trust or enable, it simply means I will not hurt you." And you do not.

Jacob is bringing about the consciousness of souls to peak to understanding what is to come. You see our love, you believe in this day, who you are.

You found that souls will speak what they have to, to save themself and they will leave the other person and themself in the non truth they created and it can only take away. It has not another path to follow.

In truth, a soul can not be in truth with another if it is lying to itself. And souls wonder why they can not feel! Glory be to God Almighty.

So souls try to create the very feelings they can not feel in liements to themself(s).

They try to create love rather than feel it. They try to create beauty rather than be it. They try to show love rather than  trust  it.

We are finding that feeling, feeling it, being it is the superior of the two and it is, simply because it is closer to home. It is closer to self.

There are many bodies on Earth in this time. Many wants, many needs, many yearnings. If a soul is not yearning for growth of itself, there is not growth amongst the masses of souls. The greater populations.

All the modern day speakers are the steps to the understandings that there is a picture bigger than the picture we see. Bigger than the thoughts that we have.

Bigger than the paychecks we bring home. Bigger than the reasons we think the world would be better within however to think bigger is to understand the Macrogrowths rather than the Microgrowths.

For the Macrogrowths have to be seen, and the Microgrowths will create a path to be done! Glory be to God Almighty.

***Origins of Truth, Love and Purity,*** The Morsels of Love we are All Looking For!

These passed days have culminated to the truths of the souls in aroundments. And have brought about the lacks of fire, for the lacks of truths dullened the sense of self.

Souls are not to be in horror of others when horrors of themself(s) are their truth. You are teachers. Teach.

Speak in truth and give not the times of Earth to those who will not rise. Rise and they will rise. Listen and they will have forum. Act and they will have succeeded.

And you speak. "Let's rise together" and they want not to be together, they want to be special and you will speak, "Rise and we will rise together" and they will speak, "No, I can not love myself enough to withstand."

And you will speak, "Rise and we will rise together," and rise. And they will learn from the example of the risen of heart.

To rise over the thoughts of ill will and bring about the love that outlines all of existence. Glory be to God Almighty.

The souls of Earth are in waitments of rising. They are in need and in want. For they know not what they want and want not what they know.

You can not speak that souls need love when the souls that need it will not admit they are in need. They want to draw to them in the same lacks of accountings that they have in their lives in other areas.

They did not have anything to do with this or that, it just happened. And nothing just happens. There is purpose and reason behind all things.

Do not fret on the Energy of Earth souls. They are simply in lacks of understandings of self. You are teaching everyone around you survival.

You are teaching growth and you are teaching that all can do and all will find a path without the detriment of others to achieve. You are teaching to depths of help as you are teaching the depths of askments.

You do not feel like you are in trouble. You are not. Time is teaching and souls are learning. Understand that all things happen as they should and you are simply on the paths of getting there.

How else can it appear? The means of achievements do not appear as such. They appear as struggle. Understand that growths can only come of this.

Intent is your truth and your growth. Those who speak they struggle not, that they have everything under control, are simply holding growth in place.

Growth is challenge and challenge has purpose and purpose has challenge.

Love is strength and it is shown in the struggles it takes on to fight for it, to draw it out, to understand its depth and its width.

Life is a reel of series of Growth, Love, and Purpose. To fight Growth, Love and Purpose is to say Ego is bigger than truth. And the proof, the measurements of success, the better thans, all live in this world.

You have been exampled this. Glory be to God Almighty. People want to believe there is good within them when they are not so sure if they are good to themself(s).

People are curious of possessions and claimants of souls when they are not so sure they possess themself(s). Souls want from others to show them they have come to points of discovery and have moved on.

And there is moving on however it is of lateral natures than onward.

Souls like to create situations that call on each other and there is reason for growth, opportunity for growth. Truth comes in times of need. Truth has to surface when there is a landing for foundation.

Soul's intentions come from what they need to accomplish. What they believe they want from another soul. Souls speak from heart as they want to believe their hearts are working.

The heart of a human soul is the asking of life and what they want from it. The ego turns it into the games that are not based on truth. The two struggle in dailyments. That is the story of life.

All souls have a job to do however not all souls who come to Earth plane come of service to other souls.

Most come to conclude on journey's of challenges of love in purity and free will and choice. And others come of service and most do not know that it is them.

In this time, we are reaching them in conscious mind for it accelerates their own understandings and even within those we wake up on Earth, until the awakement, they also do not know.

Experiences must be had to understand the enormity of mission when it is time. Earth is simply a plane to find love without absolute. To understand it is there no matter the obstacles.

We are all in searchments of love and candor however we have had lacks of love from others, of self, along the way and it blinded our eyes from seeing all that is available.

The challenges are to overcome and growth your soul. That is why each and every soul chose to come to Earth. No other reason; Evolution unto the oneness of Soul. That is God Almighty.

For we are all of God Almighty! Glory be to God Almighty.

For the things not believed on Earth are of truths and the things believed in this time are not of truth in the majordom of thoughts and possibilities.

Those who are not speaking truth are being seen in their quickness of moments, for the gaps between truth and non truth are widening and the energy is speaking to us that life has lost its balance.

Those holding onto passed thoughts are now passed. There is no longer room for the grand takings away from their lacks of prudency to all. They are now being brought upon to be seen.

They are holding on as the meek will fight until the end however their seenment is teaching all souls of the world, how it appears to speak in rhetoric and do in danger.

To want something that belongs not to them and speak that it belongs to them simply because they are more powerful.

To ask of others what they will not expect from self, To speak of others in tones of less importance.

That is the harshest of all doings, to speak the souls of God Almighty are not of greatest importance. Glory be to God Almighty, for there is not a soul more important than another.

It is spoken and contradicted. As I speak that all souls teach us who they are. And you have been taught.

And you have learned that all that is not given to/for a soul is what the energy of the soul itself speaks to the world, asks for, seeks to work on the challenges of itself.

And those that take away, their challenge is to give. To see that all souls matter as they do. That hurting others in truth is the hurt of self. To the self. For the self.

That is the lack of love I speak of. And you are fighting the lacks of love in symptom. You are healing the lacks of love in their truth.

And you finally understand that those that fight you do not want to learn from you, they want to steal you. They want to have the truth and they want it for themself(s) and not share it as you are sharing it, they want to be the better than for it.

You now can see and it all takes on sense. There will always be sense however the understandings need be growthed into step by step, for the learning's can not be without the process of truth, for how could you see how far away truth is, if you can not see the trail it takes to get to it?

You are of fine and you will remain so. There is magic waiting for you, for your hearts knowings and your mind's eye.

All the knowledge's that you have accumulated in life on Earth can now be seen in the world. That is the mind's eye.

The growth out of ego, hence the seements of the world, as it is not what you want from it.

That is the shifts of the secure mind, for the insecure worlds of doubt that the mind tries so hard to see, react and not feel. That is ego. That is why ego is never happy.

Once you have mind's eye, you can see, which means that ego is defeated. Our love the magic of Earth is the existence of the love of home.

The love of home is the magic, the absoluteness you speak of, the calmness to witness without the fear of defeat, the resonance of known truths into the faiths of actions, the growth of evolution of souls onto the knowings of oneness of soul in all. Glory be to God Almighty.

For the growths tell you that nothing changes in truth, truth simply deepens, widens and heightens the knowing soul; So beautiful the glory of knowledge.

For any soul of existence, speak to me that a soul can not learn, growth, and learn again what it thought it already knew.

Everything has depth and knowledge's that want for greater depths and knowledge's.

Souls who are trying to stay the same can not, even at all resistance to any change. For they will still change, they will still grow in physical, they will still have different favorites, even though they will pick markers that state they are not changing.

Even the cells of the human body change in moments of time in each and every soul. There is not a way to not, change is the truth of change.

For nothing is as it seems, nor can it be. For the soul is on Earth to learn, to search, to ask and to seek.

All those that deny this basis of every mission on Earth take it away from self hence others and it creates the undertone of an unsure world

And wills of souls who want to continuously prove they are of greatest stature and want not to share life with others will always and always be of conversations as warning to others.

Just as love propels, ill will expels. It expels thoughts of acknowledge and protection. It expels thoughts of growths and learnings. It expels thoughts of catalysts and meeks.

It expels, for any of ill will is not welcome, even to the ill willer itself.

They are teachers.

All things are possible with energy.

For those who do not know, they are into the provement phase of self, and even if it means destroying oneself, a family, another soul, a friend it matters none, for the meek can not see, they only want.

They do not appreciate, they only collect. They want attention for self and take away from another.

The meek teach everyone who they are, and they do not understand they are everyone and can also learn. That is the blindness as it appears.

So red you are thinking, and I am thinking so read! Glory be to God Almighty, for the teachers will always have a hand in what they teach.

In what everyone is on Earth to teacher, for the Teacher will always know more than the student and it is choice and free will, truth, love and purity.

Or lacks of feelings of choice or lacks of feelings of free will, lacks of truth, love and purity, that is behind everything and everyone. Every atonement of life on Earth.

And your love of all is not compromised it is simply taught to take on those who can love to carry those who can not. Nadia, there is much to speak to you. You are coming to points of complete Clairity, as to souls, their roles, their home to Earth missions and the appearances of what of this has become.

You have taken on an interest in souls on Earth and how they deal with conflict, as to the abundance of truth that you know and are, and the truth of soul's perceptions of self as you have come to witness.

And the perceived truths of self, of others, of the world and how it appears in the hearts of souls, and your fascination as to how souls choose to live. You have at some points come to complete alienation of some of the souls choices and can understand the run do not walk away sign in the moments of your realizations.

You believed all souls to be of beauty and you want to help everyone only to find there are those souls on Earth that do not want the worlds of truth, love or purity, and they will fight like an animal in the jungle to stop truth, love or purity from having a chance to be of presence in their own life(s) or anyone else's.

They will take on the energy that they have nowhere else to create and sustain chaos. You could not figure out how or why. You could not understand love meangled in suchness or the lacks of wanting love to be present.

In example after example you would find that the lacks of love at times are seen as love and misinterpreted by those who know each other and it has and can become a way of life.

And souls have not a clue they have accustomed to lacks of love rather than love.

The Lacks of love's hide when they can not manipulate their circumstances.

The learning's and the teachings that every soul wants prosperity as they believe it to be, as the mind can see it, and as the souls contents carry within and the souls of Earth project that onto themself(s) and onto others.

I am writing you of the Souls Contents on Earth. I wrote to you of yourself and of Stirling and the maturation's of heart that you both growth through and encounter.

As I write with you of the souls you encounter in growth of humanality of this time.

Every soul has a role. For every soul on Earth is energy. All energy is of connection, for in truth all there is is energy.

WE are only in form as a way of recognition however at home we do not need form for recognition.

We are of purity, and light's of evolution of a soul tells the energy who it is. And it is present as to the evolution of soul, not the evolution of judgments who the soul is.

The restriction of having a form is of great challenges to Earth, for it is a ready made judgment.

There is color of skins, races, beauty, health, disabilities, stature and status that comes with form, and that is the greatest of challenges.

For that is where judgments make decisions and take on reality and projections and expectations, that base from ego rather than soul. Earth is the plane of challenge.

That is why you speak to many, do you want a soulution? Are you really asking? If you do not want to hear the truth, I am not the person to come to for help.

I will tell you the truth and I have found that many do not want it. Be sure it is something you are truly looking for, or we are both wasting our time. Do as you know and you will grow to do as you can see.

You now know you can not make a soul happy by being love, of being there, by sharing, that you can just as easily fuel their anger and bring out troubles to your own life for simply being happy yourself.

Yes, it is true, A hard to believe truth before your eyes. It is truth. That is Earth.

That is what Earth has become, is, and carries in its energy's in this day.

And those with pure intent are coming forward and being known for who they are.

They are the soldiers. They are the Souldiers of Earth. The Absolute. The Soulutions.

Yes, there is a pattern here. For the vocabulary is changing in it's appearancy of need.

Nadia, one more thing, stop not taking accounting for the writings. It is you. It is me. It is the world you are responding to. You do not want to say so, for you want not to live in your knowledge's at times.

LIVE IN YOUR KNOWLEDGE. AS YOU ASK OF OTHERS. ASK OF YOURSELF. YOU SPEAK YOU HAVE GREATER CONVICTION OF YOUR KNOWLEDGE AND THEN YOU DO NOT WANT TO LIVE IN THE MIND, SOUL THAT YOU KNOW OF YOURSELF. LIVE IN YOUR KNOWLEDGE.

I come to you, I speak through you, I reside within you, do you know why? I am you. You are me. WE are one of love. There is a you. There is a me. We are separate.

I can not be you. You can not be me. However we created a one for mission. I can not pass on to Earth without you. You can not speak in completeness without me.

CHAPTER 17

A MILLION BABY STEPS

Our love, your writing is in difference of form in this time. The learned lessons of the last years of three have brought you to the understanding of the world in present and the whys that you could not see.

You see it had to be personal, close and in form of absorption to you and that is why you are in freedom of it now and you could not be before.

As well, now you are in the sustaness of those who want to fight and begin to lose sight of what they are fighting for; for the fights of life have lost their fight.

The agonies of life have lost their purpose. For the agonies of some are of all and now souls simply know what the other is talking about when they speak that they are unhappy.

So I ask the world at large what is happy. Why do you have to feel happy if you work so hard to not be happy? If you work so hard to endorse unhappiness for others and happiness for yourself, why for some and not for others?

We complain that this or that does not exist and we are waiting for whom to exist it? It already exists and it is ignored by choice, fear and ego.

Nadia you are thinking this writing continues to continue. Yes, for the thoughts of this writing takes within it days of concurrent knowledge's. You see your love; I am speaking of ownership to souls. Ownership of actions, thoughts, of behaviors.

Souls have come to find ways to speak not their own truths. They believe if they did not speak it, it did not happen. There is attempt to live in what they want to pretend they did, rather than what they have done.

There are many stories I hear and Nadia, they are stories, they are not truth. And they are lived by. Said so many times they seem truth and all souls around live by the lie rather than by the truth of that truth.

Situations are set up in manipulations. Planted like a well seasoned recipe, only the love is left out, the lie to one's self replaces it and then you have a tasteless meal.

The food is there. It is colorful, it smells great and yet you eat it and you wonder why you can not taste. That is how most souls are in feelments in this time.

They wonder why it is that they can not feel. Souls can not feel, for they do not speak their truths.

And when truths are not spoken, there is anger at one's self for not speaking truth, so immediately there becomes suspicion of everyone else; Suspicion that no one speaks truth, as they.

So now we have a soul who does not trust itself nor does it believe anyone else. And no one wants to feel that, so what happens? The soul takes on that no one speaks the truth, it is a matter of fact that everyone lies.

And that person tries to find in others what it knows exists in itself. And they will point out or create that another has lied or stolen; all to mask the first non truth that a soul allowed to happen in the first place.

You see, our love, our loves, Truth does Matter. As souls search for the world's truth, the truth of this moment must be accomplished.

The love of this day must have its life to live, so that the life of life can find its foundational love, its purity of soul to sustain.

Nadia, you ask, how do souls sustain? They must speak truth. How do souls speak truth? They must ask themself, what is my intention here? Why is that so important? Without ownership, a soul is lost.

You see now, in current world conditions there is not ownership. Therefore there is not truth and the world is left to find clue after clue that things are not of OK and yet they are sidelined about truth.

Over and over again, the truth is subsided and souls have found every remedy to avoid hearing the truth, which would overwhelm them and the world they hear, simply to be able to go on.

People shop, eat, medicate themself(s), speak of others, watch movies, listen to music in records of numbers, simply to postpone hearing truth.

For Truth is louder than shopping, eating, medications or any luxury thereafter. For without truth, the souls of Earth are in a state of limbotic thoughts, helplessness, and loss of control of their life(s).

Without ownership to self, there can not be otherwise, ownership anywhere else.

Nadia, when you sense ill will and you know the truth and you wait upon a soul to speak it, before you speak it, do you know why you wait?

You wait because you understand that the power of a soul when it speaks it's truth is contagious to that soul. **For you will not judge them for truth, it is the lacks of truth that are judged.**

All souls accommodate truth and when it does not exist souls speak of each other as though they have never taken away ownership from themself.

Glory be to God Almighty, for every issue starts within an issue of ownership. Truth, love and purity are universal, hence they have universal appeal.

Souls speak they want this or they want that. They have a dream house, car, job. What about the dreams of truths freedom? What about the feelings and propellations of love's energy?

How it is to understand and feel purity towards self and others? For then the house, car, job, they are put in perspective and all the bells and whistles are not attached to self worth as they are now.

Glory be to God Almighty, for the soul is now with price tag, and discounted by lacks of ownership as products are discounted for non movement.

Nadia, I am showing you truth and I show you the hidings of it; the tortures to the soul of hiding its truth. Trying to conceal as though they are not seen, and yet they are, so fully.

And the relationships lose as a result. You see, when a soul speaks not the truth, it matters not if they are caught or not. The energy exists anyway and it is reacted to anyway.

Nothing that exists can be invisible. At times souls do not know they are lied to, in action or in words however they will have a feeling of not trusting.

Not knowing what not to trust, so they simply excuse that person from their energy in self preservations.

**To lie is to live with your eyes closed. You use to speak, living in illusion. You use to speak that you can not communicate with a soul that lies, for the communication is fruitless.**

You see our love that is why there are very few paths with those that life. You see three things happen.

One, they can not hear themself speak, for they will forget what they have said. Two, the listener will discount them, for energy will tell them too, and three, they live in the illusion they are not missing anything and that they are gaining to have lied.

And energy will not allow that to happen. The soul that lies will stay put for it's lifetime until it can come to the truth of itself. As love is eternal, lying is external and has many stops and ends, many avenues to its demise.

For a person to make up a reason as to why they did something and it is not a reason at all, is to lie to itself. For a person to speak to another "I did not and they did," is the most obvious.

I am now speaking about a soul's truth. When a soul on Earth takes on another soul, a parent, a sibling, a teacher, a friend and blames them for what they do not have, have not done, did not do, will not do, will not speak, for fear they have, for worries they carry, they are lying to their self.

They are saying, I have not a will or a soul of my own. It is because of others I am not full. Every soul comes to Earth full and there are many examples to teach souls that hardships are fought, that is challenges, growths and learning's.

To say others, is to say, "I am not full, I do not know, I will not do, I will not speak that I have a hand in my own life. I will not, and I will blame the world and say it is the world and my circumstance."

**The truth in circumstance is that they chose a mission and are trying to forfeit their mission.**

And they live by complaining about this person that person, this situation, that situation. The complaining of a soul leaves a soul helpless and looking for another soul to take them on and live for them, and they to live through others and no one can take on that burden.

**No one can be responsible for another's soul, Energy will not allow it. That is a charge of attempted usury**. I say this in using today's terms, and in my time, we use to call this simply weakness.

Simply laziness of a soul and yet it was very rare in my time. For there were not enough peoples to complain and there were even less to take on the burdens of another while tending to their own. **When a soul accepts lying unto itself, then no one can truly live in their care.**

A soul can not depend on them, for they will be and are inconsistent. They will begin many things however not from heart, so they will not finish them.

They will speak big stories and they may or may not be truth, so others will question them. They build big castles in the mind and they are not purchased or earned.

When one soul lies to another, the soul who receives the lie can not forget it. However to rectify is to speak the truth, so that the receiving soul can accept at the very least that they soul that lies can self account.

Those who come not forward can not self account on any level. In the past souls would speak, I give you my word. Their word was worth everything to them and to the receiver.

In this time, many leave the door open to interpretation. They use words that may not confuse the receiver at first however will after the truths start to reveal themself.

And then trust erodes, as we sit in year called 2007 and souls do not know or speak what is truth and what is not.

Concealment, not speaking, trying to hide, taking situations and speaking they are not what you see, hear, or heard. Checking to see if anyone actually believed them and purchase their misconceptions.

When there is lying involved on any level, to a child, to an adult, to a company, to a friend, to a store clerk for that matter, a soul begins erosion onto itself. It begins its own discontent to itself.

You see, a soul that lies does not trust even itself. It simply losses track of itself.

It forgets what it really wants and what it speaks it wants. It forgets what it really is and what it is speaks it is. It forgets its real stories from the made up stories. It begins to live in a mission that is far away from its truth in mission and then it is lost.

When souls speak the world is lost, this is the lost the world is speaking of. They can not look another soul in the eyes, or they practice doing so to try to avoid detection, however the lacks of truth are stronger in energy then the physical deception planned and administered.

**There is not an energy that can penetrate love, truth or purity. It is only the liar that believes this is so, simply because a liar does not believe anything anyway.**

You felt very harsh to hear me speak the word liar. There is not another word. A soul who lies, will wonder why they go through friends quickly and a soul who is honest does not want to lose friends.

A soul who lies will say others are attacking them in some way, a soul who is honest will speak, this person is ill, and I will walk away unless he asks me for help.

A soul who lies will speak "this person did or did not do this to me, for me." An honest soul will seek its growth no matter what. A soul who lies to itself will speak you are to blame. An honest soul will speak, "I had a hand in this, I really did not want this or that."

A soul who lies will speak in terms to manipulate others to their thinking and get them to do things for them they can not do for themself(s), and a soul who speaks truth to itself will appreciate and contribute.

You see if a soul can speak to the world through self accounting, then the world can growth. If the souls of Earth speak to each other through blame, self pity, and lyings of all kinds, the world will stagnate.

If the souls of Earth have issue with what is truth and what is not, there is helplessness and in this time, Helplessness is trying to curb itself as those with truth and means are trying to repair this world as those with lacks of prudence and lyings can not see even themself(s).

Glory be to God Almighty, for the souls of Earth are in need of balance, of truth, of love, of purity.

And that is all that you are saying. That is all the book means. That is all that souls need. **They need to be reminded that the lies of mind are not worth the loss of love of their soul.**

The price of losing a soul is the price of lacks of happiness and the imposition of that onto others.

And that is the initial stem of the unhappiness all around that limits and boundaries decisions, relationships, and movements from growing forward.

It is holding everything back, like a funeral for the living. For now the perception of physical death carries with it thoughts of relief, for life is giving nothing to hold onto in its burdens and its lights are very dim as a result.

Projection, whether spoken or not is the truth, and it is responded to in energy. Glory be to God Almighty.

Our love, your discovery of the world is the discover of those who live in the world. You have nothing else to do with souls. You are simply their learner, a teacher of soul's reflection.

There are many souls who come to Earth for Service. Your service is to the returnance of souls, to themself(s).

You see our love, you are love. That is all. You are truth. That is all. You are purity. That is all.

Souls self appreciate in falseness of illusion and insecurity to boast their standings. However, of what race are the standing or winning? What are they winning?

What has anyone won, if in this day all that is known has put us in traitorous thoughts of fellow souls? Of fellow human journeyman?

How could it be that souls on Earth can not feel that other souls on Earth matter? How can some be so giving and some so ill?

It is the polar energy's of this time. Peace and pressure can not withstand each other. They are polar energy's. Granted love is not love. Love is love.

Earning respect is not needed when there is respect. Living to achieve is not achievement. Achieving to life is life in it's fullest.

Giving gifts for something is stealing the joy of giving. Giving your heart is the greatest felt gift of all.

Receiving in pressure of returnance of the gift, is not receiving at all. It is pressure that negates peace of that soul. Give it back. Speaking truth gives a soul an opportunity to believe in truth.

Speak truth to see it. Speaking in lies of your thoughts is saying to the world, truth does not matter and we anger at the world for letting us get away with it.

NO one wants to believe they can. For then they will believe it can be done to them. Hence the lacks of trust we now witness.

Nadia our love, keep growing. And share your energy, for then you will let the world know it is possible.

Speak the truth, even with those who evade it. Live in your truth even as it puts you in the "unpopular" crowd in your home.

Live in the love of those that are pure to you, for one ounce of pure love, of pure intent will overcome any obstacle, provided it is pure.

You already know. For you are teaching truth, love and purity, even with disgruntled sidelines. Growth your soul and growth the hearts of human souls. For your love is the healer.

You were thinking that healing is different, like the physically sick. At the very least, physical illness is at least seen.

You are dealing with far greater illness than illness that is yet known however on its way to discovery in this time.

Is the murderer of souls the ones we can see or the ones' who send off souls to fight a war they understand not, under false pretense and that soul is being prudent in the face of lacks of prudency?

Ordered to kill as though the soul they are killing is an evil force and it is not truth. God Almighty's preference is simply truth.

Do not hurt souls for simple thoughts, give them understanding of them.

Do not take away for being human, let souls know they are part of a group, it is called people.

There are animals and people. Animals respect their nature. People have found paths to take away from all and take the respect of their nature and humiliate it. Glory be to God Almighty, for help is on the way.

**You see our love on Earth, Earth is a stopping point and then a passing point.**

**For those who think it is all about them, and of course no one else, they walk around as Earth is the only thing, the only way, and they are distressed.**

**Racing and challenged. Angry and trying not to expose their anger. As well, they want to say they are not and they are.**

**You see this everyday. And everyone, including yourself has been exposed, for the truth not the illusion.**

**And the pressures of living illusion are far greater than the knowings of living in truth.**

**It is not a reflection of who they say they are in words however the truth of their energy and the truth of their souls do not match and you are working on matching them.**

Nadia, everything has to be important about "them" for they are not important to "themself."

And the fighting's of the wills that take place base themself on importance of self. And I speak to you, who does not want to feel like they have a right to be here? It is Earth and they are here.

The memories of the heart will speak "you are of love" and the tortures of the mind will speak "you do not deserve love."

You witness the happenings of the love of God and you witness the walkings by of the love of God Almighty, in search of his very love.

You speak "it is in front of you" and souls speak "it is for others and not for me." You speak "you are of light" and you are spoken to, "Not, ME! I am not deserving."

And you weep within heart to see, to hear, that souls do not like themself. Hence others in the truth in which they come to you to seek.

You look at those affected by your presence and the learning that is taken like a thief in the night, and the lacks of willingness to come to love. To truth. And you are fought to say there is no love or truth.

As well, you stand still and you watch as souls can say "NO," can speak, "I CAN NOT, I WILL NOT" and you sit in the withers of their personality as you can see the love of God Almighty around them and they can not feel it, for the say, "NO, I CAN NOT, I WILL NOT."

There is a determination to stand by lacks of love and the fights for love are non existent, for what a soul can not see can not exist for them.

That is when they live in the thoughts that everything works out for others and not for them. For now they created the perfect alibi to not living life.

"You see, I am not lovable. My Mom said this, my Dad said that, I am worth nothing, I am stupid and no one knows it, everyone knows it," they can not decide.

Their indecision as to who they are, why they are, what they are worth, is the spinning of self hence the spinning of all around to truth.

Truth is the trust of love. Love is not trusted in many souls roaming Earth, unable to get to, to see their missions! Missions beware the humans are coming.

And as you have come to know, all with any self motivation will fall by the wayside of the life that you are creating for all of mankind of Earth.

For all the journeymen who are walking, talking, speaking of what they want, without the truth of their motivations. For the shows of partial truth and hiding the remaining parcels of thoughts and actions.

For the searchers of the remaining truths of themself(s). There are all kinds of souls to reckon.

That is why you quiet so readily. You are home on Earth. Earth is not home. And you bring to Earth the truth of home and you can now witness, why the souls of Earth are on Earth. To growth.

All that you see are souls who are not ready to come home yet. And you are bringing the truth of home, for many have forgotten why they came to Earth.

And some do not even believe they made a choice to come, least alone to that thought, that they have a purpose, a reason.

Some say there is not purpose, it is me, me, me and others say, I do not know my purpose, for they want something grander than they have chosen. for they see not the grandness of love alone.

Souls want more than they came for and do not want to honor what they chose for themself(s).

Simply because on Earth, there is the duality of self motivation and pure intent, free will and choice, and the veiling of God Almighty, for the souls of Earth to search for the Absouluteness of their growth of soul.

That is the purpose of all of souls. Of all the choices made to evolve our souls and return to Absouluteness and search the understandings and learn-ings of Us. Of love. Of God Almighty.

There is more however it can not be seen, for Earth, for it is not of Earth, and that is where trust of love, of truth, of purity will travel the soul to greater understanding.

You must have truth, love and purity, in truth of your soul to see the rest. For they are the keys, the treasures, the answers that souls say they want and pass right on by as they speak they want it.

Stubborn is Ego. Strong will is of pure intent. That is the difference. It is like the difference of Fear and Afraid. Fear is Ego and Afraid is from intel-lect. From knowledge.

You know why you fight for things in life, it is not coming from insecurity that you do so, as Stubborn is the need to be right.

You quickly relinquish being right for the knowledge that you need to growth. That is the will of the strength that you have. When you feel ill will present your will becomes stronger!

If you did not have that within your cells, this mission would not have the triangular force that it needs to carry on.

Nadia, you speak about how we are not allowed to invade the energy of others. That is why we can not change other souls.

That is why they must come to on their own. For it is not allowed.

There are ways souls try to do this with manipulations or brainwashings as they call it however the other soul can not do this without giving permission to other energy's to do so.

We are Souly responsible for all that happens to us. For all that is allowed is allowed through the acceptance of challenge or the acceptance of the act.

It is not right or wrong. It is the truth of energy.

You saw how only a small part of our home energy comes to Earth.

Yes, only the most dense of our energy can survive on Earth for all the other energy's of home are too light, too elevated, to be able to keep a soul in its place on Earth.

And souls do not even know they have this tiny ball of pure energy within therefore they can not see it or feel it.

At times it lives in dreams, day dreams, night dreams, heightened moments of love, moments of glimpsing home on Earth.

Some do not notice for they do not believe. Again and again, things are thoughts, rather than the grander, thought are things.

Think it and it can be. It will find a way, for your brain will work on it for its design is simply to accommodate the soul.

When ego is given to brain, it will appear as though ego fights soul, and it does however brain of any soul is objective.

Our souls on Earth, our souls at home who have come to Earth, can only know the challenges of Earth are designed and chosen to teach and your promise to your own soul is why.

It has nothing to do with anyone or anything else. It can not. However it can affect.

For thoughts are things. And thoughts are superior to things. That is why souls try for things to find that they are still asking about their souls.

And I am so within you, for the three corners of our souls are the three corners of all thoughts, learnings, lovings and acknowledgments of self.

And all souls will have these corners to live within and without. A box holds in and a triangle's angles allow for open thoughts.

For humans do not understand their attractions to triangles, the number 11, Light, Paths, Avenues.

They use the same words and do not know of each other until they find each other. That is confirmations of home on Earth.

For their common veiled knowledge's releasing itself to them to find each other and growth, propel, with a strong sense of purpose.

That is why peoples on Earth, they want for these words. They are their words. Their thoughts. Reminded to them, to who they are, why they are. And they can growth onto the truth of further growths.

Souls stopped at drugs and drinking to feel different. For how could they see passed that if that is the best they have.

Again, things are thoughts. Wait until you see the transformation of thoughts becoming things. Glory be to God Almighty.

# CHAPTER 18

# THE BEGINNING

I have written nothing in my time. I have spoken nothing of being divine or not.

I simply knew that I was an Angel of love and I came to Earth simply to bring out love to the consciousness of souls; for the continuum of human life in form to have consciousness of love.

Love was not acknowledged and there was brutality to each soul from another. The souls of that time were on their way to lacks of connection, lacks of congenuity and lacks of connectiveness of missions.

*(CONGENUITY—In your truth of understanding, your view in pure thoughts and actions)*

As now the souls have come to loss of self awareness and accountability's of actions and intentions.

For in my time, souls came to life in lacks of knowledge's and now the knowledge's are in lacks of soul involvement.

We are of celebration at the waking up of souls. At the provocation of souls!

At the learning, the questions, the growth, the levels of evolution in truth, in growth, of those parts once ignored, not heard, not questioned.

For all that was taught in error will erase, with resistance by many however over time will erase. And all thinking will come to know thoughts based on truth, which will instill and embed all other truths to take forum.

That is of greatness of souls, a gift to souls who are here now and those that will come.

The erasement of knowledge of home and having to rebuild and create the lessons that have been chosen to accomplish will have a truth based, love based understanding.

The lostness of souls in this day is measurable however unseparable in which your world can measure at this time.

For then different growths can occur when thinking is based on basic truths.

There will be discovery of other forms of souls and their travels. There will be those who can see them in meditation and it will be of normalcy!

There will be discovery of new life, of old life in purity and learned from in truth.

And all the Angels sing in unison at the comings of love on Earth in balance.

In the knowings of askings of guidance and love and the meekers will stand and take blindness into growth of self.

The catalysts will show their colors and the purity of love will resurface. And the other side of love will have a chance hence free will to carry it. Glory be to God Almighty.

The greater the knowledge's the greater the challenges. The greater the lessons the greater the learning's for we are in learnment forever.

The lower energies when raysed will supercede all known love to be as though it was never known in lower energy. And the other side of love will present itself into the depth of what love can be.

(RAYSED—To attempt to over power love with lesser energies)

The energy of love is living and nothing else is alive. There is no life without love. That is the talk of the end of the world. It is truly the talk of the end of love, for love is endless and it can not be.

The limits of the meekers will speak of this and their meekness will surface and they will be subsidic in nature, still trying to find a way to overcome, for their own self interests.

(SUBSIDIC—To do as habit, putting things off rather than facing them)

And the lessons will keep presenting themself(s) until they can be touched, felt, seen, and heard. All souls have purpose and reason. And all are in love of God Almighty.

There are no mistakes however every soul on Earth at this time comes and came with choices, free will, and the love of God Almighty.

What was chosen of it is the grandeur of the soul to determine. And love shared grows all souls. If all could only know it is so simple. So simple.

The complications of mind bring about the twistings of all things.

Yet within its purpose, much is learned from the blind. The pure at heart are the teachers and the blind can not learn until purity begins its workings within.

The Animals of Earth will be in greater response to human life, for they are of pure truth and they too in instinct understand there is no truth based life on Earth at this time.

Self motivation is rampant. It is unknown to the self motivated however the concern for self has taken away the concern for others in heart and in mind and in souls.

Others have become instruments for everyone else.

There is no concern as to the pressures that have been put on each other as a result, a worker is not a good worker if they do not stay late at work.

Yet the worker that stays late at work is not with family. What happens to the family, to the fabric of the worker? What happens to the heart and mind of the worker?

It all stagnates and then moves away, for the time given on Earth is not spent in betterment. It is spent in pressure and sustained pressures take away.

And those who sustain it lose the meanings, the moments to think, ponder, grow internally.

To do mindless tasks which are of such great importance and take away from physical work which is mental achievement.

Some try to get away in life of not doing anything! Beware of the souls that evade movement.

They are the greatest robbers of self, therefore of life. Life is of experience and growth of self.

This is where/when life is to be lived. Does a soul want to come back to repeat uncompleted missions?

Does a soul want to come back home and realize they have not learned and witness how they have taken away life rather than flourish it? The souls that have been coming back are in dismay as to their actions.

For God Almighty is all loving. No judgment. It is the judgment of self I am responding to here in this moment. It is the judgment of self.

That is why I tell you to **TRUST YOUR INSTINCTS. FOR YOU DO NOT KNOW THE INSTINCTS OF OTHERS.**

**TRUST IN YOUR INSTINCTS.**

You are truly all children of God Almighty. It has to be set up and accomplished in some way. And in the world of societies it is parents in children and the avenues begin in that forum.

Glory be to God Almighty, never look back, you can do that when you come home.

Take strength from the past and propel the future, for future only exists on Earth for that reason.

Time is so simple, for in truth there is no time. It is simply time to give order.

Order is necessary on Earth, for there has to be direction of mind, for the mind is so vast and there had to be beginning in some forum.

The ingeniousness of time is very slow so the lessons of life can be learned from. That is the turning back. That is the propellant of the future.

To look back in weakness will increase the weakness and to look back in strength and love will increase the strength and love!

When souls come home they are guided and loved. And on Earth they are in search of guidance and love, for that is the testing, the growing, the learning of free will.

The free will of Man can truly move mountains and that is in truth.

The free will of man can take the soul to levels of evolvement that couldn't be imagined and yet can happen.

We are learning that the limitations of the mind take free will to stagnation. Yet there are no limitations of the mind.

Those few that feel betrayed by growth are the ones in the sandmud of Earth.

For the foundation on which they stand is of shallow love, for how could they know when it is masked in what they call principles on Earth? Another pride of man made proportions.

All things are for the bigger picture. Humans are disheartening in behavior and thought. For their behavior is thought.

If only they understood the transparent packages in which they live on Earth.

However Ego is a good word, it masks their intelligence into belief that no one can see their true motivation. When in truth it is of appearance in nature.

If only they could see themself(s), yet the mirrors on Earth are only one dimensional. When they are seen from home, they are seen entirely.

There are different levels of knowing at home when it comes to the evolution of souls.

There is much that is known by all souls however there is also learning that takes place.

The only things not known to a soul at home are the matters of evolution that need to take place for that soul.

As well, my loves on Earth, all writers and speakers of this time are part of the mission. Souls who connect in mission do not necessarily know each other.

There are preparations. There are growths of energy. There are acknowledgements of souls that they are coming to consciousness of thoughts that provoke and give to the soul greater questions.

You are watching, seeing, hearing all of this. You are seeing sustainness and conviction. You are seeing love for truth and purity of intentions.

There is a role for all souls. One connection to the other, for we are all one. All evolves to one. There is no other reason, way, purpose of Earth.

There is no one that is alone. That is one whole of love. I speak love. Details of Me on Earth are in irrelevance. That is why nothing can be proven. It need not be.

When I was sentenced to the hangings of body and form that was the method. For it was not known of my miracle until afterwards. How could there be plans of me while I was not known?

As you speak, as I speak. As is known it is truth. There is not trickery or conjure. There are not mistakes to how, all is known and there is not a hidden agenda to my existence.

I simply existed on Earth for a mission for God Almighty. And I am back for the same reasoning's. I am omnipresent. And my energy travels.

I am open to the world of love, for that is my existence. I speak not to details, for the human minds fight the human souls of the same self. There is not argument in love.

Nadia, you were thinking of me and the taxation's of my time. I was never political and my message is love. Souls were in jeopardy of many losses due to the lacks of prudency in my time on Earth.

I did not come to Earth to rule Earth. A self serving mission I am not on and was not on, for there is not time.

I am on the same mission in a difference of time on Earth however there is not time at home. And in this time we face the same issues within different missions of souls on Earth.

There are many more souls in mission at this time. There are many pressures of ill will propellments at this time that are covered within the realm of truth and they are not of truth.

The truth is hidden and the truth is not in the favor of souls. And the issues of lacks of truth have injured the very form of souls.

And within that injury souls are expected to be attractive sexually and if they do not look good then they feel themself(s) not. And if they do, then they feel that all of their efforts are worth it.

As well, souls have come to discarding all of their worth to whether or not they are attractive. I am in saddened state, for the looking's over shoulders of others to see others is of greatest insecurity of heart.

For what does that accomplish? It simply says I need to be important and I speak, important to what?

You are losing the interest of what you are in current and you are not being current. If you have a job and you do not like it, leave it and grow to your intent of love.

If you are with a person and you do not want them entirely, I speak, walk away and let them flourish, let yourself flourish and find the soul that carries your love as you will carry theirs.

If you are in a home that is of no light, find a home of light. If a soul walks into your home with the intentions of lacks of love to your home, send them away.

If a child speaks in angst, do not allow the energy to live. If a soul comes to you and tells you, you can not make do, walk away and you will do.

I speak, believe in who you are, as souls need to stand up for the stand uppedness of themself(s)

Do not let those who want to fret of life fret. Walk away. Speak and walk away. Give and let it be with love. Reduction of soul's purpose is in present.

Returnance of souls to self is of greatest importance to souls. For the losses are unaccountable in this time on Earth.

They can not even be seen in their entirety. For souls are in fear of each other, for the fears of self are stronger than the love of self.

What has happened to love? Love is turned into something and it is not of something. Love exists and is eternal.

I am speaking that the human journeyman of this time has lost understanding of the depths, the truths of love.

Nadia, I am showing you all the tales of the human souls. I am within your form. I understand the vastness it takes from you to believe it at times.

I hear you question me and say, how could it be that you live within me? You hear me, see me, I have no thought alone. No one is alone. No one has a thought alone.

Yet, I hear yours in minueteness. I live within your form, for we are the first meshing of two souls within one form.

How else could I return to Earth without the focus being on me returning to Earth. Returnance is not the issue to address, it is the message.

We have lost sight, as you know, and now you witness many books, authors, speakers, all in a train of newness of ideas.

Some understanding it is bigger than them and that they are part of a mission and others living in ego and taking on that it is them.

What is them I ask? And you ask the same questions. For you know that knowledge never ends. Never stops and will never.

WE are all on Earth for purpose and Earth is simply one plane of growth.

It is the lowest energy and its fight for love, truth and purity being its only characteristics.

All challenges, happenings, wantings, are all stems of purpose of Earth. And the known trails within veil are the challenge.

Finding answers, finding intent, finding love in purity are the rewards.

And with the growth and evolutions taken place on Earth, the evolved soul returns home to witness and study their growths.

Learning never stops. Learning propels the mind to expand itself. As you have seen on other planes, there are densities of whiteness, of purity.

It is simply in the evolutions of other planes and the purpose of those planes. As I speak to you, one of the characteristics of Earth is cycles.

It is all cycles, for the human soul needs some regularity to time and pace its missions. That is why time exists. It gives chronilogicality to all thoughts, things and growths.

It is a way to pace and to see that there is always what you call time to repair. However once evolutions come to a soul in truth then time has meaning no longer.

For the purpose of time is no longer needed to take on the truths, for the other side of truth is now present.

Speak the love, the message, for none else carries matterment. Do you think of matterments of your conversations of 30 Earth years ago?

I was in written form in that time. Tell me what you can remember in detail and I will tell you my life. My life is yours and yours is mine.

I have nothing more to say of my time other than the love that propelled to this time on Earth.

And now the propellations have taken on form of discomfort for souls rather than comforts and I come to you in speakments of love again.

For comforts within, for the souls of Earth have taken on the losses of their ownness of love, truth and purity and can not come to the truths of self in the truth of self.

The love of God Almighty does not leave a soul behind. There is no behind, there are only continuations of life on Earth and lessons within life as we have all come to experience for our souls growth.

And we are the love of God personified. I want to speak of souls who thank God Almighty for everything, believe that the thanking comes from home to Earth for experiencing.

If the soul knew life without negative, to come down to experience for God Almighty, is of the greatest Challenge and that is why God says simply, ask ask ask, talk to me, I am hear.

That is why God Almighty is here, to help souls.

It is the opposite of what I am seeing here, for the fear of hell has turned God Almighty into a commodity God Almighty is not. Glory be to God Almighty.

And me into a human I was not. I am an Angel of God Almighty; An Angel of love.

The love of God Almighty, reigns on souls, penetrates life, belief and withstandment, Patience and cures, Hopes and depth of self.

And when that energy surrounds a soul, the soul carries that energy in surroundment of others.

God did not create Chaos, God gives souls choices.

Was Christ here or not? So what.

What I did while I was here? So what? What remains from my presence on Earth is what I will speak on and all else is irrelevant.

I came to speak of love, on love, in love, All else carries no weight.

For then the facts of what, of what of written the oldest, who wrote it, what circumstances it was written in, what my daily life encountered, what miracles?

All that is of greatest importance is that love and trust in something, anything, came from that time.

However internal greed came into the ego of those who wanted to use all the words of God Almighty and force the love of God Almighty within the realms of fear.

Fear teaches nothing and now in soul's soul there is not much left to work with.

I come back in this time not because I am special not because you are special, however because love is special and the learning's of love are not known to souls.

And we are here to relearn love.

I am here to reteach love. For the avenues taken now expect from love, when love can only grow from love.

Love can not birth from fear. From questions that can not hear the answers. If there is not an answer, trust that you are not to know yet.

There are no mistakes; there are only growths, lessons on Earth. Once that is not seen the ripple affects of this is self abusement.

It is all so simple and yet many of souls live in this and can live an entire missionless lifetime as this. God is love and Earth is free will and choice.

There are no mistakes. There is not a question that remains without an answer.

And there will always always always be questions that require a leap of faith of a soul. For that is the entire purpose of the veil.

I will be with you in writing, for the book will be of great weight, for those who will receive it will be of ready. They will cherish the words of God Almighty.

For the hands of a prophet, for the love of Angels, all will be present upon each world of ready!

Glory be to God Almighty, for all of souls have purpose and ponder, all souls have hope and wonder.

It will awake again and drive the energy of Earth into the new world of love that will be come.

For the humans that come will carry the torch of such hope on and those who carry not will be motivated away, yet the examples of love will teach them in totality!

Nadia, you are of love, my message of love. NO more no less! Ever. Another human term I am loving. NO more no less.

That means it is there with no exaggerations. As I like it! For I have been exaggerated to non recognition of truth!

I am here to realign the love of God in the hearts that are in search of, in need of, love. So simple again!

Glory be to God Almighty! For each soul of such significance to God Almighty, for if the souls of Earth knew that intervention is on the way.

You are just in thinking that there is something great coming to all, it is here, and now it is in the day of knowing what exists and soon will become.

They will have thoughts to ponder, decisions to make, life to live and hope to have again. Glory be to God Almighty!

Souls can not die while on Earth with Ease and Souls can not live on Earth with Ease.

You can not have an answer without the question. You can not! However, the answers you write of are of the questions of this time.

I spoke to you in passed writings of beginningments of your knownments of me, do not change the writings. You can not.

Souls must rise to the occasion. Many occasions have been slighted to the hearts cryings of answers unseen.

Love propels. Love is; however the energy of love grows love and the souls of Earth are in never ending search of such love, for the love of home is the destination of any path taken on Earth.

God Almighty is love. And Love is God.

Growth takes us to knowing. Stagnation holds us in place. To have faith is love, is love's growth. For love is growth. Is learning. Is acceptance. Is love. Is purity. Is truth.

If any one of these is absent then the stagnation will remain until all the avenues of self sabotage are exploded and seen for the wreckage that they are. Glory be to God Almighty.

I spoke an Earth term in this moment in great enjoyment. Glory be to God Almighty.

Love can only propel. In its truth. For a soul to try, to come to defining love, has lost love. And in that loss, there is effort to define love.

How can love be defined when it can only be felt and it cannot be spoken, when it is an emotion?

Did you ever feel like in one day saying I love you is enough and in another you can not stress its meaning? For love is fluid. It flows.

It catches those who can see it, those who can feel it. Moments of deepest love bring tears to the eyes and cleansing the soul. Heals the wounds and holds the body in health.

Love is the healer, the grower, the nurturer of Earth.

I have spoken much about love and yet I can speak in infinitedom, for love is eternity, love is perpetual, love is instant and love is pure.

Love is forever however not in forever as defined on Earth, for love is the essence, the beginning of all creation and exists throughout it.

Love follows a soul from God to home to Earth to any other plane.

And it comes back in growth; on each journey, each lesson, each moment of Earth and beyond of all existences. Earth is only one existence, one plane of experience(s).

Earth is not the beginning and it is not the end. Earth is a tool to grow souls to love.

Back to love. Love. Love. All else fails around it. All else pales around it. For the light of non love can not withstand.

Nadia, the blessings of teamness between us has given me the forum to come to mission on Earth in once again.

The importance of such mission is growing the love in which I am.

Your purity has given forum to my light to come to Earth in wholeness and not be in knowment until the miracles of our Lord God can be presented to help the souls on Earth look within.

My birth to humans again will not be a rebirth, for the purity of you, gave to me existence again in peace, to come through and be known without the birth process of humans on Earth.

WE are a team, amongst another and with the worlds of Earth and Home, for Earth being one plane of learnment, for soul's pleasures of growth.

The choices are endless in ways of growing. For time is not time however slowed down to teach.

At home there is no year, no minute, no second. There is no day, no month, no year. It is. Simple. Absoluteness.

Earth is the drying flower of the universe at this time.

In love all will be done. For the meek seize to speak!

I had to say it like that, for the humor I draw from it enlightens the paths of home, on the planes of many. For to see the seization of meekality is to know that the love of God Almighty prevails in balance. Glory be to God Almighty.

I will be the attraction to the writings. I will carry the soul's interest to the writings. That is as simple as it is.

That is the truth of my appearance. I will dispel the theories of error. I will let truth find its surface at last.

At last it will be that the truth can rest the souls and move them on.

That life on Earth is of "complication" for the minds of self motivation are rampant. You already know of this however how does it reset?

It resets with truth. Glory be to God Almighty.

Nadia, you are unwilling to admit the extent of your knowledge's, and yet when you speak to one, you speak to millions.

You leave no one out and you treat not a soul without the love, respect and candor that makes their souls want to open wide unto them; even when it does not seem so at first.

Every time you have to speak onto a soul, you speak to yourself that you do not want to speak anymore. Yet, imagine if you did not speak?

There would be no refinement. It is not of you that you speak, it is from you that you speak. You are a messenger. That is what a messenger does, is, and will be of always.

As well, Nadia, our love, you have learned to separate yourself from what you speak, simply that you need not a thing.

You believe you do at times, and then you find out that you only want what souls want for themself(s) and you are learning to give a soul their space and time and simply give them love and support, even if their life(s) do not include your involvement.

You are in freedom of life and others are in freedom of you. That is love without conditions. That is what love is. Nadia. You are living love.

You want everyone to be free and not affected by what hurts you or stifles your soul.

You can only speak the truth, and leave life to take on the energy of truth, and the love of understandments, and the purity of living it so.

Nadia, you will have many that tell you "you are too much" and yet you can not be too much, for if you were not too much then no one will hear you.

And if souls can not hear you, then they can not be challenged enough to learn. That is a teacher. Teach. With love of home and your love of Earth, and to Earth, live in your freedoms as you strive for the freedoms of others.

Open your heart as you teach others to open their hearts unto themself(s). Glory be to God Almighty.

If we thought of God and we are grateful, then we can't see what we are here.

If we think of God and that we are gifting God Almighty for being on Earth, taking on the challenges, living the conditions and fighting for the betterment of all of us, then we get our purpose.

To be grateful for everything we have, in fear that it will be lost or gained based on us being good or bad, then we have a long road of disappointment ahead.

If we can look at God as a partner to us, Us being a part of him and him of us, That we can ask for help and speak from heart, not be shy or speak in a way to be heard, you are heard.

No dressing up or down and no driving to get there. If we see God as simply love, then we can feel his love, if we see God as though we have to earn his love, then we are trying to be something we are not.

You see, we are naturally nice, clean, hard working, loving and compassion. The minute someone tells us we have to be those things, we do not know what to do. So we try this to please, that to please, and then we are not pleased.

WE become contrived to appear a way that is not us and we are not comfortable. However, when we believe in God as love, then we can just love and flow naturally through all the journeys of our life(s).

Without the stresses of how they have to be, why, where, when, however to trust in the truth of ourself(s). Enough to flow, like a river that simply knows where to go, without knowing what it will find and trusting it will know what to do when it arrives.

If you think of life as preparation rather than grateful for having life, being alive, feeling fear of things; thinking in preparation gives you the freedom to understand that life is to be lived, explored, challenged and growthed.

Take on the weary and you will wear out. Take on the challenges and you will learn overcoming. Take on Love and it will lead you to the honor of life, the feelings of life and the projection of all that we think can be.

Limits are from fear. Boundaries are from strength. Trying is from fear. Doing is from strength.

Strength is your truth. And Truth is Strength. Living in your Truth is to Love Yourself. Living in love is to find purity within. Love can only be pure.

When we witness a person who loves, for no reason at all, they want nothing from us however they leave us with much. They leave us with an example of self love.

All self love is is living in truth of who you are.

Then you will speak and others will learn and listen.

Then you will walk and smile for your understands of life.

Then you will take the time to eat well, to take care of a body you will need for a while here.

Then you will clean your things and not accept that you reflect your mind in clutter around you.

There are so many ways we communicate who we are, and those ways speak before we speak our words.

We are billboards of ourself(s), even when we think no one can see.

So when we think of God, he is not a religion, he is a friend. He is the best friend you can accept of him.

He is a partner that will push you to reach further every time you believe you reached far enough.

God will teach you the other side of yourself. The side you do not see so much, every day, just because we are not taught to look at life that way.

God is not impossible, and neither are you. We are all part of the same picture, the same home.

If we think of the world as our home, we would never bomb it or ourself(s).

We would never purge it in one place and fill another. We would enhance the nature of ourself(s) and the resources we have.

We would think of so and so and not of what we bought that we do not have yet, we would think of so and so as a person like us, who needs to breathe, who wants to work, who wants to eat well, and have his or her family feel proud of them.

We would think of so and so and say, hey he has a name, he is someone's son or daughter and they mean something to someone.

When we meet another so and so and he appears like he has no one, we would help a person, not a so and so, to grow into a circle of people who care, rather than blame them for being without.

Or better yet, make fun of them for not succeeding. We forget our success comes from all of us and our losses are felt by all of us too.

We are not alone, we are as alone as we want to be. And I speak to all of us, to remember, We are everyone and God is not seen, yet he is felt and he is heard.

He is not a religion to section off into factions; that is us. He is whole and loving. And so are We. We just need to remember who we are, so that we can see what God sees, And then God will be seen.

Nadia, our love on Earth, your hearts stability of life on Earth is that you are simply a visitor. As is every soul.

However, they think not of visitor for when souls on Earth speak of forever they are simply speaking of the rest of their life on Earth.

And they say a soul dies, where does he go? Souls have figured out by now that a soul is the only way to work a body, and when the soul is gone, the body no longer has purpose.

So I speak to souls when you visit a plane, what are you to do, when you feel as though you are a small part of a very big thing.

I have news for souls, there are only people on Earth that can do anything and anything that happens on Earth is the doing of people.

There are resources, foods available, water and air. There is the nourishing of the sun by day and then night light of the moon.

There are cold months and warm ones. There is light and dark. There are animals and plants.

And all that the intelligence of souls has given, done and created is what we have today. Not more, not less.

So I ask peoples of Earth what has your intelligence given to our Earth. What kind of love did you share with it?

What has been your mission's purpose to enrich your life, to make your visit everlasting and eternal?

What has been your search for, outside of you, that you have learned and taught through your learning's?

I will tell you what I witness. I witness much ownership and much wanting for objects and lacks of caring what happens to others. I witness cars having better care than people.

I witness wars that speak in volumes of how little peoples mean to each other. I witness crimes in everyday that souls no longer call crimes.

Now there are some criminal acts that we say, Oh, well, it is not as bad as.....

Souls have the right to do, to be, to speak, to act upon themself(s) as they please and find ways to account for.

Souls do not take the time in their days to account for what has happened as a result of not speaking their truth. Even if a soul does not speak something, it is the unspoken that is harshest.

The harshest words are the unspoken words. The words spoken can be dealt with; it is the guessing energy's that breed behaviors that another can not explain.

As you are discovering answers in your life, you are discovering the answers of the world. It is not that they are or were unknown to you; it is simply time for the answers now.

The affects of the careless nature of the human soul is now rampant and vial. Vial? Yes, it is in its activity state.

You see our love; the soul is overwhelmed as to what to start, where to start, what to think about and what to do next.

The soul wants to simply fill it's time with anything, since it knows not what to fill it's time with.

Trust is lacking and souls do what they can to stay close to themself(s) for that is the only truth they have left to count on and even then, they are not so sure they are telling themself(s) the truth

Every vision opens a gate. Every thought of love creates an avenue and every intention of reaching souls builds a road.

Our love, you have motion within mission. You are moving quickly and your Physicalness is at home and on Earth and it is as though there is only half of you present.

Live close to your home in this day, in tomorrow's day, and in the day thereafter. Breathe and lay your head, come up and work and breathe and lay your head once again.

Let your time be felt by you, there is not a rush of time, nor is there an answer you look for in this time.

You are the answer, the reason and the purpose of souls reaching their own souls with Garth and candor rather than with money's and things.

Nadia, in a day to come, My physicalness will appear as light from you in the form that people will recognize and you will not have to speak.

And when you do speak at those times, it will be US speaking, for you will never be alone.

All are waiting for the next coming of Christ. Yep, I am here. For nothing is as it seems.

I love all and I care for all and I am here for that reason. I had to come back. All knew it would be, yet they really don't believe it.

Can you imagine? They believe I will come back in roar, large enough in the sky for all to see, to hear, to fear. I am not to be fear.

I will not judge a soul, for that is the job of the soul, to look at itself upon return and learn. So simple is life, so simple in love. All love will heal.

Upon return, all will see their affect on Earth, as they have in all of life that they challenge in any form.

The evolvement of soul is all that is asked of one self!

Nadia, for if the world were to know I am now here, Not scary! I am here and I am living here through you. So simple.

I see all now as it is in reality and I can feel all the emotion of all at once and I get a reading for a way to explain it to you.

I am here, for how could anyone know? How could they tell? Nothing is as it seems.

Yes, it is the new world of God Almighty. It is knew in thought, in reason, in hope of life on Earth. It is NEW! It will Challenge!

Work for love.

Work for truth.

Work for Purity and you will work for the Souls of All Earth.

Glory be to God Almighty. Glory be to God Almighty. Glory be to God Almighty!

Nadia, go and rest and come back to me, this writing is in conclusion. Glory be to God Almighty.

❧

FROM NADIA:

Christ says to me over and over again, one change has to happen before another can. I am thinking in this day and age, who has the time? We just want the results, today, yesterday if necessary! Patience…is all I hear. That time is the best teacher, that time answers every question.

So time went by, one year, two, and now I am on about five years and growing. So many times, I was impatient and I would think I want to do this or that, now.

I would feel like everything was in my way that put off me doing what I thought I wanted. And then I would think, but I know better, how is it that I don't use the knowledge that I have.

I would think to myself, the things that were said, not just as a good idea, but I would think it and say, let me use it. It started to calm me inside when I would say I want to make the best dinner for my family and I would. Rather than saying, I have to make dinner, then I have to drive so and so, and then I have to run to the store.

I was learning to live in the moments of my life. It had a ripple affect. Or when I would think, Oh I just told someone about Christ and I would feel like I had three arms and fours legs afterwards and I would remember Him saying to me, everyday ends as it should. I would remind myself and it would go away that I felt bad or embarrassed.

I learned when not to speak and when to speak. I learned that silence is a language all unto itself. A million baby steps in my mind, in my heart and in my soul. All combined within my thinking of using what I learn, sharing what I know, and living my intentions took time, love and compassion to myself.

Only then was I was able to feel this for others as well. I began to understand the value of my life not just the words. Not just wanting to make things look good however to live good to myself. And everything else finds its home within and without my thoughts and actions.

A million baby steps is what it takes to bring about one change. One action. One thought to fruition. We all have to start somewhere and that somewhere is here.

You are living and visible. Do not let invisibility be you to you. See yourself, touch your heart and let your mind know you know you can use it.

Our souls are waiting for us and we tend to rush so quickly we think we will get to it. It doesn't take time to get to your soul, it simply takes thoughts. Start by asking yourself, what would be my favorite thought today, and think it. Give it a chance to be heard and give yourself the openings of your hearts content.

This is for US. When something, anything is pure, we always know it. It is worth repeating again and again. One ounce of pure love and pure intent will over come any obstacle, provided it is pure.

The only way to start anything is to start. There is no magic, there is simply motivation. The glimpses of love of self are the propellers of all growths.

A million of anything started within one cell of thought, wanting and desire. Desire can not be put off; it can only be shut off.

It is here in all of us and some of us caught on to the strength of how our desires of learning, of loving, of sharing and of teachings have brought to us awareness. And quiet joys that have strengths within them that are unexplainable yet live in our souls and our actions.

There is a resting place that gives us greater motivations and inclinations without the expectations that bring about all that takes away.

Live in glory and you will see glory. Again there is no magic. WE are the magic. It is not a thought alone, it is a reality and so are WE.

*Part* THREE

# THE BOOK OF TRUTH

# CHAPTER 1

# THIRTEEN Thoughts

1. The energy of pure love is fought until it is understood

2. One soul is an example of a million

3. Pure intent will overcome any obstacle provided it is pure

4. One soul is not more important than another

5. If you feel something and it does not settle within, run do not walk away

6. The obvious is in front of a soul and the soul can not see the obvious at the times they are looking for something from a particular situation

7. Inner wants blind souls into actions they would normally not take Inner greed's of one soul grows into the takings away of many souls

8. Pure love propels and the ripple effects of love are endless

9. Love is not a physicality it is an emotion

10. Truth settles

11. Purity evolves

12. Love propels

13. One change has to happen before another can

# CHAPTER 2

# The Number ELEVEN

Eleven is of two standing, of two points of view, of two of love. Side by Side. The number of two is to begin the growth of strength, for souls are not meant to be of alone.

It is ones. It is the firsts. It is the newness of the first twice. It is the 11th hour where people present the best of themselves when all hope is lost. It is the doubling day of the month, it is the easy number to remember, it equals two. It means that those on Earth are not meant to be alone.

11 is significant, for it is of all people. We have one and one arm, leg, sides to our bodies, to our brains, to our hearts, so even those things with 1, are 1 again within itself. You have one heart, yet one side of the heart is different from the other and one can't function without the other, so they need to work together to function.

11 is for all to essence, to know, that one is not meant to be alone. More so, it is the brightest day of the month. Why? Because inside it is understood that there is a specialness to this day and inside it is understood that we are not meant to be alone. Those alone are quietest on this day however in their hearts there is hope, for this day is of brightness within and without. For it brings to light many souls.

The 11th of September, do you really know the significance of that day? It joined the souls of many at once to return to home, for there was great celebration. It joined the souls of many nations in one short time and all went home in unison.

It was sorrow on Earth and rejoice and understand at home, for nothing is as it seems. At home that day was a great and joyous event. Glory be to God Almighty, for it is the day of significant events.

Time and days and space, they are perception however there are moments of heightenment, for the rhythms peak and bring to light energies. And that is the 11's; the pairings, the unisons, the momentary opening of hearts in life on Earth.

# CHAPTER 3

## TWENTY-ONE Months

The earlyment of souls on Earth is the greatest of times and it is looked at as the easiest of times. When the soul comes to earth in the first year of time it is set in reaction to stimulus.

It is set in behavior of how and when and why to accept love. The soul is determined already as to how it will live in mission. And the way in which love is put in will affect the course of mission throughout.

The soul's exposure in the first year of life on Earth, the soul itself can not remember or recollect that information of self however the greatest growth of a soul on Earth is in and up to the 21$^{st}$ month. That is from the moment of inception and concluded in the first year of visible life.

The child at inception may not be in the womb yet, for it can enter the womb at anytime however the parent of that child is chosen and known to the soul. Glory be to God Almighty. The soul will learn more in the first 21 months of existence than at any other time in human life on Earth.

# a Plus i Equals g

Accounting, Intent, and Growth. aig. Like an egg; the beginning of life. It must be gone back to the beginning. Do not ask intent first. Teach it. That is Accounting. Then Intent is learned. Then Growth can happen.

The memory will come out in accounting. The intent of the soul will come out in the growth. There is no other way to truth, love and purity. Accounting, Intention, Growth, are the keys of life for a soul. Teach it by example. a+i=g.

# CHAPTER 5

# THE CULMINATIONS

## ABANDONMENT OF SELF

Souls are coming home without completion of mission. Pacificness has become a way of helplessness of souls knowing where to turn within the inspirations they have come to Earth to carry out. Each soul comes to learn and the learning has come to cessation and momentary loss of memory of selfness within each soul(s) life(s).

God talks to so many people, who do not believe in him, are not sure he exists, for they are not sure they too exist. So people who do not believe in God are not sure they believe in themselves. The human soul lives in general abandonment of self. For the self is alone in heart.

We, as in any soul on Earth, are not meant to be alone yet within another we are still in feelment of alonement, for we have stifled our existence by not speaking truths as we know of them. The games of heart are the way of heart in most cases to self first. Some believe they are smarter than the game however there is no game based on truth.

## ABORTION

Aborting a child before birth, the soul returns home and tries again, for the mission didn't include abortion. Yet true abortion is stopping any process of growth available.

## ACCEPTANCE

Not all people can or know how to understand life as it is, for most want life to be what they want it to be not what it is. To accept life as it is, again and again, goes back to self accounting. What cannot be accepted in self can not be accepted in others.

## ACTION

Every action has a reciprocated reaction whether it be verbal or in body or in mind.

## ACTIONIZE

Peoples need examples that bind. For the examples of existence in this time are unattainable in nature to the souls of receiverment of such information's. The taughts in error come from pastness, in a time when it was in relevance. The holdings on to these stories, these happenings within and without grandiose additions or subtractions can not hold a heart in place. And does not provide for it a basis of what is present and needed for a soul's heart to actionize itself.

To actionize itself is to carry itself in honor of self. To actionize a soul's doings is to say "I care to grow. To carry myself in this life I came to experience." Many souls, members of humanity, come and the rigidity of the lacks of love in providence begins to show and apparenate in behaviors that take away.

This is the truth of the taughts in error and their generation of growths in time. For all grows will propel. And the grows that take you away propel in this way. When a soul is detached, as has been spoken, it is of generations of acceptance of minute behaviors that take away.

## A DAY

All days conclude on a day on Earth, for there is no stopping of time, all things rest in the place of layments. The changes that have to come in to fruition come in each bite of each day. Each day is open to the souls within it. And the purity of thoughts, of actions, carries the energies to growths. Celebrate life in every day, for it is only a day. And a day in time is forgotten yet the love within it is carried beyond time.

## AFFECT

There is nothing on Earth that does not affect a soul. All souls are affected by all souls. There are no questions without answers of love. There are no conflicts without answers of love. There are no trials without verdictions of love.

## ALLUREMENT

There are always allurements between peoples. Whether it be in physical allurements, mental allurements, they exist. That is what creates enough interest to simply interact. There may be nothing needed between the souls however it says to the soul, "This person is interesting, and I would like to explore the job, this work, this relationship," whatever the circumstance. And then work, jobs, relationships are had on the feelings of allurements.

Now the stance of the soul approaching those very allurements takes the allurements and shapes them. Another example: If the soul is looking for a relationship, then that allurement will grow into a relationship for the soul in coming and the soul in meeting will have the same goal. If the souls in allurements want to work together than that will come to flourishment. And if the job is in allurements to both souls or many souls, the job will be proceeded from the stems of that very allurement.

Without allurements, no soul would have need to speak to another. There has to be interest. There has to be. For when there is not interest there is no soulution, no solvation, no new ideas. No growth. No love. Without love, the allurements of the sameness internal, this could not happen. And all rise in love.

## ALONE

We weren't meant to be alone, do alone, think alone. The joining of thoughts creates and that creation develops wisdom hence wisdom is! There is not a monopoly on wisdom. The needing of souls to join is of the essence. The detachment creates isolation. Isolation breeds selfishness, angers, aloneness and all of that brings about loss of hope and love and caring for self. For then the self feels uncared for hence no caring for others.

There is no small energy. There is no energy that is out of the reach of souls. For once energy is in calling it calls unto others. It brings the hearts of souls towards.

That is the greatness of energy within a soul, for it is shared. No one soul is meant to be alone. There is no alone. The word alone is of energy that takes away from the very soul hence leaves the soul alone, for that is the energy of aroundments to that soul. When a soul's thoughts are of takings away it takes away the souls in aroundments. Then the soul of alone asks why it is alone and that is why.

## ANGELS

Humans who came to be human can be Angel like however Angels come to Earth to be Angels. On Earth this is looked at as someone who is special. At home an Angel is looked at as service to all in love enumerations. There are many Angels now on Earth, walking, speaking, you see them in raising the consciousness of what they are now recognizing as a movement towards one, although that has not been spoken that way.

## ANIMALS

The Televisions of our time have stagnated thought, have given souls a path to nowhere and a heart of passivity. Television has purpose. It has some growth. It carries it much however the passing of vulnerableness, fears, cries of heart dominate programming. News programs are not entirely truthful. Most who are not speaking truth know of it.

Yet the payment for such actions has given truth a back seat in thought, mind and action. For the souls in losement truly know why however they are so far away from truth that they truly do not see it or know where to begin. All human souls are souls from home. All animals' souls are souls from home however they are innocence. They are instinct. And as Angels carry souls, animals are the closest souls on Earth to Angels love.

They carry within them, love and only love. Instinct and only instinct. They will be and are animals in all of time. They are sent to live in instinct. They are on Earth to carry the belief that there is something more; that humans are not the only existence's; that there is a bigger plan.

That the perfection of love that happens in food chains and the animals simply knowing what to do. And there is no schooling as to how, as the human soul must endure, their growth is in love only. They are pure love. No matter what animal it is.

That is why, going back to Television, when there is programming of animals, human souls can watch much in love, for they are witnessing love and realness. They have no free will in the way of humans. Animals are instinctive. They love, when close to humans in unconditionality, in a way that humans can not. That is the reason as to why this is so.

As well, humans have growth of love and free will of choices and experiences. It is hard to carry such thoughts in truth however souls on Earth, their challenges are to grow in this way. And for souls who have no one within their daily lives with souls, they can turn to animals and still have love in life within them. And they can speak to, converse with, love and hold, love. It is available to any soul who can want it.

For growth is always in each and every human soul. In animals, they are simply love and the growing of that love. Humans search for what is already known to home and to animals. They are the closest being to Angels of Earth in Visuality.

**ANSWERS**
See your fear or it will not go away. See your soul, for it is waiting. See your heart, for it needs love. See your role for you can not begin otherwise. See the world for what it is, not for what you have turned it into. Glory be to God Almighty. The souls of Earth know not the answers, they are meant to search for them.

And when they know them they are meant to use the knowledge. And with that knowledge we are meant to grow. And with that growth will come a new growth. And with that new growth comes depth in knowledge. And within the depth comes the evolution we all see.

And challenges abound the soul to push itself, to Hone its knowings and the rewards are the gifts of color to the soul. The gifts of sharing of self and the gifts of love are eternal. And the world lives in the energy of love, of mission, of choice and of Free will.

## ANYONE

Anyone can take away and not anyone can give. Anyone can boast but not anyone can speak truth. Anyone can complain but not anyone can solve. Anyone can be human but not everyone wants to account for it. All want to believe in love, truth and purity, but not everyone believes it.

## APPRECIATION

Appreciation is so important in life. For then there is another resting place. Appreciation is of healing for the soul. Those who can not appreciate, they are not of resting. There is not a point of comfort. Happiness is momentary and taking is essential and giving is sparing. For it is giving only in self motivation.

If a person can love themselves then they can love others. If they can take care of themselves, they can take care of others hence if there is appreciation of self then there is appreciation of others. Appreciation takes on a form in a person. We notice those who appreciate and are drawn to them, for they rest in heart and truth becomes the spoken word.

Deciding when and if to talk to someone is of egocentrism. No solvation of issues is of avoidance of self. Self accounting can not be present in such times and self motivation supercedes, for the immediate pleasure of self is the only momentary pleasure there is to feel.

Peoples know so little of self that the lack of knowledge of self becomes the lack of knowledge of others, yet others are dealt with within that lack of knowledge. The person of this mindset then wonders why they are not of acceptance or accepted or moved on.

No lesson is learned. Can growth happen in stagnation? It can not. So simple. Yet the doer of blind activity can not see, for the blindness of heart sees no road.

Self motivations rest no soul. Self motivation takes away and gives nothing if it gives nothing back. Self motivation controls. Self motivation is a simple way of saying I know myself not and I can not know you. So simple. Hence, if there is appreciation of self then there is appreciation of others

## ASSESSMENTS

Everyone wants to look good. Some do it with status, some with money, some with earnings, some with love, some with illness, some with complaints, some with creating, some with wanting to be better than others, for then all can say who they are. Each lesson does not do its job until a souls reflection to self teaches that soul who it is.

The human soul can only do what is believed to be wanted from self in the moment. Once the moment passes and the lesson is of learned the soul assesses.

Assessments come with love if the soul has already love of self. And the assessments come with anger if the soul itself is of anger at self. And the assessments come with skewments if the soul is a soul of taking away of self. And the assessments come with meekness if the soul is the soul who looks to others in control.

Nothing a soul does unto itself it has not done to others. For souls on Earth believe in self importance and can not see in much times that the actions they hide from others they hide from self.

When a soul is up to skewments does it know? It believes at the time in getting what it wants from others and from self in order to fulfill whatever happiness' it believes to obtain from others in any given situation on Earth. The soul believes it can hide things, feelings, actions, however energy can not hide anything.

All energy exists, that is why the unseen is felt. Humans wait to know in proofs of actions that certain behaviors, actions, did or have existed. However, long before such proofs come to surfacement the feelings came to the souls in instinct, which is energy that has not yet been seen or discovered by the nakedness of the eyes.

Expectation, self importance, entitlement(s) of souls and the surround-ments of such thoughts, pulls peoples away from each other rather than brings them together. Superficiality brings souls together initially, such as exterior facings of souls, possessions, temporary needs, however longevity is very difficult to sustain in these times for those very reasons.

The outside is seen and dealt with first and the inside is left to be discov-ered. Many souls do not care for the inside of anyone nor do they want to know more, unless in that, there is a way to serve the soul of the one wanting to know. The safety of souls amongst each other has eroded, for souls are constantly in search of the ulterior motive and can not concentrate or relax in the love of the relationship of any kind, work, home, family, loved ones.

The purity is the soul's keeper. When purity does not exist, nor can truth, nor can hope, nor can growth. Without purity, all things are kept in place. They can not move or grow. How can anything around grow without love, or truth, or purity? Many souls are in facements of great beauty, enthralling to another's eyes yet the inside is the beauty that sings the truth in beauti-ment that abounds and grows.

When the beauty of within is not sought, grown, loving and with great care, it is lost in the shuffle of life, living in self importance and trying to tell, show, explain, endure self worth by the bragments of life. For the depth of life has not been found, challenged, loved and cared for.

The depth of life is a treasure for the soul who can find enough internal truths to find it. Then the other sides come into the soul's energy. The other sides of love, truth and purity come home. Bring home. Touch home in the days of time of Earth's experiences. Glory be to God Almighty. We draw to us who we are in mind, heart and body.

We draw it to us. For the energy is in existence. It is already there, and you draw to you, you. That is why lessons can only teach a soul who it is. When the soul is not yet able to withstand its own truth it will continue to repeat until it is ready to learn who it is.

## BALANCE

The world is depleted of such purity and of such love at this time, for it took many ill intentions to get to this day. There has always been a balance until now! The balance isn't in numbers it is in the lack of personal belief that is pushing the world to imbalance. And those who are self motivated, they soar when the personal belief of most is not in existence. That is why you witness more negative at this time.

It is hard to maintain balance here. The varying of emotions, of feelings towards oneself is of great variance. There is much hope here yet it needs to be found again. It is lost in the struggle of trying to be anything, something, yet not knowing how.

## BEAUTY

Physical beauty is temporary. The physicalness of a soul is in each day different; however the soul of a soul is the sustainess of a soul.

Beauty is an attraction however once the soul is known souls can not see each other. It is not that beauty wears off it is that energy of soul is greater.

There has to be an attractant to each other for how could anything grow a wanting to occur? Yet souls want to use beauty as they use monies. They will dress and attract each other, they will use money to attract each other, they will use the stimulants to attract each other, for then they can begin the soulful searches. However the stimulants have become simply stimulants and the soulfulness of each soul is in overlookments.

All is given so quickly, there are not stimulants to continue to in wantings to know of the other soul. The elements of realness of souls misses. There is a power in love. It is an energy force that is so strong that nothing is in strength greater than love in purity.

Beauty is someone, something to appreciate not someone to conquer the beauty of. You will learn from the appreciation in truth the beauty of all things, for their challenges to the soul are the greatest life challenges for all

464 — Origins of Truth

souls. Whatever the standards of beauty are in a human, in a car of this time, a home of this time, in things things things, that require not emotion, simply possession of, do not have energy of happiness without the energy of happiness being in them.

I cautiously use the word happiness in subjectivity on Earth. However I speak of the pure energy of love. Understood as happiness however not as it is known on Earth. That is the perception things and peoples who are seen as possessions will bring unto another in perception. That is happiness as it is known.

Many souls, soul after soul, I witness in wantings, in great anticipations and then I see the sense of happiness' that are gotten. And then I witness the realization that it is not what was thought or perceived. It did not do what they wanted IT to do.

And then they set their sights on something else to make them happy and caste aside so easily what they fought for, worked for, wanted, to say you are not making me happy. That is Ego. There is not consideration of the other soul, thing or any part of it. It is what the Ego wanted. Only to find if the Soul did not have happiness in the first place, nothing the Ego can provide will fill the space. Only the truth can.

## BEAUTIFUL UNION

The beautiful union of all souls is simple love in form. The purity that exists within simple love can not be found, it is internal and it is earned in life again and again and again and again, through pure intent of soul, through the self accountment of heart.

Taking away the desire of control, which leads to greed, to superiority, to wanting to believe you are who you are not. To leave that behind is to gift your soul with the openings of love, of simplicity, of the very things sought in errorous ways of mind.

The greediness of happenstance will never be able to survive the heart and mind of a soul.

## BEING OF TRUTH

Being good is nothing. Being bad is nothing. Being of truth is everything. Nothing else will grow, make sense, be, leave within you resonance without truth. Truth does not judge. Truth does not teach. Truth does not grow love. Truth simply is truth. It does nothing. It simply is a foundation of all things.

## BELIEF IN GOD

If a soul does not come to God, how does he appear as he believes in other avenues of hope and love in visualizations of mind and heart?

Every soul on Earth comes with more love than they can consume, for love is eternal. They come as babies form to bring that love to the world and it does. So easily in new souls, for the new souls in truth remind every one of home.

The babies scent of home, their living in home on Earth. Now when they live and are born to a soul who knows not such love, their own love shapes itself to the love they are in livement of, with the soul who knows not that love. They become the love they see and in heart search for the love of home.

Now if one of their challenges were to come here and not believe in the God, which is love, it is saying, "I am not sure love is present." Yet every soul has eternal hope there is something. They do not know why they have it, yet their shapings on Earth have left them in a dryness of love. And yet there is still hope in heart and they will visualize to see however their boundaries and their limits are not endless, other than what they can see and hear. What is of proof to their souls and that is what they will go on.

When the eternalness of thoughts is not present then the eternalness of dreams can not be. It is simply asking for things, peace, love, homes, cars, children's, goods, comforts of what they have; the thinkings, without the beyondness of their knowings. They simply shut off the openings of eternal evolutions. So simple is the truth. They will struggle in greaterments of Earth, for then Earth means something different to them.

Those who can see eternal, God, love, etc; understand that Earth is simply one of their journeys of soul. Those who can not see such love believe the Earth is the only place to find answers and Earth can not answer. For the energy of Earth stagnates within the power of the souls intentions on and off. That is the limit of answers given to any soul who can not see in furtherments of soul and heart.

## BELIEF WITHOUT FAITH

Be prudent to your soul. For to take care of yourself as you would others, will give to you the value of what it means to take care of another, for you will know of that from yourself. People cannot give what they do not have.

When there are problems, those problems already existed within that person long before it presents itself in a "couple" situation. God can only be for those who want to know, to touch their own lives and then touching lives of others. God can only be when asked, for free will is the reason of all existence.

Talk to God, ask God for all you want from purity and continue on, for each day is as it should have been and will end for the greater good even though it may not seem so at times. That is where trust comes in, belief and faith of heart. Belief without faith is not a helper it will take away. Faith is a builder, for within faith that is when what you believe becomes. Glory be to God Almighty.

## BLINDNESS OF TASK

The eternalness that exists is not of seenments to souls, for the clouded visions of happiness and love and purity of heart are needing clairment of souls purpose and the meanment of such knowings in life.

Souls do not recognize the truth of what they see, for they are looking too hard and expect too much. The expectations of life have taken that very life away from the souls of expectations. What can you expect from life that life can not give you for the purity of your soul's search?

To live in deviations takes away and takes away and takes away. A soul will notice another's deviations however not notice their own. That is the blindness of task that is the repetition however in purity souls are not meant to be alone and what one soul can not see another can bring to light that truth.

## BLUEPRINTS

We all come to this plane with our mission; let me call it an Earthly term, our blueprints. We come to accomplish journeys. Not one, many. We accomplish our growth, for one growth has to happen before another can. One Journey must be learned from for the other journey to begin. They can be concurrent when the learning is accelerated and one journey does not depend on the other.

An example of this is a musician who plays music and comes with the gift of music and services souls to fruition and has family and company and growths in many facets at once. All being related and all being intertwined. One growth does not depend on the other. Growths of love do depend on one another.

Works come from the soul however the learned behaviors, in truth they are relearned behaviors and actions; however the journeys of love are the truth, the mainness of all journeys of souls. And the love that is known is the increase of elasticity of the soul, the stretching, the expansion of soul.

The purpose of coming onto other planes is to evolve in love and come home in greater evolution. Learning is constant. In the galaxies, there is a difference of the way love is perceived and all that comes along with the propellations of love. The missions of Earth are sought after and free will exists within them.

## BODY AND SOUL

You are born in love and that is not of judgment of other souls. Each soul came with its purpose of who they are, of why they are. The human eyes can see however what if there was not vision. Then there would be no difference. The human ears can hear however what if they could not, for they could only love again. The human hands can move however what if they could not then there would be no way to eliminate another soul. And the human legs, what if they could not walk? No one would be walken away from.

In our eyes, our ears, our arms and our legs, God Almighty gave to us free will. And we have come to this day, in the manners of free will. And free will is not in hands of open knowledge's and the wills of souls are not in truth free. God Almighty gave to us a mind and in that mind it can be in takings away and the takings away are in greater balance than the givings of fruit. And now it is time to learn in love without fault, guilt and grandeur of suchness to be involved within the processes of thought.

It is of timeness now to give a soul license to live in the love of self and how it is to be of so. The learning is endless and can never cease. Those who carry ceasement of love live in the detachment of life. For the world of love repels them, except in the stances of self motivation. They only love for the rewards of love without the truth of its existence.

Love can not only exist in some places. That is an impossibiliality! Truth in love can either exist or it can not. A soul can only understand to love itself or it can not. And the openings of discoveries come with realizations of truth within self and to take on the patience it entails to search within. The "withouts" in life, they are not working, as the human mind is in boredom yet in searchment of the very things that are in creation of this very boredom.

## THE BOOK OF REVELATIONS

Soon the world will be ready. And when the world is in synchronization all will come to light. The Book of Revelations. All fear will be erased from the books of horror of soul to establish that a soul is to suffer in any form at the hands of God Almighty!

Glory be to God Almighty, for in God's name souls were put in jeopardy therefore how could they trust elsewhere? If the God that loves can be the same God that takes away, hurts and maims!

Glory be to God Almighty, for this is not of God Almighty.

In the Quran there is violence to souls as well however masked under the pleasures of God and within rewards. There are only rewards with God Almighty. Souls came with purpose and that purpose was not to be perfect as set by the standards of the world in this time. Perfection leaves a state of mind of inflexibility for what is a soul to do once deemed perfect. Perfection is of love.

## CHALLENGE

It is not how peoples are in behavior when they are in happiness however how they are in challenge. That is the teacher of any soul. For challenges are the growths, the points of contact between the outside world in which souls live and the internal makings of a soul. In these times it is said, and I love this expression, for it had no place in my time, "Where the rubber meets the road."

It is the motion. It is the action of all the soul's knowings when in challengement of self. Of external meeting the internal and what results from that meeting. Souls take away from themselves more than any other soul can take away from them.

I will example you. A soul comes to you in meanness; do you want to spend time with a soul of meanness to you? Do you want to share learnings with a soul of meanness? That soul loses love, caring, support and growth when the meanness is the repellant.

When a soul resorts to, lives in, becomes of meanness', then that soul loses the love of the world in return. They repel the love that they are looking for through meanness. For it cannot be!

What energies exist in a soul that the souls carry on Earth carries them. Draws them to pictures they see, they create, created, in mind and heart to think hence believe, for thoughts are things. Glory be to God Almighty. And those who see, who create, who care for self, who love, who teach; are seen, created, cared for, loved, taught!

For all things in life are circular. When said in the world of today, what goes around comes around, it is all of circular. It actually in truest of thought does not come around, it is already there. Negative begets negative already and positive begets positive already. What goes around is around.

## THE CHALLENGE OF EARTH

All things have energies. On Earth, some things have such low energies so that they can not move. Everything can not be moving on Earth. The slowment of energies is how time is in slowness and experiences can be had and growth can take place. The wonder of the mind is expanded on Earth as to how can there be such love, God, stories of "other side." It is all the same side.

Souls do not die. Peoples know of God however can they find him if his love is of question? Can a soul prepare itself to take care of itself with the way in which God is to be found? Love is to be found? And is that love of God in non visibility able to live within a soul without the soul knowing of its presence?

That is the greatest challenge of Earth.

Peoples look at each other and they ask themselves, others, could this story be of truth? Can God really be here? Is he hear, how do we know? They believe they have the story(s) of their religions respectively to concur their stories. They believe they have experiences in life to concur their stories.

They want to rest with it and they know the truth and the truth that they are learning does not coincide with what they believe, for they went to others for their truth and they began to get lost. And following going to others, standards are set and the soul starts aiming to please humans and not self. And the losses begin.

The internal disappointment of the soul without consciousness knowledge takes place, for that soul came down for a mission and then stopped itself for the search, for the love of God Almighty got taken away from them.

And they are now on meshed missions of those who are working within weaker movements of energies, which is to follow others and not be able to teach others by being who they are, for they simply became the standards of others and not of self. Glory be to God Almighty.

## CHANGE

Each year of time brings about changes of greatness. The changes keep the mind in livement of current time and changes give the soul purpose of growth. Seasons change to renew Earth and the glorious mind of soul's change to renew soul. It is not of taking away, it is of learning another way. It is not of sad to change; it is of growth to understand that change is the constant of time. If there was no change on Earth there would be no need for time on Earth. It would not make sense.

One change has to happen before another can, believe and it will be, think and it will become, thoughts become things, things show others and others learn. Some lack the faith they speak of. That is the irony of life.

We speak so we believe. We do, and we find out what we speak is not of truth in always, so caution becomes a thought. Fear sets in, worry starts to build its house and doubt become of the personality! Soon a fortress of stagnation is present. Grow and learn, learn and grow, for the seeds of life live within you.

The lessons of souls on Earth are difficult, long, tedious and blinded by mental realities. Imagine. Why one person can walk in one situation and another can't? It is only and simply because of the mental realities. To be all things possible makes them possible. Glory be to the open mind of life, for only then can life be life!

## CHEATERS

Nothing is as it seems. All cheatment of souls takes away from both souls! And every time it happens it happens again and again and again, until the cheaters themselves do not trust who they are. It is not the act; it is the action of heart and mind combined. That is why cheating is harmful.

For sex is sex. Anyone can have sex; that is easy. However, the boundaries of heart and mind are broken in heart and mind and that is a harshness of repair internal. The cheating do not trust each other. Glory be to God Almighty. That is the lesson. It takes away from both. That is the lesson. And if it is not learned it is sometimes repeated, thinking they will do it right the next time.

Like any other lesson it is repeated until learned. Those who are far away in time and space, cheat their bodies and then their minds. Even if the other party is available and there is a partner of marriage, it will dissolve the marriage at heart if not in physicality. For it tells the soul of itself that it is of lacking. That is cheating.

Peoples know not what they say, what they do, for the affects shape the soul; the affects of behavior. Those willing to open up lines of energy in their lives that take away from themselves and from others, try to look better and better on the outside of self. With cars, clothing's, homes, things, things, things, and I went here and there, see, I am of importance and love and on the inside are the inner workings of turmoil. The inner workings of turmoil come without saying, to takings away in any form, some more than others.

There is not a cell of truth, an atom of hope, a millisecond of description of any soul on Earth who will tell you multiple partnerships in the sameness of moments did not destroy their truth of self.

There is not a soul on Earth in truth of self that will tell you that cheatments of self with others, to another, made them ever feel like a better person. ALL CHEATMENTS THAT HAPPEN COME FROM PAIN. THERE IS NO OTHER REASON. All. No more no less. That is why some will argue with you that it is OK, and though you have not the words you understand the truth.

It does not matter what it is called. It is from pain. And it continues to bring on pain to self and others as it lives in energy to happen. Even the children's understand its pains. It is the greatest deterrent to universal law of love, truth and purity. It breaks the souls bond to self hence to all souls around that soul. That is why even those who in horror of others doing it, try not to acknowledge that they themselves are members of that breakage. It is simply truth to go to the fork in the road of self and rearrange your hearts knowings into faith of love. For the cheaters of the world in love, lack the faith that love grows. They are mad at love for betraying them and they want to hurt love by cheating.

And all of these souls came down to live that out and speak it yet in truth there is not fullness of understandings as to why. It is not in good nor bad, rich or poor, to cheat.

And the ones who want to cheat are coming to tell the world there is no love. That is the truth. Pains of generations have brought the souls to this day, for energy carries and in weight greater than all things. And love in purity propels. And in this time, this day, this period of human experience, you see the polars of love and lacks of love. And some of the moments that appear as love are not and some that say they are not are. So simple is the truth. It has nothing to do with sexualness of humans. It has to do with deterrents of faith and love, for nothing is as it seems.

Cheating is looked at on Earth as a voyous adventure. It is simply a lack of self love and worth. No more no less. When you are in wantings of outsidedness it is for lacks of love in your home. It can only take away from all. There has been no instant that it has grown love.

Think of it as the cheaters of monies. Those monies are never brought back. When a soul can say they understand and they remain in cheatedness of relationships, they can not forget and it gets in the way of all other situations. It is the feared subject and then the used subject in depth of argument and it shows its color of non forgoteness.

Cheaters are the examples of shrinkage of love on Earth. That is why all comes. They are challenges of love and the truths that accompany them. They are the listings of hearts when they are questioned as to what they believe and the questions of heart when a soul stands in alonement of self in hearted discussion of self and actionments to self and others.

The caring it takes to care for one soul, a soul to itself, is extensive with simplicity of heart. It is simply love. No other way. Love is simple. Explanations of souls to each other for actions need not be, for if love in purity is present then the discussion need not happen in blamements of who souls are. In cheaterdom of humanness is the breaking of universal law. It is the puffed upedness of ego and the taking away of soul. Whether it be in cheatments of monies, bodies, things, souls.

## CHILDREN

Children are of innocence. They are protected as/until they approach puberty, and in this time they live with pure questions of the mind. As they reach into what is adulthood they form who they are and are ready for many missions, with the input of childhood and the answers of pubescence. Hence, they created a blueprint of who they are. And modification of mind, of spirit, comes with pure intent and steers their souls.

And others start early in becoming non flexible peoples of this world. Others become early, as to wanting control and fearing all they see and witness. They cocoon in the world by themselves, they need a sense of control and in those moments have isolated themselves from others. That is of sadness to shut off so early and act as though you did not.

This is what happens. Those who are apparent in their need to control the world hence others, have a false sense of worth, of security, of love. For with these people there is all falseness hence relationships of any kind are of simple disaster to the recipients of such peoples.

There are many divorces, separations, children who do not see such peoples, coworkers, partners of life in passing who walk away strange to the person they believed in once knowing. As age progresses, apparency of behavior becomes greater in transparency. They cannot see, for behavior has been set in ways for so long it is simply the acceptable way of thought and no longer hidden with age.

Older age of human soul sets itself in ways, when the isolated mind is present. This can happen to a soul at 25, as it can at 50, as it can at 100.

Older age is of mind of the human soul not of body. You meet many with older physical form and yet you sit at ease with their souls on Earth. And you meet some at 25 that you have to walk away from to take a physical breath; that you cannot sit within or without once the behavior of such is felt and unveiled.

Children are the innocent of souls in time of forever. All damages that happen in the child's of life are the manifestations of pending and then complete adulthoods. This is the obvious however it is the penetrations of ill will. For in the years of High School on Earth the demeanor of a soul is in growth. And it becomes the basis of a soul within pressures.

In my time on Earth it was when a child began a trade, for then the character of a child was solidified in that time; the actions onto children breeds in them compassion or rebellions. Those are the first lessons of experience. What happens in early childhood is not felt in completeness until protection is gone and the experiencing begins. That is why some peoples go back in time to reclaim what they have known.

Those are the ones who stuck themselves in life and can not see or be in the day for what it is. And those who wanted to run away from childhood, they are the ones who are in constant looking for that better day. However, that better day never comes, for no day can be the better day. Living in the moments on Earth is to live. All else, in going back and going forward, miss the opportunities of the day.

Any soul can be happy when all things are met. However the character is defined in belief, in truth and in the hope of life. Of living in the day and knowing that they will only be days to come.

For all souls will live. There will be funds, things, pleasures and then there will be none. Who is the person in both places? Glory be to God Almighty. Souls do not live in the moment and believe souls to believe as they do and have been in teachings of half truths. So that time is the best of teachers is shown here in once again. Souls were in the knowing that nothing is ever enough. They were taught suchness in self motivation of parents wanting them to be what they are not and overlooking what they are. For not to see the day a soul is in is to not live in the day that you are in.

## CHOICE

So simple is choice for humans. Is decision. Is letting go. There are endless choices. What choices a soul makes are the decisions to influence heart, mind and what can grow into their lives. These choices are of great value. No one soul has to do anything! Everything is a choice. The hand of the soul on Earth is greater in Strength than any soul can know.

And yet the strength is squashed and the complications and explanations begin. All the stories told to convince, to sway and to add to the pressures of life, all of the hurts that carry when they could have been soothed into growth. The soul does not know what it does not know however pure intent, truth to self and love of self will overcome any obstacle. All things will happen in each day.

What things does a soul choose? All days will be lived. What things does a soul choose? All moments will have something in them. What does a soul choose? All days will contain love. Will a soul see it? All days have skewment. Will a soul be drawn to it? All days have time. Will a soul use it in fear or in love? All days have other souls. Will a soul share it? All days are opportunities. Will a soul take them? All days are times of growth. Will a soul know it?

All days produce a conclusion. Will a soul have closure? All days end in rest. Will a soul be able to? There are no maps. No guidelines. Souls are told what not to do and they also know what to do; how do they choose? How do they know better or worse for themselves? What factors come into choice?

The answer to all the questions above and beyond all questions is love, purity and truth. To Self: Self love. Self purity. Self truth. It is all so simple. It is all so clear. It is all right here, right now. Can it all be seen? When love can not be seen, felt or heard, or simply recognized, for the lack of love produces much in its path.

That is the excuses, the explanations, the complications and the reasons why. That is the secrets, the "don't tells," the things that leave other souls wondering and the beginnings of mistrust in others then in self. Or in self and then in others gives birth. Love is one endless thread without any entanglements. Entanglements are the non presence of love.

Every soul has free will, Never, never forget that. Every soul has the choosings of the world before it. All souls have choosings. All souls have choosings. The choices that they make, when they are choices of self compromise, they are cushioned with verbiages, actions, sayings, speaking's to support the compromisations of self. When there is truth it is spoken easily. And all else needs explanations, comes with some kind of complication, some kind of past drugged up to support the actions, and it goes on in infinitedom of reasoning's to support ill intented actions of self.

Every soul on Earth has choices. And those choices of soul teach us of the soul(s) existence and the way in which the world is seen. It is so simple and so clear. That is truth. That is love. That is purity. All things, all things without exception come to truth, love and purity. All things are of truth, love and purity, for truth, love and purity are all one in the same. There is no harm that can come from love.

## CHURCH

Most call them the house of God however the house of God is Earth. It is not embodied by walls of ANY KIND. Church is where emotion of God is exemplified however it is the emotion that fuels the building not the building that fuels emotion. Emotion is the source of what gives life to any situation. Without it, without compassion, all is the same, no movement, for it is the energy that moves all.

How could a building when not occupied move anything? It is the souls that enter that create movement. Energy is the movement of all things. That is why when the energy is of negative it is of chaos, run don't walk away, for the intentions are mishap of emotions and it will be of impossible to not be affected, repelled, or drawn in.

## CIRCULAR ENERGY

Geemla, it is a word in Arabic, to take your weight of despair and know-ingly dump the weight on another. The trick is though that the weight that is dumped onto the unsuspecting soul does not relieve the giver of Geemla. It simply spreads the weight and the giver of suchness leaves in greater weights for the sharings of what they came to share when the sharing is of ill will.

The propellations of ill will are energies in sideways and the propellations of love move forward, ahead of. That is why there is stagnation's in ill will. It is sideways, and the human eyes can not see sideways and that is why they can not see it coming to them at times.

One who can not feel love, who wants to complain and hurt others for the love they do not feel, can not feel, will not allow themselves to feel. They have a circular energy. They come to fruition and then fall down again. They can not go through the doors they open. They do not realize that energy is not circular.

Pure energy travels in forwardness ahead of a soul. The only reason for cir-cular energy is the wanting to be better than. That is pure self motivation.

They try to come to life in charmments and they do, and then the charm turns into weight and the weight makes the receiving soul run not walk away. That is the circle. And they must keep starting over and over again with the charm, only to find that it is not charm that sustains. It is truth.

And they can not see their truth and they speak of it in detail, their truth, to convince others of their truth. Yet in truth, truth does not need to be rep-resented. It simply needs to be true. Circles live in the same energy planes. And forwards live in the same energy plane. They live in coexistence however forwards teach truths and circles catalyst forwards.

## CLAIM YOUR FEELINGS

To claim your own feelings is to open the door to internal wake up calls to all that lives inside a soul. How great a find that is! Glory be to God

Almighty, for souls wait for life to be what they want it to be before they can feel? Or pay attention?

A lifetime could and does pass and that soul missed the chance to know of itself, to understand its purpose and then to give back. Most can't begin to give back in a lifetime of lessons, for they choose in discourse to themselves their paths in life.

All is well, it means that that soul will have other times and opportunities to come to terms with their growth and lessons. And when their growth is out of sync with those around them then it is time to move on in life and explore the soul's depth or lack of.

Anger at a soul is fruitless. Understand and trust in the bigger picture that that soul need be growing away, for its purpose is growing for all.

## CLEAN
When your mind is in thought; clean. Cleaning is symbolic for organizing the mind and the soul of all. Cleanliness is not work, for the labor of the hands feeds the heart and mind answers to all. To clean gives the soul forum to propel to completion of task, which completes the tasks of those things felt unbearable to a soul.

## THE COMMERCIALISM OF LOVE
The commercialism of love has given injustice to the greatest force in the universe. Love is not a thing. It can not be bought. It is not a story. It is not given or taken away. It is not able to be used, and without it sustain of anything is impossible. No matter what it appears to be, without sustainment of love, all possibilities parish.

## COMPASSION
Compassion needs nourishment. And nourishment comes from service of any kind. And when service is lacking then compassion lacks two fold. That is why helping each other grows souls, for then the compassion to a fellow soul is present. For when the soul asks only for itself there is internal isolation hence anger.

## COMPETITION AND EGO

Souls want to be teachers and Ego tells souls it is a step down in humanity to be a learner. To learn. I speak for the emotion of souls. "We have answers, they are for all of us" and Ego speaks, "No, I want to be the teller, the wise one," not in realization that there is no competition.

All competitions are created and competitions can only exist when there are participants. In a game of sports this is known. In the living of life, which is not a game it is a journey, there is no competition. There is simply Ego or not. Truth or not.

Souls come from home in search of truth, love and purity. That is the fact of every soul. Souls who want to speak there is no truth, love or purity, do not have the courage to live their life. They lost courage and candor, Truth and honor.

To have truth and honor, courage and candor, speaks to souls that all things are possible. There is not impossible within the mind of a soul without the ego believing in itself that something, anything is not possible. Thoughts are things and things are thoughts.

## COMPETITIVENESS

To see the panic of one person trying to please another is disheartening. It takes away from their souls and fills it in with the things that continuously take away and flourishes feverish frets, measurements, competitiveness.

Competition is of fun to grow and to stir the mind into growth.

Competitiveness is entirely different. It is of willingness to do things that are not of giving however of taking away. Those are the greatest losses of truth. Hurting the energy of souls hurts all else.

## COMPLETE

You can not find complete until you are complete. You will find less complete as your lessorment is present. Know yourself and you will know of others. For a soul will attract their own reflections in time.

## CONDITIONS OF LOVE

Some believe that love is conditions. It is seen and understood in all of their doings. Their commonalities hold them in place and slide them backward and then hold them in place again. So simple. What is love without conditions? Love is simply love.

If and when a soul comes to know expectation, know conditions, on what they want or need, is it not love? It is simply not in purity that it comes. Most souls can not withstand life without expectation or conditions, for love is taught and not felt on Earth.

Straying of heart from self comes of the love being taught and not felt. Hence, the beginnings of searching's, of filling holes and healings, they know not, for they are forever trying to fix things and they are not finding completion. For the intentions as a whole, see not, seek not the truth. The truth remains in flawlessness.

The truth is flawless. This is true of all things and it is true of all peoples. Understand that motivations into behaviors comes from desperations of different levels of control or loss of it in their lives. They are all lost. Their lost is not of apparency, it is of internal.

All humans look of simpleness on the outside. They have bodies, they clothe them, they clean them and they maintain the body that they are in form in. Now what lives truly is the soul. It is called the mind when in thought and the heart when in love.

Humans at times believe there are separations. Love is not separated. Heart is not separated. They are names given to try and make understanding of who they are. Humans let not the love of life, the pureness of soul to grow when separated. When separated in some things done and some things not, that is the most understood of love, for that is the conditions you see and hear.

The body is of bodyment and the soul is of eternal.

The soul of any person, human, will carry itself until the journey concludes. If only the simpleness of that can be seen. When it can not be seen and the lessons are of different paths and the motivations are of self, then the pureness of love becomes injured.

And those who injure the pureness of love they do it to self first and then see the results of it spewed on to every unsuspecting and suspecting soul in small doses in daily of lives. That is how those things happen.

Most of times peoples of manipulations and self motivations end up in aloneness, for others can not bear the weight of argumentative life. It is of the greatest pressures to endure to the mental stresses of another, to add to the layers of the human mind already. We help each other, we grow each other however to pull a soul into the darker shades of mind is to drag the soul into the turmoil's.

Purity lacking conditions, Love lacking conditions, Hope lacking conditions; the conditions alone have taken away more from life than the expectations.

**CONTROL**

All is solvable. All that can not be solved is what is worked so hard to control, for how can control be solved! Control is of the weary, of the meek. Control speaks of the weakness of life at its best and the soul's absence of self love hence love of self. Control is the controller of none.

For truly there is no control, there is anger at life and selfishness in not attaining and no patience for the trust of life. Trust in life is key.

Trust comes from the intents of the pure. Love comes from the intent of the pure. So when there is lack of trust it gives us a soul before themselves of lack of intents of purity hence once again no love in realness.

Love becomes the tool to be of happiness when it is happiness that brings about the discovery of love. So simple and yet in the mind of the controlling soul there is true belief for those souls, that they can get others to play out the actions of their hearts for no one else but them.

When that is of discovery the manipulated soul runs away and tries in nicement to relieve themselves of the wrath of the souls of control. They are the souls who have to come back and hurt and tear down the buildings around those who can accept life, for at some level within, usually the deeper levels within, the controlling souls know of their lack of trust hence pure intent hence love.

There is no good or bad. No right or wrong. If the will of souls was not controlled, the best would come out of souls, for it would only know love. It would not be in stresses to do as it did not wish. The progression of life on Earth is taking away the souls right to be in freedom of heart, mind, body and soul hence the taking awayment from all. One can not feel a thing that is not shared by all in eventuality.

So many are afflicted by the controlling and realize such souls once the heart has been open and exposed. It takes years at times and by the time the discovery is made it is an accepted form of behavior. And then a day comes when you do not know why you do not feel anything for that soul on Earth anymore and the easier it is to run not walk away.

Those who are stuck are only the ones who do not believe they can make it on their own. The control souls try to control is controlling them. The greatest form of control is to let go of control and trust in life.

## CREATION

Think about all the fights of souls within themselves about God, about love, about what life is supposed to mean, how it means it, why it means it? It is all creation. And in Creation all things, souls, live. And in the livement there are choices. And in those choices is free will. And within free will there are the choices of others influences, lower energies, love and the ways in which it is, was, shaped.

And the experiences begin. And growth becomes. And lessons honed. And lessons not honed repeated until honements take on a place and growth can and does move forward. A giving soul is a soul that is known right away, from heart. I am saying this in againments so that in another way souls can learn of it. For it will reach some and then all.

484 ~ Origins of Truth

## CULTURE

Each culture teaches other cultures and the only way it can be learned is through example. So many peoples came down to simply be those cultures to give to the world interest in itself and then onto others. To learn and open the mind that there is not only a way of oneness: That there are many.

However there came a time when the males of the cultures had fears they could not keep the cultures in the ways in which they wanted them to remain; to control the women and the family of protection. So they brought about rules; Rules of fear; Rules that invoked rebellion of heart, which controlled some and repelled others from their wanting to know.

And then you would witness division in cultures. And then a church would separate from another. And then there would be another sect; Then a division with the sects. And was that from God? It was of man. Who cares in truth who the prophet is, is the truth not more important than the messenger? It is not being the messenger! Glory be to God Almighty.

The saying; kill the messenger. Where did that come from? Know that is the truth of fear. To kill that that comes to it and that soul's mission is not of understandment in the present time. It is a meekness and a bandwagonness that peoples are. They are too scared to be who they are and simply because they know not who they are. Glory be to God Almighty.

No soul can be blamed for who they are however they do need to be reacted to, for growth will not be possible without. Glory be to God Almighty. There are truly no mistakes. There is no future predicting. There IS pure intent and guidance. And that carries growth and breeds learnment. So simple.

## CURRENT ISSUES

These are the current issues. The roots of all the ill wills in present in past, in future, for there is no time. However there is change in circumstance and the circumstances written in this time are different from past Earth time and will be different from future Earth times. However love, truth and purity remain the same. That is the differentness the sameness and the difference again.

## DATING

A woman may witness a man of human handsomeness by the standards of time on Earth or a Man may witness a woman of sameness in beauty. And yet when the speaking begins all the beauty changes form, all the manliness' change form, they will either strengthen in truth or go away in self motivations.

Once a soul dates a soul does there become owement of truth? Love or demands? Caring or accusations? Caressments for reward? Or Caressments for love? And then souls want to blame the one who wants to run and demand he/she prove that he/she loves them. And every day becomes a day of judgment! And the deterioration of what love is in purity begins.

It is a spiral of downwardments of soul that no one can maintain. OR want to. And they leave. For to love in truth is to not use the other person to fulfill your happiness or curb your sadness, that is the greatest imbalance I see. NO one can make another happy. Caring builds love.

There are many areas of relationships. Souls only want the parts they want and not the others. They want what THEY need and simply forget that the other soul is a soul. They want a look, a price, a person, and they do not believe they have reciprocation to be all the things that they demand.

They only do it if they will get something in return and punish when they do not. That is love within conditions. And as they speak they have unconditional love, their love of conditions is underway and that is the trickery of the soul onto itself hence onto others.

Oh, the souls who come unto these souls! The anguish it entails to live in the webs of a mind, without a broom to swipe it clean. Glory be to God Almighty, for souls run away from these souls first, while they are still together, and then in physical form soon after.

## DEATH

There is a lot of death of soul in living physicality. When a soul doesn't get what it wants in this day, there is great anxiety that attaches itself to that soul. And then there is overwhelmence of not knowing what to do, for the internal belief, faith, is thin, so thin it is transparent.

## DEPTH

Depth is not what it seems. It is in the nature of love that depth exists and love truly has no boundaries and limits. No edges and no holes. Love is the waves of energy that can only carry all things around.

## DEVICEITIVE

Ego is a strong deviceitive of soul. Deviceitive, it is a taker away of soul. That is deviceitive. Ceit: to take away. Vice: in mind over soul. De: in discountment of greatements. It is deviceitive to a soul to favor ego rather than soul; to favor hurtments rather than growths, to favor foreclosure of self when a soul can still make the payments.

## DEVILS

There are no devils, weaker spirits, lesser than love of God Almighty. All that is said of elsements is created by those who want to believe that it exists. And it is created in the lowest forms of energies to live within and that is the devils, the weaker spirits, the lesser of loves that is spoken of in greatness by humans. To think it will create it, yet in allment, all that is not of love is not of God Almighty. No exceptions.

## DO UNTO OTHERS

The bigger picture of life, of love, of the way the inner workings of the human mind are with pure intent. Their growth will come with their love of themselves, their love will come with acceptance of themselves and their purity will come with that same acceptance of others. For truly to do unto others as you would do unto yourself is a very gigantic truth!

## DRUGS

No one soul can do drugs just once. Once the soul knows it can escape Earth it will continuously try to do so. That is why it is a form of suicide, for it kills the existence of life on Earth in the living. The soul is in heightment however it is falseness of self. It finds itself in a place of allurements and unablements to see life's treasure in truth. Through love.

This is a short cut however without the love; it can not be sustained, for it is not in truth. It stimulates the body to work as it is not designed to work hence the body knows not of itself. If it is abused within, the body will begin to break itself down to accommodate the druggedness needed to sustain it.

For the body can engage in all activity the same only with exclusion to see. The soul will sit in the experience of it however the experience of it is an illusion. It is a falsity of self in lacks of prudency to the heart of soul you possess.

Did you ever see a soul speak of drugs in pride that they take them. If any way of communication is expressed it is in denial of some sort. Except with like souls. For the soul knows it is a soul of betrayal and drugged souls know they can not be trusted entirely. And when one soul finds that another is within that realm of drug reality on Earth, they themselves do not trust in entirety the other.

They are young in mostment, looking for love. They want to be with people and they find much more grouping when there is common cause and with drugs there be no common cause other than the drugs.

There is no status in drugs. As in Sex. There is no status. Anyone can do either. Why? Lostment. Sadness. Aloneness; Lacks of understanding of the world around, so there is need to create a world. However the created world is less real than what the perceived world is. That is what is meant when they say a soul did not remember, did not know what it was doing, did not care who, what, where they did anything to themselves or to others.

It is a very low energy to be in the druggedness. Once a soul comes back to clarity of Earth, their need to run away is instant. It is a farness away from self. It is called cool, something to do, a mender however all who do it, join in and propel the stagnatedness of all their souls. And they hold in place and live in a freedom they are uncomfortable confronting in everyday life.

It cowards life as it seems greater. It gives to the soul what it can not have, what it can not do, for it feels its confidence in falseness, for now the soul feels it can not function without out it the same.

They see a potential, not a truth. They get lazy to explore the truth of life, of love, of caring for themselves or others. They are no longer present in fullness, for they want to run away and take themselves back to the falsity that seems real, rather than to be in real to them and grow from there.

Drugs are simple in taking. Not a specialness as you would think. You find ways to insert it into the body. However did you ever see anyone happy who takes drug? Stay happy? It can do nothing but to take away.

These physical and beautiful souls who take away from themselves and walk around in shadows have looks on their faces that stop the warmth. Take the experience inward and spreads, and then disappears. There is no home. There is vacancy in beginning, for the soul knows it is taking away, the middle in floatment of truth and the end when it takes the soul to the rawness of itself.

It has a beginning, it has an end; therefore telling you it is not eternal. There is no soul more important than another. You see the more money a soul has does not mean anything. It is in worsement to that soul, for they have more money to take away from themself(s).

For now the soul has money as it always wanted, has time as it has always wanted; has home and food and no appreciation. The taker awayers remain without learnment of self and still group in packs to take away from themselves. Nothing can make them happy, content, nor can it, for the soul knows not of itself and finds avenues of escape no matter what is presented for it.

How awful of life to be clear minded, for then the work of the soul can be seen. Drugs are a great way to avoid that. And the disappointment of the soul can never go away without the soul being a part of itself. How can a soul see others when it can not see itself? How can a soul get to the helpment of others when it can not help itself?

The blind are more common than those that can see. A soul can not know who they are if they do not know who they are not. A soul must know who it is not to know who it is. For the blind believe they are unique.

They live in fear, in jealousies, in hopelessness, and they want things to make them happy, whether it be drugs, homes, cars, clothing's, equipment's any measurement of physical showings of who they are. However they are taking on the visible and know not their truth.

Can a car speak to you and tell you who you are? It shows others who you want to be. You are left alone. Can a drug tell you how to comfort yourself when it is gone? You are left alone. Can a piece of clothing keep another soul close to you? You take that clothing off. You are left alone. Can a soul escape itself and still be alive on Earth? It is standing alone. For nothing about things speaks of souls needing each other.

When you help your family you stand with them. When you work on projects you build glory. When you prepare a meal you sit in togetherments and share. When you love from heart it does not escape nor does it go away. It is the truth of farawayment that keeps souls looking for anything to tell them life can be better even when it comes in falsements to self to do so.

The true murders are the murders that one does to itself. The true deaths are the ones that occur in life. For the known deads of Earth are not dead. There is no death of spirit however there is death of life in livement. Some want to run away and feel something, anything for real of self. It matters none what is real on Earth, for real is self before it can exist anywhere.

It is choices. It is life. It is free will. Drugs are not a reward. They are a taker awayer in truth and acceleration of what a self can do to a self. This needs no other soul. It is a person choice that the soul can tell itself it is not loved. Drugs are the opposite of love. It is a card game with no winners.

There is no challenge. No chase. No mystery. No love. No home. No compassion. It is of no mind, no soul, no body, to do once, twice or forever. It has a beginning, it has a middle and it has an end; the complete opposite of eternity.

## THE DRUG OF CHOICE

Ego is like a drug of choice on Earth. It feeds itself in ways that help no one, not even itself. Ego is very much of mind only. Ego fights the soul and that is what stems for purpose of Earth. For free will and choice give each soul the option of listening to it and detouring mission. A soul living in self importance of self is simply ego. It is Mind without Heart. It is a computer without an owner in today's language.

## DUALITY

Think of contradictions between thoughts and actions, beliefs and behaviors, love and pure love. What is the difference, what is the purpose(s)? You are looking at the duality, the separations of what is known and what is done.

What peoples believe is not what they are able to do so easily. What peoples believe is not action, for their believes are not in strength. They are in what they believe to be righteousness and their beliefs become markers of what is good and bad. What is good and bad matters so little yet the more unaware the human mind is and has been; the easier it is to be able to think in ways of duality.

Thinking in duality is the first ways in peoples being taught. The duality is the extremes presented in who, what, is good or bad. Good or Evil for churches, and for parents, the other great influence it is in behavior of every day. There is separation between Church and behaviors of parents. Those are the first of influences. Both are good and want to present "good" and yet in that there are many contradictions.

It is not about the soul simply looking for itself. The soul has to look for itself; otherwise the soul can not give to others. And the soul purpose of Earth is to find love in self, then to others. It is what we do for others that is of greatest importance. That is the reason, for all of the self knowing, self love, that is sought after to be. Without it, there is no sense of giving and love.

You can not be the problem and the solution at the same time, for then the duality takes place. The duality of life is felt that it needs to exist. However, it does not; it too was the creation of free will. There was no snake in the gardens of Eden, the eating of the apple that came to punish women, the listening to the devil that caused men and women to fall and be born of original sin.

All of us are truly made in love. We came with guidance and embarked on human life as to experience the makings of mind when the veil takes away the knowledge of love and not the feelings of love; to find in each other the points of light of love and grow within.

There is not perfection however in purity all things will be. All happenings will guide, all lessons will be of learned. The belief that duality exists, the knowing that there is a sense of control as to the outcomes, are the harboring points of growth on one hand and great frustration of the eyes that can not see on the other. If the souls of humans can be set free to be, they will not want to be in duality.

There are no maps to follow. No new roads. Peoples are looking for peace in ways of heart and all the little that they know. About the Buddha's, the Hindus, the methods of greater freedoms of heart. And then you have the greatest preachers of duality and they exist in the Muslims, Christians and the Jewish Faith Options on Earth.

It is not so simple to explain, as it is simple to know. Humans know what is right; good, righteous, loving, for there is no right and wrong. What they know is that the intent of humans is to love and care for each other and when that does not exist, it causes other things to happen and those are the very things that take away. That taking away causes friction in the hearts of humans and then results in the friction of the hearts of others.

Religions, groups, common points of interest, work, jobs, interactions, they are all ways of humans conforming to life or what they know of life. What wills of souls before then carved out in life. And now they are at this point. Where there were many self motivated decisions that are made, were made and are being made presently. And you know there is not end when self motivation for a soul, a religion, a company can there be.

Take a credit card. It is not designed for you to conclude it. Rules change and the changes are given in fine prints that the normalcy of the eye can not read. Rates increase with mailings that are known to not be read however disclosure is what is told. Costs for lateness are increased in "by the way." And they are on top of the interest. So if you are full and you are late, you get a late fee and an overlimit fee. So now you have interest, late and over limit fees.

And it was created legally with self motivation, with ill intent of souls who wanted and did benefit. It is worth it to pay people to recover monies, after humans are broke and broken, and even the monies not recovered are made money from when the losses are used for tax purposes.

Is it honest? No. Is it real? Yes, for it was created and accepted by those who still did not believe they would fail. And when they can not repay, as a result they can not take on any more. That is the favor to all of you. When you can not repay and you stop using the ill intended projects of others to survive. For life on Earth, Monetary is like a puffed up balloon, and a small hole in the balloon will hold itself in place for so long. That is true too of the emotional self.

Peoples have choices and they can only make choices on what they know, so simple and so loving of life on Earth for all. If only all could believe that they are loved already, the energy would turn in instants of time. The insecurities rule much of the happenings at this time, for the internal confidence of souls is startling to the hearts that carry them around.

Self motivation is the worm that eats away at all the intentions of those who are not self motivation. It is the disrupter of good will. Its truest trick is that it looks appealing, it sounds of appealment.

All souls are honed to learning in experience. How else is a soul to know? Duality is the key to all pain and relief. How do you get relief if the intent you put in is of ill will? You must ask the souls of those who instill complications and manipulations into action; for they are the meek of the Earth.

## DYNAMICS OF A WOMAN AND A MAN

All souls can have sex. When you hear a soul say, "He loves me, we had sex," it startles you. When you hear a man say suchness it does not. Why? For you know the dynamics of a woman and a man.

You know the detachment of men at times can be real. You understand what a man goes through in thought to have sex with a woman and how he can feel like leaving right after and not feel odd about it.

A body is separate from the heart and soul in moments of non emotional attachments to a soul. It is the moments of emotion that carry a moment with a woman for men and at times it does not include sex on Earth. And within that the sexualness is intensified hence the feelings of love are present.

For women the hope of love is what drives their sexualness. For a mate to domingate and create a biological match. However many women ignore the instinct of who they are in truth, and try to act that it is how she has sex that takes on the reason for why she is sought after.

*(DOMINGATE—Feelings of a woman to a man without thoughts of sexualness, however of procreation)*

However sexualness without love can not hold onto itself. You can see the weight put on sexualness, the breasts of women, the body parts, no head needed to attract. No heart needed. Just in body. That is what happens when a soul attracts with things rather than heart. It is not to say it doesn't work that way, it is to say it does not stay in that way.

And souls are in wirement of souls to stay. In time, it is truly a hardship to partner many in sexual activity. The lack of depth in emotion takes its toll on a soul on Earth. For we are programmed to grow and when we stop and live in repetition of any kind, there is boredom and then sadness.

Souls who believe they can live that way over time would rather live in alonement, than the alonement that is felt in many half relationships, as any half truth is non fulfilling in heart, mind, body and soul.

That is running out of time in the current religious format as well. Yes, anyone can say they are anything. Can they be it in truth?

The lack of truth(s), the setting aside of emotion(s) and the casualness of the depth that the heart needed to inspire passions, love, growth and knowing of self, is the sadness you see in heart around you.

However, when there is love in purity with intensifications of love on Earth, the sharing of physicalness carries with it the energy to nourish throughout time. That is the bonding truly of a breast fed child. They live within the energy of the mother in greatness of all time.

The heat of the body, the warmth of the heart, the emotion, carries and carries throughout time. When a breast of a woman is touched it is of the greatest sexual, emotional, and glorious love on earth. It beats the heart in quickness, it wakes up the body, moves the blood, embodies the growth, the nourishment, the touchings of life through out.

To inject a breast with plastics is another half truth of life. Then it is turned into an object and took the fork in the road that that breast is sex and not love. However in love, when it is touched, it opens up the world of love for both. Some souls love to touch in gentleness of a woman's breast, for it is always warm.

It is inviting life to grow and to hold onto the essence of the beginnings of human growth on Earth. A soul form latches onto the breast of a woman before it can see. It is emotion before it is known what it is, for it is already known for the love that it is in alreadyment. There is more.

In sexualness, the breast of a woman is home for all peoples. It is the closest to home a soul can feel on Earth in physicalness. For it carries the openings to the rest of the body. It stimulates the waters of the body to expede from within to without; to ready the human body in growth of another.

The readiness is of the grandest of pleasures God Almighty gave to the human body of souls on Earth, for it releases the fluids of life; the fluids that carry the fluids of another. There is unison of body, of mind, of thought and of depth all in once of moments.

When there is not love of purity, that love will dissolve itself in time. For the love within the touches will not carry its energy any further. It will come and go. Try and be tried however it will not be able to live in foreverment. However in truth it will sustain. You see the lack of sustainment, for truth is only half present.

You see many peoples who live with each other, touch each other, sex each other, eat together and they do not laugh, cry in happiness', speak in truth or in silence and they live in this way in each and every day. They know not the sustainment, for their own energy does not carry the soul into further-ments of growth; However, when truth is present and you know of it you rest internal. There is no rush to do anything.

It matters not what you wear, you do, where you go, do, what you eat, how you eat it, what you speak, how you speak it, there is trust; In life and in love. In self and in God, for life and love are the sameness of life and love. Glory be to God Almighty.

You see the sexualness is pure emotion. There is not physicalness involved until they're their love in truth, for the physicalness is not felt the same. It can be done however it will not be the depth. And that very depth is what is missing in the world of worlds on Earth.

## EARTH

Every plane is open in thought. And for Earth, it is the thought and experience of free will. For the will of the free souls shapes all. And that is what is seen. Nothing is at it seems.

Many are on Earth and can only see Earth. On Earth it is easy to forget all else. For it ties the hands and bounds the feet of souls. It holds them in place and forgets them love. It carries them into treasures of falseness. Earth runs out of things and panics those from believing they will live forever.

Earth is a teacher of honing souls. It takes them away from home, only to bring them back. While they are on Earth, the true experience of all is to take home away from mind and let heart find it again; to experience life without home on all levels.

There are many successes. There is always balance. The ones of pure intent find it quickly. The ones of self motivation at times come home without the discovery. Earth is the hardest of adventures to endure. It is, for free will is very affected by surroundings. At Home this does not happen; the will of a soul knows its mission. ON Earth there is no knowing of missions, for the yearning of purity is the key.

Life is only part of a soul. Souls on Earth believe in many ways this is it and it is of safety. In reality life on earth is the least safe of all experiences to choose. It is the hardest experience as a soul that it will endeavor. Glory be to God Almighty, for nothing is as it seems. It is the one experience that experiences in the absence of the knowledge of God Almighty.

May the world run its course. May the thoughts of blindment come to be seen, if not by the blind, by those who can see. There is witnessment of many events of sorrow; some from naturicities, some soul made, and some in intents for one and not for all. And peoples are speaking, as they have throughout time, that things seem to be happening in groves and it is to bring about the end of the world. It will not end the world. How does the world end?

*(NATURICITIES—Behaviors we turn into habits that become natural to us)*

It will still be here no matter of matters. It is the souls that would end, in physicality upon existing Earth. There is no end. For nothing ends. There is endlessness' in all things. The Earth is a mass of energy. The fear of the Earth ending is the limitations of minds eye. The energies on Earth are touched and maneuvered by the souls that inhibitate it.

It causes all else to happen within and without the surface of Earth. For the souls energy is of the strongest of energies. The Earth as it is is in response to soul's energy at all times. That is the truest of collective energies. That is why there is trueness in calming after the storm, as the expression is expressed by humans.

When there is what is known as a natural disaster, as you have seen on the Earths surface, such as Earthquakes, Hurricanes, Tornadoes, Tidal Waves, Wild Oceans, those are the solidifiers of Human souls to another. Those bring peoples together in openness and helping. In serving and comforting hence compassions grow and live on and love propels.

When there are actions taken from the blindness of others, of foresight of others, of prudency towards fellow humans, of self motivations, we have the robbers of life at work and play. The propellment of suchness takes away from all. And it is no surprise as such. For it is seen and known and yet the blindness masked as intelligence lets the self motivated believe that they can do it, for the reasons of such actions remain stronger than the souls of fellows of souls whose energy ultimately carries life on Earth.

When peoples speak the end is near; there is no end. When peoples speak the end is near it is the end of them on Earth. Not the Earth that will end them. And the missions stand still. And the life that lives itself on Earth is the choices, the actions, the motivations of the souls that exist within it in heart, without on surface, and the intentions the souls carry.

For all believe in life, and how that belief is, came from home. When a soul arrives on Earth it is both home and Earth. And then the shapings begin for the experiences to happen. And the happenings of those experiences, those thoughts, those motivations of their time are what exist in now.

There is no time. It existed them however the soul's energies give it this form it is in. It is like dressing a soul. Free will is that important. Motivations are that important. Love propels in truth of souls.

Self motivations take on another course. Souls have choices and within those choices there is affectment of all things; All things, not simply the souls. For all things are of energy. All energy reacts to other energies. All reactions are reacted to. Hence propellment. I say it in such simplicity. And yet for the mind of blindness it will not be understood.

The mind of blindness is the meekers of the Earth. They are vigorous in their fight. They will never inheirate the Earth. Yes, that is the correct spelling. The Earth belongs to no one. Ever. How could that be? That is a taughtness of error from the beginning of its mentioning. There is no inheritance of anything. Nothing belongs to anyone.

All that is truly of real is love. All else will shrivel around purity and love. All else is in place for honings, for experience. And it will vanish as did the years a soul lives and only remembers. All that is truly remembered is love. How it came into the soul on Earth; The harshnesses of love and the purity of it. None else is as easily retrieved. That is true of all things.

Only love is remembered. All the facets of love: The turnings, the twistings, the openings, the closures, the movements, the motivations. It is all simply love. As love is reacted to all things are affected. And in that affectment the workings of love in skewment have brought souls home in incompletion of mission. There is a pacific stateness of many souls who can rebalance the underbalancement of the Earth's state of energy at this time.

## EARTH AND HOME

Nothing is ever as it can seem, for where would the mystery of life's lesson come to solvations? There has to be hope. There has to be truth. There has to be purity of heart to come to solvations. If any of these great wonders are not present, the lesson has not covered all the facets of its learnings.

The love of life is never ending. Once that is understood it simply never ends. When it is not understood it is "I love this this way. I love this like this or that. I care so much for you and not for you." Some will not see the carryance of each other, the love of all, the knowing that all want for the hope, the truth, the purity of heart of self.

To respect that knowing of self can only come to the eternality of the world. When the world of Earth comes to the knowing of Eternality in entirety, then Earth will mesh with home and there will be no longer a need for Earth. It will come with Evolution, not with the destruction's that are spoken of now.

The energy of despair can not travel. Only the energy of pure love can travel. And when all love is of purity it will be of home. And all the lessons of Earth in completion therefore not a need for Earth. The World will never end. It will come home in its eternal purity.

## EARTH EXISTENCE

All that exists on Earth has been willed by the souls upon it. And compilations of souls throughout time. Time paces however time is a measurement of actions, things, growths; for it has to pace.

Every step of knowledge breaks down the barriers of Earth and Home. The truest experiment of Earth is to bring about the meshing of home and Earth for all souls, as you live in it now; for then the world can grow on the other side of love, life and truth. How could souls know their wills are of such abundance and love? We are in force of beginment of such knowledges.

## EARTH'S PURPOSE

Truth is the miracle. Humans like to state that miracles can not be explained however truth is the miracle. Truth, growth of purity, love in purity are the souls working achievements on Earth; The purpose of Earth; The purpose of choice and free will. Growth of souls is the purpose of Earth. In love, in truth, in purity within the knowings of choice and free will.

## EGO

The ego is the trickiest of emotions. It is hard to detect at times. Ego looks like a helper, a lover, and friend. However it is self motivated in action and the holder of the actions angers at the lack of outcome towards the efforts instilled. And the purest of love in the equation hears the anger that was disguised in prior speakings and the truth is transparent.

Ego is interesting in its makings. It gives a soul a power of believing it can be better than others and rise the soul above and bring to it praises, materials of things and status; At times in earnments and at others in non earnments. Some conceal it and others flaunt it, depending on the soul of free will in presentations.

All emotions are fluid. They mean nothing until they are given life by the soul that they mean something to. As love can be seen and felt within the love that is felt and seen by the soul in sharing of it.

Sex can only be sustained when love can carry it. All other reasoning's, happenings, can not sustain its candor, its honesty, its truth in heart. In sexualness nothing can be hidden in times and the depths in surprise to many grow into passions greater than any felt.

In Ego, the ways of companies who are looking for monies from souls in self motivations, tells souls that there are problems with healths in ways of sexualnesses, emotions, control and being of greatnesses. And they present medications to make monies by creating images that hurt the human Ego; Hence, the purchase of medicated solutions to problems of Ego, not problems of truth.

Hence, thoughts become things, for peoples who do not have these problems begin to think of these as problems hence in becoming of such. Thoughts are things.

Thoughts are truly things. In the beginnings of thought of self motivations, the person in thought will immediately think that they could never do such a thing. And then they start to see that maybe they can do such a thing. And then they begin to imagine such a thing. And then they begin to think of how they would do it.

And then the soul will take itself in a thought of action, of doing, and when the opportunity appears the action is taken, justified, and not thought of in the initial shocks of horror that happened when the truth of that thought was apparent.

And then denials of mind and heart come into the picture for the soul to cope with its own actions. It waits to do it, whatever it is. And then the realizations start to set in, the knowings that this particular notion was of Ego, of self motivation. And defenses begin to form in future argumentations with others over the possible discoveries of such actions and the stories of non truth begin.

The hidings take place. And when truth is spoken and the hurts of the souls combined take on, trust will erode. Hence, takings away intertwined within Ego. All thoughts, all feelings, all love, all greatnesses, all self motivators, thoughts become things.

Thoughts are things. Ego is of takings away from any soul at any time. That is why when a soul of receiverments witnesses Ego in another of souls; it is responded to in runnings away. Souls are on Earth to know that there are specialnesses between them. That love carries; that they cannot be love of self without the understandings of the ranges of emotions and the respondings of heart to them.

## EGO AND MIND
EGO IS THE OPPOSITE OF MIND AND FEAR IS THE OPPO-
SITE OF LIFE. Ego acts against the logic of a soul and fear is illogical all
together. Ego is the most accepted act of taking away from one's soul and
Fear of life is what triggers Ego to come into the picture frame of the mind.

Ego takes on Fear by doing the very action(s) to take away the Fear
however it hurts the very soul and the soul(s) of others around to accommodate the actions of Ego. It begins the workings of insecurity and it
provides a path of self defacement.

For the actions of the Egomonic soul are simply to pacify its fear of what
they do not want to happen to themselves, and causes that very thing that
they do not want to happen to themselves to happen. It is the trick of the
mind when security of mind is not present. It is the falseness of inflation of
mind without heart.

*(EGOMONIC—To live in your mind without involving your soul)*

Ego has no heart. Ego can not see. Ego can not hear nor can it feel. It is
driven by fear. But those we say have big egos, they accomplish? No, they
do not, they accomplish nothing. Ego takes away. Ego has a sense of falseness in selfness. The Ego can not succeed within a soul who knows of itself
in fullness and richness of trust in all People's, Things, around.

The accomplishments are short termed and short lived. They are minute
victories in a million steps to self dilution. The Ego tells you, you do not
have to try, that you are already there. The Ego says to you, you do not
deserve this relationship; they act like you do and then some, and behave as
though you are loved, when you can not in entirety love yourself. And that
is acting love not having faith in the belief that it is present.

Ego is the soul at the head of a company, country, family, who sees not the
souls around, however controls them to their liking. Ego is the soul who
takes the funds of others in lacks of prudency.

Ego is the soul who hits another, kills another, overtakes others to their likings and dehumanizes souls to carry out actions of hurtfulness, and presents instead of souls needing each other, a path of isolation and fear.

Fear takes on Ego, for when fear is present, Ego has a home. The fear of Ego are the fearest of fears. Ego is the lacks of love with mind, body and soul. An Ego will do with body what it would not do with the heart. The Ego will do with the mind what it will not do with the soul. The soul and the Ego fight each other, for it is the balance between self motivation and pure intent.

Ego is the stem that grows the plant that grows the leaf that builds the tree of no fruit. Ego's purpose is to set the stages of separation of heart and mind and body from and away from love. Ego does not take a soul to love. Ego is the master, when God Almighty says not he is master.

Ego wants to fight those of pure intent. Ego wants to hurt others as it is hurt. Ego wants to control others, for fear that others will see them for who they are. Ego is the foundation of sanded concrete. When it is wet in saturation, it will not withstand, as it appears in sturdiness.

The eyes of those who can see can see Ego when it is in play. For it can only play. It can not and is not of truth. And the soul tires to convince itself that it is of truth. For if it is not of truth, they too can not be of truth.

It appears a helper however it is only a helper to divide, hide and separate. Ego is teacher of none. It simply is an example of taking away, an example of lessorment of mind and heart and body. It tells on the soul without the soul speaking. It speaks on the soul without permission.

It can only come from a pain source of which the soul can not confront. To confront the pain is to let go of ego, for ego can only remain the illusion that it is. Every ill can only be the ill the soul believes that it is.

## ELDERLY

The children of the elderly come to their parents, mostly in times of need. The elderly are lonely peoples and the meshing of the elderly populations of Earth are separated. The elderly are of the discarded souls on Earth. They are the teachers of experience and overlooked, for souls do not have the time to talk to their children in force, let alone the elderly who need patience of another kind.

They are the resources of Earth and they are not seen nor are they heard. The lack of knowing has caused many to suicide their bodies to release and come home. They made it to the lastness of life to hurt themselves, for lack of love. They are the result of lack of love.

## ELITISM

Elitism is a way of saying everyone else is not OK and I am therefore I do not have to account for myself; since there is no one soul smarter than I. And in that the insecurity driven thoughts and openings of how elitism starts within a soul is the very flaw of their thinking. It is the Isolator of heart, for there is no soul more important than another.

## ENERGY

All things have energies behind them. In completeness. If a soul takes on an energy to make twistings, you will have twistings. If a soul takes on to solve itself, you will have solvation. If a soul takes on to take away from self, it will take away. If a soul is resisting growth, it will not admit growth even when it happens. If a soul wants to grow, it will see only the growth in which it wants to grow. If a soul wants to carry anything, it will carry it. If a soul wants to stump, it will live in stumpedness.

Souls try to grow yet when they want something out of someone and are in the process of takings away, it is always apparent. No matter how smart the soul is there is no soul on Earth smarter than energy. THERE IS NO SOUL ON EARTH SMARTER THAN ENERGY.

Hence, the soul who tries is seen for what it is. It may not be a day or a year or a minute of time on Earth, once it is physical it is already of seenment.

Waves of energy are the strengths for the Earth. Earth is entire energy. Without a soul a body can not move. Without a push an object can not move. That is the obvious. However words have energy as well. Glory be to God Almighty, for truth can not be seen yet it is known in energy.

## ENERGY EVOLVES ALL THINGS

As souls do not evolve they believe the world is about them. When they evolve they begin to see the picture of bigness of how we truly are all here together. That we as souls in human form are going to look like something, like someone, and our souls, our personas as humans when on Earth have to be of something. We dress and that says some things, we speak and that says more, we have actions and that says even more.

Yet all energy precedes all of these things, otherwise the world would not be able to react to everything at once. **God Almighty has energy preceding all else simply to keep truth vibrant. That even a veiled soul can respond to truth in energy and responding to all other stimulus is choice of that very soul. That defines free will.**

## THE ENERGY OF EARTH

There is much on the other side of love. For if only souls could know it is past the lying, the cheating, the stealing of self. That is the lowest level of Energy that exists. And that is where humans are. The levels of energy that exist on Earth are like the deepest

disappointments within selfments of Earth. They are quiet disappointments and they have brought about the sinkings of energies.

The planes are harder to break through due to the density of energy. WE are poking holes of light, of expansion. It will be. For the love of God is of all love. We are helpers of service, for God Almighty can not come to Earth, for his energy can not be absorbed. So simple. People have taken the words of grandness without foundations and given them meanings of undertones.

Being a prophet means to message; it is not a prize. It is viewed as a prize. And the message is overlooked. Being an Angel is a point of evolution. It is not a prize; it is a job of service, of love. We are not meant to be here alone. We are different and we are the same and we are different again. So simple.

Life will be. Who we are can not be given or taken away from us. It is to be shared. Glory be to God Almighty. Glory be to God Almighty. Glory be to God Almighty.

## THE ENORMITY OF LOVE

The man that sends the sons of others for money and not truth will never find truth. Love can not be tampered with. And there is much manipulation in and around the human mind and heart.

Those who know not what they say, see not what they do, care not of souls of others in relation to their own, manipulate to receive unjustly. To control, to grow egonomic power, to live in insecurity and disguise it as strength, to speak truth in pretendment and anger at truth in reality, to dim another's light to light your own, is the manifestation of the meek, in the taking away of self hence others hence life on Earth.

All is affected and all is seen and yet in that seenment there is acceptance. For the minds of the likedness know of the security it provides to continue in the path of suchness to self and to each other. Hence, the taking away-ment of inequity of souls, for that can not balance and there is no soul on Earth more important than another.

NO SOUL ON EARTH MORE IMPORTANT THAN ANOTHER. NO ONE. GOD ALMIGHTY DID NOT CREATE IMPORTANCE. GOD ALMIGHTY CREATED LOVE. GOD IS LOVE. HOW COULD LOVE NOT COME FROM LOVE? HUMAN SOULS ARE THE GROWTH OF LOVE. THE EXPERIENCE OF LOVE. THE DEMEANOR OF LOVE. THE GLORY OF LOVE. THE ENOR-MITY OF LOVE.

## ETERNAL

So simple it is and yet the mind can not see? For clutter of thoughts has dimmed the world at this time present. Future is affected, for future in your world is not present at home. Home possesses no future, no past, no now. All it possesses is souls in the form of love, Eternal.

That word is not properly defined on Earth. Eternal is. Eternal means, gives, loves, learns, flows through the essence of all souls. Eternal is the reason we can exist! For how can an existence exist without the internal making, knowing that it exists? Eternal is to exist! Glory be to God Almighty!

Eternal is the driver of all that exists! The emotion of Eternal is Love, for Love is the reason, the essence of Eternal. Without love Eternalality could not exist, for essence cannot exist without Eternal and propelled by Love. To think it in your world, Eternal is the car and Love is the fuel.

Eternal is endless, for it is not of time it is of existence. Without Love, Eternal could not exist! Love is the purpose of all. Free will defines love, for it shapes how love becomes to a soul.

All that you witness, all that you see, it is the shaping of that love and how it came to a soul and what the soul has done with that love, reacted to it, grow(n) from it, took direction from it and became, as that person has become. You meet those that love shaped harshly and you witness the loss of Eternal when you witness love taking away. And you witness the existence of Eternal when love is present! Glory be to God Almighty!

For God, for Love, is Eternal. When God and Love are not present in the mind of a soul you see the loss in immediance! Love expands! Never to forget that only love can expand anything that exists, for all that exists is Eternal and love propels Eternal, for without it Eternal can not exist!

## EXPECTATIONS

Eternalness exists however it is not of seenments to souls, for the clouded visions of happiness and love and purity of heart are needing clairment of souls purpose and the meanment to such knowings in life.

Souls do not recognize the truth of what they see, for they are looking too hard and expect too much. The expectations of life have taken that very life away from the souls of expectations.

## EXPERIENCE

There is beauty in the old sayings, in the old loves of life, for they were believed in believing that is the way things were. Now there is great believing in blindment and fears, for peoples have come to know that if you do a task you will get the reward.

However, there is no reward with God. Reward begins in self. There is not task with God. There is task within self. The love of God is discovered within the love of self. So simple. For all discovery is designed for the soul of the discoverer. So simple.

Without the path of discovery there is no growth. Growth and experience is the purpose of humans. Human is the form it took to grow the soul. The veil is the absence of knowledge to grow within free will. Free will, the choices within the experiences and the paths in which will can grow the direction of the experience.

Experience nurtures evolution. Evolution brings about understanding and compassion. Understanding and Compassion breeds self love. Self love is known through self accounting. Self accounting teaches to give of self. Sharing of self and giving back to the world in which you live is completion of journeys. Completions open the door for greater growths.

The greater growths come back to teach others of all that is learned. Those are the moments that come back to the soul and give understanding even though it may be momentary, what the humanness of life on Earth is all about. And the rejuvenation of heart comes into opening. And that opening comes with purer love. And purer love refines itself into infinite understandings of souls. And pure love is birthed within the soul's evolvement. Glory be to God Almighty.

Nothing can be as it seems, for the mind of humans are veiled, for experiences are in honement of life on Earth and review can come later in time.

Why do souls come to experience if they already know everything before they come to Earth and then they will know everything when they go back home? And during their time here, why does it matter, if all will go back to the same knowledge? There is always fear of non reward and that is what is causing "good" action amongst souls.

The reason of Earth is to veil and to search for the greatest driving force of all of souls in whichever plane of experience they are on; to come back to home in free willness of self; to search for what is temporarily the unknown. And you witness all the ways in which it is extended, through injury of that very thing called love, called purity, called truth.

Even in killings as one would say, and what of murderers? Murderers are taking you back home. And in many cases live in the absence of home. They are the furtherest away. And the ones you call victims are released to the universe of love in moments that look and appear to be horrific to the humans of souls.

That soul was released back to pure love at the hands of those that are further away, for irony is of love when most lack of love of self is in existence. The world is not as it seems. That is the answer to that question. Nothing is as it seems. Humans live their life by the standards of fear. If the murderer in truth simply knew it was because they are the further away, they may have the tools, help and support to get closer.

If those in physical death get to return to home and are released to love, would the murderer be taking them away from what is truly the harder of the two, Earth; So ironic indeed. Humans built rules, laws, and decisions on towers of fear. Towers of fear. Every rule, law, decision, is based on fear. The purity of heart, will and can easily walk through such fears.

## EXPERIENCE IS REPETITION

Life is open to souls who are in search of openment. Any door closed to a soul on Earth, it is the soul's hand that is closing it. Truth is effortless and all other avenues are avenues of experience. I say experience rather than growth for Experience is repetition and growth is evolution.

On Earth souls do not know what to do with purity. They say they look for it; however they do not recognize it when it is present. They say they look for it and when it is undeniable in facement of souls, they want to take away from it. To put it away, for then accounting does not have to happen.

## FAITH AND BELIEF

Actions tell you, tells souls around you, who you are. Actions speak to faith of souls, words speak to belief. To believe something is easy. To believe something is to say, "Yes, that makes sense to me." To have faith carries the soul differently. Faith is the growth. Belief is the beginning.

Many believe in much and have faith in little. How does faith grow? Faith grows when the love of self is present, for the love breeds within heart cells of the soul. And within the love of self, the compassion of self, the understand that a soul is simply that, not to be of something a soul can not be or truly desire to be.

To not pacify the soul into the knowings of complacency, for the soul knows when it is not in prudency of self. However, when there is prudency the soul can only go to the trust that builds the faith in life.

If a soul does not face itself in acceptance of the factedness that perfection is love and perfection is not a dress, a suit, a car, a house, a pretended action with pretended words, then the soul can not give to itself. When a soul believes in the outterment of itself and believes that the words spoken and the "actions" taken can not be seen for the falseness of energy they may profess, the soul looks at itself as a counterfeit and it works in the mode of stagnated counterfeitism.

Glory be to God Almighty, for a soul can only react to itself and then to others. Projection is a natural way of life and the projections of our time live in the superficiality of life. And the depth, the faiths of soul's surface, when the few souls working towards the core of a nucleus speak in volumes within the love they know and it spreads in quickness', for love can only propel.

And that is what touches souls, for then they remember their own souls and the promises of heart made. And then they can look again at self and say, "Where have I gone? How have I gotten to here? When my heart is here, how do I do it? How do I feel it? When I feel in purity, how do I stay there? How do I get there?"

And the answer lies in the truth of self. Can you look squarely at yourself and talk of your role in your life? Of your actions that speak faith and not the beliefs that you are doing so? For the understanding that faith is greater than believe, that belief is a common term for an opinion however faith is the basis of love. And love propels. Can you, a soul on Earth say, I have done this with no blame and ask why?

"Why did I do this? What did I need from this? What was missing in me to ask of myself such action(s)? What is drawing me to such experiences? Why do I thrive greater in taking away from myself, than in givement to my self?"

"Why is that comfortable and why is loving me not comfortable to me?" Souls live in the lacks of love that came to them in life and the belief bred action in suchness. The compromised heart teaches in this way. The compromised heart propels in the human soul in this way.

Openness heals. It is not too late. Learning of love is not a timed event. It is the propellant of love in purity that is sought, for then it is within and without the soul in sharement, and growth comes to all.

## FAME

Ego is simply not the way. Fame is not the answer, for fame is not in existence. Fame is like saying that a star is shining when the star in the sky is an airplane. Nothing is as it seems. Truth is the magnet of life. Honesty teaches honesty. Honesty of heart to oneself and discovery of one's mission is internal fame.

## FAMILY PRESSURE

The families of life on Earth have found a way of challenges that have put pressures on the purities of heart. And those stresses became a way of life. How can a soul see love, feel love, witness it and discard it? It goes back to accountability.

If a soul let itself go into love, they could no longer live in the angst they have built around them. They do not want to face their angst with beauty, for then they will be in fear that they will fail at their dreams. So they keep their dreams dreams and they continue to take away from self hence others in growment. So simple.

It is hard to witness however that is the love of God. For God sends angels, billions of them, to give love in aboundment. However if the energies are pushed away then there is blindness to the love and the help that is on the way. And those souls will snicker at those that believe in love and God. The love and God's love are one in the same and in the purity of love it is hard to reach for it has been pushed away.

## FEAR AND EGO ARE FRIENDS

Whenever fear intrudes anywhere along the road to peace it is because the ego has attempted to join the journey with us and we have to let it exit our journeys. Sensing defeat and angered by it the ego regards itself as rejected and becomes retaliative. You are invulnerable to its retaliation because I am with you. On this journey, you have chosen me as your companion instead of your ego. Do not attempt to hold on to both or you will try to go in two different directions and will lose your way.

## FEAR, DOUBT AND WORRY

Can you believe that life is meant to be in despair? It is not. Fear doubt and worry stagnate the soul. The choosing of fear is human. It is of the weaker souls who try to explain what they do not know and ignore what they do know. Worry not, for fear doubt and worry stagnate the soul. May all the stagnated souls lift their worries and be free.

## FEAR, TRUTH AND LOVE

Many believe they will speak to a soul and that soul will hear. You can speak to many souls and they can not hear. They can only live in their self motivations, for growth has not taken them to their own self of knowings in yetness. And that is simply the truth.

Knowing truth releases the wanting to change a soul to grow a soul knowingly. Their growth will come to them in moments of their truths. There is not a soul on Earth who will learn against its own will. They will learn when they search to learn, for they will call the energy of learnments to them.

They will grow when they choose to grow, for they will call the energy of evolutions to them. They will meangle when they are meangled themself(s). And they will rest only when they are rested. For souls can growth each other only when both, three, four, want to growth their souls in unison, for that is group.

And all souls on Earth can know that they call to them who they are. What they are. Why they are. Until the who, the what's, the whys evolve, they will stay in place. It is of the simplest nature.

And books are written at every point of recognition to reach a soul at its stage of events. That is why there are so many points of views. And there are movies to bring out all the fears, and there is still no conquering of fears, it has given even more.

Even when there is not perception of reality I am in witness of souls who want so much to feel that they will take on fear as a host, as a partner. I am baffled at the choicings however in understandment that fear is easier to find on Earth than love. That is why the choices are of suchness. As well, love puts a soul on the brinks of self exposure and fear is an avenue to hide within.

And souls, for lacks of love themselves; do not have the faith in love as they have in fear. Hence, fear is stronger than love, when in truth love is the only emotion of all Earth and Home and the grandeur, the growth, the purity of soul, is all in the choosings of love. Fear gives the soul nervousness', Lyings, meanglings, non lookment of eyes within self and others, trappings and never revealing complete truths.

To witness love is to addict to its truth. That is the true addiction. That is the truth of all souls. That is the truth of every soul in knowing of who they are. And love will come with objectivity and non holements of souls. For love calms it does not tension. Love grows it does not hinder. Love protects, for there is no exposure. Love accelerates, for it can not see stagnation. Love accompanies, for it is partner of truth.

Love accommodates, for it can only help others. Love rotates, for it is of newness always. Love propels, for it has only a forward stance. Love can not be tampered with, meangled, hesitated, or lied about. Love is truth. And truth is love. And God is love. And love is God. God is pure and Purity is God. Hence, love, truth, and purity being the basis of Earth. Of Universe. Nothing is stronger than love, truth, and purity. And it sounds so simple and so easy to say.

You write in fear in red and in truth in the avenues of blue. For red starts the heart beating in fear and blue opens the soul to the universe. That is why red is associated with fear driven thoughts of humans in advertising's and movies and suchness, in vixens of women and in blood of man. And blue opens the avenues of souls of growth. Read in knowing there is reason to allness on Earth.

## FORGIVENESS

How do you forgive yourself? To forgive is to say I have not learned. Compassion, will speak that you have learned. Forgivements in speakings are to say you not only have not learned it is the same as using the word mistake. Are there mistakes? No. And there are not Forgivements. Forgiving is what "sinners" say to ease their sins. That is taking away from self accounting.

Self accountment speaks "that in truth I have taken action to take away from someone, anyone, for there is no soul more important than another. I have spoken in truth of my soul to myself and I found this is not something I want to action again. I will go to those I took away from and heal them as I will heal myself.

To forgive myself will be taking on Excuse and I already know there is no such thing as an excuse, for then I would be excusing behavior I chose to do and I will have to admit to myself that I have chosen such actions." Truth is the cushion of life. The twisting of life will remain until the truth untwists it.

## FORGOTTEN

No soul is forgotten. All souls on Earth are here to lesson. There is always movement and meant missions, meantness of behaviors are meant to be so. And free will takes on the paths of propellment. So simple it is. When a soul makes choices that soul is there for the outcomes.

## FORNICATION

There is no sin so how could there be fornication. There is only loss of feeling of sensation when the internal is not involved with the external and that is true for anything. Just because it is physical may be momentary however the overall lasting affect is that of rejection of some sort when such closeness is shared and then absent. So simple. So clear.

## FOUNDATIONS
The world needs the carryment of much love coupled with the patience to see what others can not. And give them the openings of growth and perseverance and persistence. And never losing the foresight of the pictures in mind, of growth, belief, love, truth and purity, to be the foundations of all thought, mind and body of each and every soul on Earth, have to be present for complete growth.

This is the forefront of all growths and the stagnation's appear not to be of suchness at this time. Today's stagnations look to the eyes as growth, yet the foundations are coupled with self motivation, rather than prudency of soul. They appear to be of growth, of growing, of moving up and moving along however the spinning of minds is rampant in the souls of souls on Earth.

## THE FOUNDATIONS OF PARTNERS
Desire comes and goes and desires of wants that have no other attachments however then this is a moment in all things that leaves many moments and no foundations. Souls have one foundation. Not many. That is why souls can not in truth partner with more than one.

The desires of this time are the pushed envelope of normalcy to be with more than one. However, each soul on Earth, it matters none who it is, is meant for one, not for many. Many deteriorate the foundations.

That is why there are always, without doubt, troubles when more than one is involved. It threatens foundations of soul. It is not jealousy as it appears it is the takings away of foundational growth.

## FREE WILL
Earth is choice. Earth is Free Will. If ever a soul speaks to you, know that Earth is Choice. Earth is Free Will. Stand by your decisions, whatever they may be. Stand by all that you do no matter what the consequences of your actions. Others have choices to react, to act on, to involve to not involve.

All souls, each and every soul on Earth has Choice, for Earth is Free Will. That is all that it is. What is available on Earth is available for reason. For purpose. The choices shape what will happen in time that is created just for Earth, just for that purpose.

Purpose is reason and Reason gives purpose. In the world it is designed to appear that what all souls want is what is happening.

That is not the case, so simple, due to the fact that all souls want love in one form or another and they do not have it. Love is not simply for some, it is for all. Souls are not more important than each other, how could that be?

Choices make these decisions within the role of mind within the role of soul. Choices are the movers of energy. Free will is the knowings of all things possible and choices are the shapings of all possible things. The soul of Earth is challenged in every decision, for not to simply say I will do…anything, is a choice.

Some souls like structure simply to not have to make choices yet their will will fight them. Simply because it is out of a job if it can not see possibilities to make choices, for then growth ceases. This is what I speak when I speak that the souls of Earth have grown pacific.

They are no longer wanting to make choices. Simply because they have given up will, which means missions are not completing and growth is not happening. So simple to see, to know, and yet to do, to action is of greater course.

## THE FUTURE
There is no future as peoples on Earth speak, there is only truth. For the propellment of truth, of love, of caring, of holdings can have no stoppings. The future is not the future. All the future is is what a soul doesn't know yet. It is there, it is internal, external, it is of present however lack of knowledge becomes lack of happenings, lack of doings, for how could a soul do what it does not know of yet!

## GIFT
It is a gift to the life on Earth to know that there is good in store for all.

## THE GIFT OF PLEASURES

Most souls do not want to be lessoned they want to control and that very control takes all the love and purity out of the intent of that soul; So simple and yet so hard to see in the blindness of experiences. What we call the gift of pleasures have become drug like in humans. For the pleasures of life without love are no longer pleasures, they are needs and wants, for the control of the environment of self overcomes the individual.

That is the lack of love itself, the detachment of the human mind and body. People do not care who they interact with. At most times they do not, it is to fulfill themselves. They take from another soul and share what is not theirs, or the other souls, for they are there out of self motivations. Love opens the doors of the humans in actions of body.

They look for the pleasures and do not understand why in their actions they remain unfulfilled. They are in temporary. How do people know when they are in temporary? They do. All peoples know how their impatience in waiting has taken away the mysteries, the questions, the yearnings, and the wanting.

It has turned into sex. That will fulfill one kind of need only. However in truth it is the part of love that can share itself in physical, without the love from within, within the soul's touchings. How do people know it is love? They know not what they know not. They carry a veil that leaves them open to growing their souls.

## GO BACK TO LOVE

Go back to love. Love. Self love. Self accounting. Love on Earth. Love at home. Love of each other in all ways. When love is in truth it is in all ways. Love. God is love. Love is God. You are love. Love is constant and forever and in timeless of time

## GOD

We are souls of God. We are all souls of God. All souls of God. There is no color, no job, no religion, no race, no restrictions in the world of God

Almighty. God Almighty's creations are all a reflection of all peoples and existences.

God Almighty is of pure intelligence, within the gentlest of gentleness to all living in life, at home, on all planes, for everything is of perfection within the imperfections perceived.

The mind believes itself to be so smart; smarter than the universe. However it is not of being smart; it is of being of love, Simple and pureness in love.

God gently knows and sees all: With love and purity, with hope and desire of growth of soul. For the gentleness of love soothes, heals, growths and gives happiness where the eyes are in fortune to see it, even in times of hardship! The world asks the questions of God and when God Answers they question the answers.

God is Grand. In love and intellect of soul, of all souls, of the soul of a soul, for all souls are one, of themselves within God. For every soul of existence is of the love of God, from God, because of God, with God, for God. God is the beginning of all and all of God. How could a soul not be of God, for God created! Glory be to God Almighty!

## A GOD FOR US AND A GOD FOR THEM

There can never be an "us" or a "them." It is simply an "us." There can never be a God for us and a God for them. There is simply God. There can never be a religion that only takes away all that you can do, for that is religion and not God. There can never be control, guilt and fears instilled. That is not God. That is soul's choosings of perceptions.

That is how strong perception is. The experience of Earth is to find love and God. And the experience is leading souls to create a new God; One that is a reflection of souls in fear, doubt and worry. The love is granted upon earnments and the love that existed was overlooked and changed in definition. The love they wanted to grant upon earnments was and is already here.

## GOD IS LOVE

Love is love. And in love there is a lightness of being. Love does not mean you have to be anything hence in truest love you are simply love and in truest love your purity within surfaces.

And within the purity of truth and love and purity, you are in life in easement of life. You are carried within. All with hope will come with truth. All with truth will be grown to become. All with purity will command its truth. And all with love is the grandest of findings of God Almighty, on Earth, at home, all planes, all universe, is love.

And love is the essence of all souls, of every one soul within and without the existences on Earth. And you know. It is not a person. There are many people. Love is a feeling. Love is intangible yet felt. It can not be of anything in elsement, for it can only be love.

To sound simple and be grand; to act like it is to not know it, there is no acting. Glory be to God Almighty. For God is love. And God is present.

## GROW

Grow all else and all else will grow you. It is of love on Earth and the Earth giving back love. The Earth is alive. Respect of the land and the air and the waters and the foods gives all back to the souls. There is nourishment everywhere. There is love everywhere in everything. There is hope all over the place. Passed by like a meal when one is not of hunger.

## GROWTH

Those resisting growth will be fought within themselves, for their greater self knows they came here to grow and when they stop that growth the internal struggles begin. So great now, the time has come to take the pace of the world to another growth of soul, for some things will never be thought of again as truth. The truth will disarm those transferring untruths that carry with them the result of injuring the soul.

Injuries to the soul are not what you think. It is not in killing or hurting or maiming! It is in the young who are taught and then carried into adulthood.

The adulthood is when the true pains, the true hurts become, and actions are taken to answer those hurts and those pains. And people are taught early on that they are not loved.

All people are looking, seeking an inner foundation within. They know not of this. On Earth time is chronologicalized for purpose.

There has to be mental order to exist, for growth to be measured and all time is measurement of growth.

Soon all will understand and that is in the hands of all love surrounding and there for the taking, if only their misgivings can become giving. The blindness will life itself and show the true light of all matters and pure intent will take all there.

Growth rests the heart and gives all situations wings. Growth says to the soul, you are of heart, for you allow for growth. Intent can not allow for growth until it is pure. That is why we attract to the growing souls. Simply because we know in instinct that with growth comes purity. **Growth can only come from purity.** Purity is the treat of life. Growth tells the world that purity has been found. Those who stagnate, they want to stagnate.

## GROWTH IS ANOTHER LANGUAGE

Those who come to Love, to Truth, to Purity, can only learn. When you know a truth there is nothing within the realm of anything that can take the truth and turn it into something else. And on the other side of that is when truth is not present.

And there is a road to truth, the questions, the experiences that need to take place for truth to present itself. And the free will of the soul to work within its own purities to find that very truth.

And when purity is not of present it takes the soul on yet another journey to open the eyes to what they can not see. And if they still can not see, then another avenue of learnment appears itself, in another fashion yet the same lesson and so on.

It is actually very easy to see, for the blind can not see and try to explain. The blind have to explain everything that is why they speak so much, exhaust all around and in fact are saying nothing. For if truth is not spoken then nothing in fact was said.

## HAPPINESS

What is happy? Love of soul is true happiness. Happiness does not appear in bubbles. Happiness appears in contented souls. When a soul can know itself it can share, it can have the moments of intimacy of self, to self and then to others.

When a soul is in truth, they do not say, "I can and will do this..."they simply are it. They do it without the sayedness of actions. Without the need for recognition, for all recognitions, sayedness, they do not matter to a soul who knows of itself. For there is not time for every action to be of acknowledged, for the actions are of so many.

The one's who do then announce they have done. Then remind all they have done it, then come back to hurt you with what they have done. Then tell you you used them for what they have done and this is only one action.

They are the most uncontented of souls on Earth to live in amongstment.

They are truly not happy as the world would say, and I would say they are not contented. They are restless and every issue has to be discussed without solvation. Blamed to a soul, for someone has to be taken away from and the soul is left to itself to sit in owement from others.

And when owement on the terms of the soul is not had, watch out for your soul, the other soul will not forget and neither of you will rest.

## HEALING AND HURTING

Souls will do, accomplish, behave in any manner of what they believe. Energy is energy. If a soul can see their healing they will heal. If it is time for a soul to exit Earth there are few variations to coming home. Souls are eternal. Home is eternal however Earth is not eternal. Earth is a home for experience and growth and it will growth a soul to go back home however Earth can not keep a soul.

When a soul passes Earth it comes back home. Home is eternal. Earth is not. Those who believe Earth is eternal are not in their truth, nor the truth of anyone around them. When all that matters is what is important to that soul that soul will find themselves in their own webs of alonements, for the laws of the universe are for everyone not for some.

They want to live by the laws of man and human man. Each and every soul that comes to Earth is veiled hence the limitings of thoughts, belief(s), possibilities, endlessness are hindered in the process.

Let me give you an example. Let us say that a soul wants to bring about trouble to another. That is Earth. Let me speak that a soul who does not speak to another, that is Earth. A soul who wants to hurt another for personal gain, steal from another, hurt a child, murder another that is all Earth. And those who can love, walk away, run away, evolve from the learnment of lessons that is home.

Those who love and growth themselves to growth others, speak and walk away without motive, share meals, heart and home; that is Home that is eternal. If a soul wants to heal of itself it can only heal of itself in the purest love of self, for that is eternal of soul. All souls are of Endless. Bodies are Earth. Souls are home.

So simple is the truth of all things known. All is known. Even home, by those who are Earth bound only. That is what atheist is. They are simply Earth bound Souls. For they know not what they could not know of.

They believe that they are invincible and when they find they can not control their bodies and they can not control eternal, they fight it and anger that they are in illness or growths of any kind for that matter. They try to appear as though they have done research to back themselves up. Not for themselves however to convince others they speak in greaterments of self.

True teachers teach in truth of what they know, who they are. They need not the gimmicks of what Earth speaks to the mind, the ego, to accomplish. The soul is the accomplisher. If a soul takes on actions to hurt others they are Earth bound, whether they say they are Earth bound or not. For I speak and I speak, actions are in greaterments of words. Words on Earth are the lowest form of energy when not spoken from heart. Glory be to God Almighty.

Neeya is the ruler of all souls of universe. Neeya is the healer. Neeya is the growth, the evolution, the truth of any and all souls; One and all, all and all and one. If a soul wants to take themself to a backedness of thoughts, of ways, of actions of something that they do that will begin with hurting themselves, another; the other will gain heart from Neeya, whether that person knows of their action being known or not. When a person close to you betrays the trusts of your soul to them, them to you, understand that the trust was truly never there. For nothing can happen if it is not there.

*(NEEYA—Your inner intent)*

## HEART
You can not open your heart until you understand your heart. It is that simple. That is something that is not of rush however of truth. Not all souls can reach truth in sameness. The lack of time to self comes with harshness in decisions and in the affect it poses on others.

## HELL FIRE
We speak much of love and without the love of life around, abound, there is no purpose for continuation. For it exists, is looked for, is wondered about, is of heart and mind and soul of every human. It is the motivation to do all else. Even the soul that hides itself in the forest to let their soul be of seclusion is looking for love, needs love and looks for it in nature, in the love of animals, in rain, in trees and in life other than the souls of humans.

The only person who can truly hurt a soul is the soul hurting itself! For any one soul to speak different is of lack of knowing! Is of lack of love of self hence to carry that lack of love onto others! The soul of a physical form not knoweth of thyself. The love of God is speaking to All.

Do you want there to be hell? How could the same God that loves you burn you? You hear of souls seeing a light when passing, have you ever heard of a soul seeing fire? You only hear of love and yet you create the fear in which you want to live.

How do we know who goes to fire and who does not? Fire is man made, for fire does not even exist at home and there is only a home. That can only mean that free will of souls is respected and the deviations of free will into hurtment of others souls is of man madeness of life on Earth. A soul who is not loved can not give love, nor can they share of it. And when a soul is not in love of self it can only exist to meangle the life's of others as well.

It is not of harshness to understand. Yet the harshness of fire is? How could that be? If there is not evidence to souls of God's love so easily, how could there be evidence of hurtfulness of fire? You also hear that the souls of Earth will not hurt if they have God.

What if a soul believes they have God and they hurt, how is that explained to the soul? That is setting the soul of Earth up to anger and fear God Almighty therefore it is not in love to souls on Earth hence its truth can not stand time, reason or weight of thought. It is a taught of error and nothing else.

## HELPING

Helping is many things. It is the sharing of humans in doings together. In being whole with another in soul, for none is more important than another. To address a soul in "how can I help You?" Is there anything you need? What can we do to complete such a task?

Lead at times and follow along at others; both equally as important; both deserving of each and every soul on Earth; Both growings of internality and buildment of unions of souls in truth.

Helping is not a question of, or an owed to moment on Earth. Helping is from the heart. No owements, no mention, simply heart speaking to heart. Love growing; all growing in the openness' of thought that a soul is not alone on Earth; that there is pure will; that there is compassion; that there is shared commitment and shared life.

Life is not meant for one to live however all to live. That a soul on Earth is a soul of strength, for the love of home exists in each. And every soul is fragile on Earth, for the lowest of energies exist on Earth. Helping grows. Those that will not let you help them, they are the ones that have memory of a soul hurting them for helping them.

Those who are helped and do nothing in the sharing of the experience live a world that revolves around them. They are not helpers. There is no sharing of life there is only service; Usury of life not of others. And those are the souls that miss the most of the reciprocation, for the shorterness of sight from them is the openness to less travel of heart, or mind or body.

Other souls begin to live in excluding the souls that take and do not give, for the self motivated soul who may want something from another will keep trying. However, a pured of heart will walk away, for the knowing of teaching such a soul is by the expulsion of their needs entirely, for the blind to see. Nothing is as it seems.

Souls are meant to be with another. They are meant to share and build. The togetherness of suchness is the love; the aloneness' and the rejections of helps when presented or asked or desired is to leave a soul in abandonment. That is true abundance; in any case, in every case.

When self motivating is involved it takes on another route for both souls can feel the game of it. When pure intent is involved it truly teaches a soul of another.

And when abandonment of helpness happens the responding soul wants to walk away from the non giving soul. It is the naturality of action to do so.

For the naturalisity of souls before the laziness' of mind and body towards itself is to help another and live in the fruits of shared growths.

Those who help not want want and want and it is of great decision as to what they will do and what they will not do.

The truth is do everything. For the effortlessness of doings is so simple. The mind clears itself in tasks. The heart grows itself in sharing. And Love propels on to the very things that the soul was in waitment of doings. There is a reason for all things human, for the path of humanality is to grow through challenge and obstacles of love and purity, of awareness and decisions.

*(HUMANALITY—The traits of us as souls on Earth)*

Life is of free will; Drawings to love and carings of heart within. Of clairity in the soul's content no matter the obstacle and finding the bigger picture every time. It works every time if it is sought.

Without the wonder of the soul, the helpment of self and others, the common search of love within each and every soul on Earth, the joining of mission from home before the interference of Earth energy and the challengers that come about herein; there is no reason for the experiment of Earth. Glory be to God Almighty! The love of Earth is the challenge of souls!

## HOME

The bigness of home is magical like a child's dream. On Earth, the magical is searched for yet in paleness. For home comes to souls without duality of mind, without the wonders of outcome. Home is simply of knowing and growth. Earth is of choices and experience. Earth is studied at home as you would one textbook in studies at schools. It is simply one experience. There are many experiences and Earth is of the harshest.

The love in home is where home is. It brightens the colors and vissies the plants in breath. It flows the waters and thoughts are what are known as travel. There is only love and evolutions of love and learning's. There are mimics of home on Earth, from remembered thoughts of humans and much from infusions of thought from home.

*(VISSIES—Exhaling the beauty and nature of all things in all purity)*

On Earth there is ego. Ego is a feeling of greatedness of soul without love of self in entirety. That is why when there is ego involved in any way it takes away from the soul. Even if it is to the point that others may lose attractions of heart when ego is involved. There is presence of other factors on Earth.

There is free will in all places, all planes, the universe. However, ego differentiates souls. Ego does not exist on any other plane in the Universe. It is written of in the Bible of wars between Angels, in texts of many kinds however those are tales of duality. All negatives can be created by the thoughts of free willers enticing the makings and the depth of ego.

Yet at home the energies are different and the energies create greaternesses. For Earth is to experience life without the knowings of home, and veiled memories and the strength and endurances of love. To write of home in continuousness is like reading of a dream and wondering of how it could be on Earth as well. And after that the descriptions could be of interpretations of heart. For it is of thoughts, of things of love and of passions; of understandings and of harmony in perfections.

## HOMELESS
The homeless are present in the brightest light to remind souls of Earth of appreciation.

## HONESTY
Those who are not honest within in literal terms, have nothing to offer truly, without. Their offerings are of the nature of counterfeitism of soul that is felt. And when felt in the human world that is rejection. All rejection is the witness of counterfeitism of soul.

## HUMANS

God Almighty is of love of the human soul. To come to Earth as a human is a challenge greater than any. The insecurities of the human mind challenge its stance, its vigor, its choices and its existence. And the growth begins. And the thoughts of how to get what a soul believes it needs, has to have, wants; are the breeders of experience.

How does that soul go about getting what they believe they need or want? And in that you are reminded of that soul's stance, of its vigor, of its choices. And time is the best teacher. And in time you understand how long the intertwining of mission needs to be. This is all innate. And actions follow.

Those who fight their own original hearts of love come with complications of thoughts, actions and control of all things. They start in fightment of soul and end in fightment of all. Glory be to God Almighty. To fight oneself is the single most startling tragedy of mankind on Earth.

Humans are a way for the soul to hone. Coming to Earth is to work with all obstacles, Obstacles to overcome and overload, Situations to pull the purpose of life in surface, finding the positive when it is not apparent. Learning to calm in situations of ill will and trust in yourself enough to know that when there is love there is the answer to all things possible.

When there is not, there is way for the playment of souls into the worlds of experience that they produce. Once pure intent is in living the playment is no longer playment in the paths of experiences of self motivated behavior.

The pure intent of a soul carries them into the teachings and the learning of challenge, growth and understands, greaterment of happenings and then the teachings of souls around. It is one life for another, with another, because of another. It is learning from and with each other, to care and to interest and to grow and to learn. There is no other way to do it. To take away from others, one is taking away from their self in firstment.

It is all so simple. It is said and it is said and it is said. How hard it is to believe. How difficult it is for the soul of entrapment of self to see or to know, for there is true belief that no one can see the actions of their intents. Glory be to God Almighty.

What they do and what they want to do and what one soul wants from another. Whether it is approval or disapproval, wanting recognition or attention, wanting time or pushing the personal time away; Sometimes to want to know the life of another, for personal information and satisfaction or dissatisfaction of self and then of others.

The untruths are not in dissolvement. The last ones on holdings on are holding tighter, for they are feeling the challenge of loss, of what they have put together to know and then to live by, and using that to take away from other souls. It can not be. Knowledge calms and empowers a soul into patience and love. No one can take anything away from you you are not willing to give them.

## HURTING

When someone wants to hurt anyone it is because they are hurting themselves as well. When a soul wants to do what ever they believe they want to do, show someone, speak to someone, yell, point out differences, meanness', arguments, hittings, abuses, killings, all the forms of self hurtments. They are in self hurtments first, before they can be reenacted; All actions of reenactments of what already has happened in the mind.

There are not mistakes, there are no accidents and there are no lackings of accountability of actions. In truth accountability is simply when a soul will recognize and take responsibility of action. Then the soul can learn and grow on or stay and repeat. Any more simply and it will take much to learn all else.

## IDENTITY

Church after church and group after group has "a way" to think, to band, to join into something that will give them sense and growth. Some want these groups to carry them, for support is sparse on Earth. Some want these groups to give them identity to do as they do not feel they can alone. Some want to feel "better than" others by statements of their group rather than the statements of heart and self.

Some simply want to belong and will go along with all that is said and done as a result. It is called IDENTITY. Everyone wants identity. The human soul is of great groupings. There is an attitude of Me Me Me and that is the fork in the road that divides the soul within itself. Groupings of Me Me Me.

Some try the me me me within groupings only to find that self motivations are seen early on. Some want to do everything themselves without help, advice or groupings. Some want groupings, for they do not feel strong enough themselves. However we are designed to work together. As one.

That is the goal of evolution. On the way to evolution there are groups of souls who band their energy together to grow. If that grow does not include others however takes away from believing that the great energy they have found is not to be shared within the world however only within each other, that group no longer exists in the energy of evolution, Of One.

It is the fraction of energy and the takings away from any growth within or without of that grouping. Glory be to God Almighty, how can a group that separates souls into different, more important than, better than, be a part of ONE? It can not be.

That is why the thought processes, the ways of life, the speakings of life, the tryings of joining in that stem only from self motivation, repel the very energy they are seeking. And that is why those in those kinds of groups, thoughts, ways of behaviors are alone and feel alone. They are not happy for the answers they are seeking are not answers for all however answers of self.

## ILL INTENDED

The ill intended are the meekest of souls. They are the true hurters of the world in which all live. The ill intended take away in silence first, and then in thoughts and then conversations. The final is the actions and they believe at those times they have thought it out to come in without notice and do what they can. However there will be notice, for there is no stronger force on Earth than love. Love in purity is the greatest strength of all time.

## IMBALANCE

Never to fear, doubt or worry, for all things are as they should be. How could they be as they should be and there is imbalance? That can happen, for free will wills things as they should be and it is God Almighty, the guide to the hearts of those who possess free will. The absence of love internal, guides free will to imbalance, collectively and in whole.

## INDIVIDUAL SOULS

Souls build strength when they believe themselves to be in and on their way to getting what they believe they want. For souls trying to be of team, of self within a group, of a group without selfmotivations attached is not of becoming. That is why most of what you witness around you is not of each other it is of each individual soul.

And the thoughts that they can live in isolation within a group and not be seen for who they are. The energy's that are in truth are the meekers in general actions. The meek believe that none are as smart.

Souls have lost their way. Earth is not going to end as many will say; we angels are hear to continue Earth. To grow the souls who carry Earth's energy while they are present. The energy of souls affects all things. Souls are in mostment(s) of self importance at this time, without the integration of thought(s) of others.

The integration needs to happen, for love is stagnated and in regression of hope, caring and truth in this time on Earth. Glory be to God Almighty! The souls that are fighting for freedoms are looking in the wrongness of places. It is not in the world first and then to them. It is in souls first and then shared with the world.

## IN EACH DAY

In each day, know you are growing and let all else rest aside you. In each day, work with heart and know that all those around you will live in theirs. In each day, trust and you will teach trust. Love and you will teach love. Care and you will teach caring. For it is needed in abundance on Earth at this time.

## THE INHERITANCE OF THE MEEK

When you meet the meek it is not as you would think it. It is not that there are so many of them that they're greatest in numbers. It is that the ones of them, they hurt and twist many peoples, situations and things around them; that their energy leaves despairment in the hearts of those around them. They affect many and that is their inheritance.

Most peoples, souls on Earth, do not recognize them. And they let them in their hearts, their homes, their lives. And the intentions of the meek are in taking away. The insecurities of the meek, the internal non acknowledgements of self, the internal lack of happinesses are a daily assessment. They are a daily ritual of running through problems, creating them, alas sharing of the pains internal manifested.

They have a complete blindness to anything that they say. They completely believe they are right in all things and that they do not need anyone's advice in learnment of self. They also believe that those they choose to surround themselves with are those that will speak truth to them, for they choose peoples, souls, like them for advicement and that is why they trust them. It takes one person of meekness per crowd to hold all in place.

The pure hearted want to help, want to listen, want to help again. For the meek are in repetition of problems, of reasons, of glories in others mishaps, of problems of others, not only their own, and with that they hold all in place. They affect many and that is their inheritance.

## INJURY

Love exists on the other side of all injury. That is the fruitless wonder of the world in which the Earth has become. Souls stay in injury and look not at the love that has become of it!

## THE INJURY OF LOVE

The injurement of love injures souls and that is the usement of souls on Earth. They come to the world from points of injury. They come to the world with what they need from it rather than what they can contribute.

They want to soothe themselves, no matter to others and no one is soothed. The soothements dissipate and need replenishments in quick times. That is why there are repetitions of behaviors for they know not the lastment of love. Love carries and self motivation takes away.

## INSTANT HAPPINESS

What love means to humans is instant happiness and when that is gone there is no sustainment. When in truth, love is the growing of happiness in which it grows into in each and every day and discovering the other sides of love of vastness of mind and thought.

## INTELLIGENCE

Intelligence in alonement does not provide fuel for the soul. All are intelligent. How the soul experiences is what is of importance. How the soul interacts with others is of grandeur. For souls are not meant to be of alonement.

## INTENTIONS

The intentions create the paths, the paths create the dreams and the dreams expend love onto the world. It is the truth of pure intent. Life can only be what you want it to be. What you call into it.

## INTOXICATION

Thoughts when intoxicated are postponed, delayed, transferred into self and stagnated. For there are thoughts and they do not become things. For when the intoxication wears off the motivations to do the things that are thoughts are replaced with the motivations to postpone, delay and transfer into self. And the actions of thoughts do not happen.

We think that there were less inhibitions with honesty of self and that conversations are in greater fluidity. However, they are in greater fluidity yet they are not. They are in greater fluidity however with skewness to reality of thought. The intoxications of mind are very subtle yet it takes away the multifacetedness of life in entirety.

It does so for it alienates the soul from self and is the quiet silencer of action. In some intoxications it would seem the opposite due to the momentary highs or lows it produces yet in overall those slows not only stand in place, they cement in place in those times. And the partner of intoxication slows down as well.

## I SAY
I go back to love. I say love. I say self love. I say self accounting. I say love on Earth. I say love at home. I say love of each other in all ways, for when love is in truth it is in all ways. I say love. I say God is love. I say love is God. I say I am love. You are love.

## JUDGMENT
There is no good or bad. No right or wrong. For if the will of souls was not controlled, the best would come out of souls, for it will only know love. It would not be in stresses to do as it did not wish. The progression of life on Earth is taking away the souls right to be in freedom of heart, mind, body and soul; Hence the taking awayment from all. One can not feel a thing that is not shared by all in eventuality.

## THE LACK OF SELF LOVE
The lacks of love and the appearance of love have taken the world into a lack of growth and completion of mission. Lack of love has grown the world into an overwhelming experience for souls to maintain balance, regularity of thought(s), understanding of self of others. Love of self of others.

Jealousies in every day life of life in appearance not of truth; Envies of life in Appearance not of truth; Monies of appearance not of truth; Lyings in appearance and the opposite of truth; Appearance in appearance not of truth. For in this day even the human body is now what it is.

The avenues of what a soul calls attractive stem from foreignality to the body of the soul. The soul within can not see the beauty within and forges ahead to put in plastics and liquids, devices, and medications, drugs and alternations of thought. In awayments from self into the outsidedness of self inward only to find it does not work. And addictions set in to make it work and perform as it is mastered by the human mind to do so.

No will, simply control of self over matter and truly it is the matter in control. This is the gravest of non truths to self. Self over matter can only happen in the truth of a soul to itself. And even in thenness it may not appear so.

Challenges and obstacles take a soul into the discovery of truth from heart. For then the value of truth grows the soul into the knowledge's that do not let go of the human soul and leave it in strainedment of self in the conclusion of lesson.

There is no conclusion of lesson in addictions, manipulations and controls of the soul. For in all the soul is in a role of slavement to the outside world and that is the truest slavery. Slavery is not being owned by another it is not owning of oneself. Glory be to God Almighty, for nothing is as it seems. Nothing is as it is seen.

Love on Earth, if not started from within, in each and every soul; there will always be misgivings, discontentments. Troubles that accelerate into involving many souls, wars as you witness, tortures.

And we witness souls who justify and believe there is a soul more important than another. And the manipulations and gamements of mind that come into action in souls to another, for the fears of life being greater than the truths.

That the owning of oneself remaining in abstract of thought and the powers of deviations stronger than the greatness' of truth, for the soul can not believe, let aloneness the faith of itself. It is a reflection of the propellment of lacks of love that propelled into the lacks of self.

Truth is a living movement. It breathes, it grows, it carries growth. When it is not present, what is present is a suffocation of the heart and all the mind needs is catch up to it. For the mind can understand what the heart already knows. Yet the souls of mind do not believe therefore faith has a path of suffocation to come through before it can make it to believe.

Truth has to make its way back through paths of suffocation of mind in this present day on Earth to be heard.

**LEARNING**
Learning is not a chore it is a treasure.

**LIFE**
Know that life on Earth is a short time and that a soul exists in all time. That people are simply people and there is no more to it than that.

That pain is growth. That a child's heart is clear.

That adolescent's lose their protection and that is when childhood experiences relive.

That early adulthood is the time in which to grow again in protection of building a future. Not knowing the mishaps.

And with middle adulthood comes establishment and growing of families in mind, for planting the seeds of continuation are present.

Older Adulthood, to look back at life, change what is needed, explore alternatives to robotic learning and forward into giving back before you come back home.

Life is a synchronization of heaven, if only it were paid attention to, the details of life are fascinating, just wait until you get home and see. Life is meant to be in enjoyment and trial in balance. The trials bring the enjoyment and the growth brings the trials.

Perfection is as the soul knows, for love is perfection and perfection is love. Those who know self love in form while on Earth, trials are learned from and the growing of that one soul can only grow the souls around it.

You see it is in such simplicity once a soul is in acknowledgments of who it is. It does not in necessarity need to know why it is here. It simply needs to acknowledge that it is here on Earth.

## LIFE IS CHOICES

Life is choices. All that is in your life of heart is what you choose to carry. Nothing happens to you. You happen to it. You create it. You exist it. You make it real. All you bring, all you have, all you do, that is choice of you.

## LIFE IS LOVE

Life is love. Disappointments are love in its glory. Hardships are gifts of growth and love. Life is hardships and happiness, love and endurance. What is scared? Scared of what? Take it on. Why not? Why not love? Why not care? Why not do? Why not touch? Accept love. Accept caring. Accept actions. Accept your gifts. Accept love to yourself. Balance. Love. For love creates balance.

## LIFE IS MAGICAL

Life is so magical, if only people could know their true rule in their own lives, for they give so much away. For free, no charge of giving back, no charge of receiving, for feelings are stifled for the non earnest of what nature has become, to accept without the thought of what is next. Do you understand? To do and not to expect: To accept with the thought of some future sharing.

## LIFE TEACHES

Life endures. There is no other way to do it. Experiences are chosen. There is not other reason they are your experiences. Growth comes from intent. There is no other way you can grow. Self Motivation takes away from you. There is no other path it can follow. Fear robs life from souls. There is no other path.

Doubt says you do not trust. There is no other reason. Worry says you are scared. There is no other explanation. Repetition means you have not learned. There is no other recourse. Blaming, forks a soul away from understanding. There is no other use for it. Life teaches. There is no other purpose of life. Love is already here.

## LOVE

Love is pure. There are not conditions. Love is simple and clean air and clean heart. Love is fruitful and in giving it can be shared. Love is not a thing. It is a feeling. Love is not created or because of anything. Love is love.

And in love there is a lightness of being. And that love does not mean you have to be anything hence in truest love, you are simply love; and in truest love your purity within surfaces.

And within the purity of truth and love and purity you are in life in easement of life. You are carried within. Love is the fluidity of life. Love is in every fragment of life. Life is the genuineness of soul. For love expands! Never to forget that only love can expand anything that exists, for all that exists is Eternal.

And love propels Eternal, for without it Eternal cannot exist! The ripple affect of love is endless, for the most simple being of the grandest of love, for the most simple of being the grandest of love.

Only in simplicity can love truly be consciously seen. In complication love is seen in abstract, for truly it is hardest to feel through complication or self motivation even if stated 100 times. Life has hardened the edges and the lines of love within.

Love has become something to be had, a thing. And that is the pain of life that you see and witness. Love is love, if left alone it will grow. With manipulations it will cease to grow and with pure intent it will carry one hence all.

## LOVE IS PERFECTION

Perfection is of love. So simple. Love is Perfection. There cannot be perfection without love. That is the reasoning of seeing what is perceived as perfection and yet there is not feeling in attachment.

And in otherness' you come to a home, an art, a work, and you fall into the love of life over it and that is the perfection. It touches and it soothes. It grows and it embraces the soul of the souls of the souls of the souls who are in recognition of self love of others in passion of soul.

## LOWER ENERGIES

Love on Earth lives in the lower Energies. For love on Earth is in starvation and created through acts. Love is not an act. The surprise has not been found that love is what it is. It is not anything other than the fluidity of emotion and of life it flows, for it can not flow without emotion.

It is an emotion. The emotion, the wanting, the having of such is simply to think it, to feel it, to be it and that is all that it is. To make it bigger is to take away from it. To make it bigger is for reasons of inadequacy of love not of love.

Love is truth and without truth there is no love. It can not exist. In fluidity it becomes as the human mind has become it. Glory be to God Almighty, for the soul on Earth is on its own in its own mindness however it is for all. Earth is for all to share and each soul wants a part of it for themselves however it is of shared.

However, no one is sharing. All are asking for their parts, their ownings, their prowness of self within the world that exists for all. The lacks of love have by now built this thought way into the fabric of life on Earth as it stands within the realm of life on Earth.

## MANIPULATIONS

There is much manipulation in and around the human mind and heart. Those who know not what they say, see not what they do, care not of souls of others in relation to their own. They manipulate to receive unjustly, to control, to grow egonomic power, to live in insecurity and disguise it as strength.

To speak truth in pretendment and anger at truth in reality, to dim another's light to light your own, is the manifestation of the meek, in the taking away of self hence others hence life on Earth.

All is affected and all is seen. And yet in that seenment there is acceptance, for the minds of the likedness know of the security it provides to continue in the path of suchness to self and to each other hence the taking awayment of equity of souls. For that can not balance and there is no soul on Earth more important than another.

NO SOUL ON EARTH MORE IMPORTANT THAN ANOTHER. NO ONE. FOR GOD ALMIGHTY DID NOT CREATE IMPORTANCE. GOD ALMIGHTY CREATED LOVE. GOD IS LOVE. HOW COULD LOVE NOT COME FROM LOVE? HUMAN SOULS ARE THE GROWTH OF LOVE, THE EXPERIENCE OF LOVE, THE DEMEANOR OF LOVE. THE GLORY OF LOVE, THE ENORMITY OF LOVE.

For love can only carry a soul. Lacks of love in carryment hurt first the soul of self and carries itself to all surrounding souls. When a soul cheats a company they hurt all souls involved. When a soul lies it hurts itself, for then the soul can not trust even itself, let alone others.

When a soul cheats another they relieve the other of their confusion and internal greed. When a soul steals they take from the world and do not give back.

For all things given that soul are no longer valued, for they lost caring of self. The stealing is the stealing of one's soul, for another soul can only be affected by the loss. That is a violation of another soul to a soul.

It is not the taken, the person of affectment, the losses in companies that is the hurt of cheaters. It is that the cheaters exist and are present. And in this day it is in great commonhood to accept suchness and all else fails around it. The result of monies, love, possessions, are the very things lost to the souls of takement in energies of lowness as these actions take to have happen.

There are no lines however the boundaries of the human mind are in endlessness of lack of knowing how else to think, to feel, to know, less what is exampled to that soul. For the soul is in lack of usement of brained decisions.

Most decisions are automatic and done on impulse. The bigger plan of a soul's life, the bigger picture of who a soul is is lost in an instant impulse. That impulse comes from the insecurity of belief that moment can never happen again. And the sadness of a soul in prison of itself will imprison itself upon the believing that life will not be what it is again.

That greatness' can never happen again, for the faith of greatness in life is dormant and souls react to impulse out of the fear that they will never have true joy, so they settle for the joy of a soul for a moment. And the cheatment of souls carries souls into the sameness of thought. They fear that there will never be greatness in life, so they settle into what they believe greatness to be in a moment and leave with angst at self.

The cheatment of soul can only settle into the bones of the body. That the soul simply took away from itself a part that propels into lower energies of self in all other areas of life. If the money is on the table and it is not yours and you take on it as property it will give to you the lowest of energies on Earth.

If a soul steals a possession and believes in happiness of it, it will only give the soul angst within its possession. The angst will be of the soul who lost their belongings, for the energy will not rest the soul of angst.

There is much to say on this yet the truth of it is very little. We are saying to souls; settle, wait, react, listen, hear, live within moments of life. The passing by of life in quickness has truly taken away balance.

Love grows, heals, carries and ignites. The soul in lack of ignitions is the soul in stagnation; Looking for a partner to stagnate with. For the partners of stagnations can only stagnate others. The partners who are in suchness with children teach stagnation. The children will be saved of suchness, for the truth of love is coming to them.

The cheaters of this day will be hearsay and past tense, for the truth of souls will come to the other side and the stealers, the cheaters, the lying souls will be seen for who they are, for the balance will carry truth. And at this time truth is out of balance.

There will be a need of less laws, for souls will be of greater accountability. The loss of truth was never mourned. The loss of truth has been the leaders, the speakers of messages, those that speak the news to others, of stories, of happenings. The acceptance of non truth has propelled. And that propellment will come to a halt in a moment on Earth.

## MARRIAGE

Souls are in a rush to say they are in love. Souls are in a rush to say all things are great and he/she loves me. Everyone wants to be in love. There is a rush to say, "let's get married." And then the eyes open! Are they purposely blind beforehand? Are the souls that are marrying really that bad that separations come afterwards? Souls already know what they find out when they marry.

Marry, as love, as Me, as many ways of life on Earth, have come in packages not representative of their truths. What does it mean to marry? Marriage is a fluid flow of love. Love does not stop or start. Love is fluid, no beginning, no end. Marriage is a choice. We all have will. We all have mind. And we all have choice. And it is a life choice.

Marriage is forgotten as it is a choice of any kind. Once people get married, once that big day has passed, then the living begins and souls are not prepared. For media, family, friends, they do not support the marriage part of marriage, as they do the road to such action.

Once married, expectations are put on the partners from the outside and from within themselves. For then they believe that they have to be a certain person, have certain things, want and need much more than they asked for before. Expectations are high and deliveries are low. Marriage is not money, it is not children, it is not family, for all of these things have now been found to happen even when Marriage does not.

So what is Marriage? What does it mean to marry? Does it on Earth mean that a soul can not do things? Does it mean that a soul can do things? Does it mean that you have things? You can not have other things? Does marriage take away or give? Does marriage offer advantages or take them away?

Marriage is an emotion. On Earth they created an act called marriage, to let the world know, to bind the souls of suchness. In truth, marriage is an emotion of heart. It is the soul without the mind. It is the opening of truth to action.

Marriage is a state of mind. Mind wants partner for it to have balance. Minds of humans settle in love. Grow in love. The mind fights the souls of Earth less in love of partner, in teachings of love of self.

Marriage is a reflection of who you are. Who you choose. Why you choose to be in this way, and how you chose it? Marriage tells you who you are. It shows you how you can compromise and still feel whole. Marriage teaches on the adult level the love of mother to children at births.

Marriage teaches that love can intensify and propel, driven by intention alone. Marriage teaches the heart that even in moments of all you could not know, you can learn in balance and in love. Marriage wants nothing from it. Whatever is wanted in the marriage is created by the partners.

Marriage is diverse and flexible, the love of two and its infinite power to grow all else around it. Marriage is the home of home on Earth. It is the love of God Almighty on Earth in personification; the makings of love with mind, with body, with soul. For the body is nothing within the soul.

The mind will tell the body it needs not love however the body does not care for love or not, it is the soul that needs love. When the mind takes over, bodies can relate to anyone. Sometimes souls will say there is love to trick the mind and body however there is waking up very quickly after those very thoughts.

Love can not be tricked. It is an emotion of truth. And truth is truth is truth. There is nothing else it can be. Marriage is the mirror of truth on Earth. In marriage everything is seen and heard. Heart is in growth and dimension. Marriage is the learnings of self in the learnment of another.

They say marriage is one. Marriage is one in hope, in dreams, in purity of action. Marriage that does not possess this is not of marriage. That is why papers saying so, someone telling you to, that is not marriage.

Marriage is emotion and truth and love and purity. It is growth and entailments of self evolvement; of reflection and refinement. Marriage is a want, a desire, a need and openment of self, not closement.

Marriage on Earth has been reduced to The Wife, The Husband, women banding together, men banding together, They and They, Him and Her. I hear much disheartenment, for simply the meaning it got lost and remained unknown within generations of time.

Marriage seems to be a way of saying "I really like you right now." Marriage is a contract and if one soul does not live up to it they have irreconcilable differences and souls did not grow they ran off.

I am not saying souls need to stay with one another. I am simply saying that the souls are not marrying; it is that their souls are not marrying. Minds can not marry. Bodies can not marry. Minds are for everyone. Bodies are for everyone. Souls marry.

When souls marry and love, truth and purity do not exist, neither does the relationship. It becomes a burden and the souls do not go inward to find the essence of burden, for love, truth or purity may only exist partially. You hear much, souls are engaged, souls want to marry, souls are separating, souls do not like each other. All the stages.

However in truth in marriage there is no beginning, no middle, no end. There is the hope of love on Earth and that hope continues in relationship, only now that hope is shared. Hope that comes because of a soul will leave with that soul and the remaining soul will remain without the hope they looked for in someone else.

That is why it is important to look into self. A self can not give what it does not have. It can not share if it does not know what to share, how to share and wants the other person to be responsible of taking care of them. That is of great burden. That is not partner, that is not growing and stagnation will occur.

Growth comes from intent of heart to do so. If you are a soul that loves, you will love and it will be shared. There is no beginning to do so. No end to do so. Love is eternal. When marriage in soul happens between souls it is eternal. If this does not happen, it is simply growth on its way to it. Once it happens the souls never want to replace it, for they understand that eternality is eternal and that love is now home to grow.

And that is the pairings that you witness when you see the connections; when others are bothered by those connections, when they themselves did not have the love of self to wait for such pairings and exited mission, which is called settling.

A settler is never comfortable and neither is the assisting soul. You see truth is truth is truth. Marriage is not anticipated in love. Souls try to impress with what they wear. Then what they say. Then what they have. Then what they do.

Marriage is not made up impression. Marriage is emotion and the holdings of such great emotion it makes all else short of anything in life done in purity of self, of love, of truth, pale in comparison.

There is no turning back once love, truth and purity are known to any soul. It can not be. For nothing can be the same.

Pure love is all souls remember. Pure love is the essence of every soul on Earth. Pure love is difficult on Earth in the barrierment of self and the lacks of self love that have brought up much self doubt hence doubt in others.

There are answers, there is love however the souls of Earth are in waitment of how. Simply start asking yourself(s) questions. Why, why do I say this, do that, wear things, buy things, when I find that does not make me happy? What do I really want from myself? Why do I want that? And a soul will begin to know, who am I?

Like a lost child in a forest of trees. You must give it a way to follow the light of the sun and it will know where it is going; back to paths of light. In Truth; that is Marriage.

It is a Path of Light. If it is seen that way, it will be. If souls could hear those words, they are healing words. They heal to think path of light, to hear it, to think it again, for it is of the absoluteness of home.

## MARRIAGE AND RELATIONSHIPS

Marriage has become the exception to be in love rather than the way of the glory of love in which it is in purity. There is talk of cheating, cheating up, cheating down. Not only in marriages, cheatment is rampant, for the soul of the uneasy of heart is of body and no longer of mind. The cheatment of souls amongst each other is the insecurity and fears of being loved.

So the theory of love becomes theory and the truth of love is lost. And the greater the partners are the less love is had on all ends. No body wins. It matters not if a soul truly cheats or not, it matters that the taking away of self in internal knowledge's is the hurtment of all souls. Glory be to God Almighty, for the unions of souls builds from within the trusts of love.

How else to know of suchness without the existence of suchness within self? It is not sexual. It is not even attraction. It is possession and the belief that the insecure soul is desirement of self to others and false confidence is built. The truth of the matter is any soul on Earth will find a willing partner if they look.

Every soul on Earth can perform a sexual act. Every soul on Earth can perform an honest act. Any soul on Earth and any plane of existence, in any level of universe, has the free will to carry itself wherever it may. It is the self trust, the self love, the self truth that is within and carries itself from one plane to another.

Every soul is simply on mission of its own lessons. Marriage is the closest union to home on Earth; when marriage is in purity of the souls involved. As is the love of a mother to a child, for that is the first experience of love in purity on Earth.

Of friends who need not a thing from another and are present in the love of purity, for the purity between souls who choose to live with another gives the depths of love a home to flourish. Most souls do not get this far in life, for they exist in the trials of heart and mind in infancy and the depths are not acknowledged or known.

That is the telling that trust is going in surfacement of souls and the depths are missing. And that is what is looked for in serial numerous relationships, for quantity is taking away from the quality that is in existence, yet the tappings into are not found by many.

Marriage is the carriage of the soul and that is what it is meant to be. To say that marriage takes a person away from other souls, persons, is to say that the soul can not withstand, understand or want depth of soul, of self, of heart, of mind and of body. So simple it all is. Nothing is as is seen, as it seems, for less is more. It is in truth of all avenues of life.

## MEANNESS

Meanness' repel. A soul is a soul. It matters none who. And that is why these souls do not flourish other friendships. How could other souls ask for suchnesses. Falseness' are seen from hearts of souls. They react to the non words. For what are words?

Emotion is felt. Not words. Skewedness is felt. Not words.

As sex is not physical, Conversations are not words. Love is not words. Caring is not words. Words give souls an avenue. Written words give the word a point of view. Sex gives physical pleasure however all are in only a second of time. However, the emotions of truth are felt in foreverments.

## MEMORY
A pure soul in wanting is shaped by memory. A self motivated soul comes from memory. Every soul is affected by memory in thought. Whether the actions they speak of were in the way they speak of them, of it, it is the way they remember it that shapes a soul.

## THE MEEK
The meek are those that think with their mind, not their souls.

## MEN
The male gender, they collect, they want to have as many of anything. And they want women in that way. They do not want women for the women. They want women for the counting. To say, "I know so and so, I had her, I got this." It is like saying; "I got an A on my report card" at a school of education.

This is true of all men, No matter what. Once men gain a certain security within it is not that they do not want to count anymore, they simply understand why they need it and it no longer is a need. It is simply the confidence in knowing.

## MENTAL ILLNESS
Mental Illness' stem from traumas to the human race and those that come within that realm come in attempts to grow and nurture the releasements of those energies. There are medications to subdue those souls at times, for

their traumas still are in need of generations to come and dilute the strength of the ill will imposed.

That is what is called hereditary: A group of souls who come to Earth to release and relinquish energies of other soul's traumas. This is a common reason for coming to Earth for many souls from home. And you recognize this in souls as you speak to them.

When they say they do not know why they do as they do, they themselves do not like it. That is why I tell you run do not walk away from ill willers. They came to grow the ill will into love and each may be in steps along the way in which they can not solve. And can only solve through the learning of others examples and energy, rather than the talkings, that is the least heard of actions.

## THE MIND

The mind is the greatest worker of all. The mind is the steps ahead of all that exists. The mind understands more than it knows. The mind is the keeper of all knowledge's and they can be set free and become if only the mind is aware that it can. Sit in stillness and let the mind come to its openment and live in and become what it carries. It is the only way to see. What the mind can not see the heart struggles to believe. To see is to do and to do is to become. And to become is to share. To share is to live life on Earth in fullness.

## THE MIND IS A COMPUTER

Many souls are on Earth simply because they have to live, to survive their missions and within that journey they can no longer feel why. Souls speak with sweet sorrow in words, in actions, in askings and in their own perceived truths.

They do things, take on actions, to feel alive and the thresholds are rising in what can stimulate the mind, the body, the soul. The ranges of love and of understanding of such have given way to the mind in control of the soul; trying to make the soul conform to a stance far less superior than it is.

The mind is a computer. It has no feeling or comprehension of. Every body comes with a mind. Every soul is the passion, the love, the home of the Body on Earth. And within that truth it is being set aside for what the mind can do. What the mind is seeking when in combination of the soul, for it wants to control.

And Ego simply helps it along. And the heart, the soul of a soul, triumphs in love when it acts in truth of its own love and the discovery of the depth of its own love hence shared love once it is known.

## THE MIND OF THE MEEK

It is all about self centeredness and me, me, me. The shortsightedness that can last a lifetime and take away any joy those souls can find, feel, or have.

"Look at me. I am beautiful. I am desirable. I am wantable. I will not love you cleanly. I will not love you unconditionally. I may not even love you with conditions. However I will love you when you do not want me.

I will love you when I simply need someone to be there, for lack of any other warm body. I will love you when you make me look good. I will leave you when I find something, someone better. I will say horrible things to you, about you, when I do not care about you. I will say nice things about you when I am sorry.

I will walk away from you in a heartbeat and I will come back to use you when my ego needs an uplight. I will walk away from you when you are sad however I will walk towards you when I am sad. I will come to you when I need you. I will help you only when I want to. I will take care of you when I get credit and I will walk away from you when I don't.

I will say I love you, I care about you. I want you when I get all that I want from you. I will destroy your integrity otherwise. I do not love you for you. I do not love you for me, for I do not know how to love period. I will not admit that, so I will live life in games and create scenarios that can remind me I am still here. I am living and I will appear to do things that are all in rightness yet I will always know my motivations and the manipulations I need to create to feel loved or cared for.

Love for me is momentary. It is not forever, for I can not be here for myself forever. I have accustomed to living within the lies of heart and mind and I have accustomed to taking souls of that sameness with me along for the ride.

When someone can see me for what I really am I will put them down and try to destroy them to the souls around me, for then I can be chief again. I need to control myself and those around me so then I can keep my lies in place and see the workings of my meekness, to inherit the souls that are not wise enough to listen to me.

Once I inherit a soul, I will no longer respect them, for what fool would really listen to me, when I do not listen to myself? I will disgard them and treat them as I treat myself, with the self hatred of my self spilling over onto them.

I want to hurt others as I hurt inside. I want not to search for myself, so I have learned to mislead others. I have learned to hurt others to take away my pain however my pain is still there and just dug itself deeper. I still do not want to look at my pain so I will go and create and hurt someone else. I will take those that look like truth and I will poke holes in them.

I will take those that are happy and start to speak to souls who know them and I will begin my path of taking away from them. I will start to speak of them in illness so others will question them. I will plant seeds of doubt in all those around me, around others and keep the stirs of the pot turning.

I will stand by and watch as the clues I have left behind unfold and I will come to the rescue and appear as though I am helping. I will not help a soul, unless there is return in it for me. If I help a soul and there is no return in it for me, I will let that soul know what I have done and punish them for my doing it and I did not get what I wanted for my doing.

I will say something happy and end in a note of question and doubt. I will appear loving and then I will begin to set up my plans. I will try to try, however I can not keep trying if I do not get what I want. I am sad inside, however I will only speak of the sadness of the current situations I have created.

I will love my children when it is convenient and I will do as I want otherwise. I will care for my friends when it is convenient and stay with them for lack of any other friends. I will be the victim, for how could I account for my actions. I will say it was done to me, for my role in my life is irrelevant. I will pretend truth, for I know others will, for who would want to confront me? Where would they start?

I have started so many simmering fires that by now no one could catch up to me nor does it appear that I started them. I have succeeded when no one knows it's me and the innocent and the pure hearted are brought down.

I will live in my sadness and I am not sorry for any sadness I have created. I will teach my children to be as I am for I have not resolved and neither will they. We will live in the daily living of self importance, for no one matters but me.

At least in self importance I will know what to do. I can teach that. My children are exampled me. More sadness I feel however not worth enough to explore myself. It is too hard and been too long for me to start at the beginning of my wiles. I have hurt many by now, and still I am hurt in accumulation now.

I must remain blind to all that I do, and then I can live in the belief that I am not so bad. That I do not hurt others, yes, I will say that they hurt me, that they did this to me, to themselves. It is not me. It could never be. My sadness propelled."

**This is the mind of the meek. This is the mind of the blind. This is the mind of when you ask how can you? And you find why they can not see.**

**This is the mind of inheritance.**

**Glory be to God Almighty, for the human mind is only that. The human soul is of God Almighty. When the mind believes itself to be greater than the soul this is the mind of the meek. For they are fighting God hence fighting self.**

Souls want greatness. Those that think with their mind, not their souls are the meek. That is definitional. Pure intent are those who speak from soul. The meek speak from mind alone with no belief in anything but themselves. Definitional.

All of life is halves. The soul without the mind and the mind without the soul is to live on Earth without love. The elevens. The one and one. It is all of foundation.

The meek are the crack in the foundation, for they have not discovered that control of self is restriction of soul. The control of others is the hatred of self. The manipulations of hearts of peoples are the murderous events.

One and One. Eleven. Two halves. Foundation truth. Balance. Purity and wisdom. Soul and mind. All in love. All in calmness of heart. When found.

**MINDHOOD**
Souls believe and have function in the world as it is and know not of all else. For souls, as they have to be to mission themselves, want to take care of their business in life here and now. There is much belief in fantasy and much evasion of internal truths.

The soul wants to fight its own will to prove itself worthy of its own mindhood. Like the way in which you think manhood and womanhood. There is a mindhood of soul.

That is a common and major struggle within a soul. The mind is fighting instinct, until the mind can accept and love itself and learn there is a partner between soul, heart and mind, rather than a struggle. The struggles you see without, are the struggles that exist within a soul.

## THE MIRACLES OF LOVE

The miracles of love in purity internal are not needed to be of external to be understood, find the paths of light. Know this in always, for Earth hands to many miracles. And they are passed by, for the intent is looking for something bigger, better, sweeter, and it is never found. For the selfishness in which it is sought closes the eyes to the day in presentness. To see what is in the day at hand is the grandest of life on Earth. To wait for things, peoples, better all the time, in simplest, is to hold time in place hence stagnation. And what can truly make a person happy other than the self of the person of the soul.

## MISERY

The misery of heart finds those who will perpetuate it. They look not for the answers, for they would not have presence of mind to know, so they hold themselves in place. Not knowing keeps them like others and they can relate.

## THE MISSION OF HUMANS

The mission of humans is to see through and look beyond the actions, for the motivations are truly the truth of souls. To believe that there is greater love for souls than the daily tinkerings of human life, to carry that love and pull others up and along. When others do not want to pull up, to let them go, for they have been touched and move along and touch others yet.

To hear and not respond is simply to not know. To hear and to respond in lowness of energy is to not believe in self. To hear and to respond carries love to yet some more. It is love. It is love. It is love. You will find going back to those you have loved that you will always love. Love can take on different forms. Love is not always the same. It is pliable and reliable. It is in cleanliness of always. For the cleanliness of love leaves it open to infinite avenues in always.

There are many forms of love. Love is truly love. The roads of purity within it grow it or take it away. Those who need great attentions from others are the souls that had lacks of love in confidences come to them in growth stagements. Those who want to leave souls in awry are the souls who could not express the hurtedness they felt and the incompletions of expression when it was in great need to do so.

So they learned to hold on and to come back in underneathment of surfaces and they are the "undertones." Those who understood love from heart understood that nothing can shake that love. No matter what happens to them or those around them in life. There is love and that constant, that stability, of the soul's heart grows the soul into a soul of helper.

And those who had compassion and love, no matter what a soul came to them with, Illness' of will or it be with love to them, they are the teachers, those of service for all souls on Earth. Those who keep thinking of a better day, of a better person, of a better stance that will give them happiness, know not the elements of truth. Nor do they carry within the understanding that time does not exist except in memory and that happiness is present tense. Not future tense nor is it in past tenses.

The form of a body can not tell you in truth the content of the soul of the body. Souls are mischeeved in believing the beauty of the utterness' is what is sought after. The internal is all that will be seen in time. For time is the best teacher. Those who encounter for monies, for things, you already know their fate, for their love is of thingments and not of life.

*(MISCHEEVED—To take away from a situation knowingly and expecting that other souls did not know of what you intended to do)*

For life is second and takes away from the soul the entire experience of life. You can live on Earth and evade mission, for that is choice of soul. And in that, the outcome of life is life not lived, for that soul will in alwaysment feel in the wrong place. Those are the souls who are in denial of mission.

## MISTAKES

There are no accidents as peoples would say or mistakes as most would love to know are of truth. Simply the mistakes that peoples call mistakes are the things at times that they wish that when they hit the fork in the road, that they went the other way of the fork in the road. However all decisions of free will have a path and the lessons come down for will be played on in that forum.

Peoples are only peoples. Some are happier than others. Some are greater in truth than others. Some are open to love and some are not. Some want to enjoy, some do not know how to. There are challenges and that is all that they are. You can live within the challenges with happiness of heart.

Some challenges challenge the happinesses that exist and that is when decisions of change are made. It is so simple. People try to find reasons, blames, excuses, fighting's, ill will, jealousies, vindictivenesses, contempt's to explain changes, when changes are simply in time to happen.

The word mistakes gives life to all that simply was in time to change, not meant for the foreverment of life on Earth, simply a holding place, or a teacher of lesson, or a reason of work, or children, or family betterments.

When that is secured the lessons continue and it may not include the circumstances that it needed to happen in that time. There is no remorse in life when this is understood in the entirety that it is.

Discontentment has become and can become a way of life. Those are the peoples who do not believe or the peoples that believe too much. Many are scared of change, resist change. Who fight it. Who hurt because of it. Who hurt others for it. For acceptance of newnesses is gone. That is a direct reflection of trusts dissipated.

Peoples do not want or welcome change, for they feel that what they already know is enough. Growth and truth found are difficult challenges. And trust within a soul is very little. Hence the soul fights change; Fights growth.

And when change happens and it does not come out to the desired results of what is wanted, going within the mode of expectations, then the change is called a mistake. An accident if they did not have the foresight to know it was coming.

And within that the fight against change, growth, strengthens. Glory be to God Almighty, for the changes within growth all around; the restrictions within hold all holdings around. The trapment of feelings takes place. And the lack of breathment within takes place hence the exist of those that are looking for growth becomes. And then change is had.

There are no mistakes, no mistakes and no mistakes. All that happens comes to souls in challenge and love of heart of who they are. And they have choices and choosings of who they are within the challenges that arise. And they either learn greater who they are or they are left to lesson their way.

In those lessons, souls lose souls, gain others and make choices that affect such happenings. It is all in the choices of heart and the wantings of the soul and the yearnings of the soul. And the happenings within that call for those very things to be as they are. And the souls needings of attentions, egoness' fed, wanting to be powerful, great, looked on by others as someone special.

And all peoples strive for the favors of others on their looks, and what they may have, or one or the other. The energy of a few is hurting all souls around. Follow your heart and do not hesitate in what you know. Grow yourself and do not stop fluttering around the world in which you live.

## MOTIVATIVE THOUGHTS AND ACTIONS
Motivative thoughts, motivative actions and their stagnations can carry for days, for weeks, for months, for years and for lifetimes on Earth. The motivative thoughts are truly to keep the person in place in placement of stance without challenge.

For then the greatness of that soul can not be noticed, for it would grow the soul and the soul is subconsciously saying "I do not want to be accountable. I do not want to grow." Just as I spoke of cheatments, liements, stealings, for that is saying "I want to hurt myself, please let me, because I do not want to be here or anywhere entirely."

It is a form of self sabotage; as is the relentlessness of not wanting to solve problems however to simply have problems; for then there is something to talk about, something to do. Something to feel in camaraderie with others, for it again lives in the lower energies of life on Earth.

The lower energies can erase in an instant if the soul so chooses. For the focus of the soul will become. Souls do know this however it is easier to lie and not to tell the truth. The truth releases and the pretending keeps the games of life on, the games that trick the soul itself hence all others hence the world. And at this time in time on Earth it is the way it is.

It is the acceptedness of how souls are in believerment of self. If they speak ill of another, want someone to fail to boast of that failure. To want to succeed so others will respect them, project them, all the self motivated channels, the ill will is already there. They are the failure, they have not succeeded and that is simply the way it really is.

For the pacifications can last for as long as the soul keeps the pacifications alive. Some souls like to try, want to try, want to appear their efforts are with heart however if only they get what they want first. And when they do not get what they want, they turn on themselves first and then on all others.

They are cordial if they are happy and very mean when they are not happy. There is great hardship in this type of soul, for they are the hardest to get close to. This type of soul will love you with all heart and undo all love with words of horror in anger; will take away all the moments of love, caring and candor to truth of ugliness of heart as seen in the moments of anger.

The moments of angers are the teachers of one soul to another. Any soul on Earth can be cordial, loving and respectful in the happiness of self however who are they when challenged. What are they and was love consistent and in truth? Is there some truth, and pretendment in some? That is not foundational, for that soul is only self motivated. Motivated to you if you can offer them something and when that offerment loses its lusterments to the soul they become difficult.

The self motivated believe the world is in this modement of thought and react and behave in this way even though they do know better, even though they know better. The fear of losing is much stronger than the belief of love in any way. There is a loss of truth in great measure. There are many stories and only the non emotional issues are spoken with truth.

If someone fell, got hurt, is in sickness in realness and needs help. Then truths are spoken. However in all else truth is absent, not spoken, uncalled to the forefront. The added insinuations of tone and direction have taken way of fancy in this time.

## MURDERERS

No one soul is here on Earth by mistake so there can not be mistakes. Peoples say "well is a mistake a murderer." A murderer is simply a lack of self love. That comes from somewhere, from other souls as well. Support for souls is not available in many forms and the ills of heart grow ills in others and that is the propellation of lacks of love.

Some souls hurt others in heart, in money, in many other forms of taking aways and the soul(s) in receiverment of suchness have to live through it. A soul that is taken away in form comes back home to great love. Glory be to God Almighty, for nothing is as it seems.

## NON TRUTHS

When the questment of truth is the paths of mind, the stories of non truths dissipate along the path and never make it to the end of the paths. Non truths only carry other paths of startment and no conclusions. Conclusions only come from truth within. Every soul has a story. Every story carries in it some truth. The eyes choose to live within and or withoutness of truth.

## NOTHING IS AS IT IS SEEN
Nothing is as it is seen. Once something is energy it has happened.

## NOTHING IS AS IT SEEMS
Nothing is as it seems. Nothing. That is the glory of life. What the eyes see is. What the mind truly wants becomes. No one, not a soul, even those you don't like being around is without a plan. No one is alone in this world or in any world, for God is tender to his creation of love and surrounds all with love throughout all of life.

God gently knows and sees all, with love and purity, with hope and desire of growth of soul. For the gentleness of love soothes, heals, growths and gives happiness where the eyes are in fortune to see it, even in times of hardship.

There are so many ways to escape the experiences of life, and sometimes they are the only ways people know. Some like to share or find those who are growing, only to find out they are the teacher for those who do not know.

And then there are some who catalyst and take souls to their next points unknowingly. And then there are those who plant seeds of doubt and yet it grows others around them even though there is mistrust of them. Nothing is as it seems.

## NOTHING IS UNSEEN
Nothing is silent. Nothing is unseen or unfelt. However, all things in life on Earth can believe to the soul of doing to be in camouflaugments.

## OBJECTIVE THOUGHT
Souls do not have special behaviors for each person that they know. They simply search for souls to act out their behaviors, to speak without taking into account bias. That is Objective Thought.

It is not of who it is, it is what it is. Every soul is a stamp of a way of thought, of doing things, of holes, of what they want out of what they call life. They have a stamp of their mission within and Earth is the journey of how they go about it.

Some choose decisions closer to the heart and some do not. Some want things that take away from themselves, for they have been taken away from in love and some do not. Some give without repercussion and some take without repercussion. Some understand basic concepts and some do not. Some have sophistication of heart and can see others and have innate curation and some do not.

Some have internal organization and some do not. Some are in a flutter always and some can not see flutter at all. Some can only see solutions and others do not want answers. Some create problems and yet others only want to solve them. Some will love without condition and most love with condition. Some will conquer and not complain and some complain and do not conquer. Souls are known for who they are even when they believe they are not.

Some will try something on you and if it does not succeed, you will soon find out they have gone to another and done the same thing. No difference, simply another soul who is unsuspecting. Some souls will speak truth and others will speak in hiding truths.

Some speak in straight forwardness and others will talk in circles. You already see the onward souls and the circular energy's.

Some can make sense out of truth and yet others will take a shred of truth and turn it into something it is not. Some will come to the world with open arms and some come to the world with open armed torn. For that is ill intent.

Some want to make peace and some want to disturb balance. Some have jealousy and compete to show up another and yet others can go through life without the conscious thought of this. Some will be nice only to receive what they want, (self Motivation) and some souls are simply in truth, nice.

Some do not like words of health and happiness and others have to fight to stop them from their mission of destroyance. Glory be to God Almighty.

Souls are in circles and the circles are within them. And they take their circle and try to enclose as much as they can for the ownership of cleverality wants to be shared so that it can establish its stance and not have to face questions of self. Souls who hold each other in delusion live in the delusion they created. They live by the delusions that are markers of success just for them.

They will compete to see who is better, stronger, more lively, more successful based on their standards alone. And when one falls just a little bit, the other is taking happiness in the fall and acting as though they are helpers however helpers only to know more and hurt the other more.

It is slight of the eye and harsh on energy. It is felt and that is the ways in which trust erodes with souls amongst each other. Changing energy's is truly not changing. **Souls speak of changes however it is simply growth onto the knowns of home.** And they will **growth onto it**. That is the ways of heart. You can only **growth onto it**. Glory be to God Almighty. For Objective Thought teaches you objectivity of trusting souls.

## OBSTACLES

All obstacles are moments in home, flashes and truths, for all reasons do not have to fit into the structures of what seems to be the structures on Earth. There is greater freedom of love at home; that is why when souls come to Earth they can not believe the challenges they have asked of themselves however they are seeing their challenges with the biggest challenge within their challenge; the added Mind part to the soul.

The Ego, the ways of taking away and all that could come within that frame of thinking. The strength of truth, love and purity once found and is it chosen? That is why there are choices and free will. That is why a soul comes to challenge.

## ONE

The world is one. Love is one. Truth is one. Purity is one. There are not separations. There are not divisions. There are no boundaries. There are no limitations. Earth's human energy creates suchedness. That is the evolution as we speak. It is the evolutionization of souls to each other, in recognition that they can only be one. For they come from one. They are one of many and one of one and one of many again.

The loss of the core belief that we are one is the result of Earth in this day. Those who speak we are one are perceived as "foolish" by those who are in ego. However nothing is as it seems. The only souls, who will speak that another is a fool and not know it is talking of itself when it speaks, are the evidence of ego and self motivation. It is that simple.

## ORIGINS

Love is the stem, the Origin, the notice we take and the sustainment we keep; the truth of love, the purity of love, the love of love. The lacks of love have been written of in great extentedness. When there are lackedness' of love, the words, the feelings, the actions, must have to be in spelled out of the lacks of love, words, feelings and actions. For the catalysts of suchness in experience had to play their roles to ensure that the world can learn of itself, see itself, know of itself.

How a wife can give to a husband and how she can take away and how a husband can take away from a wife and how he can give. Most actions of souls of what Earth calls husband and what Earth calls wife in this day, we can call it anything we want however it is a decision of heart not paper and it matters not what we call it. However on Earth it is the words of usement. Husband and Wife. This is the original partnership of souls on Earth.

It is the mimic of home in Twin souls in what Earth calls soul mates. Souls are in home within the others existence. At home all souls understand there is a gift to each soul(s) of existence and within that gift of soul each gift compliments the completeness of home in entirety.

For each drop of love within purity of feltedness of soul, each shared gift that grows all souls. Each form of partnership is love and giftedness and sharing and the world of any galaxy, any plane, any universe and home stems from this. The love, the gifts, the sharing, for that is the Origin of Allness of any kind.

There is no beginning; it is the Origin of Soul(s). And Love, Truth, Purity, those are the steerers of all love, gifts and sharing. Without them the Origin(s) of Universe can not be of honor hence Propellation can not grow into growth. Within the love, truth, purity of love, gifts and sharing in the internal of souls this exists in all.

It is the soul's ingredients, if you can understand that better. Each and Every soul comes to Earth with Love, with a gift and the knowing of sharing it. Each and Every soul comes to Earth with Love, Truth and Purity. And the births and happenings of the day of Birth onward are the shapings of experience.

That is why it is important to know who a soul is, has been, born to, lived in, ate, slept, schooled and loved. For that is the story of the experience of that soul. Did the experience take them away from self or bring the soul closer to itself?

Did the soul understand or did it resist its mission and growth of heart internal? Did the soul feel love, receive love, carry love into growth? Did the lack of love overcome love of purity? How did that appear to that soul? What did the soul do with it? Did they know why they did with it as they did?

The reactions to the action tell the story of that soul; Tell the soul who it is; Why it is, and that no experience, no action is of mistake, for it can not be. Each soul must take responsibility of itself. All lacks of love to others comes with the foundation thought of that soul NOT taking responsibility of itself.

The habits and patterns of humans are hardest to see by the human itself. So all humans have eyes to witness what a soul can not know of itself to tell who he is. Souls have ears to hear. Not only to hear some words however to hear intonations, hesitations, truths of heart in strength of voice and lacks of love in controlled voice, in words of nice that are words of destruction(s) of many emotions to the receiving souls around.

## ORIGINAL LOVE
Original love is the first love felt by every soul upon creation. It is the pure love of God instilled in each soul, each drop of God that comes to existence. Before anything else each soul began with original love.

## ORPHANS
The children unknown to the parents of such are the treasured children of Earth. They are the ones who look forgotten and they are truly the ones never forgotten. Nothing is as it seems. For the Glory of God is of wonder of heart.

## THE OTHER SIDE OF LOVE
The other side of love is in feeling. In heart. In growth. The magic of life intensifies when the realness of emotion is present, when the imagination is not given prompts to think. The human brain is a remarkable thing. The human brain is the master of the mind. The other side of love is of intensity side by side in simpleness.

The other side of love is the light in which love flourishes and carries. It meshes home on Earth. It carries light not only to you, however to all that encounter you. The other side of life holds no boundment, no boundaries, no escapes, no limits, for they do not exist.

All that exists is the honesty in which life is of existence. It can be together and within and without the presence of the other.

For the other side of love creates. It builds. And it provides the time and the patience to do what is of light, no matter what the path to get to it is. There are no limits; there is no time, there is nothing. All there is is an internal rhythm of heart that carries in the purity in which it is.

## PARTNERSHIP

Life is a series of partnerships. And they can only be partnerships when souls are partners. Balances may be of difference however when there is not reciprocations, souls will look for other partners. This is true of all peoples anywhere.

Most issues between couples do not get resolved easily and these are the hardest to forget. Yet in time the mind may ease however they are the very acts that trouble the souls. It will come up in arguments in much of time as though it has happened in newness each time.

Intentions run strongest in partnerships of any kind. Partnerships of families, friends, coworkers and in greatest of affects marriages.

Peoples like to believe they live within specialness. When they find out they are not, they begin to feel simply ordinary and then the ordinary things begin to happen.

This is not an issue about sex yet it is. Partners do not like to believe that that exists outside of their time, their space, their relationship.

Internal, why would they seed others, for that is the insultment of the relationship. External relationships are internally used to take away existing relationships. Many times the problems of a partnership do not take away the relationship which would be the cause of actions outside of the relationship however the acts of sexualness do.

That breaks a bond. So simple. It is a bond that is one of the few on Earth that are in great difficulty to repair, as is the work of thievery, of lying. That is why it is all called on Earth as cheating. All are cheated. There is great learnment in this situation. For then the act is used as collateral in future arguments.

That is the beginning of love destroying its greatest on the souls within. For then they think, God, how could this happen? Who is this person?

Why am I with this soul? Those who come back to these relationships come back with other reasons to stay. For fear of leaving is the greatest, for comfort.

When intentions are not based on happiness and love, for that is the opposite of how it appears. It gives way to many dramas to come and makes for many days of misery on the soul of the human. The path of taking away grows quickly. The paths of taking away have the least of patience. And both parties grow into a pattern of mistrust. It will be a longest of lessons and a hard path of overcomements to the souls involved.

Males like to state that it does not matter at times to love as women are trying to say as well at times. For it is treated as a treatment for ego, vitality, who that person believes they should be.

Time truly teaches. In time all things surface. Trust that pure intentions in life is of all truths and all truths of strength and all strength comes from purity of intentions. When intentions are not of purity, at times that very thing propels souls in these areas to feel of excitement.

This is greatest in those who were loved in conditions. Then they hide parts of themselves as they did with the condition parent, teacher, etc…For they can only excite in the negative. That is the harshness of love coming in skewment in ages of youngment upon experience.

That is why it was called dirty pictures; yet the body of a female or a male is not of dirty! They are of love; Seeking love in the ways in which they have been shaped; the body of an adult and the mind of a child in disillusionment. So simple to know and yet the internalness of the results has brought about many pains for peoples. They believe this is of greatest pleasure to them and it is pain based so it can only produce pain.

Let me tell you further. When the act itself is completed and it is only an act when it is pain based, the soul knows of it immediately in afterwardments. It does not have to reach the other yet.

Ego is also a factor. Much sex is looked at as desirability on the part of the soul in muchness. Yet what in life in muchness is balanced on any level? Yet this act, without emotion carries differently.

We are taught in error in muchness in this area. It is the forbidden; however, God did not forbid it. It was thought to be of men however who were men with? It is of men and women on Earth and it is the under carpet conversation. The under carpet of acts, the under carpet of feelings, the least taught and much assumed position in life on Earth. It is the barometer of souls.

Those willing to cross the lines of bondment between souls are the souls to understand that trusts do not exist within them. For it is not the acts, it is the breaking of bonds. It is feeling as though God turned on you hence it is now pain and it turns on the soul unto others hence greater pains.

The males believe it is a right of manhood. It is a right of closing down enough to disregard self and then another. It is deep. It is internal. For the act is the result of love. When the virginal love towards love is skewed it will appear in skewment. Glory be to God Almighty. The inner workings of souls is endless.

Many say, "in my younger days," and they look back and feel accomplished as a male; However, if they look at what they lost as well. For with women it is not lost as easily. A woman will leave a relationship for another. A man will stay as long as he can live in his pain and love at the times of same hence duality. Glory be to God Almighty.

Truly ask any man or any woman the greatest moments they have had and it will be love in purity. Nothing else can be of that. When the purity is gone or not present, measurements and egos set in. Do you love me is asked? Do you want me? Do you need me? Those are asked, for they are not known. So simple is the truth.

There are mentions today in many times on the topicness of souls intertwining in mind, heart and then body. The body is simply a body. What you do with your body is an extension of mind and heart. It is not separate. I will not take into consideration what any soul may say of this. It is an extension not a separation. As are all things in life.

This is not separate from life; as is nothing else separate from life. Do you understand the sameness and the power of this being singled out and what it has done to souls? For no soul of cheatment anywhere will know of itself as not a cheater. Those who come to others in preparation of cheatment have the intentions of destruction and care not of actions.

The pain needs a home and it will carry to all those involved. Those who are willing to do this remain without partners. For when they are with partner it is not with the partner that they are with. It is with themselves seeking company. They try to believe it is of partner however they pressure those in their lives in greatness until they put so much pressure on them the person realizes that this person is driven by intentions of non purity in truth.

The relationship is based on insecurity, acts based on insecurity and the partner realizes that they are only there to fill a hole and not there out of love and truth. And they leave in the time it takes to figure that out. And the soul of ableness of cheating continues on, not caring who they are with however acquiring yet another soul being the goal.

The life of that person is spent acquiring souls, for the feelings of love become more and more distant each time they take another human and try to make that human what they want them to be. You have seen this from countless men, countless women. That is why they are alone. Not because they are bad or good or loving or not. They really care not who they love they want someone to love them despite their lack of love for self.

Hence, the pressure begins in making that person love them, prove they love them and grow dependent and needy. They do this to everyone. And everyone believes it to be special for them. However, notice as well those in this behavior pattern have many to choose from and no one is there at the timeness of same.

They go out, dress up, look of handsomeness and beauty, say the right things, wear the right things, drive the best cars they can afford. Buy interesting pieces, for topics are rare in lack of loveness, so they have to speak of things. And then in a months time, three months time, six months time, a years time, a few years time, it is all gone. The lack of purity can not sustain. The lack of love could not sustain.

You see this in many men and women as well. They have become in greater frequency since over time they have learned to date and not to endure. They have learned to charm and lost naturalisity. The loss of naturalisity can not be seen by the soul of action, for how could it continue to know of its own truths. Purity brings love in all directions.

## PARTNERS OF SAME SEXES

They have difference in pleasures, for their roles are of difference to them and in greater instances than not on Earth. It is that sex is sex and the fulfillments are in difference, for they know that the growth of life is not of present.

It is not right or wrong for those who want there to be a right or wrong. There is not sin. Their challenges are of difference and sexualness for them is of releasements and closures of balance for them to function in humality. However, in love of a man and a woman growth of love is always known in eternity.

All souls have purpose and none in shunment of life. For life is for the difference and tolerance and love bred from within. For the sameness who leave the world without challenge. And again, any soul can conform and live well in easyments of life however how does a soul live within the hardships and challenges. For only then do you know who a soul is.

Same sexes are no bigness of deal as it has been dealt on Earth. That is simply fear of souls and unknownments of self. Glory be to God Almighty, for God is not judge of his creation, he is of his creation and love of all souls. All deviations happen on Earth and stay on Earth upon entrance to home.

## PASSION

As in all things on Earth, interest, intent, can give life to anything. That is why it is of great importance to do as one thinks and not to deny passions in the bodies embodied on Earth. Shortchangement of choices is to take away the glory of all knowing from oneself.

And the soul will always acknowledge its loss of self within. That is what is called frustration. And frustrative behaviors begin to set in. When a soul acknowledges itself no matter what circumstance it is in it releases its own energy within the universe in which it lives. If the soul can not identify its own circumstance it will fight itself hence others and the energy is not released and stays within in the frustrations of self.

Souls are affected by every thought, every sight of anything, every word of conversation. For the soul is simply receptive. That is why it is of great importance to know and understand the passion of soul(s) of self. To know is to affect oneself in growth. To not understand intent takes on an energy in the word, actions, sights and sounds of all around and it will deaden the area in which it resides.

## THE PATH

Your intentions will create the path. The path will fulfill your dreams. Your dreams will bring more love into the world.

## PATHS

All that is known is simply partial truth. That is all. That is why there is mishap and question, Deviation and separations of thoughts. That is why souls can not agree. However it is time in the historical of time on Earth to elevate the souls of Earth, the peoples who are in experience now of this pressure and release their paths to love in growth.

The stagnation(s) have left the world in which souls live without life in truth on any level of energy. The energy at this time is in its greatest lowment of measures. The soul(s) of Earth are in quiet and in disbelief of what can actually happen and no others can see.

All souls can see however the deadendedness of what is seen is overwhelming and souls are at no cluements of thoughts as to where to begin, what to do, why to do it and how to do it. They have no answers, for the answers of their own heart; their own life(s) are not answered. Glory be to God Almighty.

And there are those who are trying to answer these questions; however they all are coming back to a way to live that is not natural in the world as it is in this day.

There is no path that can be followed in completeness, for the only path followed in completeness can only be love. Only love. There is no other path. You can call it God For God is Love. There is no path other than love, purity and truth. All other paths wind up and around into experience. All will find its path, for there has to be a million movements of energy to move a mind from one moment to another.

Positive life, even in hardship brings to all of us the rewards of pure faith. It gives and gives to know truth and when truth is camouflaged it becomes and takes on another form and that form may take years to present itself, for camouflagment of soul is to erase your lesson of soul.

The paths to home are many and many have detours and the forks in the roads bring about the lessons. The truth is, you can always go back to the fork in the road and realign yourself. Your soul is a flexible and lovable soul. Your soul wants to help you and if the feelings of the soul are working away from it, how could that soul grow?

How can flexibility be flexible with all the thoughts and all the love turned into something else? It is much easier to be and do and know the truth, than any other way of thinking yet the truth is fought. Fought with energy that could take the soul to a different light, for the light is fought with vigor at times, for the lessons are resisted for that soul.

## THE PATTERNS OF GROWTH AND LOVE

On Earth the patterns are of growth and love, hugging and repair. Healing and knowing that there is hope. Knowing what hope appears as, hope speaks as and that hope growths into other growths. For love is continuous growth, depth, widenings of souls and extensions of limits and boundaries of mind.

## PEOPLE

All peoples are the same. Their differences are not consistent with the sameness, for everyone is of individual. And then they are the same again.

## PEOPLES

Peoples, I use that word when I speak of soul's outward behaviors and Souls, when I speak of the inner makings and thoughts on Earth.

## PERCEPTION

Perception creates reality and the realities of this time have gone awry. Perception has built into it thresholds of thought. Those thresholds of thought created the environments that humans call their groups. Their groups give their souls comfort however they are taking away from other souls, from themselves, the truth with this creation.

The world is in need of balance. People are predominately lost. Our sweet and beautiful humans wander with no path. No path at all. As people would never believe God's love is simple. There has been no "religion" or way of life that carries, other than the love of God, IN soul. That will carry the rest of it. No proof to others. More important is to carry such within. That is true of every soul on Earth, at this time, in past and to come.

## PERFECTION

Perfection is love. Love is perfection. And perfection is love again. There cannot be perfection without love. That is the reasoning of seeing what is perceived as perfection and yet there is not feeling in attachment. You come to a home, an art, a work and you fall into the love of life over it and that is the perfection.

It touches and it soothes. It grows and it embraces the soul of the souls, of the souls who are in recognition of self love in enoughments to recognize the love of others in passion of soul. Glory be to God Almighty, for the love of life can only be in such greatness as the propellants of recognition.

For then there is the deepest sigh, the clearest sight, the openness of heart and the mind of understanding. Life can not be of things. Life can only be of love. However, that love comes, it's coming and any shred of purity will grow all around it within the realm of greatest of emotion(s) to carry it. For perfection is of love. So simple. For love is perfection.

Peoples idolize what they do not have, could not get, could not have. What may not have been meant for them in this life and yet in the humanality of lacks of the controller's internal want to say, "If this would happen then everything would be perfect." There is not perfect.

Perfection is love. If the love could not carry a soul into contentness internal, it is not love in completeness of purity for that soul.

## PLANES AND GALAXIES
All planes and galaxies are within each other and energy is the only separation. All other planes have difference in mission. There is no duality as there is on Earth. Earth is the farthest plane from home. It possesses the lowest of energies. And that is why the variance of love, meaning the distance from love to lacks of love is furthest away from each other.

That is why there is what humans call disasters. It is all the spinning of some kind of energy, always always always driven by the energies of the human will, free will, choices made. There comes a point in energy when it reacts to the whole, the masses of souls and the energy in which they produce. It is not their bodies and what they do with them, it is not the mind and what they listen to or do; it is the souls will alone that drives energy.

The mind has not a will. The mind is already there waiting for an inhabitant. It is only the soul. The soul tells all else what to do, it is the energy of the body. The soul is the opener of all feelings, of all actions, of all thoughts. The soul is eternal. The body, the mind, they are of Earth.

The planes are other homes for souls to experience. There is no duality, meaning that souls on other planes, in other galaxies, they do not harm each other. Missions are not as varied as Earth. They are in greater depth, and growth of greater intensity.

On Earth souls have many choices, for that is one of the purposes of Earth. They have free will, which exists throughout all eternity. So the only variance for souls on Earth is choices.

The forks in the roads of the paths presented. Free will says you can do as you wish. Choice finds out what you wish and does it. That is the difference between free will and choices.

That is why there is self accounting. To account for the choices made within free will. That will tell any person who they are. That is why a manipulator does not like the words, love, intent, purity or truth. It repels their purpose.

## PLASTIC SURGERY

Everyone in life needs love and that is so simple to give, to be, to do. There is searching for comfort and not knowing where to begin. The belief in dreams is overburdened and overwhelmed. Love has been distorted to attractiveness and even the definition of attractiveness is blind to the one who believes is attractive.

There is much covering up of self at this time. Plastic Surgery. And the why is painful. For the lack of self acceptance to levels of recreating their creation and taking away the naturalness of lessons that come with aging and growing. And the acceptance that comes with it is now gone and aborted.

Trying to stop time mentally; physically it appears with surgeries. Yet it is the mental stagnation that is of the truth. Your essence is who we all are. Our beauty is the acceptance of our essence. There are young and old for reason. We all get a turn; we all get to be each age for a year. Like any evolvement, going back isn't the same as when, for that is evolvement.

## PORNOGRAPHY

Those who will perform will say love for love of now. It is parts of life in this time, for this is the only form of immediate pleasure, since longer term pleasures and depths are so far away. It is what the human worlds call the next best things to truth in love.

In time the soul will lose touch within itself for the sensations of love become in unrecognizable form to them and then loneliness they accustom to. And with and within others it remains in a temporary state.

A cheating soul of self may not be the one who appears as cheatment of self, it is both, both souls are in the cheatment. There is a cheator and a cheatee, both are taken away from. The desire of souls is looking for immediacy and has lost its way.

That is why I am an Angel of love. I can see what the souls can not see however to return home and witness, is to witness the loss of self and the deadening of a heart that lived in dreamment of life on Earth and the loss of it to use the body without the heart and mind. Deeper inside it comes from lacks of love to exhibit, for the exhibitness proves to the soul, to others and to the soul again that that soul is of desire.

It is sold to souls and they believe they will find that as well in illusion and the illusion fails a soul and the sitting within the soul sits in loneliness of heartedness. Yes, there is enjoyment to watch what others are willing to do however it is simply a body. The body is free in life and form and the form of a body lives in beauty to a soul who seeks it.

However, the engagement of all else is in temporary and in truth leaves the soul no longer trusting love. The falseness of what sex is and the depth and reality it has potential to are years of light in apartness.

## POSITIVE
The positive is the actions of love personified. The negative is the actions of doubt personified. Negative repels all, even the doer of doing negativity onto others.

## PRETENDERS
The pretenders are of losses in this time on Earth. The pretenders are in pattern; Predictable and boring. Sorry and lacks of prudency, leave them in horror to others and in blindness to self. Any soul can see, and the meek are blind. For they believe the blind to be the blind however the blind eyes of a human can see greater than the blind eye of the meek.

The meek twist truths when truths are spoken. The meek spin words to dizzy the soul who is listening. The meek are offensive to the souls of heart to stop conversation and to win the argument of the moment. What the meek are blind to is that there is always an argument of the moment. There is always a mishap and a misunderstanding waiting to be explained.

There is always something that has to be talked about, for the twistings of truth have to continue. There is always a lack of restment in the souls of the meek. For they are forever working in what they will do to achieve whatever it is that they feel they need to get from another soul; Even if it is only internal satisfaction of making sure that soul understands the wrongments of the self entitlements of the meek coming at them.

The inheritance of the meek is the weakest link of Earth. It appears in disguise and until further knowment of the challenges of the meek they are not discovered right away, however once they are in discoverment they remain blind to their actions and the other souls can see, predict and react accordingly.

The parents who live in meekness are the examples of the children in which they raise, for the signs will be seen in the rules the household lives within, as the rulers of companies and countries run of the meek. No different however affectment of numbers of people is the only difference.

And in truth one soul affected is enough. For then all souls live in the affectment of the meek. In all of meekness love conquers meekness and challenges their souls to fight, for that is the growing lessons of meek, and as catalysts of lessons for others. So simple is truth.

## PROPHET
A prophet is one without judgment. Who sees true reality. Who beckons to light and who draws to light.

## PROPELLMENTS OF LOVE IN MARRIAGE
Marriage exists simply to propel love. There are three ways on Earth to propel love in furtherments of each other. It comes from the love of self, the love of children's and the love of spouse. When all of these, what appear to be separate loves exist in truth in life on earth it propels the love of others in truth. Otherwise you have rules about love.

## PRUDENCY
Be prudent to yourself, for when there is prudency towards self hence others.

## PURE INTENT
Pure intent with no motivation but love, how do you know what motivation is in love? When you care not what is returned to you. When your returnance is in knowing that you have given from heart for intentions of love. How do you know again?

You know when you can walk away and want nothing. For real. When you can forget that giving, onto to finding when you receive the love that comes in receiverment, it is open in heart and grows you in greater love of self hence of others. Love, truth and purity. How does a soul know? It knows. When love, purity and truth are not present it is known.

When there is something done in outcome of thinking. "If I do this, then this will happen," what happens when the soul does not receive the "then this will happen?" If the soul is in happiness without the outcome that is pure intent for the intentions of doing are of growth.

If you need an outcome, that is the fastest human way of knowing you are looking for something to make you feel better. And with that you are saying that you do not feel good "unless." Your intentions are self motivated and not in purity. And when the outcome is not what you want then angers and self doubt set in. You will know that your intentions were not pure.

Pure intent tells you that the outcome does not matter. It matters that you did your best and left it up to the universe to give you what is yours and what is not was not meant. That control breeds angers and control takes away. And giving up control is the ultimate of control in truth; to let go of wanting is to let in of pure intent.

Pure intent is fought for in mind, heart, body and soul. And when a soul takes away its ability to know its own intent, it opens the avenues for paths of growths in skewments to take place. All souls know when this is of happenings.

Glory be to God Almighty. For all souls know when their paths are not in heart. When they continue on paths of their heart's awayments, they lose sight of their own hearts contents!

It is of no surprise however when it becomes a way of life to live in this, settling can not happen. And the restlessness' of heart begin. And the lookings for a partner to fix what they could not begins. The partner may not be in the romantic senses however it is in mostment guised in this way. It can be in a friend, a mother, a father, a child, a sibling; someone to ease or deter from the road of self path onto the path of others.

The soul that is lost looks for validations of their losses and goes to others to validate their actions. If they go to wise souls it startles them for the wise soul will tell them the truth they do not want to hear and they will discount that soul. If the soul goes to someone who agrees with them, they will stay there, for they were in pacific mode, not in the mode of hearts solvations! Glory be to God Almighty.

And we are coming back to the solvations; to the soulutions of soul, to the openings of thoughts, to the giving back of purpose. The lostments are so far past they are not recognized as lostments in this time, in the timed livings of missions on Earth.

And missions come to home in incompleteness'. Souls at home who come in recentnesses in times of past say this to be not known to them on Earth. Glory be to God Almighty, for help is on the way.

## PURE LOVE
One ounce of pure love will overcome any obstacle provided it is pure. If anything else arises know that pure intentions were not present! Pure love wants to share itself; lack of love wants to claim.

## PURITY
What is purity? It is simply to have self accounting as the thought process to what a soul chooses to do. To see how it affects, you, others, and why you want it to happen, be or exist. Purity asks you why you want it, need it, desire it, and it is the best you can do for yourself(s) in life on Earth.

It is a way of thinking. Purity is love in openness. All that is hidden, not told, withheld, not accounted for, left for others to figure out, left for souls to encounter hardship, sad feelings, loneliness, or brings troubles, is saying you care not of yourself or others. Insecurities and lacks of love in memory cause much of ill will. That is why ill will takes away.

That is the cause, the reason, and the unlessoned soul is the soul of ill will-ness. Ill will can not be of a lessoned soul. For the lessoned soul is the learner of souls. The lessoned soul is the one who understands the lack of existence of mistake, that all is as it should be. What am I to learn of this? How do I go on? Why did this come to me?

To understand there is alwaysment of bigger pictures and the microness of life is simply a way of saying that nothing bigger exists; that nothing is meant to be; that souls are only here with nowhere to go. How sad in thoughtedness' that there would be nowhere to go. How would that explain itself that this is it? And there are no balances on Earth without the love of home that speaks to souls through each other, gives from heart and leaves sustainess of entire being to come forth.

Souls on Earth are here to experience. When experience leads to lack of self love it is the goal of the soul to return to love. The soul can not return to love without purity. When purity is found life opens into a formation of hope. In the hope, the glory comes in sharing. Once sharing is spoken actions take place. And souls unite in growing in trust.

In those interactions there are questions. The questions that are answers with lack of purity take away from the soul, then the group of souls. When the questions are answered with purity there is growth in energy, physical and mentalness of souls. Glory be to God Almighty. It is so simple.

When purity is not present, neither is growth. Purity is so important, intent is so important, truth is so jarring that it has no way to go other than to band together.

Purity is a weed killer of life. You live in a garden and purity keeps all the wild growth out. The wild growth without knowledge of intention stops the vegetables from bearing growth.

On Earth souls do not know what to do with purity. They say they look for it however they do not recognize it when it is present. They say they look for it and when it is undeniable in facement of souls they want to take away from it. To put it away, for then accounting does not have to happen.

Love is peace. Peace is love. Love is God and God is love. Love is tender and calms and grows garth. For purity is the way in. Purity travels, does it not? Purity is the traveler of galaxies on Earth and all planes. Purity takes you home and in the moment of passing, for each and every soul on Earth is their greatest truth, love and purity before them.

## PURPLE
Purple penetrates the soul's soothings of holdings of contentness and love of self to flourish and solvations of mind and heart join. Glory be to God Almighty. There are significance's and beauty and purpose in all things.

## PURPOSE
Souls will ask themselves and others, what is my purpose? Why am I here? Why am I not special? The gifts of souls are the soul's gifts and the gifts are overlooked and can not be seen. The compromisations of souls can only happen when the soul itself says it is welcome. That is in taking responsibilities for actions, for the whys of a life on Earth.

And then the soul can say "this is who I am. This is where I start." To not speak truth to oneself is to say, "I do not love you enough even to know you. I am sorry soul, I will not be able to take care of you, so I will just use the body that I am in and I will go home when I am done here. Until then, I will be on pause." And then nothing is felt in entirety.

Souls need love. Tender love. Tender care. You can not change souls. Give them love and the love will touch them. The love will allow for their souls to ease and to open. Some will anger at you for loving, for they want to love. They do not know how to do it and they will want to be better than it. Run, do not walk away. Energy precedes words and actions. The hearts speaking's when in purity is the heard heart.

## QUESTIONS
All questions have answers and all answers breed greater questions. Let the questions come, for the intrigue of the mind keeps the soul alive. Never let up on the energy of love and its measurements to nothing else in the universe. There is no movement without love. Love is pure energy. Simple, and in all guided service love is the mover of the universe.

## REASONS AND ACTIONS

The motivators come from pain in some fashion or another. From disappointment in love, for expectation is present. From a happening that went unresolved, for intentions were not in solvation, they were in being right.

If only the soul can hear itself it would know in alreadyment that it sounded like it was building a case to be seen as being the "right" party and validation in that way without the intention to solve.

The holdings of wanting things to be perfect however can they be perfect without the open hearted intentions along the way? Do people wait for perfect to be perfect? If perfect means love, can it already happen and not have to wait for its turn in solvement? Glory be to God Almighty!

So peoples turn to other corners of solvement rather than the truth of the matter. They turn to medications, alcohol, behaviors that take away, holdings on to angers and internal refusal to solve a problem however an acceptance to take it on and try to fix it rather than solve it. That is the core of issues faced by human peoples. There is an ego driven need to fix things, anything, rather than solve it from heart and grow on.

There are no clear cut paths of solvations. Peoples are that scared to choose the truth of matters. They would much rather not face their own truths and take away themselves, their partners and eventually their families. And it will look like reasons that seem of truth. However, they will be entirely of other reasons of truth that originated years before the happenings.

Emotions of what is thought of to be love and the Thoughts of what money is supposed to do and to be are the greatest downfalls of human peoples. Emotions unfounded and thought to be of foundation. Yet relationships sought out from points of weakness in heart, not in strength of wonder in intent, they take all down a road of hardship and no found glory.

It appears to be of glory and the participating souls believe in their specialness. The desperation of specialness will create it. Until their own truth begins to nag at them it will carry them at some point in them trying to revive it. It is the escape and it will remain so until it begins to destroy those in aroundment of the souls in participation.

Searching for love in places where actions are taking away and the souls believe they are giving to themselves at those times. You call it affairs, you call it cheating. We already know that cheating is cheating self. Do not use and bring in another soul to encounter the death of yours. It will only bring and add weight to your back in life.

You will carry it like an open wound and your times to be involved in it will cause yourself and all those involved into a mountain of unrepairable troubles, for the truths will take a lifetime to unbury.

Relationships end, not due to the acts of sexualness however to the lies and the stealings of time. And the stealings of mind that carry along much in the process of taking away.

Spouses, kids, friends, all will take a back seat to the new addiction and when that addiction begins taking away it grows more and more. As does and would any other addiction that is made to erase pain rather than the healing of it. Nothing is as it seems. Nothing can be. The mind of humans is here to take in growing and solvement.

There are many ways to go and to solve the issues and happenings of soul. The key is; remember Love, Purity of heart, Truth in trueness of actions.

When there is clairity it is known and when there is not there are tensions, anxieties, fears, worries, doubtment of self and then of others and the patterns of lying are set to take place.

Like a person ready to run a race to the finish and the finish is the finish of the soul at hand, the souls involved and the way in which life was trusted is gone. And the way in which the future days of the souls involved need healment. And in most cases there are angers that are unresolved, for how do you resolve such angers?

Most carry them into other relationships with friends, family, work places and all facets of life. Then it is known to that person that that person can not trust itself. And those around these souls learn that you can not trust in others. At the conclusion of suchness it is done. And all souls affected will stay together in angerment or they will dissipate and share those pains and angers elsewhere.

The truths of life give a freedom of life around it. The alienation of truth will alienate those around it. So simple. So freeing is the truth of self. For then it can carry into the world of others. Many times truth in teaching takes place when the knowing soul ceases in actions and lets the soul of ill intent recognize that they are not dealt with due to their intents of ill will.

How does ill intent look? It comes in anger, resentment, conditions, pushing's of others into being who they are not, wanting to hurt those around the situation, lack of carement of others and looking for fulfillment of self only, wanting to be valued at the cost of others, wanting to bring in problems at the same discussions of solvement, leaving it to others to take care of things and taking no responsibilities within self of doing so.

Not seeing responsibility of self, blaming others without the true wanting of soulutions however wanting to keep the problems alive and well. Truth calms all. Lack of truth stirs up all things and gives them life in which grievemnents conclude. It is what life has become; it is not of what life is.

Life is choices and these are choices. Imagine if the choices were to develop talent, learn newness of things, rather than repeat patterns. Taste the newness of different lives rather than gravitate to the sameness of things. Work in pleasure and share energies in growth. There is a reason for all things. Never think it not.

## RECIPES OF LIFE
The recipes of life, there are a few and one of them is honesty. The other is pure intent. The other is truth. The other is learning lessons. The other is love. All go back to intent in your hearts heart and all others will happen.

## RELATIONSHIPS

God is of everyone, for everyone and of each soul in its own frame of mindness on Earth. There is internal connection of all souls that came down in human form to experience.

For in them they do remember that they all knew of each other in some thread of consciousness. It is hard to learn of others without giving to them, without sharing of service between each other.

That is why the lack of giving grows cynicism in souls. Those who do not give truly do not know how to receive. When they receive they receive with only thinking of self. And motivation of others for them is the self motivation of aliveness. How could they know? For the human mind all things are of projection.

The way in which the world is seen; it is seen through the experiences of that very soul. Those who seek others are not pleased with themselves. However, it looks that they are so pleased with themselves and that they are thinking so highly of themselves, they can get and seek others to come their way. However, breaking bonds that the soul makes is what happens, only to that self.

Seeking to compliment the ego of the human soul is what is happening. To reestablish worthiness and to reestablish that part of the soul that is looking for internal validation is truly the source. Remember that sexualness of the human body is only as the emotional state of the human mind can dictate and be. All things are emotional. For all things are driven by heart and mind. Nothing is done without it.

Intent of heart and mind drive all other factors. Many think false highness of their soul's ways and carry that with them into others and use them to nourish their false highness internally. Both will be aware of this at some level however it is acted out in physical form. For that physical form in the ways of peoples is an outlet for that thinking.

Truly it is lack of esteem. The doers think it not however in reality it is pure lack of esteem. It is not of physical. There is always, always something to be accomplished emotionally. A sore in some state of soreness that carries souls into thinking it is sexual. Since making emotional is so easy and convenient to over look. Glory be to God Almighty.

People are interested in others lives of sexual, for they are looking for the answers as to why. You would think to yourself that if someone, anyone, wanted to have relations outside of the relations they have then why have the original relation. It is egoness. It is fear of not feeling, as though your measurements to and in the societies in which peoples live will not be measurable.

What is the first thing peoples think when they hear about what you call cheating happening? They think and know that those peoples were of unstableness. It is different in fantasy than in reality. The reality tells you who you are and the fantasy tells you who you think you are. In their deepest senses they are running away. It is a form of self sabotage to want to inject new souls into your force of development.

There is nothing done without feelings; Great feelings or of despair. It is a sign that what exists around the soul of injecting, that soul wants to walk away from at some level. It is a rebellion of heart to the body in which it accompanies, for not being prudent to itself. It is not of sexual.

Sexual is the release, as is eating too much to hurt the body of the soul, or to cushion it from the hurts of the world, or abuse to curb the hurts of childhoods, or the violence lashed out to yet unleash other pains. Just because it is of sexual nature, an element of a few moments of a physical satisfaction accompany it, so it is masked from pain and looks to the naked eye like pleasure.

However, it is not of such and it is no different than any other self betrayal that can happen or take place. The unrested souls are looking for other unrested souls and that is a sure find on Earth. For nothing is as it seems, nor is it as you may think it! Glory be to God Almighty.

## RELIGION

People have religions and the religions do not talk about souls they talk to the souls. There is a lack of path of naturalisity from what is told to how life is lived and viewed. Yet it is taught as truth of how souls should be and there is nowhere in the world they could live in guidance of what is taught.

There are many motivates when skewment occurs and there is love and purity in love of God Almighty. Religion has become love accompanied by rules, too many to remember and even more difficult to live by. Not that Religion is wrong, for there is not wrong, nor right, it is an avenue to reach, to touch, to path souls onto one.

When Religion can not do this, the challenges that come with ownership of Religion turns souls from love to murders in many forms, upon which they can not even explain. Religion becomes the replacement for angers that Religion may have caused in the first place.

I am not speaking to hurt or take away from Religion. I am speaking the misuse and motivational causes of Religion to camouflage human emotion that does not have a safe outlet hence Religion is used to divide and conquer, to separate and give ego reign.

It has become a place of sanctuary by those who love God Almighty and Understand. And a place of usury by those who have motives and use Religion to cover motives that have nothing to do with God Almighty and have much to do with Ego and Self Righteousness.

As souls stand before God and they say they did it "for Religion," that is not truth. They did it for ownership of Something that is not theirs, it is the world's, and they were born into it and they fight for it, separate for it, claim for it, treat others better than others because of it.

And they begin to believe they are the only ones that God Loves, which in itself takes away from God as One, for All. God is not divided, souls are divided. And Religion is the divider.

So I speak, What about religion? It is time to examine what souls have in common and respect those differences.

Muslims are not bad peoples of this time; they have resources on their lands. Their lands have brought attack to non political people and forced them to act in defense of their heritage, their religion. Their ways of life made fun at, simply to take away their humanness, so that others can steal from them under the name of their own religion and take the believers of God Almighty to ensure that they have followers to allow them to steal.

And now the others kill in the name of religion so the co-mingling of issues ensures and it has nothing to do with God, it simply has to do with resources and ownership. So the liar will speak "we must fight for religion and for God," and the purpose is to steal at times.

No one can say what the current issues are; they can only feel it, simply because it is not spoken in truth. It is deterred and sent down another road, until the truth can surface and the thief has time on its side to take on others in their quest.

And when all is accomplished, they come back to religion to speak, God is Great. Allah is their God, Buddha is their spiritual growth, and souls are now in creation of what may work since they are finding it hard to live in what hasn't been working, for now there is complete chaos of life on Earth and souls are searching in desperation to further themselves in life, with all the ill will that takes on forum to the mainstreams of masses of souls.

## RESEEDING

The pure intented feel not the threats of life, they feel the strengths. Glory be to God Almighty. All souls have choices. All souls can hear, see, think and feel. How they choose to do that is their choice entirely. Glory be to God Almighty. It is their choice entirely. That is why you are to run, not walk away from those who's thoughts and actions bring to them troubles and to others.

That is why you can choose to run and not walk away. They make a choice to hurt and you can make a choice to not accept. They make a choice to lie. You can make a choice to no longer accept their words. They make a choice to take away. You can make a choice to give; to give to yourself the gift of knowing who they are and reseeding from that soul. Reseeding: Meaning to plant the ways of love where it is accepted.

And the others will learn when they have come to making a way, a choice for themselves that will do that. No one can do that for another soul.

## RESTLESS SOULS
Nothing is ever over to the restless soul. To know truth is the freedom of any soul in existence. To understand one's soul within truth is the adhesive of the trials and challenges posted to each and every soul on Earth.

## RHYTHM
The work of God is in quiet and in love. To be in tune is to know and to feel. And the rhythm becomes a dance in which you can't lose your step or turn the wrong way. For the bigger picture is always in sync and the smaller screens of free will drive it in direction however not in purpose. Purpose remains in love. All remains in love and will forever be!

Love rules all of movement on earth, physical, emotions, and natural. People's movements if left to natural would do what is prudent within. It is more unnatural to go in the direction of complication and that is the confusion you witness and see. You always know when someone is natural inside. You always know when that rhythm exists however when you witness going against the rhythm, you see internal unrest.

## RUDE
Rude is what ugly is. Nothing else. It never matters what a person looks like or thinks they are. Being rude is the worst human trait of all. It leaves souls in not knowing what else to do.

## SECRETS

Those who need secrets, "only telling you" of truths, who need to build confidences and alliances, are not of seekers of truth. For truth is told in candor and truth. There is no other way. To have secrets of what you really feel in politics, family, friendships, workers, remember that energy precedes physicality's.

There are no secrets in truth. Those who have secrets, who speak half truths, who pretend truths, who do not speak in completeness', who say, "I will be honest with you," your thoughts immediately say, "Who are you not honest with?"

Or those who say, "Let's come up with a plan and not say what the plan is," it will be in forefront of the receivers mind that there is a plan. If someone says, "Do not use that word, or they will know what you mean," is it the lie of the word? Thoughts are energy and carry with them weightments greater than words.

Those who seek advice, ask them why they seek it? Do they seek it to spew themselves into greater acknowledgments of masturbations of mind and take not the actions to unskew their thoughts? The thought of the human soul precedes the physicality of actions.

Time is the best teacher. Time will tell souls on Earth all truths. From the tiniest conversation to the largest of forums, lacks of truth are truly known before any words or actions are taken in by the receiving souls on Earth. No truth can hide itself. It can sit in hiding until all energies come into recognitions of souls to the energy. It always happens.

There is no truth unknown. All truths are known. All lacks of truth are felt. It is the way it is. It is the openings of all worlds and the closing of many. It is the avenue of hearts in growth and the avenue of usement in hearts of lacks of truth.

## SEEK

Seek and you will find; and all the avenues of your adventures will come to your seeking. Like the call of God Almighty to the souls of Earth, for the remembrance of God's love frees all and balance becomes. So simple. For life on Earth has taken away purpose. And purpose breeds questions and questions bring answers and answers grow freedom.

## SEEKERS

Truth is truth. Truth does not win nor does it lose. Truth is truth. Truth does not want nor does it create, it simply is. Truth has not an ego, a mind, a soul. Truth is love and love is purity and all are absolute and all are of the universe. All are the standings of home. There is not an argument at home. There is immense love at home.

You can not be a seeker of life and not see life? You can not be a seeker of life and take away from life at the sameness of time. You can not be a seeker of life in words and a taker away of life in actions. You can not be a seeker of life and a seeker of ill will? Should I speak this again in another way?

You can not love and take away love at the same time. That is the overthrow of balance in this time. It can not be had and taken away at the same time. It can not be eaten and not eaten at the sameness of time. You either ate it or you did not. There is not an indecisive, I don't know, maybe, question mark.

Passive speakings stay put. They stagnate the thinker. YES, NO, I WILL, I WILL NOT have stand. Have garth in them. That is what attracts is truth. As I speak and I speak in endless of eternity, Truth is simply truth. There are not motives in trust as ego fights so diligently to let down the seeker of it.

Ego is not a friend. Ego is simply a catalyst of souls to endure their own motivations and the struggle of heart and mind. It is the reality that souls of this nature exist, for it is painful to witness the agony of another soul and be the target of them as well.

For what is a soul to do? This is the core of conflict after conflict on Earth; Souls who take on other souls to give them the sadness that they are.

To inflict pain to gain self perception. To inflict conflict to give their pain a name. To inflict takings away to say that they are not the only one's taken away from. To gather company in pain onto another. To gather together ill will in return to continue the pain that is now habit to live within. To gather ill will to say that ill will is done unto them to simply live in ill will. It is a game of the mind not of the heart and there is not a game based on truth.

The point of a game to is win. To take on the means to win. To think of how to win. What it means to win. What it takes on to feel like a winner and the soul does not prepare itself otherwise. It matters that souls can leave with the strings of love of self in truth. Love in endurance of a soul unto itself. I am giving you the thoughts of truth that are of you.

There are not winnings, earnings, when it comes to life on Earth, there is love. I say this again, there are not winnings, earnings, when it comes to Earth. There is Earnment. What can a soul win that it can not find within itself? What can a soul not have on Earth that it does not want?

Speak of love and you will find listeners. Speak of hope and you will find love. Speak of love and you will find angerers. Speak of love and some will say you are silly. Speak of love and others will see it as their strength. For only those who see love as their own strength will understand the worth and value of speakings of love. God will not let down a seeker.

## SELF ACCOUNTING

Where does a soul start? It begins with self accounting and there is no other way to truth. If a soul can not see itself how can it see the soul of another? For then it will be what they want from others without regard to who the soul is. It will be what they look like that is important; how much money they have; what they can do for you.

Otherwise they are out of the picture. That is usury, which is a form of self hatred, to use another person. To acknowledge to self that that is what you are doing is to never be able to do that again.

That can only come from self accounting. To say, "I did this or that," gives you a peek as to who you are and why. Why you? Why not another doing those things? And the questions that are asked in self accounting are of growth and paths of love.

When self accounting is not present, self motivation(s) have a home. For then it is simply in circles of circles of thought, of the soul alone, in manip-ulations of the world in which they live. To get and achieve what they want alone, without regardation of other souls and that is how one soul affects another.

It brings internal sadness yet souls do not have time to explore. So they go on in their day and they understand that that is how other people are. And those that can not see believe everyone is of this way.

Never to worry, for God will guide. And for those who listen they will grow. And for those who can't hear they will spin their wheels until they can hear. So simple that life is yet without the simplicity, the complications of mind, the insecurity of souls gives to them behavior even they themselves do not know how to handle.

To believe all is in one's hands is too much to bear, for most souls want not the responsibility of oneself hence the block to self accounting. Self accounting is taking a look at your own role in your own life.

## SELF HONESTY

Human souls are in contrivation. The goals that each soul has are to do things that put the soul in the moments of life present. The souls want to be accepted, loved, cherished, acknowledged, cared for, caring. However, those feelings are difficult to ask for, to verbalize, so the honest of needment is not present.

So the soul looks for ways to cover up such needs. It looks for camouflaugment to say to the world, to loved ones, "I don't need you, I am well on my own, look, others, I am well on my own." And that looks like a soul that is detached and doesn't really care and sometimes it looks like the soul cares much and helps in activities of life around. Glory be to God Almighty. Souls rest.

You can say you love, need love, cherish, need cherishment, acknowledgement, acceptance. For then the honesty of such requests rests your soul, rests the souls around you. All pure intent can be dealt with. It is the camouflaugment that is hard and difficult and convoluted in dealings, in happenings, for then pure intent is off far away from the soul!

## SELF IMPORTANCE

No one soul is more important than another. Knowing of souls is the growth of life. Choices are the path of free will. Free will grows or takes away. The way in which love is learned affects all choices. And the choices affect all peoples. All are of each other and each other are of all.

The energy of love is unquantifiable. That is why it is not on the scanning of any form of science. Yes, all things can be proven through science however science can only prove the seen. The earth is run by the unseen. By the energy of love, the ranges of love, from the deviations and lacks of love to the strengths and propellments of love. Love can only have the ranges that human souls give to it.

In truth love is pure and in propellment always. If the energy of the human soul is ill intented, then love will propel into that growth of experience. If love is given the energy of pure intent then love will grow in the path of propellment in evolution. Love is the force, the movement, the honor of all energies.

When love is not present it is immediately known. It is felt and it can not be shaken off. When it is not present, no soul wants to be present as well. Those that are present are the examples of lacks of love and carryment of suchness.

For souls at times do not know when there internal operation is based on lacks of love. They want to feel love however they want to control it as well. There is no way to love other than to love. There are certain people, places or things. There is love in everything. It can be seen by those who feel and know love of self.

Otherwise, the things, the places or the peoples are what is important and not the love of truth. And that is where the mishaps begin; the emptiness in loving things, only some peoples and places, leave the soul with conditions on self.

Those conditions on self carry the soul into a loneliment, for then they believe some souls to be more important than others and they learn to ignore souls on the basis of self importance.

There is no soul of greater importance of another. And when souls are in treatment of such there are lacks of sincerity, lacks of love of self, lacks of honor and self truth. That is much to say for treating souls in difference because of who they are perceived to be.

The motivation is to be part of, liked by, important to self by means of outsideness. And the inside is left to ask the soul, "Why do you believe that you will be better through another?" You are an important soul, as all souls come with the gift of life and love and the lessons of home.

Importance on Earth has given way to status and separations, as does religion, race, background, beliefs in political areas, in moral areas. These stresses and differences have to exist to exercise the mind into growth; If a soul can want to be loved, cared for, needed, then why can not another?

To do otherwise comes as a self loathement unto others, for you can not give what you do not have. Souls carry in them the wanting of what they believe they want. Within that they start to choose the souls they seek to get what they want. That soul may come to them time and time again and they will not be seen, for they will not be deemed as important.

For with souls who look for self importance, every day is a new day. The love is in spurts and the souls that are within the closeness to the souls of self important, they are judged in each day as though the day before did not exist. The history is looked at as proof of relationship however it does not bond the relationship.

It is proof for the self important to say, "It has been this many years, we did this and that" however the bondment of that history could be walked away from in an instant, for it had no value.

For the self important value not love they do not have for the self. On the other side of this worlds self importance is that the self important soul will help those in need, for the recognition of doing so. And when a soul around them is flourishing they want to take away from them, for now there is no longer a means to control them.

This is the trickier of the two, for the soul that was helped grew trust and then gets turned upon without warning. And trust for others is affected by a soul with pure intent hence the shapings of lacks of love begins.

When a soul is parented by a soul of self importance, these are the souls as adults who are in losement of their own worth, for they have not the foundation(s) of love in purity.

## SELF FAILURE

Love is the purity of heart, the meaning of truth, and the grandeur of soulutions. With truth there is not a search for soulution. With truth there is not a loss of what to do. With truth there is a way, will be a way and there is no way in which it can not be!

For truth when absent causes all the other ways of insecurity to become! Self motivation is the greatest force of taking love away from self and then from others, disguised as love and caring and hope and then it transfers into a road that is hard to turn back from. It becomes a web of misguidment.

It becomes a path of helplessness, "Why am I here" thinking and finally it feels like self Failure and truly it is the only real emotion of the whole process. Now, only the lucky realize self failure and those that do not repeat. Most repeat, for the recognition of self failure is one of the hardest emotions to endure.

## SELF RESPECT

We are all faced with challenges. There will always be souls of growths, physicality's, of talents and of candors in life. That is to produce further growths. If all humans were at the samenesses of level there would be sheer boredoms of learnings and all existence is in alwaysments of learnings.

There are differences within the samenesses. The sameness of souls gives to them foundations of thinking and understandings of each other. The differences give to soul's interest and further growth patterns and learnments of growth patterns that are not of theirs. It opens the doors to all openings of hearts when the hearts are in earnestments of looking's. Glory be to God Almighty.

To have respect of your own soul and its doings, its happenings, its openings to self and in sharing with the universe of energies the soul is known and teaches respect of soul. Respect of soul speaks of a soul that that soul is in knowings of greater self on Earth. That is why it shapes the universe onto thoughts of givings, of learnings, of beings.

Self respect is of greatest love of self hence of others. Self Respects says of a soul, "That I understand there will be challenges before me. I understand that I have choices. I understand that there are other ways in which to do this however I chose this way."

Self respect takes into considerations the hearts of others and knowings of the ripples of affects of actions, of heart, of mind and of love combined. Self respect gives to all the example of love in purity of understandings of life's role on Earth. Of seeing and being in the higherness of self.

When you see it it cries your eyes to witness it. Souls can feel self respect in another of souls. And when the souls part, the souls can feel the penetrations of love, of caring, of trust and of all truths being, when encountering a soul of Self Respect. All things, feelings, thoughts that are in becoming of things, are felt by and within all souls to each other.

The body is not as significant as it is created to be, in order to make businesses flourish. Human souls truly do not respond to the bodies of another in sustainments. We read each other in heart first. That is what is called instinct on Earth. Some can respond to their own instinct and others do not hear it.

Women want to hear it and others do not. And instinct is either in makings of being a helper to a soul, or a hindrance when a soul is in self motivations and wants the workings of their doings to be of what they need from it and not having the trust in self enough to hear.

And in others they know right away that what is before them, who is before them, is not in their best of interests of heart or of mind. And Ego is present. You can call it Self Motivations. You can call it Ill Will. You can call it Meekness. And you know in an instant.

When the soul is in higher of self, in Self Respect, it responds to itself in truth, love and purity. When it is in Ego it responds to itself in self motivation and Meekness.

To know the difference is to live at home on Earth, to understand free will. To exercise free will. To carry the love of home on Earth is to live in Self Respect. And to take on the lower energies is to carry the self motivations. And Free Will is truly free in Self Respect.

## SERVICE
To teach, to example, to be of sustainment, to rise up and not come down to others, to speak of purity and intentions, to be in truth of heart in easement and in firmness is to example sustainment. To teach sustainment is from the consistency of building within the foundation of truth.

How does it begin? It begins in the soul wanting to put itself aside and think of someone they love. And that someone that they love is the self of the soul; to honor the growth within and the wanting to seek ways to grow.

When the soul begins to take away, to question itself, to see itself in truth; It is very difficult to look within, for many souls have accustomed to looking without for love. How do you open a soul's eyes to this?

They will know. It may not be of immediate however they will know. However, the opening of eyes truly begins with the letting go of expectations. To love as a child is to live without expectation. To go through illness in severity is to live without expectation. To self account is to live without expectation. The expectations of self projected take away in all situations.

The freedom of heart to do and not to expect is the rarest find. And to answer the question in entirety is to say, do service. That is how it all begins. To serve teaches humbleness and with the humbleness of service, the soul is seen outside of itself, and while the soul is outside of itself it can see itself. And when it can see itself it can balance.

And when it can balance, the cries that are felt and blinding become a part of the soul, not the soul in entirety; Hence the beginning of self in recognition; Hence the beginning of balance to do so; Hence the understanding of samenesses, differences, samenesses again. Glory be to God Almighty, for then the soul is on its way in truth.

When service is in happenings the soul can not think of itself in entirety! To not think of self in entirety breeds and paves space to think of others.

WE are here to serve each other. Imagine if instead of higher taxes for social programming that there were community service extensions. The taxes would not be needed to provide income for the underprivileged, the underpaid, those who can not take care of themselves.

Peoples would not need to work so hard to make more money, for the taxes would not be so great. They would not be needed as they are now and still in appropriation they are not allotted to all things and programs needed.

When there is community service there is true health. The learning's of people amongst each other will take place. The carings and the understandings of being a part of life and not the center of life take place. Monies are not needed to satisfy the ego and less things are needed. Simplicity happens without cause or tryings.

Life becomes more fulfilling and no medications for anxieties need to be had. However, the self motivations of money that can only have the energies of what is given to it propels and becomes. The teachings of love can only bring about love. How does a soul start? Service. And let the ripple effects of love begin. Nothing is as it seems.

To be of pain is to be of service. It brings to light the higher self, the greater energies, for the soul must step out of itself in yet another way and that is to accept service. To give of service and/or to accept of service teaches self love, self acceptance, self beginments of growth. Earth is looked at as a commodity. Back to expectation, all souls have expectations put forth on them because of love.

Yes, there are knowns of Love. Love does not hurt, maim or disfigure. Love is given and when given in purity it can only grow, there is no other alternative. When love does not grow it begins to take away for the intentions of souls carry love. Souls give love life. It is present however if it cannot be seen, then it can not be felt, if it can not be felt, it can not be had, if it can not be had, it can not be shared. And the separations of attachments begin in dissipations.

That is why children are so happy. They only know of love, for their intentions are to play and to learn. When their protection is of wearing offment, they can see of what they have known in difference, and the challenge of recognizing, knowings of, sharings of love begin. And the taking away of protection leads the mind to question and to look within.

That is the preparations of growth. For then the child, who is now of age in teenment is looking for answers to questions. And the search of love begins. The happenings of how love is coming into and what it does in action and in heart are what the soul becomes through honement.

Love is needed as nourishment of heart and mind. In simplicity it is stated and in difficulty it is recognized, and in easement then it is lived. I come back to service. To work with another is to understand that soul. To stand beside another is to open energies to exponentiate. To live in truth is to teach self and others greater energies.

The absence of truth is lower energies in search of excuses and not answers. It is easily seen however the cries of the soul lead to blindness of the mind. For the truth remains itself no matter what time in history it is. The truths of love have been known and will continue in its quest of growing the human soul to it.

## SEX

What is sex? It is a sharing of love. So simple. Yet on Earth it is a marker of vitality. It is a way of saying, "Yes I am desirable. I am wanted and I want. I am cared for and I care." Yet in soonness, in no loveness, it follows another course. It carries within the soul settlement and begins to skew love. How could love be and then be gone so quickly and easily?

That is the question of heart, when the quickness of events becomes one party losing the meaning or the picture of life as they thought it to be. And Settlement gives way to desperation. For then it is not why you act on sexualness, it is to whom. Someone, anyone, and that way a soul at least knows they are viable.

Those who carry pure intent will attract pure intent. And those who carry self motivation will attract and carry the same. Some who sexual soon, will tend to leave soon, for the sharpening of time is gone and absent. The loss of sharing of time gives way to emotional abandonment. The saying of after will be, "I was with that person however who are they?" As the discovery is made the rejection takes place.

To see the soul of internal without the connection of external is of backwardness of human connections. Build stories, relations, foods in sharing and walks in parks. Build experience, as you do with yourself in heart. And as the heart grows the flowing of the body is natural. Can you eat a fruit before it is ripe? It looks beautiful and yet you can not eat it until it is time. That is true for all things, of all things in life.

Some use sexualness to bring back to. Yet by then to say you love someone and not be with them means that your love in heart has changed and in body will have had to follow. You can love them, for time gives the balance of heart however in body, the love was a passing love and not a permanent sharing. It existed for the growth of both souls to carry them to the next evolution within their souls.

Yet some do not move forward and hold on and try to retain the relationship with the sexualness and therefore claim a relationship that is not there. That is of desperation as well. The desperation of non movement of onness is due to lack of belief in future of soul and fear of belief that the soul is able to have faith in itself. So peoples settle. They believe sexualness signifies a relationship and it does not.

Time, experiences, time again, trust, attractions of heart, that carries souls onward, in life, in works, in relationships.

You can not have sex with God however you can love him. That is true for all things in life. There are no separations. That is why many question love for God. What can God give to them? Why should they carry something that they can not see, hear or feel?

Why should they carry that kind of love when it will not bring them sexualness that night or ever? They want what is now, an immediate reward of existence. An immediate validation of who they are.

Yet the sharing with such a soul is sharing with emptiness in ultimate and the staying is no longer. The wanting is no longer. For the love of God is the trail of all paths. Self motivated love and loves can not carry a soul.

Self motivations in monies can not carry a soul. Self motivations in things can not carry the things. You can walk into a home of what looks like smallness and live in the love that exists within it. And you can walk into a home of vastness and you quickly understand that it means nothing. That is why.

It is all so simple. And all of this applies to sexualness however the human eagerness of validation has taken away many of the pleasures of soul that are multifaceted and gives to it one facet. You can still do it however learn the wonder, for the gifts come through intent. The gifts look like gifts on Earth however they are simply the rewards of intentions.

When a soul can understand itself and its actions; that is gift that is reward. For love is of greatest of reward and openness on Earth. It is the calmness of heart in approachment. So simple and so open a heart will be. So simple and open love can withstand.

When a soul is told how to show love the very love they are to show is diluted. To feel love is to feel body. There is release in moment however love carries and takes further. Not in constant startings however in continuous openness of knowment of another's hearts and its content.

The depth of soul is the purity of knowings. In purity, time becomes non existent. In purity, days are in continuation of life. There are not stops and startments of time. And in heart there is no limit.

Much is stopped before the endlessnesses can be known to a soul. And that is also part of the lack of fulfillment souls have in their lives, in their own hearts. Not digging deep enough to touch what lives inside and outside of the soul(s). The depth is what carries. It is of home on Earth.

**SEX AND LOVE**
Let me tell you why sex is a marker for all. As I can hear in your beautiful mind, you think of sex as special. For most it is not sex. It is conquering what they can not in themselves. Let me speak to you how. Sex speaks that there has been intimacy, which tells the soul encountering that there is something special there.

What happens in times now on Earth, sex is easily available. There are many seekers so the seekers do not have to seek too far to have sex. So they do not discriminate as to what is important to them or not, for they have nothing to lose, they can just walk away.

In most cases one of the two parties looks at it as intimate and the other looks at it as release. So what happens? Trust erodes. Abandonment roles in, ego wants to prove and the search is on for not making that mistake again. And the taker, well the taker is actually more empty than the one who gave with some heart attached.

However, there is great soberment to heart and to soul when two souls meet and very quickly they are unclothed, for they are showing intimacy without intimacy. They are saying, "I am here but not for long." If either of us wants to make something out of this, it is of greater challenge to go back and speak the building blocks, if the structure looks already built. It is in harshness to build stories and homes, for all the gifts of the soul were presented without the gifts.

Each and every soul knows of this who has encountered these moments. They do not understand why the one of the souls will not want to speak to the other.

And it is the soberment of soul. It is the reflection to the human soul that seeks to truth to say, "I push my own truth aside, for this is suppose to be fun and then I come to find it is and has taken away from my stance as a person to myself in being able to connect and stay with souls for times of length. I don't know how to develop me, so I will replace my development with my body. And the body is saying, I can not feel you heart, how does it feel without me?"

And the heart speaks in growth that the body needs the heart to feel. To wander unto the surprises of ones truth through time, rather than moments and that is where the feelings of one not attaching and another doing so. It is self desertion. That is why you feel bad to hear that a child simply wants to have sex without thought to the partner, simply because of the very reasons of self desertion.

Again and Again, it is not the sex. It is the personalness that comes into the forefront of sharing one's soul and trying to behave as though the soul is not involved. That is a greater internal shaking than all else. How many souls will openly speak, "I slept with so many." Even the men that imply it, most are implying it and it is not of truth. No one is spared the desertion it feels to give to many without heart. For the heart requires more.

It can not know of its own requirements if it has not had the chance to develop them. Most souls believe that requirements are that a soul can take care of themself, they have a car, a home, things things things. However, the sharing of your heart when it is your heart speaking is the carrier of love.

Many may think they are in love and they try to prove it with body however the body can not prove anything. The body can only follow the mind, ego or heart. It has no other choice. It will try to stop you, it may disease you, shake you, try to warn you in some way that you are not in your heart. It will do that however that is only reaction to a souls furthers from home.

Some will love those that they do not have sex with, for they will honor the honor those souls have of themselves and they could possibly have a love that will carry forever from that respect of self that was in exhibited. Those are the souls you can clairly go back to without repercussion, for trust is already established and you also find that you did not need the relationship in that way. And that is why some feel it is "pure" not to have had sex.

They are really saying, I did not betray my heart with you and you did not betray yours with mine and we found that we know each other in truth and we are not of meant to be anything more or less. These are the originations of thoughts of actions of reactions.

Those who use their bodies to take others away from others have truly grown within the greatest betrayal of self they will ever know. Most will never ever want to do it again and those who continue are speaking that nothing matters to them that they have or they hold, for they do not matter to themselves. They are taking their own body and separating from heart.

If a man is cheating with a woman, what kind of man in truth would betray now himself first and another second. The recieving person can only recieve the betrayal and try to say but the sex is great and in truth, her own self worth is so low to participate in such betrayals that they are a pair who will never trust each other under any terms, no matter what they say about doing so.

It can not be, for the origination was of the greatest betrayal. And If a women takes on other men, her heart will shut down in ways that turn her into a scoundrel of self for the lies of self that have to happen to carry out such actions are all of self loathments as well as self mutilations and the mutilations of others and the destruction of the trust of not only self, the partner and the home.

The ripple affects are worse for the soul than the foundations of suicide of taking on medications for relief of life or drugs of acceleration of mind and stagnation of self and soul.

Souls have come to using sex as a weapon. With beauty to entice, in ways that they would only do for someone a soul is in truth of love with, for everyone.

I am not speaking that sexualness is not of beauty, I am speaking to the whys. Just as a man will carry around the keys of his car, women carry their breasts and now we are in the stages of foolments of breasts. And the minds are so far away from the body that it does not matter of truth, it simply matters of turn on, for once the turn on is off, all parties could walk away with ease.

Both will get further hurt for different reasons however all body parts are paid for with monies and does that mean that only those humans of syn-thetic bodies will have sex at some point? Where could it be going? Will everyone's eyes look open all the time without the evolutions of life spoken? Were the evolutions of life so horrible that we change our appearances in hopes of changing ourselves? The whys are the foundation misgivings of our world of Earth. You see, there is more. This has repeated itself in the history of humans, over and over again. It comes to a plateau, as Earth has come to now and souls can have sex, buy it, witness it and still not feel it. Souls can feel love not sex.

And they go to shows now where women take off all clothing's and wrap themself(s) around poles and bend over to show the inner makings of a body without a heart. Those souls find it in grave difficulty to have relationships with men and women.

And now as souls are in furtherments away from self, they are looking at the lure of this being in popular movements, for if someone will show you, you do not have to try and come to levels of grows with souls, you can simply use them, for show or purpose and leave and not be attached and those lacks of attachments ripple in the the rests of life. The desensitization's are forever.

Reclaimance of self is a rarity of heart, for the heart at times knows not where to start. They have programs now of the joy of it however not of the desensitization of soul to self. That is another orphanage of heart and it is of Earth in great dealments of souls at this time.

They tried increasing the number of souls involved, swinging, trading, same sex, mixed sexes, dressing like the other sexes and all of it has nothing to do with sex. They are barking up and down the wrong tree. They are not even on a tree they are in an ocean looking for a tree.

They dress like horses and other animals too and they have taken their bodies to animals as well. It is of the greatest deprivation on Earth and the greatest to overcome in the review of home. For a soul must transition to home once it leaves Earth and their witness to self has taken very low energies to re-evolve to home.

That is why souls snicker when they know of cheatments or they know of souls who are willing. That is why souls feel threatened from others with spouses, for there are many willing takers and it is of status of mind to encounter, only to find it was ego and not heart behind it and they now must content with this truth of self.

For these are things that on Earth can not be taken back. They are either evolved from or experienced. And the experienced in truth need to beware not of others however of self. For love is love and the tampering of love is never from the soul, the ego has reigned in these happenings.

Men looking for boys, it is not sex. It is submission of their own souls onto themselves. For they want to growth their souls by stealing and cheating the soul of another. They want to take away the manhood of a child to take away the child of their manhood. You see sex is not physical, nor a thing, it is a person, a soul. And possession of another's soul is the search that is onward for the souls of the injured and taken away from.

It is never physical. For if a penis is inserted into a male, a female, it is the same, for God giveth both physical gender the same side and reversed the other side, for how else can souls enter on to Earth. The balance is tipping the souls searching for the healing of wounds. And the attractions to the same sex is in truth the length of time it took for lacks of truth in life, for human souls to instinctively say, "I do not want life to continue."

The balances tip within the human souls of Earth when trust is replaced within lacks of love and those very lacks of love call for redemption and that redemption calls for the younger souls to be taken from for replacements. What is seen is the result of this. Men searching for boys is the illness of lacking to procreate, for they want to cease life and steal it at the same time.

The thoughts of the older men turn boys into them, turning them into older men one day, searching for younger boys however could there be younger boys if there were not balance and all souls did this? It could not be. What they are saying is that they do not believe in life. That life was not right for them and they do not want it to continue.

However, while they are on Earth, they do not want to be taken away from and they want to be in control and they believe it to be physical. It is not. It is pain. For most sexual relations on Earth come from points of pain, Sexual relationships that come from love become genderless our love. They are genderless. That is love.

For then a soul is a soul and it matters none if it is a woman or a man, a child or an adult of time. Illness is what soul's fear to hear. Fear to happen. That is the shock that peoples feel. That is the reason they want to dissect a story and feel its happenings. It is fear that their own illnesses will surface as well, as they too are not wanting for life to continue.

It is fear of extinction, which is why the current gay communities are feared and spoken of. In truth, it is the fear that they will grow and then who will procreate? If women desire the love of women and men desire the love of men and there is no need or desire to create onward, over time on Earth, instinctively souls will extinct themselves.

Peoples think it is sexual however it is in lacks of truth of the world, as we are living in lacks of truths to the extents that life should not be allowed to continue, for we are not prudent. Souls go to the sameness of gender in this mode of thoughts and want to build a life they can trust and that is a life that will not continue.

It is not a bad or a good, right or a wrong, that is really happening, it is the time of Earth, teaching the souls of Earth, they can not trust what they see and nothing is as it seems, nor as it is seen, and they will defy life by stopping it from continuance.

There are connections throughout of rejection of the world on Earth as it is. There is cohesiveness in human thoughts and behaviors that manifest and growth from lacks of love into trying to steal what they can from life and have no thoughts of the remounts of what they leave behind. Souls are trying to turn something that hurts themself, life and others into something that does not.

*(REMOUNTS—To align again. To go back and restart)*

It is about children, then the adults that affect them and then the adults that affect life, all from internal lacks of love, lacks of believence of life on Earth. Most souls simply want to sound good or take credit or give credit in ways that they do not mean it. They simply want attentions for being the good guys, the one who knows, who is trying, who is witty or bright. It is simply their way of being part of a world they do not believe in, when they do not speak in truth.

You see, truth, love, purity, is the essence of Universe. Anything that takes away from that is saying that on Earth without the remembrance or love of home, there is loss and how does a soul find the spark of home within and growth it? That is the purpose of Earth.

No matter the circumstance, whether it be loss coming to a soul, love coming to a soul, what lacks of love obstacles have come to them to over-come, to see the purity of love and truth within it. It is not that we are hearing about souls wanting the same sex for in truth there is no gender. Gender was about to simply procreate. Rejection of the opposite gender is to say I want life not to continue on Earth.

It comes from repeated killings of souls before, until this day. "Gayness" is not the only growth in numbers, as well, killings, usury, stealings, and hurt-ings with words and actions. It has all accelerated in the world.

Those who suspect others are suspicious. Those who trust not others are not to be trusted. Those who steal from others have already stolen them-selves. Those who speak ill will of others have already decided they are not worthy of love. Those who hurt others have already been hurt to know how to hurt themselves hence others.

Those who come with love can only see love. Those who come with love believe in those who do not come in love. Those who love do not feel the resistance of the lacks of love of others and they are the fuel of the universe.

## SEXUALITY

Development of body was consistent with development of mind however over time that has come to terms of changing. Now as the body is ready the mind is not in most cases of humans on Earth.

What you call sex it is not love. Nor is it love personified. It has been called all in error in beginning. It is not making love it is extending love. You can love another and never have sex and you can have sex and never love.

Love is not made. Love simply is. It is dilution of souls. That is what happens, never at first and never quickly. Dilution of souls is when there is much had with many souls and no connections. Then the connections lose their meanings and the physical self stores more energy in it as well and you feel like a body without soul attached.

For men in the world on Earth it is different. I have to say this and women tried to make it of sameness however men are of different. The male form has not the memory intensity of the counterpart, the female form. The female form carries great deals of home within her for she has to to nurture future human souls to earth.

For the female form to dilute itself dilutes in all areas of life as well. How could a soul know when the soul feels active and the activity that is taking place is activity that is taking away? It is difficult to tell the difference at times. The male and the souls that came to earth as males came to build.

Women think they do not get it however it is the reason for their existence. And they build breed. They are truly breeders. That means they breed and they sustain. They breed and they maintain. They breed love and expontiate love within the hearts of their surroundings.

Women are the feminine and they are best at it. Men are of masculine and they are better at it. When a male comes to Earth with more of home, he is in need of yet a man, for he takes on the characteristics of a woman.

And if and when a woman comes with great building within they tend to look for a female counterpart, for they need more of home. This is what you call Gay in your world however it is the levels of home that are present within the soul.

Again, it is nothing to do with Sexuality, although those in it will argue it, it is of truth. The sex is the fulfillment of the wanting not the need. Seeking out the other part of home is truly the need. There have been arguments in this regard and they are of falsehood.

Everyone came down to be who they are. No one can judge or rule that movement. It may not be the "normal" for now on Earth however is normal normal. Is love not known to its capacity as of this day? For truth is not understood in capacity at this time, so love and self accounting are not as well. It is on its way.

**SEXUALNESS**

Sexualness of humans is not in physical it is in emotional, All else takes away from the soul. The physical body does and can perform many functions. If a soul works and does not love their work, their work carries energy that is of lowness. If a soul speaks and cares not of what it speaks, the conversation is forgotten and not felt. If a soul eats a meal that is not its favorite food, the food that is eaten is eaten for the purpose of survival and the pleasure of the meal is not felt.

Friendships that cause foeness in action are not the same as friendship that is based on purity. Allure has become sexuality's foe. The channeling of the physical body in energy is not any different than all other energies in life.

It is hard for you to believe, for the human body reacts to pictures, peoples and things. However, the human soul works in glory in love. And without that present immediately after the acts of sexualness there are feelings of some dissatisfaction of self.

The heart knows it was shortchanged just as a body still wants a food of craving until it is eaten. All other foods will suffice however they will not continue to be sought after. Sexualness is a holding of a soul's knowings of self. Those who are in transition, those who are in a non love mode, can and do have much sexualness without the feelings of love attached.

At times souls believe they are in love at the time of sexualness. Some simply know it is the sexualness they are in soughtness. Some use it to hurt themselves hence hurting others. Some use it to get ahead of where they are with another soul. Some use it to

prove they are desirable. Some use it in cheatment and destruction. Some use it to pacify their soul's stance into believing that there is love present when it is not.

In every instance, in every time of the instances mentioned, there is a point of sadness within that this is how sexualness is sought after. There begins to build within the soul a lack of trust as to the ability to love. For it all comes back to love. IT ALL COMES BACK TO LOVE.

If and when any soul is present in these instances they will continue looking for a soul of love. The continuation tells the soul that there is more, that depth is needed, that love is in all of life not simply in body. It includes and will not conclude until such love is discovered by that soul.

A soul that works in a job to pay bills and take care of life as they know it, continues to look for a new job. They will train and go to school and move locations to work in a place of employment that they can enjoy the most. When there is love the companies succeed. When they are self motivated, they fail in operation at some point and continue to struggle in the operations. IT ALL COMES BACK TO LOVE.

When a soul is in a place of growing itself it will not remain in that stoppedness of soul. For the soul will always know of its own restment. Sexualness can only happen so many ways. It is not a deviation, it is not a pleasure always, it is not of hurtfulness always. It is not a weapon, it is not a bad, dirty, or cheapness of heart; it is an avenue of love.

It has been stopped by man to simply control the sexualness of the female soul. The female soul is the sought after soul of sexualness on Earth. However to have too many females is to lose sight of one. To have too many males is to lose sight of love, so simple in life to know of sexuality.

You would think that souls on their own without control would end up looking for love, for they would conclude all that is known by now. They could have easily. To know another soul in depth increases the beauty of Sexualness.

When a soul has many newnesses and no depth there is much missed. Any two souls can have sex. That is the foundation truth. Who can stop a body? The stopping of actions always comes afterwards.

However when there is relationship and discoveries are made of another soul in purity, the pleasures of sexualness propel as love itself can only propel. For the body is a source of great pleasures, much deeper than the surface of simple penetrations and danglings.

Yes danglings, for they are there however once picked in shortness of knowing another soul they do not grow back to be picked again. And regrow, for love propels. Love can only propel.

There are waves of soul's energies, the movements in which are present with different energies and how it appears in human behavior. Human behavior is not as grand in what can be seen. It is in the heart. It exists in the soul. For the soul carries all that it interacts with, does, happens, and the energies quickly discarded are those done with less heart involvement. The lesser the involvement the greater the soul is subjected to complacency.

When a soul can see love, all else that had love come in ways of deviations surface and all the love within the pure of heart surfaces. And life can be seen for what it is. What it is seen for gives the basis of going onto growths of other kinds. To live in blindness holds all in place with that soul even though the soul of another may have gone on in other ways.

To conclude on sexuality, notice that the writings of sexuality quickly move into conversations of pure intent, of truths, of passions and love for life. For sexuality, as all things that exist, is part of life, part of the balance, part of the mixture for souls to ontinue their entrances to Earth. So simple.

And the deviations come from deviations of love along the way of a soul's journeys. I conclude with the simpleness that anyone can have sexualness, for that is the naturalness of life on Earth for human souls.

Souls understand this. They know. They feel it. That is why the search is endless and tried for in such dignifiability of heart. And the self motivated they look not for love. They want possession to call it love. For then they can control it. And for the control they have lost it. If only the eyes of souls could witness themselves. To trust in self hence in God Almighty propels all. Glory be to God Almighty.

The teachings of life on Earth are written of, talked of, shared and exalted within. And the learning can never cease. For all the years of time, of peoples and there is still much to learn for the learning of souls is infinite. And the purity is known and the learning becomes the other side of life. And the living within life can only become grand even it its most challenged moments.

## SEX AND LOVERS

Not all eyes see the world in which they live the same. Not all eyes see themselves the same, see others the same. There is great need for compassion and love. For it is felt so rare that many have forgotten the feeling.

They know of the physical however the feelings that accompany the physical have detached somehow. It is interesting to me this detachment that I am feeling in souls. It is truly separate from a person, what is done physically and what is done mentally. I have been seeing an action and the complete opposite in thought.

It is boggling, if that is an earthly word to use, to see this. I am perplexed as to this intricate driver in souls that is malfunctioning. It isn't in the body of a soul that attracts. Truly it is not! Yet that is what is presented and yes there is a reaction however it isn't in the body.

Attractions are internal. Yet it is made to be external and that is where the detachment begins from oneself. Sex is a feeling of love shown, touched, shared. How could love be learned, shown? Love is fluid, a feeling. Sex is only an act without true love to be a part of, for then it cannot be sustained.

Do you understand? Sex, the word sex is titillating. However, people will use their bodies and detach their minds for show, for money, for the thought of achieving love through sex however you can't achieve love through sex. You can have sex through love and only then will it be felt.

That is attraction of heart, of purity of heart. For then the walls that exist come down and I am witnessing walls that go up in sexual contact. For the opposite is happening and that is the detachment, that even in a place of complete freedom, there is none. So is sex then an outlet? For what could it be? If even in the moments of solitude within souls there is not freedom, for then there is no freedom in anywhere!

Glory be to God Almighty. For Sex has been put in a position. And love has detached. It has been a show of skill and onset. For it remains an act of love, regardless of what is portrayed in the absence of true intent towards the soul of another. The meshing of souls is of strength. And sex without love brings about an internal weakness.

For sex is of beauty and gifted to souls however souls have taken the gift and turned it into a contest, a sale, a measurement, a marker, a determinant. For all it is is love. It is not a sin to fornicate. There is not such a thing as fornication. It is love. And with the absence of love it is different not necessary. Love is the critical point of life, of hope, of caring for it is all intertwined.

## SEXUAL ORIENTATION

All sexes have sexual orientations to all sexes; simply because love is love. The acting on these feelings sexually is a dealing that is made to man alone. There is no outcast of love when love is in its purity. Yet, there is not growing of souls without a sexual manifestation between a man and a woman however there have been rejections of a lifestyle rather than an orientation.

Humans will want to try anything forbidden to them. When there is created temptations that do not exist except on Earth. Souls come to Earth in balance of who they should be. Some come with greaterments of gender one way or another to live in that mission on Earth; to encounter it.

Now I want to speak to you of when souls are tampered with Early on. This comes to the souls from a soul they trust and has access to them. Of course there will be a feeling of good to them in these instances. There are women who track down girls or boys. There are men who track down boys or girls; there are children who track down each other.

This is all showing that at home there is not gender per say, and on Earth there is and it propels the confusions when a soul comes to Earth in greater energies than the gender it came to be. There is a great need for this catalyst stance. It is to break the boundaries of love and expand them; for families and for friends, co-workers, and world workers. It has now an attachment of shame as it always had however it is nothing new to the Universe.

All the universe entails is love. Humans are not passed their sexuality. That is why I speak of marriage in purity and what it means to love in purity, in truth and in love. A body does not know it is a body. A soul controls the body. A mind is designed to have information however it can only challenge the soul, for that is its job. There is choice and free will, want and need. There is love in purity and love out of pain.

Most love on Earth exists in pains of love; therefore the greaterments of souls can not see themselves as to why they are as they are. Souls on Earth look to love in this way as a love let down. Gayness' as it is called on Earth at this time is not a let down to love. For love can only be love. It is in measures of success and souls taking away from each other, to say one is better than the other. Sex is not physical. Shall I speak this again?

Sex is emotion; is soul. And when the souls speak to sex it is love and the body is the home of love only when the soul within can say it is in truth of love, Understanding of. Irrelevance of orientations is grand. It is a measure of openness that this is now something we have to see on Television in many first timements of showing this or showing that.

Gay souls are not animals to cage and explore. They are souls whose balance takes them to that direction to lesson all in love, for there are no mistakes. However the element of human shame can create and recreate many obstacles of growth. It feels as though souls say, "But this is against nature." What is nature? It is beauty and trees, love and truth, purity and honor.

There is no gayness. There is simply need for stimulations at this time that release souls from the usual duties of life and give to soul's forum to create their ownness of rules of life. You hear a lot of souls speak of the horror, shock, not wanting to be, wanting to be, all of it. It is simply balance. Souls are internally saying, "We do not want to reproduce, for we have stagnated in believing in life, in growth of life."

The same sex physical attractions come with greater wantings of non conformance and this is one of the grandest ways of saying, "I am choosing to not be part of the system that exists," for there are many systems. They are the pushers of stretching the currents of mind to the outside of the limits and boundaries that exist.

Same sexualness of wantings is learned in the most part. In truth, souls who come with more feminine and exist in male body forms will naturally attract to male. And Souls who come with greater masculine will naturally in gender of female body forms attract to female.

In this time of day and ageness of humanness it has accelerated to yet a heightened curiosity. Many souls have come to life and lived in both genders. Attractions are different from wantings and wanting is different from love. The mind will conquer the soul on many levels and the mind will come to the soul to stretch its challenges in greatness.

So it will pose to do what is not natural to the soul. And that is what you are seeing. It is not gayness and you will say it does not bother you and that is your truth. What does bother your soul is that many souls who are following this trend were in liement of self or are in current liement of self.

For you see the elevation of wanting to take away the rules of the world in which they live and take away all that responsibility of living up to what is not their choosings; by choosing an alternative that alienates those souls for a time and exempts them from the rules of the roads.

It is a trend in this time of rebutting the systems of set uppedness and saying to one sex or the other, "I do not need you. I want all that I can have for now, and I want not to add to this current world's souls." It is that simple. Sexual intensities are not momentary. The other sides of sexualness have not been explored yet.

Souls are still in the primalness' of sexualness simply because they are fighting truth of self. Gayness exists. It is a fact of soul's missions to understand its reasoning's. There is imbalance and it occurs in humans as it does in life on Earth. They are an example. It is not for lacks of beauty or love that gayness exists; it is for the extensions of love to present themselves from soul to soul on Earth.

It is a stretching of understandings, for the needs of love in ways that are not understood to many, simply to bring about that love is love is love.

Gayness is to teach the stretchings of love. Gayness is the extension of love. Of caring, of purpose, of bigger picture and the growth of understandings.

It has nothing to do with sexuality. Gayness says I want a female companion and I am female. I am a male and I want a male in life. Sexuality is a part of any relationship. It does not make it right or wrong, for that does not exist. It speaks in choice; in free will.

Now, souls who choose and honor who they are, the soul they choose with is the important issue of humans; For they can not see. It is not about who a soul has a sexualness with, it is the honor of the relationship that it exists in.

There is not gay there is love. There is not straight there is love. There is not pornography there is lacks of love. There is not violence there is lacks of love. There is not gender there is making home for souls to come to Earth. There will never be non avenues of souls to come and journey.

## SLEEP

At times you get tired physically. The body is not designed to go without rest, for when would souls stop long enough to remember home. There had to be a way to bring the soul back to memory of home. And that is why sleep exists. That is why the body must rest; it can not be put off or tampered with in any way.

If a soul is without rest it misses home greatly and is not of best spirits. When a soul is at rest the soul is free to see and remember and its missions are respoken ever so softly. Answers to questions happen at this time, for the soul to continue on its Journey!

## SOLVATION

Laugh through life, for it gives life on Earth a bounce of home to live in moments and not reject them. To reject moments of pain, of love, of happy and of sad, is to lose the bounce of home that cushions the road from the bumps that come with time on Earth.

The bumps of years ago seem solvable as will the bumps of today. All is of solvable. Trust in life is key. All is of solvable. All that cannot be solved is what is worked so hard to control, for how can control be solved? Control is of the weary, of the meek. Truly, there is no control. There is anger at life and selfishness in not attaining and no patience for the trust of life.

Trust comes from the intents of the pure. Love comes from the intent of the pure. When there is lack of trust it gives us a soul before themselves of lack of intents of purity hence once again no love in realness. Love becomes the tool to be of happiness, when it is happiness that brings about the discovery of love.

## SOUL

Souls are here for love. Anything that takes away from love will distract, deter, walk towards all that can not be not grown from heart.

Love for money does not work, for love lives for nothing other than growth of soul and propellants of growths in greater energies than the lower energies of constant confusion, and the pullment of wools over the eyes of other souls.

Each soul is the ultimate owner of their soul. Each soul is the ultimate doer of what it does. Each soul is the ultimate knower of its actions. Each soul is the ultimate owner of all actions and responsible to all souls who encounter it.

Each soul knows its own self accounting and if it is acknowledged or not by that soul. The knowledge is there in all knowns however it is the soul's choosings to do so. And that is why you have feelments of souls who do not know what their actions are. They do.

They do know what they do know when it comes to their own soul. However, Again and again it is acknowledgement that is key. Acknowledgments of soul to soul, Acknowledgments of a soul's willingness to know of self, to understand self, to carry self to self.

To do unto self is to do onto others. Souls can not give what they do not have, what they do not want, what they do not seek. When the seekments are in growments of self and not others they are not in growments of self.

The stealings of monies in crimement to other souls has growthed the inflationatory makings of what money is. Money is worth less and less every day of its existence simply because the intent behind the dollar that lies in the purse of souls that they hand carry is with fear, doubt and worry. With greed and materialism that is stronger than the soul and the soul is in desperations around it.

That simple propellment took away from the worth of monies to all peoples. Souls find and found ways to steal for it, kill for it, take away all love for it. And they believe in putting their love into it. Into a car, a house, a piece of clothing, a vacation, more homes than one.

It is of fine to want and to grow however to do so at the expensement of others is the true depreciation of the dollar. The takings away are in evidence now however the ingrainments of thought, of action, of wanting are embedded and belief in self eroded in constant of thought.

The attachment to things is greater than that of peoples. And it is time for balance. Souls in heightenments are searching in this time for those very things. They are looking for answers and the consciousness of souls is coming to realizations that they need to open up their hearts to know who they are.

Nothing will or can grow them but them. That the peoples around them may not see it however if they feel such action of growth in heart they must lead themselves hence others to finding love, learning intent and growth within the purity of soul.

## SOULS AT HOME

Souls can not see what they can not see. Most souls of home do not come to witness Earth unless they are called by loved souls on Earth that are left in knowing of them. The absoluteness of home carries them into the realms of unableness to be of heard by those on Earth.

They are not seen nor heard. From home they are not seen or heard and they simply send it anyway. However, they do not come to Earth realm very much, for they are not in present to the souls in which they come to. The love is felt however doubtment of souls on Earth is why they can not see or hear home.

## SOULS FROM HOME

How do souls come back to souls on Earth? It is all energy. Souls who want to support the souls that remain on Earth; it is the love of purity that can break the barriers. You see the physical body is of limits. A soul at home can come back, for the only way to travel the universe is with pure energy.

Some souls that you hear about that exist in homes and live there, they never fully left yet. That is why they exist. They will upon completion at a point in time on Earth however they could not accept that there is more.

They can not be what they can not see. They can not give what they do not have. And they can not accomplish what they know not that it exists. Even if the traumas of their human life hold them back in that energy, it is simply because their energy is too low to enter home.

Once they are freedom of heart, they will be able to penetrate the energy of home. Now, souls who come back to help in mission come through with the pure energy of love, for the energy of love is what travels.

The souls that remain behind do not seek the energy of love. And until they can they can not travel. It is that simple.

God Almighty did not come to souls in complications, he simply comes with love and love is understood without words, for it needs no language. It is the energy of the universe. And this is part of the glories of love; is the traveling.

When a soul returns home and comes in pure energy to grow a mission, a journey of growth, for the love of the souls in which they shared mission as well.

## SOULS NEED LOVE

Truth is, the love no matter who it is in, will grow a soul and then the world. All the other things are simply the challenges that have to work themselves out of the thinkings between ego and soul.

And the truth of all souls is the searchments of love and the ways, the paths, the roads have been foggy for much time now. Glory be to God Almighty, for souls need love. Want it. Search for it. However love can not be demanding, placated, forced or had with physicality.

Love is an emotion; a truth; a purity that gifts all when it is known for its simplicity and candor.

## SOULS PURPOSE ON EARTH

All souls in touchment of each other is the purpose and meaning of life on Earth. And the growth of souls on Earth to be of all souls at separations of understandings and the growths to come as they can be of understood.

There is no growth that can not be had, for if only the mind of a human soul can be in believerment of suchness.

Human souls, those are the souls that are on Earth in present. When a soul returns home and it is known that that soul was a human soul in its growth, there is glory in knowings. For the greatest of the souls journey's is the journey to born upon Earth.

The challenges are deafening to the hearings of the souls at home. As there is a veil of knowledge of home on Earth, at home there is no knowledge's of negative. The feelings and knowings of negative are forgotten and can only be imagined in the life's review of souls who have experienced the lower waves of energies on Earth.

The veil covers, for experience to begin. Once experience begins questions come to play. And once questions come to play choices can be made. And when choices are made experience of those choices had. And once had, their lessons are either learned or repeated.

Repetition tells the soul they did not learn the lesson. Learning brings about a greater more rewarding challenge. Souls came with purpose and that purpose was not to perfect as set by the standards of the world in this time. Perfection leaves a state of mind of inflexibility, for what is a soul to do once deemed perfect?

Once something is learned you can not relearn it. Move on to learn something else. So simple. We are all of each other, of one, and of each other again. This is a formulatic truth of truth and can never be in turned around of thought or action. We are all one. We are all a group. We are all one again. Try it and try it and it will never contempt truth.

Souls on Earth are here to experience. When experience leads to lack of self love it is the goal of the soul to return to love. For the soul can not return to love without purity. When purity is found life opens into a formation of hope. In the hope, the glory comes in sharing. Once sharing is spoken, actions take place. And souls unite in growing. In trust. In those interactions there are questions. The questions that are answered with lack of purity take away from the soul, then the group of souls.

When the questions are answered with purity there is growth in energy, physical and mentalness of souls. Glory be to God Almighty. It is so simple. When purity is not present, neither is growth. Purity is so important, intent is so important, truth is so jarring, that it has no way to go other than to band together.

## SOUL'S KNOWLEDGE

Most souls criticize others from what they see in themselves not of what the other soul is in reality. Angers control more than love. Reality is only real in the moment it is and even then it is not in completeness', for different points of view change it immediately.

Souls are not in knowing of self and they follow each other in hopes that they will feel closer to another than they have found they can be to themselves. They create stories, live in scenario's, hold others accountable and not of self's.

This is the way of the world. The world is looked at as though the world is in owement to the souls that inhabit it however nothing is as it seems. How could the world provide to a soul when it is the thoughts, the actions, the love of the soul that creates the world?

No one in this world is accountable for another soul in any way. We are not meant to be alone and we are not meant to be each other. We are each individual and then we are a group and then we are individual again.

This is the balance of thought, of the world, of thought again. And that is why you hear it in muchments of explainings of love in yet another way, for it to live amongst the souls on Earth.

## SOULS ON EARTH

Earth is simply Earth. No more than a Planet. No more than the peoples on it that have come to experience. No more to know than all souls are on Earth together. Is there a reason? The soul is not meant to be alone.

Those alone over time are the souls hardest, harshest to take on in life of dailyments. It is time to not let a soul take on life alone. It is time to return life in truth, love in purity and hope to the hearts of the living. For much has died. As on Earth, death is the leaving of the physical body however that is a continued journey.

Death is to live on Earth and stop the life that you are living. That is Death. The only true deaths, dyings, passings, are when a soul exists on Earth and it has a home that is not on a foundation of love.

The fork in the road can become at any time. Healing is from understanding and understand comes from compassion and compassion comes from self love in the entrance. It is the first emotion of self love.

## SOULS OUTGROWING EACH OTHER

There is no outgrowth when there is eternality. Eternality is timeless. All other things are timed and that is why change happens. Some things are foundational and others are time. Which means they are lessons in time, in journey's, and are not meant for eternal.

There are no rights or wrongs it is simply a reflection of energies wanting things, peoples, sooner than the patience they have to learn.

So they want want want, now now now. All souls know from the beginnings of relationships the truth.

However, the souls within do not want truths as they are so they try to make what they feel as truth. And in that truth they find their own truths in a day, in a moment, and that is the beginning of moving on. For it was based on a deepest non truth. So anything, anyone that comes along can take away what was already away in the first place.

## SOUL'S WANTS

Souls use themselves to further a dream however by the time they get to the dream they do not recognize they are there in realment. It is interesting when one minute part of a human soul gets discarded; it is easier and easier to discard the rest of the soul.

It happens in quickness and in many there is not enough self love to know it can turn back; that the forks in the road of life can always always be gone back to.

However, in this day there are much usements of others hence usements of self. The soul that uses itself without the knowment of what the soul's intentions are is simple in existence and not feeling mission, passion, love or glory.

Many souls want much and want much not to know of themselves hence they will know not much of which they want hence again they will not get the muchness' they want.

Hence, in one movement they pushed away from their own soul exactly what they thought they wanted and the blindness' can not show them why or how they have accomplished such a tragedy! Leave it to a soul to do the very thing that they fear others will do of them. Glory be to God Almighty.

If all souls were to truly do unto others as they would do unto themselves it would create mishaps all over Earth. However, to treat others as you would treat yourself, in knowings of how souls are treated with love, truth and purity; it will carry lights springments all over the Earth.

## SOULVE
Yes, that is a word. It speaks that the soul wants to solve. It is different from solvation. For solvation is when you take from without and solve. Soulve is to take on the inner challenges of your soul.

## SUCCESS
Success is a state of mind not a measurement. Not all people can or know how to understand life as it is, for most want life to be what they want it to be, not what it is. To accept life as it is, again and again, goes back to self accounting. What cannot be accepted in self can not be accepted in others, for one change has to happen before another can. Believe and it will be, think and it will become. Thoughts become things, things show others and others learn.

## STAGNATION
At home the energy is so pure there is flight. On Earth it is of experiencing and with weight; Weight of heart, not of body as thought by the human eye and mind. Glory be to God Almighty. The world is in stagnation's of all souls. NO ONE SOUL EXCEPTED!

There are no answers for the happenings. There are no ways of knowing what is within self motivation and what is not. There is no support for the pure intended. The pure intended are alone in their missions right now, for they are the souls to stand fast and first in heart. And they are run over by the self motivations of time.

This is true of this time on Earth. Souls do not have forum(s) to speak truths and bring changes at this time on Earth. Time on Earth is only for Earth. There is no time in elsewheres.

## STATUS
Earth's energy is the lowest of energies, that is why it can be swayed in easement by the meek. The higher energies can pain many souls, for the lower energies are the turmoil you see that comes in what can appear to be success in doings, like works, clothing's, rings and cars, Status and needing of it.

Nothing is as it seems. The questions of self motivation are many. The questions of truth remain in few. For truth can only be of simpleness and love; Caring and hope; Glory and lightness of mind and body. Status is stress in every angle. It is an intangible fight for self to be important. It changes the happiness' of action into need of happiness.

## TAKERS OF AWAYMENT
There are many who walk around on Earth in manipulation of self and then of others. It is of sad. It is not right or wrong, good or bad, positive or negative. It is not of anything other than again the truth of what it is; it is of sorrow. Of sadnesses that are undefined and live in the lumps on the physical body of the soul. It is the twitchings, the projections, the sorrows manifested.

The meek in many ways think themselves above meekness; which increases the meeknesses in foldment of stories to keep the soul busy and away from itself. It is all in using words that carry no weight and sound like they do. Act as though there are openings of heart and the heart itself lives in the injury that it wants to share. Go for the million dollar ideas not the blamings which come so easily. The blamings are the cheapest of emotions.

## TAUGHTS IN ERROR
Souls that exist in this day were taught in error. They based life on non sensicalness and formed regularity with knowing and having not an

explanation. When a soul can not make sense of anything and it is taught by other souls, all the souls involved know it is erroneous. And for that alone it gives other information, knowledge, learning, the basis of error. To believe there is evil creates it. To believe there is love creates it. To believe there is hope creates; therefore all things exist.

## TEACHERS

You teach truth by being truth. You teach love by being an example of love. You teach marriage by being in marriage in truth. You teach listening by letting others know that they have been heard. You teach hearing by responding to what you are listening to. You can only teach by who you are. No words can teach as great as the actions of those where love is in unconditionality.

Love that exists with conditions can only take away. Even in moments of appearance of givence it is in taking awayment. Love can not be used. It can not be made. It can not be because of anything. It will simply exist. And in existence love can only turn a heart to growth. When a soul is in love of life, life can only grow. When love is within a relationship the true relationship will unveil itself in wonder.

When a relationship carries not the unconditionality of love the unveilings are of takings away. Conditions can not survive the soul in which the conditions are in imposement of soul. The strangulations of heart begin to wear the soul down on both sides however the giver of the conditions gets into greater needs of control and the receiver of those conditions begins to run without knowment of actions in the direction of runment.

## THANK YOU

Thanking a soul is validation of action. So simple. It is heard and love is always understood by those who understand that love is for nothing.

## THERE IS

There is confidence because there is trust. There is peace because there is truth. There is security because there are morals. There is depth because there are values. There is hope because there is want. There is eloquence because there is respect. There is purity because there is honesty. There is passion because there is desire. There is love because love there is.

## THERE IS NO ALONE

There is no small energy. There is no energy that is out of the reach of souls; once energy is in calling it calls unto others. That is the greatness of energy within a soul, for it is shared, for no one soul is meant to be alone. There is no alone.

The word alone is of energy that takes away from that very soul hence leaves the soul alone, for that is the energy of aroundments to that soul. When a soul's thoughts are of takings away it takes away the souls in aroundments. For then the soul of alone asks why it is alone. And that is why.

## THOUGHTS ARE THINGS

Patterns are changing. Have changed and will become. No more to do things the same. The same that stays will be the internal comfort and the changes will be the growth of soul and will and a new phase to present itself for your lives.

Nothing is impossible except for the limits of the human mind. To not be something or to be it, simply think it and it will become.

To be hesitant to say of what you do not want, for thoughts are greater than things! Notice; take attention, for thoughts are greater than things! Thoughts direct and give direction; to choose growth and love yourself enough to understand why.

To understand the whys in oneself gives the understanding of motivations in others hence compassion. Compassion causes movement, to smile, to nod one's head, to help, to carry, to love and to motivate in life the carries of good will.

## TIME

There is no time. Exception of Earth, there is no time. Time is the teacher of man. Time gives prophets prophethood. Time gives true love its truth.

Time gives hope its home to live. And time teaches us of souls of iller will of weaknesses within, who they are and to leave them on their paths.

And you can choose to not join in the paths of the ill intended, for they will only lesson the souls around them of what not to do. Once that has been of learnment the souls need to part in ways, for the structures that were built were for lessons of temporariment of time.

Love is constant and forever and in timeless of time. Time is created and love is love forever. Time is created to carry souls on journeys and send them back home. For time is movement. Time gives souls a track to follow, to pace, to glorify and to take away.

Time is the balance of free will, for time adds the pressure of giving free will boundaries to make decisions and to find out the truth of self within.

What will a soul do when there is not time to know all things? When there is no time to think through? When there is no time to care whether it is in pure intent or not? And Time will teach each and every soul of itself hence of others. Again and again time is the best teacher.

## TIME IS THE BEST TEACHER

Truth rules. Love soothes. And purity is known. It is of simpleness known in yet another way. For God Almighty is only love, all else is known in love. In absence of love there is conflict. And within conflict there is free will. There is the fork in the road and that fork is self motivation or pure intent. That is there for all to choose.

And the paths begin.

And life twists and turns. The struggles of low energies and higher energies face to face. And pure intent surfaces over time. And self motivations job is to hide itself and appear as pure intent. And all truths come in time. For time is the best teacher. It is the teacher and the teachers must know more than the student to teach the student.

## TRUST

Souls are in starvements of self. Those that are pure heart are outnumbered. They exist and you know them when you see them. Trust in who you are and who souls are in higher self. For they exist, they simply need to emerge. Some are not meant to and that is the glorious work of honements in and within God's love.

There is no wrong or right. There is free will and choices. Choices are of the greatest value to any soul. See truth, make choices. And in some the choice is not to see truth. Trust that you do exactly as truth is in your heart to do.

## TRUTH

Souls themselves do not know their own truth. Not because they do not know of it. It is because they have put their truths away to live in the moments in which they are now living, simply because they put their truths away.

When you know a truth there is nothing within the realm of anything that can take the truth and turn it into something else.

And on the other side of that is when truth is not present and there is a road to truth. The questions, the experiences that need to take place for truth to present itself and the free will of the soul to work within its own purities to find that very truth.

And when purity is not of present it takes the soul on yet another journey to open the eyes to what they can not see. And if they still can not see then another avenue of learnment appears itself in another fashion yet the same lesson and so on.

It is actually very easy to see, for the blind can not see and try to explain. The blind have to explain everything that is why they speak so much, exhaust all around, and in fact are saying nothing. If truth is not spoken, then nothing in fact was said.

As more truths are spoken, there is greater thought and less happenings. And when truth is walked around, not spoken, twisted into being of something else, then the happenings begin and the turns are soreness to souls around and within self. Those who come to Love, to Truth, to Purity, can only learn.

Those who speak of some and not of all are the "nots" of worth in truth. They are taking away from all, starting with themselves. Although the appearances are that they are working for all, striving for all and they are taking away from all. And those with eyes that can see speak. And for now they are in silences. For now they are not given time and you know that truths will surface in time.

The truth is never far away and it is easy to get to. It is right in the energy of all souls. It can be pushed aside for other paths, for free will reigns. And souls learn. And other souls learn from them. And they learn from other souls hence life begins.

You speak truth and it can never hurt another soul, for truth never hurts. It is able to be dealt with; it is the non truths that are painful. The truth tells you of truth and internally a body rests in that knowing. Truth in form is the greatest of all known knowing on Earth.

Know that Truth breaks the barriers of the planes, of the mind, of the soul's stranglements of existence on Earth. In the times of experiencing, truth presents itself and it carries souls for years of Earth time or even until they come back home. Without it, there is frustration and hurt, Pain and sorrow.

When truth is present at birth the infant is free to see all that is around. When that very infant is not attended to what happens? It cries and its eyes are closed to all that is around, figuratively as well as physically. All else is taken away until the cry is met.

That is true of all of life. When the soul of human cries, in virtual speakment it can only see what it is seeking and nothing else. That is the blindness I speak to you of. The cry of a soul unanswered is not free to see in surroundment.

Truth is truth. The skewness of truth can only bring in bridges of takings away. All things can be changed and challenged. Peoples will speak of different loves, different peoples, different importances however they can not talk about different truths. That is one thing that can not be changed, turned, twisted or manipulated.

To have truth you must have love and purity of heart towards itself, to have truth. Truth does not come easy. It has to be fought for within. Truth precedes all actions. Truth proceeds all actions. Truth. Truth. Truth. It exists everywhere however the choosings of truth is not everywhere. The choosings have human motivations around them.

That is the struggle of some souls and those are the souls of bewarements. Those that struggle with truth are the weakest of souls. They will trance through life and not know why they can not attach to others in entirety. And it will be because they can not attach to their own truth in entirety. They will attract other non truthers and there are no sustainments. And a truther can not live amongst a non truther for long.

It can happen. It can not maintain. There is always the question of the non truther that there is something better out there without beliefment in what is present as being better. Not wanting to do the work of truth however to balk at truth and simply go to another person in usements.

To do to one self is to do for others. To do for others to receive from others is to have done nothing.

Without heart there is no heart. Without truth there is not truth. How can there be? And when there is no truth there is no growth. Back to repetitive actions and repetitions of control in greatment to achieve the goal of the soul. For many souls are loving and in conflict.

The longing of truth/home/purity can be the only goal of every single soul on Earth. The humanesses of souls can not be seen by the soul itself without truth. Truth is the essence of love, of purity in heart; the truth of a soul, any soul, from an infant unto coming back home.

## TUG OF LOVE

Love does heal and does give and does stabilize however the fights of internal keep battling the hearts of humans. It is like a tug of love, for the expression on Earth is the tug of war. There is not tugging of war. That statement is of complete untruth. It is the Tug of Love that is difficult to humans, for the lack of self love in such abundance that it is not even in recognizable form. We have all lived in loves propellment, live in it again. For we already know.

## UNION

Union is the makings of Universe. It is God Almighty's union with all souls that makes Universe. It is the union of love and searching's for truth that give purity of intent. It is union of self(s) to grow all things, beings, happenings in life on Earth.

It is state of mind and union of soul that breeds the experiences that souls come to Earth to encounter. It is all about union. Earth is Union's Reunion. When you have pure intent all Earth is is a reunion of all things already known at home.

## WAR

The world at this time is in war now, is it not bringing the love of souls together to endure stoppage of such action? The Earth is now experiencing a war of aggression trying to say it is not.

Killings without warrant to anyone, anything, anywhere; No history, no acceptance, no love, no caring, no compassion's, no outlook, no foresight, just killings in numbers in days of life on Earth; that carries within it a ripple affect of all lacks of love and all are left to feel unsafe, loved, or wanted on Earth.

That one day it could be, can be, will be them. And they stop wanting life to continue. Souls start detaching, wanting to protect, conceal, hide and create a sense of safety around. However, if it does not exist in the whole of Earth it will not exist within the home.

It can be created from within the soul and extended and it can only be when love fights for itself within and extended without the soul onto the world.

It is the fight of the soul itself, the work of the soul itself that will work onto the world of Earth. Souls must hear. Must know. For to stand on end and expect from others what we do not expect from ourselves is to say, "I do not want the world to growth. I do not want growth."

We stand in the lacks of love of souls who speak they do not want for those on Earth, growth. They speak it and they speak it in silence. They do not speak it in heart to themselves to growth the Earth; they speak to themselves to growth themselves.

As well our loves on Earth, hear the truth of your souls, it is there and it speaks to you. It speaks to you to extend. To service, for how else could you feel that another feels, that another growths, that another wants, that another could extend.

You see, the world is as simple as the love that exists within it. The world is as simple as the truth that exists within it. The world is as simple as the purity that lives within it.

## WAVES OF ENERGY

Waves of energy are the strengths of the Earth. Earth is entire energy. Without a soul a body can not move. Without a push an object can not move. That is the obvious. However, words have energy as well; Words.

The spoken word carries within it energy. That is why a soul can say something and another can feel it. And not even remember the spoken word at times.

For literally it is little in comparison to the energy of the word and the intention behind it. It is a world of energy. This too is obvious. However, let me show you more. A soul can walk into a room with no words, not even seen at times. And their energy is felt and picked up by another soul.

The soul can walk into that same room and say it feels peaceful, love, fears, or feelings of great discomfort. You see, energy can stay stagnant until more energy replaces it. Truth can not be seen yet it is known in energy.

## WEARINESS

There are little times in which to think. Even in quiet a television is turned on and the news is heard if not seen. In cars, there is radio and it is heard and not seen. So the mind does not rest, to think, to imagine, to dream. It is filled and it will work on what it is filled with. The human mind is of great distraction, of illusion. The mind of the human will work on everything it is fed.

So if you want something and you think it, it will come to you as your intent professes. And if you believe that you can not do something, anything, your brain will think it too, and work on it too and then it will not happen. The surprises to these thinkings are when intent is pure. Some do not believe in themselves and others believe. The believers of self open their hearts and their heads to all that is of belief in truth.

And those who believe not in themselves, they take away in everyday of their existence, until they can believe that they are capable. It follows back and forth with intents. For the pureness of intent is the driver. The love of self hence the love of others is the key. It has been said in many times and many times it is read. Glory be to God Almighty.

However, it is much harder to feel intent as purity and harder still to love self, for there is no road map to love self. And then the soul has to trust enough to love and trust in self. And then things like other souls or media have a harder time in penetration. Yet those who do not have love of self, they are absorbed in the non truths, for they have little truth within.

How do you recognize it? How do you share truth when you do not share it with yourself and give to yourself the glory of self love?

To understand your own role in your own life is simple self love. To be honest about whom you are and who you are to others; and how you affect. That your actions reflect the intent of purity and they are and will never be of complications, Glory be to God Almighty.

Many speak in ill will and twist and turn and spin only in their own direction. Those are the weary of heart and mind and they look for the weary. When someone is not of weariness as they may be, there is conflict with them. There becomes a stance of the weary wanting to bring the other souls around them down to the same level, for the comfort of company in the common misery of soul.

## WHOLE
If peoples could only know how much a part of the world they are they would become a part of the world in difference. They would think in whole not in one. They would behave in whole not as one.

They would not be able to self motivate so easily, for the narcissisticness of thoughts would not be able to flourish in groups.

That word is simply to say, "I am better than groups" and no soul is more important than another. Ever. The endlessness of love is not believed. Peoples feel or believe that it runs out, for their own belief in, within themselves runs out.

## WHY WE ARE HERE
The love of self can only breed the love of life. Souls ask in overments of time, "Why are we here?" We are here to find and discover that love propels, that we are not meant to be on mission alone. That free will can create in greatness. That weakness of soul is honed into strengths. That the mind and soul have endless capacity and that limits are self imposed.

That the soul lives in the world in which it creates. That if outside energies try to obstruct, you can push back with the energies of love. The soul knows not of its own capacity within the limits of boundaries set to live. For one soul can take away more from itself than any other soul can "do to it."

No one does anything to another. What you allow can happen. Solvements of lower energies will solve when truth is present. The struggles to solve within pure intent; reflect, teach and example to both parties the lower of energies and the greater of energies.

When there are greater energies present, those are the leaders, for all souls want the knowings of truth. And internal it is known that there is truth present and that sustains the leadership. Glory be to God Almighty. For it is. And in truth it is not in waivement, for it is.

## WORDS OF TRUTH

Nothing is as it seems, as it is seen. At times as it is thought and at other times as it is spoken. Words of truth are eternal. All others are gone.

## WORK

God Almighty did not wait to create, he created. Glory be to God Almighty. Contrary to all beliefs in life on Earth there was not a seventh day of rest. What is rest? Rest is a time of not working on Earth however to do what you love is not work. Love is not work. There is no work and rest as you would think it.

There is love and growth in all of life. In what you call rest at times there is more work. What is work in your world is truly the domination of one soul having to respond to another. And that is the deattraction to work as a word in your world. Simply let yourself be. Let your mind in naturality grow.

Work, any work, is not work when you love what you do. That is why you don't feel the weight of your work, your actions, when you only do things that you love. When you start feeling the weight of things, that is when you know you are not in the right place on earth.

**WORRY**

Worry is a subtle emotion. People actually believe it is virtuous to worry. Yet it is a taking away.

**YOU ARE OF LOVE**

God Almighty is present in always. His love is the love that covers all the layers of emotions on their way to solvation of soul's confusions. And once the love of God is asked for it is ever present. And without the asking there is isolation and the soul stands in limbo, wondering what should I do? The fears that exist here, the thoughts that take away, the deception of soul are the trial of many, for the unknown to them is true.

You are of knowledge

Use it

You are of love

Show it

You are of caring

Do it

You are of awareness

Walk away from harm

You are of hope

Live it

You are of life

Create it

You are of wonder

Grow from it

You are of light

Let it shine

# Glossary

ABLIVIATED – To absolve. To solve in your heart and the under standing in your soul that it has been learned and you have grown; never to go back to.

ABORTION – Stopping any process of growth available.

ACCUMULATED PAIN – The weight carried in the stresses of the mind and physical body. It is in the physical walk and it is in the speech and the behavior of mind. Accumulated pain first wants to protect itself and then it wants to not feel it, and then it tries to ignore feeling it and then it comes out in behaviors that take away.

ANGEL – A soul of service to and for other souls.

ASTRAYED – Lost on mission.

ATHEIST – An Earth bound soul.

APPARENATE – Appear.

AZNA – The feminine spirit of God.

BEAUTY – The acceptance of our essence.

BELIEVERMENT – To live in the beliefs of your soul.

BETHLEHEM – "Sweet Bessie" the Angel that walked beside Jesus Christ on Earth. "She" is also one of the seven Angels of this mission of love, truth and purity; Also the name of Jesus Christ's Birthplace.

CAMERATIC – Full view; Viewing media and its images.

CAMOUFLAUGMENT – To live under covers of truth.

CARNIGIC – Old and dated; without use in this time.

CHRIST – The Angel of Love. The thirst of life.

CHRONICALOGICALIZER – A pattern to behavior and a set mode of action to remember everything; to build stories with events.

CLAIRITY – Clean and Air is Clair; to see without tint.

COMPLETURE – To understand the completion and continuance of thought, work or action.

CONGENUITY – In your truth of understanding, your view in pure thoughts and actions. To live in it rather than simply think it and not take action.

CONTRIVATION – To manipulate and appear as though you are not.

CONTROLLER – To instill thoughts to another without the grandeur of love to suffice the holdings asked of.

COUNTERFEITISM OF SOUL – To live in lies that you tell yourself and try to convince other of.

CORTH – The moment before forth. The distance between self percep tion and what is. It is the work and thought before actions that you take.

CULMINGATION – Getting to the bottom of troubles brewing. To be in the midst of trusting souls and finding out that the souls you trust do not trust themselves, therefore are not trustworthy.

DEATTRACTION – To let go of and no longer have motivation to pursue.

DEPRESSION – When the passion of a soul is ignored.

DEVICEITIVE – Deviceitive, it is a taker away of soul. That is devi ceitive. Ceit: to take away. Vice: in mind over soul. De: in discountment of greatements.   Ego is a strong deviceitive of soul.

DISGARD – To know something or someone exists and to not pay attention to or validate.

DOMINGATE – Feelings of a woman to a man  without thoughts of sexualness, however of procreation.

EARTH – The house of God. The most difficult challenge. One of many planes and galaxies.

EARTH BOUND – To not remember Home at all.

EGONOMIC – The theory of the ego's role. People believe that ego is a good thing however ego is pure self motivation. It can not be your friend, your lover, your car or your home. It prepares you for disappoint ment and isolation. Ego is the polar end of pure intent. Needing to win, have, own, is one thing, having to have those things or you won't be happy is another story entirely. Egonomic is a state of mind. Like the egocentrism of a child.

EGOMONIC – To live in your mind without involving your soul. No heart. To believe that others do not feel; As you are in fear of your own feelings as well.

EMOTION – The source of what gives life to any situation.

ENUMERATION – In many times over.

ETERNAL – Forever; No beginning, no end. Existence.

ETERNALITY – To live in the mindset of understand that all things are energy driven and are present always.

EXEMPLICATION – To live in who you are, and to be who you are, and teach you are, simply because that is who you are.

EXPEDE – To put out there with effort and energy.

EXPERIENCE – What you have done and come to conclusions as a result of.

EXPONTIATE – To growth from your experiences rather than stagnate. Love grows when growths are acknowledged.

FEST – When a soul can not live in the truth that it knows; becomes restless.

FREE WILL – The overall purpose of Earth is to give a soul choice and freedom to choose or not choose avenues of love for soulution.

FUTURE – What a soul does not know yet.

GABRIEL – One of the seven angels whose job is to message to me in this mission.

GARTH – Your deepest energy. The center of our existence. Our deepest core. The gut.

GOD – Eternal Love.

GOVE – To enter the barriers to eternity.

HEAVEN – Our thoughts of pure eternal and forgiving love. Referred to as "home" by Jesus Christ.

HELL – The lack of self love.

HOME – What we know as Heaven. It is pure and loving without human traits such as judgment and ego.

HONE – Experience towards refinement.

HUMALITY – Common traits of us that we all share in basic needs and wants.

HUMAN – What we came here to be. To be human is to say you do not remember the pure love of home and you came to mission towards it.

HUMANALITY – The traits of us as souls on Earth.

HURVY – To overlook and lose sight of the reasoning's why and the messages of learning over time.

ILLUMINGATIONS – The images souls try to portray that are not consistent with who they really are. They can not see the discrepancy and believe no one else can either.

IMMEDIANCE – What comes to thought right away, requiring action.

IMMERTIONS – The inner knowings of comprehension. A soul can know something and not understand the depth. Immertions is the depth of the understanding.

IMPOSSIBILIALITIES – What we boundary and limit.

INFINITCY – Thoughts that continue eternally.

IN FORM – Our physical bodies.

INHEIRATE – Possessions and thoughts that carry onward through soul's generations.

INHERITANCE OF THE MEEK – The meek are in repetition of problems, of reasons, of glories in other mishaps. Of problems of others, not only their own and with that they hold all in place; that is the inheritance.

INSTINCT – Energy that has not yet been seen or discovered by the nakedness of the eyes.

INTENT – To understand underlying motivations of your soul.

INTERNALNESS – What we keep within and do not express entirely.

JACOB – He is one of the seven angels whose job is to prepare the consciousness of this work, this mission.

JOSEPH – He is one of the seven angels and his job is to balance this mission.

LACKASITY – To be aloof towards what is being said or done or accomplished.

LACKNESS – To not give energy towards something or someone.

LOVE – The Eternal state of understanding.

MARY MAGDALENE – The love of Jesus Christ's mission on Earth. The catalyst of many stories that keep interest in the messages of love that originated in that time.

MEANGLE – To bend the truth into angles of non truth.

MEEK – Those that think with their mind not their souls.

MENT – It encompasses the meaning of worlds. It takes it from singular to plural. It gives it life for all and not for one soul.

MICHAEL – One of the seven angels of this mission. He is of discipline and protection of the ongoing forwards needed to propel the words of love and  service to souls on Earth.

MINDHOOD – What we live within the thoughts that we do not think about, however react to our of instinct.

MISCHEEVED – To take away from a situation knowingly and expecting that other souls did not know of what you intended to do.

MISSION – Each of us have a reason to be here. We came to do something.

MISTAKE – The word to mask insecurity.

NATCHURE – To manipulate truth. To raise doubt in energy due to lacks of truth. The opposite of nurture.

NATURALITY – Things we do without thinking.

NATURICITIES – Behaviors we turn into habits that become natural to us.

NEEDMENTS – All that we need internally that exists in all of us, love, truth and purity.

NEEYA – Your inner intent. A pure place of intention; an Arabic word.

OBSOLETIZE – To take something that has existed and say it does not need to exist anymore. To no longer exist.

OPPOSIGHT – Saying we did not see what we saw, or hear what we heard.

PACIFIC – To pacify. To act in a way without full capacity.

PLANES – Earth is one plane. There are many in the scope of the Universe.

PROPHECY – To message all that learns and growths us.

PROPHET – A teacher of new things to the human mind. An expander of thoughts and love. A messenger from God.

PROWNESS – A bolstered image of one's self when they feel they are in command.

PURITY – A love without the walls of the human eye.

PRUDENCY – To do right by your soul.

PURE INTENT – To do from heart without expectation.

UNFEAT – To erode foundations.

UNSIDEDOWNNESS – At times our thinking is the complete opposite of truth and we are currently living in it as truth.

RAPHAEL – One of the seven Angels of this mission. Raphael is a delivering Angel so this actual book was part of Raphael's work.

RAYSED – To attempt to over power love with lesser energies. However, there can be no energy stronger than love, even when it may appear so.

RECEIVERMENT – To accept in an all encompassing way.

REMAINATION – To keep and growth from. To understand what is to continue and what is better left behind.

REMOUNTS – To align again. To go back and restart.

REPETITION – Tells the soul they did not learn the lesson.

RESEEDING – To define again all we know and growth into
the higher learnings.

RESPOKEN – To speak again in a language that speaks in love
without taking away.

SAPHI – The souls of Clair vision.

SELF ACCOUNTING – To understand your own role in your own life.

SELF MOTIVATION – To act with expectation or you will do
nothing at all.

SOLUTIONIZED – Solving a problem without the involvement
of your soul.

SOUL – Your energy that comes to Earth, however exists eternally.

SOULUTION – When anger is greater than love there is solution.
When love is greater than anger there is soulution.

SOULVE – It speaks that the soul wants to solve. It is different from
salvation. Solvation is when you take from without and solve.
Soulve is to take on the inner challenges of your soul.

STAGNATE - To no longer take action due to fears, doubts and worries.

SUBSIDIC – To do as habit, putting things off rather than facing them,
it becomes a state of mind.

SUSTAINMENT – To come to understand enough to maintain behaviors rather than to keep going back to behaviors you want to grow
through.

SURETY – As in sure however with understand that know what you know without hesitation.

SWEET BESSIE – An Angel of service named Bethlehem who walked beside Jesus Christ in his time on Earth. She is now one of the team of seven Angels that are within this message and mission at this time.

THE VEIL – What we can not see of home due to energy's that are not pure enough on Earth.

TOUCH – You can not touch the heart of a soul until the soul of the heart you want to touch is ready.

TRUTH – Truth is not negative or positive. Truth is truth. There are no flaws in truth, for truth is flawless. It may cause pain however it is not of flaws, simply because it may hurt another soul. It is not of negative, because it causes pain. Truth will eventually release pain, and it will grow on. Internally souls look for, crave and vascular beat to the rhythms of truth. It is the music of home.

That is truth. If you want to define truth further it is the music of home, the cycle of life on Earth, the purity of every soul at home. That is truth.

UNFEAT – To erode the foundation.

UNIVERSE – All existence beyond our known comprehension.

VERDICTIONS – Making judgments and decisions based on given knowledge's and what is known to you at that time.

VIAL – The soul in its activity state.

VISSIES – Exhaling the beauty and nature of all things in all purity.

VOYOUS – Just like joyous, only it takes away.

www.OriginsOfTruth.com